AF540434

THE RIGVEDA AND THE AVESTA
THE FINAL EVIDENCE

THE RIGVEDA AND THE AVESTA
THE FINAL EVIDENCE

SHRIKANT G. TALAGERI

ADITYA PRAKASHAN
New Delhi

© SHRIKANT G.TALAGERI

First published: 2008
First reprint: 2010
Second reprint: 2015
Third reprint: 2018

ISBN 978-81-7742-085-2

Published for Aditya Prakashan, 2/18, Ansari Road, New Delhi – 110 002.
email: contact@adityaprakashan.com
website: www.adityaprakashan.com

Printed at Replika Press Pvt. Ltd.

To

MY MOTHER
SHAILA GANGADHAR TALAGERI

and

MY FATHER
GANGADHAR SITARAM TALAGERI

Contents

Bibliography

AMBEDKAR 1990: **Dr Babasaheb Ambedkar Writings and Speeches**, volume 7. Ambedkar, B.R. ed. Vasant Moon, Education dept., Government of Maharashtra Publications, Mumbai 1990.

ARNOLD 1897: **Historical Vedic Grammar.** Arnold, E.V. In JAOS (Journal of the American Oriental Society), New Haven, Connecticut.

BHAGWAN SINGH 1995: **The Vedic Harappans**. Bhagwan Singh. Āditya Prakashan, New Delhi, 1995.

BHARGAVA 1956/1971: **India in the Vedic Age: A History of Aryan Expansion in India**. Upper India Publishing House Pvt. Ltd. Lucknow, 1956.

BLAŽEK 1998: **Is Indo-European *Hekwo 'horse' Really of Indo-European Origin?** Voclav Blažek. In Studia Indogermanica Lodziensia (Sigl), Vol.II, Lodz, 1998.

BRYANT 1999: **Linguistic substrata and the indigenous Aryan debate**. Bryant, Edwin F. pp. 59-84, in "Aryan and non-Aryan in South Asia: evidence, interpretation, and ideology" (proceedings of the International Seminar on Aryan and non-Aryan in South Asia, Univ. of Michigan, October 1996).

CARNOY 1919: **Pre-Aryan Origins of the Persian Perfect**. pp. 117-121 in The Journal of the American Oriental Society, Vol.39, 1919.

CHANG 1988: **Indo-European Vocabulary in Old Chinese: A New Thesis on the emergence of Chinese Language and Civilization in the Late Neolithic age**. Chang, Tsung-tung. Sino-Platonic Papers Number 7, January 1988. Department of Oriental Studies, University of Pennsylvania, Philadelphia, 1988.

CHATTERJEE 1970: **The Origin and Development of the Bengali Language**, Pt.I. Chatterjee, S.K. George, Allen and Unwin Ltd. (first published by Calcutta University, 1926), London, 1970.

CHILDE 1926: **The Aryans: A study of Indo-European Origins**. Childe, V. Gordon. Kegan, Paul, Trench, Trubner & co. Ltd., London, 1926.

DESHPANDE 1995: **Vedic Aryans, non-Vedic Aryans, and non-Aryans: Judging the Linguistic Evidence of the Veda**; Deshpande, Madhav. pp. 67-84 in "The Indo-Aryans of Ancient South Asia", ed. George Erdosy. Walter de Gruyter. Berlin, 1995.

DYEN 1970: **The Case of the Austronesian Languages**. Dyen, Isidore, in "Indo-European and Indo-Europeans", ed. by George Cardona, H.M.Hoenigswald and Alfred Senn, University of Pennsylvania Press, Philadelphia, 1970.

ELST 1999: **Update on the Aryan Invasion Debate**. Elst, Koenraad. Aditya Prakashan, New Delhi, 1999.

ELST 2001: **The Saffron Swastika**. Elst, Koenraad. Voice of India. New Delhi, 2001.

ERDOSY 1989: **Ethnicity in the Rigveda and its Bearing on the Question of Indo-European Origins**. Erdosy, George. pp. 35-47 in "South Asian Studies" vol. 5. London

ERDOSY 1995: **Preface** to "The Indo-Aryans of Ancient South Asia: language, material Culture and Ethnicity", edited George Erdosy, Walter de Gruyter, Berlin-NY, 1995.

FRANCFORT 2001: **The Archaeology of Proto-historic Central Asia and the Problems of Identifying Indo-European and Uralic-speaking Populations**. Francfort, H.P. pp. 151-163 in "Early Contacts between Uralic and Indo-European: Linguistic and Archaeological Considerations", ed. Carpelan, Parpola, Koskikallio Suomalais-Ugrilainen Seura, Helsinki, 2001.

GAMKRELIDZE 1995: **Indo-European and the Indo-Europeans: A Reconstruction and Historical Analysis of a Proto-Language and a Proto-Culture**. Gamkrelidze, Thomas V. and Ivanov, V.V. Mouton de Gruyter, 1995, Berlin, New York.

GNOLI 1980: **Zoroaster's Time and Homeland: A Study on the Origins of Mazdeism and Related Problems**. Gnoli, Gherardo. Instituto Universitario Orientale, Seminario di Studi Asiatici, Naples, 1980.

GOLDMAN 1977: **Gods, Priests and Warriors: The Bhṛgus of the Mahābhārata**. Goldman, Robert P. Columbia University Press, New York, 1977.

GRIFFITH 1889: **The Hymns of the Rig-Veda**. (tr.) Griffith, Ralph T.H. Munshiram Manoharlal, rep. 1987, Varanasi.

HENNING 1978: **The First Indo-Europeans in History**. Henning, W.B., pp.215-230 in "Society and History — Lectures in Honour of Karl August Wittfogel", edited G.

L. Ulmen, Mouton Publishers, The Hague-Paris-New York, 1978.

HOCK 1999a: **Out of India? The linguistic evidence**. Hock, Hans H. pp.1-18, in "Aryan and non-Aryan in South Asia: evidence, interpretation, and ideology" (proceedings of the International Seminar on Aryan and non-Aryan in South Asia, Univ. of Michigan, October 1996).

HOCK 1999b: **Through a glass darkly: Modern "racial" interpretations vs. textual and general prehistoric evidence on *ārya* and *dāsa/dasyu* in Vedic society**. Hock, Hans H. pp.145-174, in "Aryan and non-Aryan in South Asia: evidence, interpretation, and ideology" (proceedings of the International Seminar on Aryan and non-Aryan in South Asia, Univ. of Michigan, October 1996).

HOPKINS 1896a: **Prāgāthikāni**. Hopkins, Edward W. pp. 23-92 in JAOS (Journal of the American Oriental Society), Vol. 17.

HOPKINS 1896b: **Numerical Formulae in the Veda**. Hopkins, Edward W. in JAOS (Journal of the American Oriental Society), Vol.16.

HOPKINS 1898: **The Punjab and the Rig-Veda**. Hopkins, Edward W. pp. 19-28 in JAOS (Journal of the American Oriental Society), Vol. 19, July 1898

HUMBACH 1991: **The Gathas of Zarathushtra and the Other Old Avestan Texts, Part I: Introduction, Texts and Translation**. Humbach, Helmut. Carl Winter, Universitätsverlag, Heidelberg (Germany) 1991.

KUZMINA 2001: **Contacts Between Finno-Ugric and Indo-Iranian Speakers in the light of Archaeological, Linguistic and Mythological Data**. Kuzmina E. E. in "Early Contacts between Uralic and Indo-European: Linguistic and Archaeological Considerations". Ed. Carpelan, Parpola, Koskikallio. Suomalais-Ugrilainen Seura, Helsinki, 2001.

LAMBERG-KARLOVSKY 2005: **Archaeology and Language — The case of the Bronze Age Indo-Iranians**. Lamberg-Karlovsky, Carl C., pp 142-177 in "The Indo-Aryan Controversy — Evidence and Inference in Indian history", ed. Edwin F. Bryant and Laurie L. Patton, Routledge, London & New York, 2005.

LAROUSSE 1959: **The Larousse Encyclopaedia of Mythology**, tr. by Richard aldington and Delano Ames from Larousse Mytholgie Generale, ed. Felix Guirand. Auge, Gillon, Hollia-Larousse, Moreau et Cie, the Librairie Larousse, Batchwork Press Ltd., 1959.

LUBOTSKY 2001: **The Indo-Iranian Substratum**. Lubotsky, Alexander, in "Early Contacts between Uralic and Indo-European:

Linguistic & Archaeological Considerations", Suomalais-Ugrilainen Seura, Univ. of Helsinki, Helsinki, 2001.

MACDONELL 1963: **Vedic Mythology**. Macdonell, A.A. Indological Book House, Varanasi. 1963 (reprint).

MAIR 1998: **Die Aprachamöbe: An Archeolinguistic Parable**. Mair, Victor H., in "The Bronze Age and Early Iron Age Peoples of Eastern Asia", Vol.II. (ed. Mair, Victor H.) The Institute for the Study of Man (in collaboration with) The University of Pennsylvania Museum Publications, 1998 (*Journal of Indo-European Studies*, Monograph no twenty-six in two volumes).

MAJUMDAR ed. 1951/1996: **The Vedic Age**. General Editor Majumdar R.C. The History and Culture of the Indian People. Bharatiya Vidya Bhavan. Mumbai, 1951.

MALLORY 1989: **In Search of the Indo-Europeans: Language, Archaeology and Myth**. Mallory J.P. Thames and Hudson Ltd., London 1989.

MALLORY 1997: **Encyclopaedia of Indo-European Culture**. Mallory J.P. and Adams D.Q. Fitzroy Dearborn Publishers. London and Chicago, 1997.

MAYRHOFER 1979: **Altiranischen Namen.** Mayrhofer, von Manfred. Osterreichische Akademie der Wissenschaften, Vienna.

MEILLET 1906/1967: **The Indo-European Dialects**. Meillet Antoine (tr. Samuel N. Rosenberg). Alabama Linguistic and Philological Series No. 15, University of Alabama Press, 1967.

NICHOLS 1997: **The Epicentre of the Indo-European Linguistic Spread**. Nichols, Johanna. Chapter 8, in "Archaeology and Language, Vol. I: Theoretical and Methodological Orientations", ed. Roger Blench & Matthew Spriggs, Routledge, London and New York, 1997.

NORMAN 1995: **Dialect variation in Old and Middle Indo-Aryan**. Norman, K.R. pp. 278-292, "The Indo-Aryans of Ancient South Asia", ed. by George Erdosy. Walter de Gruyter. Berlin, 1995.

PARGITER 1962: **Ancient Indian Historical Tradition**. Pargiter F.E. Motilal Banarsidas, Delhi-Varanasi-Patna, 1962..

PARPOLA 2002: **From the Dialects of Old Indo-Aryan to Proto-Indo-Aryan and Proto-Iranian**. pp.43-102 in "Indo-Iranian Languages and Peoples" (Proceedings of the British Accademy), ed. N. Sims-Williams. Oxford University Press.

PROFERES 1999: **The Formation of Vedic Liturgies**. Proferes, Theodore. Harvard Thesis, April 1999.

PROFERES 2003: **Remarks on the Transition from Rgvedic Composition to Srauta Compilation**. Proferes, Theodore. In "Indo-Iranian Language and Peoples", Oxford University Press, Proceedings of the British Academy.

SKJÆRVØ 1995: **The Avesta as source for the early history of the Iranians**. pp. 155-176 in "The Indo-Aryans of Ancient South Asia", ed. by George Erdosy. Walter de Gruyter. Berlin, 1995.

SOUTHWORTH 1995: **Reconstructing Social Context from Language Indo-Aryan and Dravidian Prehistory**. Southworth, Franklin C., pp.258-277 in "The Indo-Aryans of Ancient South Asia". ed. George erdosy, Walter de Gruyter, Berlin-New York, 1995.

TALAGERI 1993: **The Aryan Invasion Theory and Indian Nationalism.** Talageri, Shrikant G. Voice of India, New Delhi, 1993.

TALAGERI 1997: Talageri, Shrikant G. pp.223-231 in "Time for Stock Taking: Whither Sangh Parivar", ed. Koenraad Elst. Voice of India, New Delhi, 1997.

TALAGERI 1998: **The Indus-Sarasvati Civilization: Significance of This Name**. Pp.103-108, in "Revisiting Indus-Sarasvati Age and Ancient India" (being papers presented at the WAVES conference, Atlanta, Georgia, USA, October 1996), ed. Bhudev Sharma & Nabarun Ghose. WAVES, Meerut, 1998.

TALAGERI 2000: **The Rigveda: A Historical Analysis**, Aditya Prakashan (New Delhi), 2000.

TALAGERI 2001: **Michael Witzel: An Examination of his Review of my Book**, in http://shrikanttalageri.voiceofdharma.com

TALAGERI 2005a: **Sita Ram Goel — Memories and Ideas**. pp.239-346, in "India's Only Communalist: in Commemoration of Sita Ram Goel", ed. Koenraad Elst, Voice of India (New Delhi), 2005.

TALAGERI 2005b: **The Textual Evidence: The Rigveda as a source of Indo-European History**. pp.332-340, in "The Indo-Aryan Controversy — Evidence and Inference in Indian history", ed. Edwin F. Bryant and Laurie L. Patton, Routledge, London & New York, 2005.

TARR 1969: **The History of the Carriage**. Laszlo, Tarr. tr. Elisabeth Hoch. Arco Publ. Inc., New York, 1969.

TAVADIA 1950: **Indo-Iranian Studies: I**. Tavadia J. C. Viśva Bharati, Santiniketan, 1950.

THIEME 1960: **The 'Aryan' Gods of the Mitanni Treaties**. Thieme, P. in JAOS (Journal of the American Oriental Society).

THOMAS 1883: **The Rivers of the Vedas, and How the Aryans entered**

India. Thomas, Edward. The Journal of the American Oriental Society, 1883 (p.357-386).

VISHVABANDHU 1935-1965: **A Vedic Word Concordance** (16 volumes). Vishveshvaranand Vedic Research Institute. Lahore/ Hoshiarpur

WINN 1995: **Heaven, Heroes and Happiness: The Indo-European Roots of Western Ideology**. Winn, Shan M.M. University Press of America, Lanham-New York-London, 1995.

WITZEL 1986: **Tracing the Vedic Dialects.** Witzel, Michael. in "Dialectes dans les Litteratures Indo-Aryennes", Paris (Fondation Hugot), 16-18 Septembre, 1986.

WITZEL 1987: **On the Localization of Vedic Texts and Schools.** Witzel, Michael. in "India and the Ancient World – History Trade and Culture Before AD 650" ed. by Gilbert Pollet, Orientalia Lovaniensia Analecta, vol. 25, Departement Orientalistiek, Leuven.

WITZEL 1991: **Notes on Vedic Dialects.** Witzel, Michael. in ZINBUN, Annals of the Institute for Research in Humanities, Kyoto University, 67(1991).

WITZEL 1995a: **Early Indian History: Linguistic and Textual Parameters.** Witzel. Michael. pp. 85-125 in "The Indo-Aryans of Ancient South Asia", ed. by George Erdosy. Walter de Gruyter. Berlin, 1995.

WITZEL 1995b: **Rgvedic History: Poets, Chieftains and Politics**. Witzel, Michael. pp. 307-352 in "The Indo-Aryans of Ancient South Asia", ed. by George Erdosy. Walter de Gruyter. Berlin

WITZEL 1997a: **Sarama and the Panis – Origins of Prosimetric Exchange in Archaic India**. Witzel, Michael. pp. 397-409 in Joseph Harris and Karl Reichl (eds.), "Prosimetrum: Crosscultural perspectives in Narrative Prose and Verse". D. S. Brewer. Cambridge

WITZEL 1997b: **The Development of the Vedic Canon and Its Schools: The Social and Political Milieu.** Witzel, Michael. in "Inside the Texts, Beyond the Texts", ed. by M.Witzel, Cambridge 1997 (being the proceedings of the International Vedic Workshop, Harvard univ., June 1989).

WITZEL 1999: **Substrate Languages in Old Indo-Aryan**. EJVS 5-1, 1999.

WITZEL 2000a: **The Languages of Harappa**. Witzel, Michael. Feb. 17, 2000.

WITZEL 2000b: **The Home of the Aryans**. Witzel, Michael. in "Anusantyai, Fest schrift fur Johanna Norten zum" 70, Geburtstag. Ed. Almut Hintze, Eva Tichy, JH Roll, 2000.

WITZEL 2001a: **Autochthonous Aryans: The Evidence from Old Indian and Iranian Texts**. Witzel, Michael. (EJVS)7-3(2001)

WITZEL 2001b: **WESTWARD HO! The Incredible Wanderlust of the Rgvedic Tribes Exposed by S. Talageri,** at http://users.primushost.com/ĭndia/ejvs/ejvs0702/ejvs0702a.txt

WITZEL 2005: **Indocentrism: autochthonous visions of ancient India.** Witzel, Michael. pp.341-404, in "The Indo-Aryan Controversy — Evidence and Inference in Indian history", ed.Edwin F. Bryant and Laurie L. Patton, Routledge, London & New York, 2005.

WITZEL 2006: **Central Asian Roots and Acculturation in South Asia: Linguistic and Archaelogical Evidence from Western Central Asia, the Hindukush and Northwestern South Asia for Early Indo-Aryan Language and Religion**. in "Indus Civilization: Text and Context", edited by Toshiki Osada, Manohar Publications, New Delhi, 2006

WOJTILLA 1999: **The Sanskrit Godhūma Apropos of a short Incursion in Indo-European and Indo-Aryan prehistory**. Wojtilla, Gyula. Akademiai Kiadoi, Budapest, 1999.

Preface

This book is entitled "**The Rigveda and the Avesta: The Final Evidence**" because it is intended to conclusively complete both the historical analysis of the Rigveda commenced in my second book, "**The Rigveda: A Historical Analysis**" (2000), as well as my examination of the Aryan invasion theory and the problem of the original homeland of the Indo-European family of languages commenced in my first book, "**The Aryan Invasion Theory: A Reappraisal**" (1993) [also published, *earlier*, by Voice of India, with three additional chapters of a political nature, as "**The Aryan Invasion Theory and Indian Nationalism**" (1993)].

When I started out on my first book, I was impelled by the conviction that the Aryan invasion *theory* taught in our school text books as *fact* had no logical basis, and was so totally opposed to everything that our traditional ideas of our history and heritage told us, that the matter required deep and detailed investigation, particularly in view of the blatant political misuse of the theory by various divisive political forces. However, neither then, nor at any other point of time along the course of the journey have I *ever* allowed my personal views to obscure or distort my perception and conclusions about the correct interpretation of the facts. So, even when my writing may occasionally have been handicapped by a lack of knowledge about some particular other books written on the subject, which therefore may have resulted in some deficiencies, those deficiencies have always been of a minor and incidental nature, and have never led me into the wrong direction. I can *confidently* (opponents may say, *arrogantly*) say that this book will set the seal on the controversy, and prove beyond any *reasonable* doubt that India was the original homeland of the Indo-European family of languages.

One person that I have to genuinely thank for this is Michael Witzel, the Wales Professor of Sanskrit at Harvard University. Throughout this present volume, I will be criticizing him sharply for the elements of fraudulent scholarship, and dirty politics, that he has introduced throughout the bitter debate on the subject, and for all the lies and manipulations that he has been guilty of in the process. But, at this point, I must admit that if he had not done all these things, I would never have been impelled to go as deeply into the matter as I have done after my second book, and this third book would not have been what it is — perhaps I would never have seen the need for a third book. His name will, therefore, necessarily be cropping up throughout this book.

My first book, in 1993, received some very favorable reviews, and even enthusiastic support, in various Indian circles. But western scholars, and Indian AIT scholars and writers, by and large, chose to refrain from reacting to it.

My second book, however, produced sharper reactions from some western scholars and writers. Even now, of course, the majority of AIT scholars, Indian and western, involved in the AIT (Aryan Invasion Theory) vs. OIT (Out of India Theory) debate, or simply involved in the academic study of the Indo-European problem, still chose to treat silence as the safest form of defence, and continued to behave as if they had never even heard of my books — after all, it is easier to attack and ridicule the nonsensical notions and wishful writings of more casual or biased OIT writers than to deal with a logical and unassailable new hypothesis backed by a solid phalanx of facts and data. But, a smaller but significant number condescended to mention my name, only to dismiss me, either as a non-academic upstart who had the gall to think he could challenge eminent academic scholars, or simply as a politically motivated polemicist whose writings had no scholarly value.

While polemical discussions on the subject have raged on, mainly on the internet, between critics and defenders of my writings, they have been notable only for the incredibly consummate skill with which my critics managed to keep the discussions moving round and round in circles, centered on trivia and badinage, involving personal details concerning myself (from my alleged political opinions to my alleged lack of academic status, skills and qualifications), while completely skirting the objective issues of fact and data concerning the subject on hand.

The pathetic level of these discussions, and the degree of arrogance, virulence and venom spewed by the AIT protagonists, backed as they are by an immensely powerful array of vested interests, is frightening as a sample of the kind of academic environment prevailing today. But there is really no point in trading abuses or witty repartees with every (to use a typical Indian-English phrase) "time-pass" writer, whatever his academic status, who chooses to shoot off his mouth on the subject. I will only be dealing with Witzel's shenanigans throughout this book, wherever called upon to do so.

But the fact is that the debate is no more only a debate between the AIT and OIT sides; it is more of a debate between subjective polemics, entrenched prejudices and dogmas, and academic vested interests, on the one hand, and objective analysis, rational logic and honest, open-minded scholarship, on the other. In this debate, the egos and prejudices of many OIT writers are as much a source of strength for the AIT side as they are a liability for the OIT side, not only in providing plenty of grist for the disinformation mills of the AIT writers, but also in contributing to keep the OIT side divided and effectively prevented from arriving at a rational agreement in their viewpoint.

In this context, I will mention only one OIT writer of this kind, because he has chosen to make his personal resentment public: the Greek writer Nicholas Kazanas. In his article "The Rigveda Date and Indigenism", June 2006, on p. 10, he writes: "**Indeed, in recent years also many publications advocated indigenism: Sethna 1992; Elst 1993; Frawley 1994 and with Rajaram 1997; Feuerstein et al 1995; and others**". In the footnote to this, he writes: "**S. Talageri should perhaps be included but despite having some good ideas, this author knows no Sanskrit and has no training in Archaeology or other related disciplines and so goes astray constantly**"

If Kazanas had merely refrained from mentioning my name in his list of writers who "advocated indigenism", I would naturally have ignored the matter; but Kazanas chooses to make certain comments, and I will, only for this once, condescend to respond to them:

To begin with, whether or not Kazanas agrees with all the views expressed in my writings, and irrespective of his personal opinions of me, how can Kazanas claim that I do not fit into the *single* criterion mentioned by himself: of being the author of a publication which "advocated indigenism", i.e. of being an "OIT" writer? What am I then to be classified as: an AIT writer? I would not, even in childish retaliation, seriously argue that Kazanas himself is not an OIT writer, any more than I could argue that he is not Greek, or he could argue that I am not an Indian. In fact, how many of those, named by himself in his list, would seriously agree with him, not only on my exclusion from a list of writers who "advocated indigenism", but even on the deeper question of whether I "go astray constantly" and whether my work is therefore unfit for consideration? And even, let me add (even at the risk of sounding arrogant), on the basic question of whether *their own* names can be there in this particular context while mine is expressly excluded?

Secondly, do *all* the scholars named in his above list know Sanskrit (and *Vedic Sanskrit* at that), and do they *all* have "training in Archaeology or other related disciplines"?

The truth is that Kazanas initiated a discussion with me by e-mail, from 26/2/2005 to 28/4/2005, in which he tried to point out mistakes in my book (TALAGERI 2000). I am always extremely grateful to people who point out mistakes (whether printing mistakes, or mistakes of fact, data or reasoning) in my writings, since it helps me to correct those mistakes; and, as I told him in that e-mail correspondence, I prefer to have alleged instances of serious mistakes and errors in my writings to be pointed out to me now, when I am alive to be able to either justify myself or to correct those mistakes, than to have them bandied about much later when I am dead and gone and no more able to reply. But, the discussion took an unfortunate turn, due to unreasonable remarks and arguments from his side, and I noticed that it was starting to move round and round in circles (like the internet discussions mentioned above); so we mutually, and (at least on my side) as amicably as possible, decided to close the discussion without bearing any resentment.

Apparently, Kazanas could not leave it at that. He had ended his side of the discussion with a Witzellian thrust, telling me that I was not really qualified to discuss, or write on, the subject since I "do not know" Sanskrit. One year later, in his above article (see quotation above), he again takes up the attack from that point. On the same grounds, he will be summarily dismissing my analysis of the evidence of the Avestan names, in this present volume, on the ground that I "do not know" Avestan.

[Significantly, in his mail to me dated 12/04/2005, Kazanas had written: "**I changed my views about IAs and the RV date because facts compelled my mind (and your 1993 opus helped greatly)**". And now I am not even to be counted among writers who "advocated indigenism".]

There is a saying in various Indian languages: "you can wake up a person who is asleep, but you cannot wake up a person who is only pretending to be asleep". I will, accordingly, henceforward only be concentrating on waking up people who are asleep, and not waste my time in trying to wake up people, from either the OIT side or the AIT side, who pretend to be asleep.

ERRORS IN MY EARLIER BOOKS

For various reasons, I feel it necessary to say a few words, and to give a few details, on errors and mistakes of different kinds in my earlier books:

1. The first mistake I made in my first book (TALAGERI 1993) was in having the book published in two versions. The paperback Voice of India edition, entitled **"The Aryan Invasion Theory and Indian Nationalism"**, was published slightly *earlier*, with a political section (Section 1 in that book) with three chapters. The hardcover Aditya Prakashan edition, entitled **"The Aryan Invasion Theory: a Reappraisal"**, was published a few months later *without* those three chapters (so that section 2 of the VOI edition became section 1 in the AP edition), and with a foreword by Dr. S R Rao.

The mistake did not lie in my making my political views clear (although, as I have clarified in the preface to the reprint in 2003, I would rephrase many of the sentences drastically if I wrote those chapters now; and my political views are more precisely expressed in TALAGERI 1997 and TALAGERI 2005a.): the chapters were absolutely necessary in order to clarify the political misuse being made of the AIT in Indian politics, society and academia, and the logic of those chapters is unanswerable.

The mistake lay in the fact that the different titles gave the impression that I had written two different books, and this left me prey to different emotions: embarrassment, when introduced (at *that* time) as the writer of two books, guilt when I thought of anyone possibly having purchased both books and wasted their money, and a bemused feeling when anyone earnestly assured me that they had read "both" my books.

In hindsight, the three chapters should have been published as a separate booklet.

2. In addition, the book contained quite a few printing errors and other minor errors in the VOI edition, only *some* of which were corrected in the AP edition later on in the year.

The reprint of both the editions, in 2003, did not, however, correct these errors. For example, on p.188 of the VOI edition, the sentence "**which *cannot* occur in the medial position in a word**" has been corrected in the AP edition, in 1993 itself, to "**which *cannot* occur in the initial position in a word**", but was not yet corrected in the 2003 reprint of the VOI edition. However, most such errors were probably not even noticed by the readers, and in any case, did not make much material difference to the main thesis.

3. On some basic points, my second book, **"The Rigveda: a Historical Analysis"**, published in 2000, contained a drastic revision of some aspects of what I had written in my first book. My first book dealt with all the different kinds of arguments on which the AIT is based, and hence was more important as a complete introduction to all aspects of the problem. But, the second book represented a *more direct* study of the literary evidence (which, in my first book was more based on second-hand references: Shendge, Bhargava, etc.), and also of the linguistic material, all of which led to a clearer perspective and some rethinking on many points.

The main rethinking, of course, was on the question of the geographical aspects: it was clear that the (almost) consensus view, that the Rigveda was composed in the Punjab, was totally without any basis in the geographical data in the Rigveda. In my first book, I had blindly accepted this view; but an actual examination of the data showed that the Rigveda was composed in the region of Kurukṣetra, to the *east* of the Punjab, and that the Punjab was originally the home not of the Rigvedic Aryans (the Pūrus), but of their western neighbours, the proto-Iranians (the Anus). This fundamental shift in perspective led to many related corrections in the course of analysis of the Rigveda.

There are many other minor points, pertaining to the literary, linguistic and comparative mythological aspects of the problem, which have undergone rethinking or revision in my second book. I will not go into them here: suffice it to say that where the second book contradicts the first on any point, the second is to be taken as right.

To give one example, in my first book, in the course of pointing out the connections between the Teutonic *Vanir* and the *Paṇis*, I wrote: "**It is not, as we have seen, merely a similarity in names (else we could have tried to identify the Greek *Pan* with the *Paṇis* due to the chance resemblance of the names), but in identity and incidents**" (TALAGERI 1993:390). But further research, in the course of my second book, showed that there actually *was* an *even closer* correspondence, in identity and incidents, between the Greek *Pan* and the *Paṇis* than between the Teutonic *Vanir* and the *Paṇis* (see TALAGERI 2000:486-491).

Likewise, in my first book, I assumed (TALAGERI 1993:370, 375) that the Druhyus in the Dāśarājña battle hymns specifically referred to the Celtic and Italic branches (rather than, as I realized later, to the residual elements of a large amorphous group of branches to whom the Druis or Druids were the common priestly factor), and that these two branches were therefore present in the northwest at the time of the battle and were among the later emigrants. However, I realized later that they were among the earlier emigrants (TALAGERI 2000:260-282).

Even more important, I realized, on my own examination of the Rigvedic evidence, that while the Purāṇas were reliable insofar as some of their basic data was concerned, they were quite unreliable when it came to placing the different kings/ṛṣis from different dynasties/tribes/clans in their relative chronological positions vis-à-vis each other both within the dynastic lists as well as between different dynastic lists, so that five different scholars who try to collate the lists arrive at five mutually incompatible versions of the dynastic lists. Historical or mythical persons (kings or ṛṣis) whom the Rigveda indicates as belonging to the latest Rigvedic period are placed in the earliest periods in Puranic mythology, and some of them seem to be present in every period. Therefore, I decided that the Rigveda would be the sole authority for unraveling the ancient-most history of the Vedic Aryans, or the Indo-Iranians or Indo-Europeans in general, and that any data from any later text (including even post-Rigvedic Vedic literature itself) is absolutely null and void where it seems to contradict the evidence of the Rigveda. It will be noticed, in my last book as well as this present one, that I accept supporting evidence from any other text only when it helps to logically explain certain aspects of the Rigvedic data without contradicting *other* Rigvedic data.

4. My second book also contained many printing errors and some careless mistakes on my part. There was a personal reason behind this [apart from the fact that both my earlier Books (TALAGERI 1993, 2000) were totally handwritten on sheets of paper, and sent to New Delhi by post, since I was quite computer (and even typewriter) illiterate at the time, and typed out by the staff of the publishing house]: my father suffered a massive heart attack in late 1999, and I was desperate to have my book completed when he was still hale and hearty. When the print-out sheets of the completed book were sent to me for proof-reading and corrections, I did a quick (literally a one-or-two-day) job of it, and sent them back to the publishers at once. However, the publishing took its regular time, and the book arrived out many months later. Fortunately my father was able to see, and read, my printed book (he left us, to our eternal grief, on 11/6/2002), but it seems now that a few more days of more careful and minute proof-reading would have made little difference in the date of publication of the book.

Most of these mistakes were corrected in the first reprint of the book in 2004, and I give below a list of all these corrections for any reader who may be having the first (2000) print. The mistakes are classified below as Chart changes, Data changes, Phrase changes, and Spelling corrections:

4a. Chart changes:

p.34: "25-28, 30-32" should be in the "ATRIS" column [in the first print, it is wrongly printed in the "VIŚVĀMITRAS" column].

p.78: In the chart on this page, the uppermost and lowermost sections should be divided into three parts [in the first print, they are wrongly divided into two parts].

p.104: On the chart, the column for "VII, Early I" should extend only up to "Asiknī" [in the first print, it wrongly extends up to "Vitastā"].

4b. Data changes (original erroneous data in brackets):

p.4: I.1-11, 24-30 (eighteen hymns) [I.1-12, 24-30 (nineteen hymns)].

p.4: (twenty-seven hymns) [(twenty-six hymns)].

p.26: I.60.6; IV.1.4. Vājambhara is clearly an inverted form of Bharadvāja. [I.60.6; IV.1.4].

p.53: 8 6+ 3(joint) 2 — 3 [8 6+ 3(joint) — 2 3].

p.98: Anitabhā Rasā [Rasā].

p. 113: I.126.7 [I.126.6].

p.169: (24 verses) [(23 verses)].

p.170: twelve references [eleven references].

p.170: eleven of them [ten of them].

p.:170: IV.7.1, 4 [IV.7.1].

p.457: IAW, p.193 [AW.p.193].

p.474: IAW, p.203 [IAWA, p.203].

p.492: Everyman's Dictionary [Everyman's Encyclopaedia].

p.492: the Vanir...a race which seems to have preceded the Aesir in Scandinavia" [the Vanir, with whom they had first fought and afterwards allied themselves"].

p.492: EDNCM, p.3...224 [EDNCM, p.3.].

p.503: in four including two oldest Maṇḍalas [in seven including three oldest Maṇḍalas].

p.519: Maṇḍala VI with Zhob [Maṇḍala IV with Zhob].

4c. Phrase changes (original erroneous phrases in brackets):

p.xxiii: the Maṇḍala number (in Roman), the hymn number, and the verse number from each other [the Maṇḍala number (in Roman) from the hymn number and the verse number].

p.xxiii: groups of hymns [sections of hymns].

p.xxiii: groups of verses [sections of verses].

p.21: These ten families are identified on the basis of the fact [The basis on which these ten families are identified is the fact].

p.31: verse 12 of [verse 12 to].

p.81: reflect one, the first, of the two [reflect one of the two].

p.90: their own interpretation [their interpretation].

p.94: horizon was western Uttar Pradesh [horizon was eastern Uttar Pradesh].

p.95: "becoming acquainted" [becoming "acquainted"].

p.113: *in fact strong corroboration* [*in itself strong corroboration*].

p.130: with Balhikā and Gandhāri [with the Gandhārīs].

p.145: in which they came [in which the Yadus came].

p.187: *in the Punjab-Haryana region and southern and eastern Afghanistan* [*in the Punjab-Haryana region*].

p.191: Rigvedic India (see map opposite p.120) [Rigvedic India].

p.229: southern and eastern Afghanistan in the west [Afghanistan in the west].

p.230: *the oldest parts of the Avesta* [*one of the oldest parts of the Avesta*].

p.230: and the Indoaryans had not yet migrated southeastwards [and had not yet migrated southeastwards].

p.243: the Aryans who migrated into India were *not* the original Indoaryans [the Vedic Aryans who migrated into India were *not* the original Vedic Aryans].

p.245: baton [torch].

p.257: priesthoods survived [priesthoods flourished].

p.295: hunt out [hunt down].
p.303: hunting out [hunting down].
p.328: are baffling [is baffling].
p.412: And so he neatly [And he neatly].
p.426: towards our earlier book [to our earlier book].
p.426: to its existence [to the existence].
p.447: and the Āngirasa in the rest [and Āngirasa in the rest].
p.455: suspected as an addition [suspected to be an addition].
p.465: mentions rivers west of the Indus [mentions the rivers of Afghanistan].
p.465: every single river of the west [every single river of Afghanistan].
p.468: names of rivers to the west of the Indus [names of rivers in Afghanistan].
p.468: not just of the western banks of the Indus [not just of southern and eastern Afghanistan].

4d. Spelling corrections (page numbers in brackets):

concordance (ix), Sudhee Subrahmanya (ix), quotations (xvi), put in (5), Vavri (9), Vaivasvata (11), Medhyātithi (11), Brahmajāyā (16), Bhāradvājī (17), Kāśirāja (18,118), Vasukra Vāsiṣṭha (31), references to Kutsa (31), Purumīḷha (38), Dīrghatamas (55), Śrutaratha (65), Kaṇva (75), Dṛṣadvatī (99), Maṇḍalas III and VII (103), Gandhāri (113,120,131,132,225), ṛṣis (134), my speech (136), Indoaryans (137,260), contact (137), described (142), in question (143), is distinctly (147), predominant (158), initiators (165), deified (168), 1st millennium (181), Raγa (184), Yašt (184), Kurukṣetra (187), Kurrum (190), movement (198), possibilities (199), latter-day (201,204), Ārjīkīyā (208), settled (214), particularly (222), Avestan (244), Mississippi (246), absolutely (249), depicted (253), rescue (253), ultimate (293), recognizable (295), cannot (302,344,411), sṛṇi (312), attempted (319), appears (324), *mē (325), the bards (371), antiquity (372), Azerbaijan

(375), among (377), eighth Āditya (379), Ambedkar (388), Panjab (430), mountain passes (439), than Book 6 (455), indicated (463), Mānuṣa (509), glorious past (518).

5. All the above are changes or corrections made in my first reprint (in 2004) of my second book, "**The Rigveda: a Historical Analysis**" (2000). Some significant mistakes remain uncorrected:

The first and most important mistake is the one pointed out by Witzel (WITZEL 2001) in his otherwise pointless review of my book. In discussing the order of the six Family Books of the Rigveda, I quoted the testimony of the Aitareya Brāhmaṇa (VI.18), that six hymns (21, 30, 34, 36, 38-39) in Book 3 are late additions into the Book, and that these six hymns contain a total of 68 verses (TALAGERI 2000:73-74). *Actually, these six hymns are **III**.30-31, 34, 36, 38, 48, and they contain a total of 81 verses.*

The second mistake, pointed out to me by Kazanas in his correspondence with me, was the omission, in my list of references to the phrase sapta+sindhu in the Rigveda, of one verse:**VIII.24**.27. This was particularly unfortunate, since **VIII.24**.27 is the *one* verse in the Rigveda which the majority of western scholars accept as a direct reference to a land or region called Sapta Sindhavah (analogous to the Haptahəndu of the Avesta), while the others are indirect references, meaning "seven rivers". In that list (TALAGERI 2000:114), *I inadvertently omitted **VIII.24**.27, and erroneously named another verse, **VIII.96**.1, which in fact does not contain this phrase.*

A third mistake, not yet pointed out by anyone, is in the list of references to camels in the Rigveda: I have given the verses as **I.138**.2; **VIII.4**.7; **5**.37; **46**.22,31 (TALAGERI 2000:122). *The actual verses are: **I.138**.2; **VIII.5**.37; **6**.48; **46**.22,31 (given correctly on another page TALAGERI 2000:225).*

A fourth mistake, a printing error, is in the chart of Family-wise Hymns and verses (TALAGERI 2000:34), where the

Bhṛgus column for Book V shows verses 44.10-12, when it should be a blank space.

A minute and diligent search may, it is possible, unearth a few more such errors in printing of the verse numbers. Fortunately, such errors (regrettable as they are, and certainly a reflection on my proof-reading) do not change the thrust of the data, arguments and conclusions in the smallest bit.

Moreover, these careless mistakes are *just* that: careless mistakes. This is completely different from the kind of deliberate lies, obfuscations, sharp turnarounds, deliberate distortions and misrepresentations or concealment of data; etc. that we see, for example, in the writings of Witzel. Not one of my errors has been a deliberate one, calculated to hide weak points in my case, or to fool my readers into believing that my case is stronger than it is: in fact, the effect of the errors has been, if anything, to show my case in a *less* strong light. For example, the chart of the rivers on p. 104 mistakenly showed the geographical horizon of Book VII extending from the east as far west as the river Vitastā, when actually it extended *only* up to Asiknī.

And it was just this kind of mistake that Kazanas chose to pounce on in his e-mail discussion with me (February to April 2005), referred to earlier. I was genuinely grateful to him for pointing out that in my list of references to the phrase sapta+sindhu on p. 114 of my book, I had omitted the most important reference, **VIII.24**.27. But it turned out that far from trying to be helpful, he was only out to insinuate that I had *deliberately* concealed this reference with some ulterior motive in mind. And the more I tried to point out how ridiculous it was to suggest that I would be trying to conceal evidence which was in my *favour* (and, in fact, if I had ignored the other, indirect, references to the phrase sapta+sindhu, and only taken into account the direct reference in **VIII.24**.27, which is the only reference generally accepted by the western scholars as referring to a region named "Land of the Seven Rivers", then my geographical case would have been even stronger: I could have pointed out that not only western areas like Afghanistan, i.e. *Gandhāri*, but even the area where the Rigveda is alleged to have been composed, the Punjab, i.e. *Sapta Sindhavah,* is referred to *only* in the Late Books, while place names of the East, *Kīkaṭa*, etc., are referred to in the Early Books), the more he insisted on continuing to make an issue out of it.

Even so, I am genuinely grateful to him for pointing out the mistake, and to Witzel for pointing out the other, more important, mistake regarding the hymns referred to in the Aitareya Brāhmaṇa VI.18; and I will be grateful to anyone else who brings forward to my notice any similar mistakes in this present volume (although it has been my effort to try not to make similar careless mistakes this time). I will be happy if they do so in a friendly and helpful spirit, but the exercise will not be any the less welcome even if it is done with unfriendly or hostile intent: *the point is that mistakes should always be corrected.*

ABOUT THE PRESENT BOOK

I should, in general, let this book speak for itself. But I want to make certain points first in this preface.

A. This book, with much new and conclusive evidence (combined with all such evidence from my earlier books as will be necessary to repeat here), will conclusively prove once and for all the following points:

1. The Rigvedic people, the Vedic Aryans, were settled in areas around and to the east of the Sarasvatī river in at least the third millennium BCE, with areas further west being outside their geographical horizon, and they only started migrating or expanding westwards around that time. These Vedic Aryans are identifiable with the Pūru/Paurava tribes of Indian historical tradition.

2. The proto-Iranians, with other related groups (the proto-Greeks, the proto-Armenians and the proto-Albanians), were

settled in the areas to the west of the Vedic Aryans, and started expanding westward around that period. These related groups are identifiable with the Anu/Ānava tribes of Indian historical tradition.

3. The Druhyu tribes of Indian historical tradition were settled in areas to the west and north of the Anu tribes, and had already, earlier, started expanding northwards into Central Asia. The speakers of the other known branches of Indo-European languages (proto-Anatolian, proto-Tocharian, proto-Italic, proto-Celtic, proto-Germanic, proto-Baltic and proto-Slavic) are identifiable with these collectively named Druhyu tribes.

4. There are other important tribes in Indian historical tradition: the Yadus/Yādavas, and the Turvasus/Turvaśas, settled well to the south of the Vedic Aryans, and the more difficult to pinpoint Ikṣvākus/Tṛkṣis, settled to their east but apparently very much involved as allies of the Vedic Aryans. These probably included Indo-European groups, whose speech forms were not included (for the lack of detailed records) in the reconstruction of the proto-Indo-European linguistic paradigm, and may also have included various *other* linguistic groups (proto-Dravidians, proto-Mundas, etc).

Till now, my above points have been assiduously ignored by committed AIT scholars, as well as by academic scholars in general who may be believers in the AIT (the Aryan Invasion Theory; or, for those who prefer such circumlocutions, the Aryan Migration Theory, or the Aryan Trickling-in Theory) simply because they have still not comprehended that there is any serious alternative in the form of an OIT (Out-of India Theory). But, if they continue to do so after this book, they will be doing so only at their own peril.

The committed scholars who have expended years or decades of scholarly effort in research aimed at forcing inconvenient and mutually contradictory facts into the unwilling contours of the AIT, and in forcibly interpreting every old and new piece of data from the point of view of the AIT scenario, will naturally represent a formidable array of vested interests which will do its best to prevent any change in the status quo. But I think, in the long run, they will only be placing themselves in the category of the geocentric theologians and church "scholars" and "scientists" who opposed Galileo's heliocentric theories in the seventeenth century. It will be better if they open their eyes to the actual evidence and carry out a thorough reappraisal of the interpretations they have placed on the historical facts and data. Else, within a few decades, their writings will cease to have any practical value in this field of studies.

I am not placing myself in the category of Galileo, but I think the OIT represents as revolutionary a change from the AIT in the field of Indo-European historical studies, and in fact world historical studies, as the heliocentric theory represented from the then prevalent geocentric theory in the field of seventeenth century European astronomy. And, however much the entrenched AIT scholarship may succeed in stifling the truth today, they will not be able to do so for too long.

And the sad part is that many of these scholars are indeed very much more greatly academically qualified than I am (in their much more detailed and fundamental expertise in the fields of linguistics, archaeology, Vedic language studies, etc.), and therefore, *once they turn in the right direction*, they should be able to uncover much more evidence, and solve many more unsolved problems of history, than I could do. It is a tragic waste of scholarship. And a real tragedy that over a century of elaborately constructed and voluminously researched theories and writings should one day become defunct.

And this is not my ego speaking. The facts stand out loud and clear: the Rigveda and the Avesta, two texts clearly accepted by the western scholars as the ultimate sources for the textual evidence regarding Indo-Iranian history, unanimously and massively present a picture which points in only one direction, and yet scholars have manufactured long and complicated stories out of thin air, based on zero evidence from the texts, which claim to point in the opposite direction.

Asko Parpola's long and detailed papers on Indo-Iranian prehistory in Central Asia and beyond, and Witzel's ludicrous fairy tale (see TALAGERI 2000:458-460) about the migrations "from Iran" of Vasiṣṭha and his clan, are two cases in point. Witzel, in fact, even finds "linguistic evidence" for his fairy tale: see section 1G of Chapter 1.

Witzel's tomfoolery is in keeping with the kind of voluminous "evidence" that has been culled from these texts in over a century of mindless scholarship, right from the time that a single word, *anās*, meaning "mouthless", occurring only once in the Rigveda (and never again after that), was interpreted as meaning "noseless", this was then taken as meaning "flat-nosed", this was then further taken as being a reference to their enemies by the Vedic Aryans, who were of course themselves endowed with noble pointed noses, and this was then finally taken as evidence of the conquest of a flat-nosed native Indian race by Nordic Aryan invaders from outside.

Contrast this with the evidence in Section I of this book, where we see a uni-directional pattern of distribution of references: a huge body of classes of names and name elements, abundantly found in the Avesta and the Mitanni-Kassite data, is also abundantly found in the Rigveda. But while these names and name elements are found in at least 386 hymns in the Books classified by western scholars (including Witzel himself) as Late Books, they are *missing* in the Books classified by them as *Early* — *except* in 8 hymns in those Books, which, again, are among those singled out by these western scholars as *Late*.

Can such massive, overwhelming and uni-directional evidence be denied for long, whatever the academic and media stranglehold of the committed AIT scholars today? Obviously it cannot.

The only circumstance in which this evidence can continue to be denied is if the continuing world trend towards mind-control reaches the limits and proportions depicted by George Orwell in his book "Nineteen Eighty Four". In this book, the world has been divided into a handful of totalitarian states, where mind control has reached the ultimate limits of possibility. The protagonist of the novel, Winston, works in the Ministry of Truth, where his duty consists of doctoring *all* early records *completely*, even in matters relating to mundane events and data of the past, so as to bring them in line with the latest whims or dictates of the totalitarian authorities, so that no evidence exists that the records ever showed anything other than the matter now intended.

In such a world, every single copy of the present Rigveda and Avesta could be *completely* wiped out of existence, and *all* memories of it wiped out of *every* record and *every* mind, and a completely New Rigveda and New Avesta be created; and the substitution would be so absolute and so complete that no-one would *ever* be able to suspect that any other texts had ever existed. This New Rigveda, for example, would contain data which would provide massive, overwhelming and uni-directional evidence for the AIT: it would be so structured that demonstrably "earlier" parts would be *loaded* with Western geographical references, references to spoked wheels and Iranian-Mitanni cultural elements, and *completely lacking* in Eastern geographical references; and would even perhaps contain graphic descriptions of "self-proclaimed" immigrants or invaders conquering eastwards into India, and battling with statedly "native" enemies with clearly Dravidian or Munda names!

But unless such a situation arises, the academic world will ultimately have to deal with the evidence as it exists today, and as it has been analysed in this book, and will have to, more or less, accept the conclusions reached in this book.

B. In this book, I have adopted some new practices.

I have been criticized (WITZEL 2001b) for adopting a system of references, in my earlier books, consisting of footnotes with abbreviated titles of books. I do not find this criticism very relevant, and see nothing wrong with the system adopted by me. But I see no reason to make it a prestige issue, and, therefore, I have now adopted the more common system of references, consisting of giving the name of the author, the year of publication of the book being quoted, and the page number of the quotation, immediately alongside the actual quotation.

I have adopted the above system of references for the sake of convenience, but I have not adopted, and will never adopt, the fraudulent system of providing long bibliographies containing the name of every single book ever read by me (not to mention books not read by me but culled from the bibliographies of other books). The *only* books in my bibliography are those books actually quoted by me, and those referred to in any significant context.

The following is the system of transliteration used in this book:

k kh g gh (n)
c ch j jh (n)
ṭ ṭh ḍ ḍh ṇ
t th d dh n
p ph b bh m
y r l v ś ṣ s h ḷ

a ā i ī u ū ṛ e ai o au

I will not be using separate letters for the nasal sounds of the first and second series (except in the combination jñ), since these sounds do not generally appear except in positions before the other letters in the same series.

Likewise, in transcribing Avestan words, I will generally use the following letters, due to problems of font (thus з to represent the long vowel ∂, etc.):

a ā ∂ з e ē o ō ā^{o} a^{n} i ī u ū

k g γ x č j t d δ θ ṭ p b f n η ṇ m s z š ṣ

I have not bothered to represent certain rare sounds in Avestan, since they are not necessary within the scope of this book.

C. Finally, in this preface itself, I wish to express my special gratitude to certain friends for their consistent practical help (in the form of articles and papers), advice and moral support: namely, Dr. Koenraad Elst, Vishal Agarwal, Dileep Karanth and Sudhee Subrahmanya.

This book, as always, is dedicated to my parents: my mother, Shaila Gangadhar Talageri, and my father, Gangadhar Sitaram Talageri. My father, as I already pointed out earlier, is no longer alive to give me his advice and moral support, and I *very deeply* regret and mourn his absence.

Shri Sita Ram Goel, the *one* person without whom my earlier books would never have been completed and published in the first place, is also no more with us; and I feel his absence also *very deeply*.

Finally, just for the record, I must also mention the names of my beloved nieces, Sanjana J. Kamat (daughter of my sister Sandhya and Jayant Kamat), and Shriya S. Talageri (daughter of my brother Sanjay and Swagata Talageri), who, along with my mother and my late father, are the most important people in my life.

Section I
Chronology and Geography of the Rigveda

Chapter 1

The Relative Chronology of the Rigveda – I Personal Names in the Avesta

The Rigveda and the Avesta are the two oldest "Indo-Iranian" texts. The joint evidence of the Rigveda and the Zend Avesta testifies to a period of common development of culture, which may be called the Indo-Iranian period.

According to the AIT (Aryan Invasion theory), this period preceded the period of composition of the Rigveda and the Avesta: the joint "Indo-Iranians", in the course of their postulated emigrations from South Russia, settled down for a considerable period of time in Central Asia, where they developed this joint culture. Later, they separated from each other, and migrated into their historical areas, where they composed, respectively, the Rigveda and the Avesta, both representing the separate developments of this earlier joint culture. This joint Indo-Iranian culture is, therefore, pre-Rigvedic.

However, as we shall see, the actual evidence in the texts does *not* support the above picture. As we have pointed out in our earlier studies (TALAGERI 1993, 2000), the proto-Iranians were originally inhabitants of northern India — originally, in the pre-Rigvedic period, of the Kashmir region, and later, in the Early Rigvedic period, of the Punjab. In the later part of the Early Rigvedic period, conflicts in the time of the Vedic king Sudās led to large-scale Iranian expansions towards the West. In the Middle and Late Rigvedic periods, the bulk of the proto-Iranians were settled in the westernmost parts of the Punjab and in Afghanistan, with *continuous interaction* with the Vedic Aryans. The Avesta was composed in the Late Rigvedic period, and the joint "Indo-Iranian" culture common to the two texts basically represents this Late period. An examination of the evidence in the Rigveda and the Avesta, as we shall see in this and subsequent chapters, overwhelmingly and very conclusively supports this picture.

In this chapter, we will examine the evidence of the Personal Names in the Avesta. Personal names constitute a very important factor in the analysis of any culture and civilization. Personal names vary with time and space. The personal names current in any society are a definite indicator of the cultural environment of that society, and a very important factor in placing that society in its proper perspective in terms of time and space. This is true even in the modern period, where there has been very great mobility of names in a world that has, to a very great extent, become a "global village". And this was very much true indeed in the conservative periods represented by these two texts.

In India, for example, most personal names are derived from Sanskrit. Yet, it is clear that Sanskrit based names like Balasubrahmaniam, Venkatachalam, Meenakshisundaram, Venugopalan, Ramaswamy or Maniratnam (let alone distinctly Tamil names like Ilangovan or Nedunchezhiyan), even if we omitted the –am/-an endings, would never be mistaken for Punjabi, Bengali or Maharashtrian names, and would be immediately recognized as Tamilian, or at least "South Indian", names. Likewise, Rajinder, Satinder, Jaspal, Harpal, Gurpreet and Manpreet could only be Punjabi names; Abhrakanti, Himanshu, Tapan, Sudhendu and Jyotirmay could only be Bengali names; and Pandurang, Shantaram, Bajirao, Vilasrao, Santaji and Sambhaji could only be Maharashtrian names.

Even within the same community, the trend of names changes with the times. In my own Chitrapur Saraswat community, for example, two centuries ago, we almost exclusively had (male) names ending in –aya and –appaya: Annappaya, Nanjundaya, Ramappaya, Santaya, Shantappaya, Venkateshaya, etc., names unimaginable among Chitrapur Saraswats today. Three to four generations ago, the –aya endings had almost disappeared, but we had names like Bhavanishankar, Shankarnarayan, Manjunath, Pandurang, Sitaram, Keshav, Dattatreya, Kashinath etc., again names which it is impossible to imagine would be given to a (Chitrapur Saraswat) child today. This was followed by a generation of names like Ashok, Vasant, Suresh, Jayant and Mohan, names still current, but not the likeliest names to be given to children today, and not common to the earlier periods either. The current trend is names like Rahul, Rohan, Akshay, Yash, Abhishek, even Kabir and Vedant — names common in Hindi TV serials, and which would have been absolutely impossible two centuries ago. The changes in trends, in female names, would be even more striking. But, almost all these names, through the generations, are Sanskrit based ones (with rare exceptions like the above Kabir) — only the trend has changed: earlier, the names of traditional gods and local deities predominated; this was followed by simpler historical or common Sanskrit names; now, we have "trendy" names borrowed from other communities represented in the entertainment media, or words simply picked up from Sanskrit dictionaries.

The personal names in the Avesta definitely show a cultural environment in common with the Rigveda. But, as we shall see, the common trends in Avestan names are not in common with the Rigveda as a whole, but common exclusively with the *Late* parts of the Rigveda, which squarely places the Zend Avesta and its culture as contemporaneous with the texts and culture of the Late Rigveda, and definitely *posterior* to the texts and culture of the Early Rigveda and the Middle Rigveda.

Names in the Rigveda and Avesta are generally of two types: simple names and compound names. Compound names consist of (generally) two hyphenated or hyphenable elements: a prefix with a word, or a word with a suffix. In most of the cases, the compound name is a combination of two independent words. Technically, these can not be called either a prefix or suffix (since a prefix or suffix is, strictly speaking, a grammatical element which can not function as a word by itself); however, for convenience, we will, in this chapter and elsewhere, refer to the *first component* word as a *prefix*, if it appears to be used as a regular first component word in combination with different other words, and to the *second component* word as a *suffix* if it appears to be used as a regular second component word in combination with different other words. There are also, less commonly, names (in the Rigveda) which basically consist of two word elements, but which (as per the accent) do not fall in the same category as compound names of the above type which may contain the same word element, and these must be noted, separate from the compound names, as single words.

We will examine the Avestan names (a complete list of 422 names is given in M. Mayrhofer's exhaustive study "Altiranischen Namen") under the following heads:

1A. The Early Rigveda — Rigvedic Names.
- A-1. The Early Books.
- 1A-2. The Avesta.
- 1A-3. The Middle and Late Books.
- 1A-4. Certain Basic Words.

1B. The Early Rigveda — Iranian Names.
1C. The Middle Rigveda.
1D. The Late Rigveda.
- 1D-1. Composer Names.
- 1D-2. Names in the Text.
- 1D-3. Other Words in the Text.

1E. Three "BMAC" words in Rigvedic Names.
1F. What the Evidence Shows.
1G. Footnote: An "Iranian" Vasiṣṭha?

1A.
THE EARLY RIGVEDA — RIGVEDIC NAMES.

The Early Rigveda was much earlier than the Avesta (which was contemporaneous with the Late Rigveda), but we do find name-elements in the Early Books of the Rigveda (Books 6, 3 and 7) which persisted through the ages and are found in the Late Books (5, 1, 8, 9 and 10) as well — and therefore also in the Avesta.

1A-1. The Early Books.

In the Early Rigvedic period, we find that suffixes as such had not yet come into vogue in personal names, or, at any rate, not suffixes in common with the Avesta. But we find five prefixes of a very basic nature: the basic adjectival prefixes su- (good) and deva-/diva- (divine), the basic adverbial prefixes puru- (many, much) and viśva- (every, all), and the basic prepositional prefix pra- (forward). These elements are found in the most important names of the period:

Su-: Su-dās, Su-mīḷha, Su-hotra.
Deva-: Deva-vāta/Deva-vat, Deva-śravas, Deva-ka.
Diva-: Divo-dāsa.
Puru-: Puru-panthās, Puru-mīḷha.
Viśva-: Viśvā-mitra.
Pra-: Pra-tardana, Pra-tṛda, Pra-stoka, (Pra-maganda?).

[The name Puru-kutsa, found in **VI.20**.10, as I have pointed out in detail in my earlier book (TALAGERI 2000:66-72), is a late name of the Late period, and along with the name Trasa-dasyu, constitutes a father-and-son pair of names that has been *interpolated* into the Early and Middle Books of the RV in exceptional circumstances. This is mentioned here because it is an important point. However, this fact in itself is actually *irrelevant* to our particular examination here because, even if the lateness of the name is denied, it would still be only one more additional name in our above list.]

The above names are found in the Early Books as follows (the names in brackets being the names of composers, including the names in their patronymics):

Book 6:

16. Divo-dāsa-5,19.
26. Divo-dāsa-5, Pra-tardana-8.

27. Deva-vāta-7.
31. Divo-dāsa-4, (Su-hotra).
32. (Su-hotra).
43. Divo-dāsa-1.
47. Divo-dāsa-22-23, Pra-stoka-22.
61. Divo-dāsa-9.
63. Su-mīḷha-9, Puru-panthās-10.

Book 3:

1-14, 17-18, 23-62 (Viśvā-mitra).

1. Viśvā-mitra-21.
18. Viśvā-mitra-21.
23. Deva-śravas-2-3, Deva-vāta-2-3.
53. Sudās-9,11, Pra-maganda(?)-14.

Book 7:

18. Su-dās-5,9,15,17,22-23,25, Deva-ka-20, Deva-vat-22, Divo-dāsa-25.
19. Su-dās-3,6.
20. Su-dās-2.
25. Su-dās-3.
33. Su-dās-3.
60. Su-dās-8-9.
64. Su-dās-3.
83. Su-dās-1,4,6-8.

1A-2. The Avesta.

Names with these prefixes are found in the Avesta as well, and we also find other names with the word –śravas (as in the early name Deva-śravas above) as a proper suffix:

Hao-/Hu-: Haosrauuah, Haošiiaŋha, Hučiθrā, Hufrauuač, Hugu, Huiiazata, Humaiiaka, Humāiiā, Hušiiaoθna, Hutaosa, Huuarəz, Huuaspa.

Daēuua: Daēuuō.ṭbiš.

Pouru-: Pouru.baṇgha, Pouručistā, Pouruδāxšti, Pouru.jira, Pourušti.

Vīspa-: Vīspatauruši̅, Vīspa.tauruuarī, Vīspa.tauruuā, Vīspa.θauruuō.ašti.

Fra-: Fraŋhād, Frasrūtāra, Fratura.
-srauuah: Haosrauuah, Bujisrauuah, Vīδisrauuah.

1A-3. The Middle and Late Books.

But the profusion of these names in the Avesta does *not* show a particular connection with the Early Books, since these prefixes are found in names in the Middle and Late Books as well, and they are found in the Late Books in even *greater* profusion than in the Early Books.

In the Middle Books, we find only some references to some of the earlier names:

Book 4:

15. Deva-vāta-4.
26. Divo-dāsa-3.
30. Divo-dāsa-20.
43-44. (Puru-mīḷha, Su-hotra).

Book 2:

19. Divo-dāsa-6.

In the Late Books, apart from references to the earlier Su-dās (in **I**.**47**.6; **63**.7; **112**.19), Divo-dāsa (in **I**.**112**.14; **116**.18; **119**.4; **130**.7,10; **VIII**.**103**.2), Puru-mīḷha (in **I**.**151**.2; **183**.5; **V**.**61**.9: **VIII**.**19**.36) and Viśvā-mitra (in **X**.**89**.17; **167**.40), and in the patronymics of the composer names of their descendants, etc., we find (besides the name Puru-kutsa, found in **I**.**63**.7; **112**.7; **174**.2; **V**.**33**.8; **VIII**.**19**.36) the following *new* names not found in the earlier Books:

Su-: Su-śravas, Su-bharā, Su-rādhas, Su-nītha, Su-dakṣa, Su-deva, Su-dīti, Su-medhas, Su-mitra, Su-bandhu, Su-parṇa, Su-kakṣa, Su-hastya, Su-kīrti, Su-vedas.

Deva-: Deva-atithi, Deva-la, Deva-āpi, Deva-rāta, Deva-muni, Deva-gandharva, Deva-jāmaya.

Puru-: Puru-ṇītha, Puru-māyya, Puru-mitra, Puru-medha, Puru-hanman, Purū-ravas, Purū-vasu.

Viśva-: Viśva-manas, Viśva-ka, Viśva-sāman, Viśva-vāra, Viśva-vārā, Viśva-carṣaṇi, Viśva-karmā, Viśvā-vasu.

Pra-: Pra-pathī, Pla-yoga, Pra-yoga, Pra-yasvanta, Pra-gātha, Pra-bhū-vasu, Pra-jā-pati, Pra-cetas.

We also find the word *śravas* (apart from the name Deva-śravas itself, repeated again as the name of a late ṛṣi Deva-śravas Yāmāyana, the composer of **X**.17) as a proper suffix in names: Su-śravas (Avestan Haosrauuah), Upama-śravas, Dīrgha-śravas, Pṛthu-śravas, Satya-śravas.

These names are found as follows:

Book 5:

11-14. (Su-tambhara).
20. (Pra-yasvanta).
22. (Viśva-sāman).
23. (Viśva-carṣaṇi).
24. (Su-bandhu).
28. (Viśva-vārā).
35-36. (Pra-bhū-vasu)
36. Purū-vasu-3.
44. Viṣva-vāra-11.
79. Satya-śravas-1-3, Su-nītha-2.

Book 1:

24-30. (Deva-rāta).
31. Purū-ravas-4.
53. **Su-śravas**-9-10.
59. Puru-ṇītha-7.
100. Su-rādhas-17.
112. Dīrgha-śravas-11, Su-bharā-20.
116. Pṛthu-śravas-21, Viśva-ka-23.
117. Viśva-ka-7, Puru-mitra-20.
151. Puru-mīḷha-2.
183. Puru-mīḷha-5.

Book 8:

1. Pra-pathī-30, Pla-yoga-33.
4. (Deva-atithi).
5. Su-deva-6.

10,48,62-66. (Pra-gātha).
23-26. (Viśva-manas).
23. Viśva-manas-2.
24. Viśva-manas-7.
46. Pṛthu-śravas-21,24.
59. (Su-parṇa).
61. Su-dīti-14.
68. Puru-māyya-10.
70. Puru-hanman-2, (Puru-hanman).
86. Viśva-ka-1-3, (Viśva-ka).
89-90. (Puru-medha).
92. Su-dakṣa-4, (Su-kakṣa).
93. (Su-kakṣa).
102. (Pra-yoga).

Book 9:
5-24. (Deva-la).
84, 101. (Pra-jā-pati)
97. Puru-medha-52.

Book 10:
17. (Deva-śravas).
22. Viśva-sāman-1.
33. Upama-śravas-6-7.
39. Puru-mitra-7.
41. (Su-hastya).
57-60. (Su-bandhu).
65. Viśva-ka-12.
69. Su-mitra-1,3,7-8, (Su-mitra).
70. (Su-mitra).
81-82. (Viśva-karmā).
95. Purū-ravas-2,5,7,11,15, (Purū-ravas).
98. Deva-āpi-2,4-8, (Deva-āpi).
105. Su-mitra-11, (Su-mitra).
107. (Pra-jā-pati).
121. (Pra-jā-pati).
129. (Pra-jā-pati).

130. (Pra-jā-pati).
131. (Su-kīrti).
132. Su-medhas-7.
133. (Su-dās).
139. (Viśvā-vasu, Deva-gandharva).
146. (Deva-muni).
147. (Su-vedas).
153. (Deva-jāmaya).
161. (Pra-jā-pati).
164. (Pra-cetas).
177. (Pra-jā-pati).
179. (Pra-tardana).
181. (Pra-tha).
183. (Pra-jā-vān).
184. (Pra-jā-pati).

1A-4. Certain Basic Words.

It may be noted that the prefix Daēuua- in the Avestan word Daēuuo.ṭbiš, above, is used in a different sense than in the RV: while the Rigvedic *deva* means "god", the Avestan *daēuua* means "demon". The name Daēuuō.ṭbiš, therefore, means "deva-hater". This is one of a group of five Rigvedic words which are of special importance in the study of Indo-Iranian history (already dealt with in detail in TALAGERI 2000:154-160, 176-180, 206-208, 250-254, etc.): *ārya, dāsa, dasyu, deva* and *asura*. These words are found in Avestan names as follows:

Airiia: Airiiāua.

Dā°ŋha: Dā°ŋha.

Daŋhu/daŋзhuš: Daŋhu.frādah, Daŋhu.srūta, Ātərədaŋhu darō.daŋhu, ∂rəzauuaṇt-daŋhзuš.

Daēuua: Daēuuō.ṭbiš.

Ahura: Aṣāhura.

Two other basic Rigvedic words that may be included here are the words for "man" and "hero(ic man)": *Manus* and *Nara*:

Manuš: Manuš.čiθra.

Nara: Narauua.

The words ārya and asura are not found in the RV in personal names (although -asura is found in later times in the names of demons), but the other words are found as follows:

Dāsa: Divo-dāsa (here, in an earlier benevolent etymological meaning of the word. Later, the word acquired an unfavourable connotation, and is not found in personal names in the rest of the Rigveda or subsequent Samhitās, until, in far later times, the word was again introduced in personal names in the new sense of "servant, slave" in names like Rām-dās, Dev-dās, etc.).

Dasyu: Trasa-dasyu, Dasyave-vṛka- (like the Avestan name Daēuuo.tbiš, in a hostile sense, meaning "tormenter of the dasyus" and "a wolf to the dasyus" respectively).

Deva: Vāma-deva, Su-deva, Śūra-deva, Saha-deva (apart from the names with Deva- as a prefix, already listed above).

Manus: Manu/Manus (in the name of the mythical Manu Vaivasvata, as well as a ṛṣi Manu Sāvarṇī or Sāmvaraṇī).

Nara: Nara (the composer of **VI**.35-36).

Finally, we must note two names:

First, the name of a very important historical personality of the Early period, whose name seems to have echoes in the Avesta: *Vasiṣṭha* (the composer of most of Book 7). In the Avesta, we find the following name or epithet: Staotar-vahištahe aṣahe. However, this has nothing to do either with the Rigvedic Vasiṣṭha *or* the name Vasiṣṭha: the related words vasiṣṭha=vahišta simply mean "best", and the Avestan name simply means "reciter of the (Gāθāic formula in Yasna 27.13) aṣəm vohū vahištəm".

Second, the name Vadhryaśva (the name of the father of Divo-dāsa). This name seems to have echoes in the -aśva names found profusely in the Late Books and the Avesta, and is probably the precursor and inspiration for those names. However, it is distinct from those names as shown by its accent, which treats it as single fused word rather than a hyphenated compound word like the rest (except for the analogical formation Vṛśaṇaśva in the Late Books).

1B.
THE EARLY RIGVEDA — IRANIAN NAMES.

Apart from the names given above, we find certain other names, in the Early Books of the RV, which can be identified as Iranian names. These are the names of two related kings, (*Abhyāvartin* Cāyamāna, *Kavi* Cāyamāna), one priest (*Kavaṣa*), and four tribes (*Pṛthu/Pārthava*, *Parśu/Parśava*, *Paktha*, *Bhalānas*).

It must be noted that:

1. *All* these names are found in just *three* hymns.
2. None of these three hymns has been identified as late or interpolated: in short, they are all early hymns.
3. Not a single one of these early persons or tribes named is mentioned again in any hymn in the Middle or Late Books, although some of the words occur again in the names of other later persons.
4. All three hymns pertain to important historical battles in the Early Period, in which the Iranians (well before they appeared in Afghanistan in the Avesta, and further north and west in later periods) are located in eastern and central Puṇjab.

In *addition*, there is one hymn (which may or may not contain interpolations, since this hymn also names two other persons otherwise located only in the Late Books) which names another ṛṣi or priest (*Uśanā*), and his father (*Kavi* Bhārgava), who play a very important role in later mythology built on the Indo-Iranian conflicts (as we shall see later in chapter 7).

These names are found as follows:

Book 6:

20. Uśanā-11, Kavi (Bhārgava)-11.
27. Abhyāvartin (Cāyamāna)-5,8, Pṛthu/Pārthava-8.

Book 7:

18. Paktha-7, Bhalānas-7, Kavi (Cāyamāna)-8, Kavaṣa-12.

83. Pṛthu-1, Parśu/Parśava-1.

All these names are Iranian ones: the names of the royal *Kavi* (Cāyamāna), and the priestly *Kavaṣa* and *Uśanā* (son of *Kavi* Bhārgava) are the Avestan names *Kauui* (kings of the Kauuiiān dynasty), *Kaoša* and *Usan* (son of *Kauui*). The tribal names are the names of the historical Iranian *Parsua/Pārsa* (Persians), *Parthava* (Parthians), *Pakhta* (Pakhtoon) and *Bolan* (Baluchi) tribes. The name *Abhyāvartin* is not immediately apparent as an Iranian name, but all the evidence points to this conclusion: Abhyāvartin has the appellation Cāyamāna (like the king Kavi, adversary of Sudās in the Dāśarājñā hymn **VII**.18 above), he is called a Pārthava or Parthian (Kavi of **VII**.18 is also apparently a Pārthava, since the Pṛthus are again mentioned in the RV in the other Dāśarājña hymn **VII**.83 above among Sudas' adversaries), and all three elements in the name are present in Avestan names (*Aiβi*-x^{V}arənah, Ā̄-iiūta and Fraš.ham.-*varəta*).

Kavi (Bhārgava) and Uśanā (his son) are named again later in the Rigveda. Also, the name Kavaṣa is found again in the name of Kavaṣa Ailūṣa, a late composer, and the name Paktha occurs again later in the name of an individual person:

In the Middle Books:

Book 4:
16. Uśanā-2.
26. Uśanā-1.

In the Late Books:

Book 5:
29. Uśanā-9.
31. Uśanā-8.
34. Uśanā-2.

Book 1:
51. Uśanā-10,11, Kavi-11.
83. Uśanā-5, Kavi-5.

117. Kavi-12.
121. Uśanā-12, Kavi-12.
130. Uśanā-9.

Book 8:

7. Uśanā-26.
22. Paktha-10.
23. Uśanā-17.
49. Paktha-10.

Book 9:

87. Uśanā-3.
97. Uśanā-7.

Book 10:

16. Kavi-11.
22. Uśanā-6.
30-34. (Kavaṣa).
40. Uśanā-7.
49. Kavi-3.
61. Paktha-1.
99. Kavi-9.

1C.
THE MIDDLE RIGVEDA.

In the Middle Rigveda, or the period of the Middle Books of the Rigveda (4 and 2), we find one prefix peculiar to the period, the prefix *Soma-*, common to the Avesta:

In the Avesta, we find one name with this prefix: Haomō.x^{V}arənah.

In the Rigveda, we find two names: Soma-ka and Soma-āhuti, both found *only* in the Middle Books.

Book 4:

15. Soma-ka-9.

Book 2:

4-7. (Soma-āhuti).

We also find here names of four important Rigvedic personalities, who are *not* named in the Early Books, but are found referred to *profusely* from the Middle Books onwards and are referred to in the Avesta as well: *Turvīti*, *Gotama*, *Trita*, and *Kṛśānu* — in the Avesta: *Tauruuaēti*, *Gaotəma*, *θrita* and *Kərəsāni.*

They are found in the following hymns in the Middle Books:

Book 4:

1-42, 45-58. (Gotama).

4. Gotama-11.
19. Turvīti-6.
27. Kṛśānu-3.
32. Gotama-9,12.

Book 2:

11. Trita-19, 20.
13. Turvīti-12.
31. Trita-6.
34. Trita-10,14.

In the Late Books:

Book 5:

9. Trita-5.
41. Trita-4,10.
54. Trita-2.
86. Trita-1.

Book 1:

58-64, 74-93. (Gotama).

36. Turvīti-18.
52. Trita-5.
54. Turvīti-6.
60. Gotama-5.
61. Turvīti-11, Gotama-16.
62. Gotama-13.

63. Gotama-9.
77. Gotama-5.
78. Gotama-1,2.
79. Gotama-10.
85. Gotama-11.
88. Gotama-4,5.
92. Gotama-7.
105. Trita-9,17.
112. Kṛśānu-21, Turvīti-23.
116. Gotama-9.
155. Kṛśānu-2.
163. Trita-2,3.
183. Gotama-5.
187. Trita-1.

Book 8:
7. Trita-24.
12. Trita-16.
41. Trita-6.
47. Trita-13,16.
52. Trita-1.
88. Gotama-4. (Gotama).

Book 9:
31,93. (Gotama).
32. Trita-2.
34. Trita-4.
37. Trita-4.
38. Trita-2.
77. Kṛśānu-2.
86. Trita-20.
95. Trita-4.
102. Trita-2,3.

Book 10:
8. Trita-7,8.
46. Trita-3,6.

48. Trita-2.
64. Trita-3, Kṛśānu-8.
99. Trita-6.
115. Trita-4.

It may be noted that all these personalities are Vedic and *pre*-Zoroastrian:

1. Taurvaēti, in the Avesta, is an early figure, the father or ancestor of Frāčiia, who is the one being praised in Yašt 13.115.

2. Likewise, θrita is specifically mentioned, in Yasna 9.10, as an ancient personality belonging to a period *far earlier* to Pourušaspa, the father of Zaraθuštra. (Trita, in the RV, belongs to a branch of Angiras priests, the Gṛtsamadas, who converted to the Bhṛgu rituals, and came to constitute a new family of priests, the Kevala Bhṛgus, one of the two main families of priests in the Middle period).

3. Kərəsāni is mentioned in hostile terms as a king opposed to the Āθrauuans or Iranian priests. (The Vedic Kṛśānu is an archer in the Soma regions of the West, guarding the Soma).

4. And Gaotəma is described as a sage who engaged Zaraθuštra in debate, and was defeated by him. (The Gotamas, alongwith the Auśijas, constitute the other of the two main families of Vedic priests in the Middle period: the ones who militantly represented the Angirases in that period, and whose hymns contain references which can be interpreted in relation to historical Indo-Iranian conflicts). But this Gotama, contemporaneous with Zaraθuštra, is clearly not the (Vāmadeva) Gotama of Book 4: he is named Nāiδiiā°nha Gaotəma (the first word is usually translated *literally* by the scholars), which, in Vedic terms, would be Nāidhyāsa Gotama, and has been correctly identified by many scholars (e.g. T.R. Sethna, in his "Yashts in Roman script with translation", Karachi, 1976) as the (Nodhās) Gotama of the late Book 1 (composer of **I**.58-64, Nodhās is mentioned only in **I.61**.14; **62**.13; **64**.1; **124**.4).

In addition, we have in the Avesta the name *Gauuaiiān*, containing the name of the gayal (Vedic *gavaya*, mentioned in **IV.21**.8), a bovid native mainly to northern India.

And Michael Witzel identifies the name *Dṛbhīka* (**II.14**.3) as the name of an Iranian tribe *Derbhikes*: if so, we have one more Iranian tribe named in the Rigveda as evidence that Iranian tribes found centuries later in Iran and Central Asia were present in areas far to the east in earlier times.

1D.
THE LATE RIGVEDA.

Finally, we come to the bulk of the "Indo-Iranian" names: i.e. of the names and name-elements (prefixes and suffixes) common to the Avesta and the Rigveda. First, a list of the Avestan names and name-elements shared by it with the Rigveda, apart from the earlier names and name-elements already seen:

Aēuua- (Eka-/Evā-):Aēuuō.gafiia, Aēuuō.sarəd.

Aiβi- (Abhi-): Aiβi x^{v}arənah.

Āiθβiiu/Āθβiia (Āptya): Āiθβiiu, Āθβiia.

-ana/-aiiana (-ayana): Asabana, Aštō.kāna, Dānaiiana, Frāšaoštraiiana, Friiāna, Gaoraiiana, Jīštaiiana, Varakasāna, Viiātana.

Aošnara (Uṣīnara): Aošnara.

Arəna- (Ṛṇa-): Arənauuāčī.

-aršti (Ṛṣṭi-): Bərəziiaršti, Pərəθuuaršti, Tižiiaršti, Vaēžiiaršti, Vīžiiaršti.

Aṣa-/-ərəta (Ṛta-): Aṣa.nəmah, Aṣasairiiā°ṇč, Aṣasarəda, Aṣasauuah, Aṣastū, Aṣa.šiiaoθna, Aṣauuazdah, Aṣāhura, Aṣāuruuaēθa/Aṣāuruuaθa, Aṣāuuaŋhu, Aṣō.paoiriia, aṣō.raočah.

Astuuaṭ.ərəta, ūxšiiaṭ.ərəta.

Aspa-/-aspa (Aśva/Aśva-/-aśva): Aspāiiaoδa, Aspōpaδōmašti.

Arəjəṭ.aspa, Auruuaṭ.aspa, Čāθvarəspa, Dāzgrāspi, Dʒjāmāspa, ərəzrāspa, Frīnāspa, Habāspa, Haēčat.aspa,

Harəδāspa, Hitāspa, Huuaspa, Jāmāspa, Kərəsāspa, Pourušaspa, Siiāuuāspi, Tumāspana, Važāspa, Vīrāspa, Vīštāspa, Yuxtāspa, Xšōiβrāspa/Xšuuiβrāspa.

[Also, according to Mayrhofer, the following names, which appear in the Avesta without the suffix –aspa, are actually cursive forms of –aspa names]: Aētauuāspa, Aiiūtāspa, Frauuāspa, Friiāspa, Rauuat.aspa, Spitiiaspa, Tusāspa, Zairitāspa.

-asti (-atithi): Aiiō.asti, Gaiiaδāsti, Pouruδāxšti, Vohuuasti.

Ašta- (Aṣṭa-): Aštō.kāna.

Auuahiia (Avasyu): Auuahiia.

Baēšata- (Bhiṣag): Baēšatastūra.

-baṇgha (Bhanga): Pouru.baṇgha.

Bərəz(i)- (Bṛhad-): Bərəziiaršti, Bərəzišnu, Bərəzuuaṇt.

Bзṇduua (Bandhu/-bandhu): Bзṇduua.

Bi- (Dvi-): Biiaršan, Biuuaṇdaŋha.

Buδra (Budha): Buδra.

-čiθra (Citra-/-citra): Atərəčiθra, Frāčiθra, Hučiθrā, Huuarəčiθra, Manuš.čiθra.

-əṇti (-anti): Rāštarə.vaγəṇti, Uxšəṇti/Uxšiieiṇti.

-ərəδβa, (Ūrdhva-): -ərəδβa.

ərəxša (Ṛkṣa): ərəxša.

ərəzu-/əraza- (Ṛjū-): ərəzu, ərəzauuaṇt, ərəzauuaṇt-daŋhзuš.

Fraš- (Pras-): Fraš.ham.varəta.

Frān- (Prāṇa): Frāniia.

Friia/Frī- (Priya-/-prī): Friia, Friiāna, Frīnāspa.

Gaiia (Gaya): Gaiia.

Gaṇdərəβa (Gandharva): Gaṇdərəβa.

Gaora- (Ghora): Gaoraiiana, Gaori.

-gu (-gu): Auuārəgu, Dāzgrō.gu, Hugu, Paršaṭ.gu, Vīdaṭ.gu, Yaētuš.gu, Zainigu.

Ham- (Sam-): (Fras.)ham.varəta, Ham.barətar-vaŋhuuam.

Humāiia (Sumāya): Humāiia.

Huuarə- (Svar-): Huuarəčaēšman, Huuarəčiθra.

-iiasna (Yajña): Mazdaiiasna.

-iiazata (Yajata): Huiiazata, Sūrō.yazata.

Karapan (Kṛpa): Karapan.

Karšnaz (Kṛṣṇa): Karšnaz.

Kasu/Kasu- (Kaśu): Kasu, Kasupitu.

Kərəsa- (Kṛśa): Kərəsaoxšan, Kərəsauuazdah, Kərəsāspa.

-maēša (Meṣa): Daβramaēši.

-manah (-manas): Nərəmanah.

Māiia-/-māiia (Māya- /-māyya): Māiiauua, Humāiia, Humāiiaka.

Mazda- /-miiazdana (Medha-/-medha): Mazdaiiasna. Nərəmiiazdana.

Nabānazdišta (Nābhānediṣṭha): Nabānazdišta.

Nərə- (Nṛ-): Nərəmanah, Nərəmiiazdana.

Paiti- (Prati-): Paiti.drāθa, Paitiiaršauuaṇt, Paiti.srīra, Paiti.vaŋha.

Paršaṭ- (Pṛṣad-): Paršaṭ.gu.

Pauruua (Paura): Pauruua.

Pərəθu- (Pṛthu/Prthu-/Pṛth-): Pərəθuuafsman, Pərəθuuaršti.

Raočas-/-raočah (-rocis): Raocasčaēšman.

Aṣəm.yeŋhe.raočā°, Aṣō.raočah, Vərəsmō.raočah, Vohuraocah.

-raθa (Ratha-/-ratha): Aγraēraθa, Dāraiiaṭ.raθa, Frāraiiaṭ.raθa, Skāraiiaṭ.raθa.

Saēna (Śyena): Saēna.

-sarəda (-śardha): Aēuuō.sarəd, Aṣa-sarəda.

Sauuah/-sauuah (Śavas-): Sauuah, Atərəsauuah, Vouru.sauuah.

Sā°ŋha (Śāsa): Sā°ŋha.

Siiāuua- (Śyāva, Śyāva-): Siiāuuaršan, Siiāuuāspi.

Srūta-/-srūta (Śruta-/-śruta): Srūtaṭ.fədrī, srūtō.spāda. Asruta, Daŋhu.srūta, Dūraēsrūta, Frasrūtāra, Vīsrūta, Vīsrūtāra.

Spiti/Spit- (Śvit-): Spitāma, Spiti, Spitiiura.

-stū/-stūt (-stuta): Aṣastū, Ahūm.stūt.

Sūrō- (Śūra-): Sūrō.yazata.

-stura (Sthūra-): Baešatastūra, Pairištūra, Aoiγmatastura/ Ōiγmatastura.

-tanū (-tanu): Pəṣō.tanū.

-taosa (-tośa): Hutaosa.

θraētaona (Traitana): θraētaona.

θri- (Tri-): θrimiθβaṇt.

-uuaṇt/-mant (-vanta/-manta): Aršauuaṇt, Bərəzuuaṇt, Gaomaṇt, Isuuaṇt, Stiuuaṇt, Taⁿθriiāuuaṇt, Viiaršauuaṇt, Vīuuaŋᵛhaṇt, Viuuarəšuuaṇt, Xᵛanuuaṇt, Zbauruuaṇt, θrimiθβaṇt.

-ura (Urā): Spitiiura.

Uruāxšaiia (Urukṣaya): Uruāxsaiia.

Usij (Auśija): Usig.

Uštra/-uštra (Uṣṭra): Uštra, Arauuaoštra, Auuāraoštri, Fərašaoštra/Frašaoštra, Vohuštra, Zaraθuštra.

Uxšan/-uxšan (Ukṣan-): Uxšan.

Kərəsaoxšan, Srīraoxšan.

Vaēdaŋha (-vedas): Vaēdanha.

Vaŋhu/Vohu/Vaŋhu-/Vohu/-vaŋhu/-vohu (Vasu/Vasu-/-vasu): Vaŋhu, Vohu.

Vaŋhu, Vaŋhuδāta, Vaŋhu.fədrī, Vohu.dāta, Vohu.nəmah, Vohu.pərəsa, Vohuraočah, Vohuštra, Vohuuasti, Vohuuazdah.

Aipiuuaŋhu, Aṣāuuaŋhu, Fradaṭ.vaŋhu, Gaopiuuaŋhu, Ham.bərətar-vaŋhuuam, Jārō.vaŋhu, Mazdrāuuaŋhu, Nəmō.vaŋhu, Srīrāuuaŋhu, Aipi.vohu.

-varəta (-varta): Fraš.ham.varəta.

Varāza (Varāha): Varāza.

Varšna (Vrṣan/-vṛṣan): Varšna.

Varšni (Vṛṣṇi): Varšni.

Vi- (Vi-): Viiaršauuaṇt, Viiātana, Vīsrūta, Vīsrūtāra, Vistaru, Viṭkauui, Vīuuaŋᵛhaṇt, Vīuuarəšuuaṇt/Vīuuārəšuua.

Vīdaṭ- (Vidad-): Vīdaṭ.gu, Vīdaṭ.xᵛarənah.

Virāza (Virāṭ/Virāj): Virāza.

Vīuuaŋᵛhaṇt: Vivasvat.

-xratu (-kratu): Spəntō.xratu.

Xšaθra-/-xšaθra (-kṣatra): Xšaθrō.činah.

Xᵛāxšaθra.

Xuṇb- (Kumbha): Xuṇbiia.
Yima (Yama): Yima.
Zairi- (Hari-/-hari): Zairiči, Zairiiaṇč, Zairita, Zairiuuari.
Zaraθ- (Jarat-): Zaraθuštra.
Zrazdā- (Śraddhā): Zrazdāti.

All the above names, except Usig and Nabānazdišta, are from Mayrhofer's list. These two names, for some reason, are missing from that list (although both are clearly names of persons, and Usig is named along with Karapan, which Mayrhofer accepts as a name).

These names, or names containing these name-elements (prefixes or suffixes) in common with the Avesta, are found in great profusion in the Rigveda, giving evidence of a period of common cultural development: the common "Indo-Iranian period" represented by these two texts.

We will now examine the case, with regard to these names and name-elements, in greater detail, under the following categories: composer names, names in the text, and other words in the text.

In the following lists, the elements common to both texts are italicized. When the two elements in a compound name are separately, but not together, found in both texts, they are both italicized. When the entire compound name, with both elements, is found in both the texts, the name is emphasized in **bold letters**: (note also the name **Su-śravas** earlier).

1D-1. Composer Names.

In the Early and Middle Books, we find *only the following one name*:

Book 3:
36. *Ghora*.

And this hymn, **III**.36, is one of the six hymns in the Rigveda for which we actually have a categorical mention in the Vedic texts themselves about the hymns concerned being interpolations or late additions into the text: i.e. hymns added into the original core Rigveda of the Family Books (2-7) at the time of inclusion of Books 1 and 8 into the collection. The Aitareya Brāhmaṇa VI.18 specifies these six hymns: **III**.30-31, 34, 36, 38, 48. [See TALAGERI 2000.73-74. In my above book, I had erroneously given the hymn numbers as 21,30,34,36,38-39, for which I faced sharp criticism from Witzel, in this case well-deserved. However, the point made by me, about the original Rigveda of the Family Books having been arranged in order of ascending number of verses remained valid, since the verse-count of the six Books would then be 429, 536, 589, 727, 765, 841].

In the Late Books (5, 1, 8, 9, 10):

Book 5 (39 hymns):

1. *Budha*.
3-6. *Vasu-śruta*.
9-10. *Gaya*.
20. Prayas-*vanta*.
24. *Bandhu*, Su-*bandhu*, *Śruta-bandhu*, Vipra-*bandhu*, Gopa-*ayana*.
25-26. *Vasū*-yu.
31. *Avasyu*.
33-34. *Sam*-varaṇa.
35-36. Prabhū-*vasu*.
45. *Tri*-śoka.
46. *Prati-kṣatra*.
47. *Prati-ratha*.
48. *Prati*-bhānu.
49. *Prati*-prabha.
52-61. **Śyāva-aśva**.
62. *Śruta*-vid.
67-68. *Yajata*.
73-74. *Paura*.
75. *Avasyu*.
81-82. **Śyāva-aśva**.

Book 1 (40 hymns):

12-23. *Medha-atithi*.
36-43. *Ghora*.
44-50. *Pras*-kaṇva.
100. **Ṛjra-aśva**.
105. *Āptya*.
116-126. *Auśija*.

Book 8 (50 hymns):

1. *Medha-atithi*, *Medhya-atithi*.
2. *Medha-atithi*, *Priya-medha*.
3. *Medhya-atithi*,
4. Deva-*atithi*.
5. Brahma-*atithi*.
10. *Ghora*.
14-15. *Aśva*-sūktin.
23-26. Viśva-*manas*, *Vi-aśva*.
27-31. *Vivasvat*.
32. *Medha-atithi*.
33. *Medhya-atithi*.
34. Nīpa-*atithi*.
35-38. **Śyāva-aśva**.
43-44. *Vi*-rūpa.
46. *Aśva*.
47. *Āptya*.
48. *Ghora*.
49. *Pras*-kaṇva.
50. Puṣṭi-*gu*.
51. Śruṣṭi-*gu*.
53. *Medhya*.
55. *Kṛśa*.
56. *Pṛṣadh*-ra.
57-58. *Medhya*.
62. *Ghora*.
68-69. *Priya-medha*.
75. *Vi*-rūpa.

80. *Eka*-dyū.
85-87. *Kṛṣṇa*.
89-90. **Nṛ-medha**, Puru-*medha*.
92. *Śruta*-kakṣa.
98-99. **Nṛ-medha**.

Book 9 (23 hymns):
2. *Medha-atithi*.
27. **Nṛ-medha**.
28. *Priya-medha*.
29. **Nṛ-medha**.
32. **Śyāva-aśva**.
33-34. *Āptya*.
35-36. Prabhū-*vasu*.
41-43. *Medhya-atithi*.
68. Vatsa-*prī*.
72. *Hari-manta*.
80-82. *Vasu*.
94. *Ghora*.
95. *Pras*-kaṇva.
97. *Vasu*-kra, Karṇa-*śrut*.
101. Andhī-*gu*, **Śyāva-aśva**, *Sam*-varaṇa.
102. *Āptya*.
103. *Dvi*-ta, *Āptya*.

Book 10 (90 hymns):
1-7. *Āptya*.
10. *Yamī*, *Vivasvatī*.
14. *Yama*, *Vivasvat*.
15-19. *Yama-ayana*.
20-26. *Vasu*-kṛt, *Vasu*-kra, *Vi*-mada.
27-29. *Vasu*-kra.
37. *Abhi*-tāpa.
42-44. *Kṛṣṇa*.
45-46. Vatsa-*prī*.
47. Sapta-*gu*.
54-56. *Bṛhad*-uktha.

57-60. *Bandhu*, Su-*bandhu*, *Śruta-bandhu*, Vipra-*bandhu*, Gopa-*ayana*.
61-62. *Nābhānediṣṭha*.
63-64. *Gaya*.
65-66. *Vasu*-karṇa, *Vasu*-kra.
72. Dakṣa-*ayanī*.
75. *Priya-medha*.
76. *Jarat*-karṇa.
77-78. *Eka*-dyū.
90. Nara-*ayana*.
96. Sarva-*hari*.
97. *Bhiṣag*.
98. Ṛ*ṣṭi*-ṣeṇa.
101. *Budha*.
102. Bhṛmya-*aśva*.
103. *Prati-ratha*.
104. *Aṣṭa*-ka.
109. *Ūrdhva*-nābha.
111. *Aṣṭā*-damṣṭra, *Vi*-rūpa..
112-114. *Vi*-rūpa.
115. Upa-*stuta*.
118. *Urukṣaya*.
120. *Bṛhad*-diva.
122. *Citra*-mahā.
128. *Vi*-havya.
130. *Yajña*.
132. **Nṛ-medha**.
134. Yuvana-*aśva*.
135. *Yama-ayana*.
139. Viśvā-*vasu*, Deva-*gandharva*.
144. *Ūrdhva-kṛśana*, *Yama-ayana*.
147. Su-*vedas*.
148. *Pṛthu*.
151. *Śraddhā*, Kāma-*ayanī*.
152. *Śāsa*.
154. *Yamī*, *Vivasvatī*.

157. *Āptya*.
163. *Vi*-vṛhā.
166. *Virāj*.
168. *Vāta-ayana*.
170. *Vi*-bhrāj.
172. *Sam-varta*.
174. *Abhī-varta*.
175. *Ūrdhva*-grāvā.
179. *Uśīnara*, *Vasu-manas*.
186. Vāta-*ayana*.
188. *Śyena*.
191. *Sam*-vanana.

1D-2. Names in the Text.

In the Early Books, we find only one name:

Book 7:

33. *Yama*-9,12.

In the Middle Books, also, we find only one name:

Book 4:

30. *Citra-ratha*-18.

Both these hymns, **VII**.33 and **IV**.30, pertain to historical battles between the Iranians and the Vedic Aryans: the first to the Dāśarājña battle, and the second to the battle beyond the Sarayu. And, even more significantly, both these hymns are placed by the western scholars (eg. in Oldenberg's classification of the hymns) among the *late or interpolated* hymns which do not fit into the numerical principles of arrangement of the hymns in the Family Books.

In the Late Books:

Book 5:

10. *Gaya*-3.
18. *Dvi*-ta-2.
19. *Śvit*-ra-3, *Brhad*-uktha-3.

27. *Tri-vṛṣan*-1, *Aśva-medha*-4-6.
30. *Ṛṇan*-caya-12,14.
31. *Avasyu*-10.
33. Māruta-*aśva*-9, *Sam*-varaṇa-10.
36. Purū-*vasu*-3, *Śruta-ratha*-6.
41. *Āptya*-9.
44. *Evā*-vada-10, *Kṣatra*-10, *Yajata*-10-12, *Śyena*-11, *Śruta*-vid.
45. *Tri*-śoka-30.
52. **Śyāva-aśva**-1.
61. **Śyāva-aśva**-5, *Śyāva*-9, *Vidad-aśva*-10, *Ratha*-vīti-18-19.
74. *Paura*-4.
75. *Avasyu*-8.
79. Śucad-*ratha*-2.

Book 1:

18. *Auśija*-1.
33. *Śvit*-ra-14-15.
35. *Yama*-6.
36. *Vṛṣan*-10, *Medhya-atithi*-10,11,17, Upa-*stuta*-10,17, *Bṛhad-ratha*-18.
38. *Yama*-5.
44. *Pras*-kaṇva-6.
45. *Pras*-kaṇva-3, *Vi*-rūpa-3, *Priya-medha*-3-4.
51. *Vi*-mada-3.
83. *Yama*-5
100. **Ṛjra-aśva**-16-17.
112. Pṛśni-*gu*-7, *Śruta*-rya-9, *Aśva*-10, *Tri*-śoka-12, Upa-*stuta*-15, *Vi-aśva*-15, *Pṛthi*-15, *Vi*-mada-19, *Ṛta*-stubh-20, Dhvas-*anti*-23, Puruṣ-*anti*-23.
116. *Vi*-mada-1, *Yama*-2, Agha-*aśva*-6, **Ṛjra-aśva** -16, *Pṛthu*-śravas-21, *Kṛṣṇa*-23, *Vi*-bhindu-20.
117. *Kṛṣṇa*-7, *Nṛ*-ṣad-8, *Śyāva*-8,24, *Vi*-mada-20, **Ṛjra-aśva** -17-18.
119. *Auśija*-9.

122. *Auśija*-4-5, *Śruta-ratha*-7, Iṣṭa-*aśva*-13.
126. *Śyāva*-3.
139. *Priya-medha*-9.
158. *Traitana*-5.
163. *Yama*-2.
164. *Yama*-46.

Book 8:

1. Nindita-*aśva*-30, *Medhya-atithi*-30, Svanad-*ratha*-32.
2. *Medhya-atithi*-40, *Vi*-bhindu-41.
3. *Pras*-kaṇva-9, *Kṛpa*-12, *Paura*-12, *Śyāva*-ka-12, *Priya-medha*-16
4. *Śyāva*-ka-2, *Kṛpa*-2, *Priya-medha*-20.
5. *Priya-medha*-25, Upa-*stuta*-25, *Kaśu*-37.
6. *Priya-medha*-45.
8. *Priya-medha*-18, *Medha-atithi*-20.
9. *Vi-aśva*-10, *Vi*-mada-15.
12. *Āptya*-16.
19. *Śyāva*-37.
21. *Citra*-17-18.
23. Viśva-*manas*-2, *Vi-aśva*-16,23-24, *Sthūra*-yūpa-24.
24. Viśva-*manas*-7, *Aśva*-14, *Vi-aśva*-22-23,28-29.
25. *Ukṣaṇya-ayana*-22.
26. *Vi-aśva*-9,11.
32. *Priya-medha*-30.
33. *Medhya-atithi*-4.
34. *Vasu-rocis*-16.
35. **Śyāva-aśva**-19-21.
36. **Śyāva-aśva**-7.
37. **Śyāva-aśva**-7.
38. **Śyāva-aśva**-8.
45. *Śavasī*-5, *Tri*-śoka-30.
46. *Pṛthu*-śravas-21,24, *Aśva*-21,33-21,33.
47. *Āptya*-13-15,17, *Dvi*-ta-16.

49. Nīpa-*atithi*-9.
50. *Paura*-5.
51. *Sam*-varaṇa-1, *Nīpa-atithi*-1, *Medhya-atithi*-1, Puṣṭi-*gu*-1, Śruṣṭi-*gu*-1, *Pṛṣad*-vāṇa-2, *Pras*-kaṇva-2.
52. *Vivasvat*-1, *Ṛjū*-nas-2, *Prṣadh*-ra-2, *Medhya*-2, *Eka*-dyū-2.
54. *Paura*-1, *Kṛśa*-2, *Sam-varta*-2, *Pras*-kaṇva-8.
56. Pūta-*kratu*-2,4.
59. *Kṛśa*-3.
68. Puru-*māyya*-10, *Ṛkṣa*-15,16, *Aśva-medha*-15,16, Pūta-*kratu*-17.
69. *Priya-medha*-8,18.
70. *Śūra*-deva-15.
74. *Śruta*-rvan-4,13, *Ṛkṣa*-4,13.
75. *Vi*-rūpa-6.
77. *Śavasī*-2.
80. *Eka*-dyū-8.
85. *Kṛṣṇa*-3-4.
92. *Śruta*-kakṣa-25.
103. Upa-*stuta*-8.

Book 9:

43. *Medhya-atithi*-3.
58. Puruṣ-*anti*-3.
65. *Vi-aśva*-7.
113. *Vivasvat*-8.

Book 10:

8. *Āptya*-8.
10. *Yama*-7,9,13, *Yami*-7,9,14.
12. *Yama*-6.
13. *Yama*-4.
14. *Vivasvat*-1,5, *Yama*-1-5,7-15, *Vi*-rūpa-5.
15. *Yama*-8.
16. *Yama*-9.
17. *Yama*-1, *Vivasvat*-1,2.

18. *Yama*-13.
20. *Vi*-mada-10.
21. *Yama*-5.
23. *Vi*-mada-6-7.
24. *Vi*-mada-4.
31. *Nṛ*-ṣad-11.
33. *Mitra-atithi*-7.
39. *Vi*-mada-7.
47. Sapta-*gu*-6.
49. *Śruta*-rvan-5, *Bṛhad-ratha*-6.
51. *Yama*-3.
52. *Yama*-3.
55. Viśva-*manas*-8.
58. *Yama*-1, *Vivasvat*-1.
59. *Uśīnar*āṇi-10
60. *Ratha*-proṣṭhas-5, *Yama*-10, *Vivasvat*-10.
61. *Nṛ*-ṣad-13, *Vi*-taraṇa-17, *Nābhānedišta*-18, *Aśva*-ghna-21.
63. *Gaya*-17.
64. *Yama*-3, *Gaya*-16-17.
65. *Śyāva*-12, *Vi*-mada-12.
73. *Priya-medha*-11.
80. **Nṛ-medha**-3.
92. *Yama*-11.
93. *Prtha*-vāṇa-14, *Prthi*-15, **Māyava**-15.
96. *Ṛṣṭi*-ṣeṇa-5,6,8.
97. *Yama*-16.
98. Śan-*tanu*-1,3,7, *Ṛṣṭi*-ṣeṇa-6,8.
99. *Auśija*-11.
106. Ni-*tośa*-6.
115. Upa-*stuta*-8,9.
120. *Āptya*-6.
123. *Yama*-6.
132. **Nṛ-medhas**-7, Su-*medhas*-7.
135. *Yama*-1,7.
148. *Prthī*-5.

154. *Yama*-4,5.
164. *Vivasvat*-2.
165. *Yama*-4.

It may be noted that many of the above names and name-elements common to the Avesta and the Rigveda may be common names and elements which originated among the Rigvedic Aryans and spread to the Iranians, or originated among the Iranians and spread to the Rigvedic Aryans. Or they may, in either text or both the texts, refer specifically to Rigvedic Aryan individuals (like the names in Section C) or Iranian individuals (like the names in section B): here the Iranian Yima is clearly the original of the Rigvedic Yama.

In any case, there are several *other* names in the Rigveda which have been identified by various scholars as Iranian: for example, Michael Witzel (in his "The Languages of Harappa", 2000) and Gamkrelidze (in his "Indo-European and the Indo-Europeans", 1995), identify certain names in the Rigveda as Iranian. These include, (along with names common to the Avesta and the Rigveda, already listed here, like *Kaśu*, *Kṛśa*, *Pṛthu-śravas*), the following names of individuals, *all* of which are restricted to the *Late* Books:

Book 1:

51. Vṛcayā-13.

Book 8:

4. Kurunga-19.
5. Caidya-37-39.
6. Tirindira-46, Parśu-46.
23. Varosuṣāman-28.
24. Varosuṣāman-28.
25. (Varo)suṣāman-2.
26. Varosuṣāman-2.
32. Anarśani-2.
46. Kanīta-21,24.

Book 10:

86. Parśu-23.

1D-3. Other Words in the Text.

There are some words, found as names and name-elements in the personal names in the Avesta, which are *very important* in that text. But these words are *not* found as names or name-elements in the Rigveda, although the actual *words* themselves are very important in the Vedic language and in subsequent classical Sanskrit. But what is of significance is the distribution of these words in the text of the Rigveda: an examination shows that these words, part of the common "Indo-Iranian" heritage, are *completely unknown* to the Early and Middle Books.

The first category of such words is that of *animal names*: the Avestan names include names with *Aspa-/-aspa* (horse), *-gu* (cow) and *Uxšan/-uxšan* (ox); and, as we have already seen, compound personal names with *Aśva/Aśva-/-aśva*, *-gu* and *Ukṣan-* are found in the Rigveda *only in the Late Books*. Other names include those with *–maēša* (sheep), *-ura* (lamb), *Uštra/ -uštra* (camel), *Varāza* (boar) and *Varšni* (ram): these words are *not* found in personal names in the Rigveda, but they are found simply as animal names: *meṣa*, *urā*, *uṣṭra*, *varāha* and *vṛṣṇi*. And every single occurence of these common "Indo-Iranian" animal names is found only in the *Late* Books (in fact only in the non-family Books 1, 8-10):

Book 1:

10. Vṛṣṇi-2.
43. Meṣa-6, meṣī-6.
51. Meṣa-1.
52. Meṣa-1.
61. Varāha-7.
88. Varāhu-5.
114. Varāha-5.
116. Meṣa-16.

117. Meṣa-17,18.
121. Varāhu-11.
138. Uṣṭra-2.

Book 8:

2. Meṣa-40.
5. Uṣṭra-37.
6. Uṣṭra-48.
34. Urā-3.
46. Uṣṭra-22,31.
66. Urā-8.
77. Varāha-10.
97. Meṣa-12.

Book 9:

8. Meṣa-5.
86. Meṣa-47.
97. Varāha-7.
107. Meṣa-11.

Book 10:

27. Meṣa-17.
28. Varāha-4.
67. Varāha-7.
86. Varāha-4.
91. Meṣa-14.
95. Urā-3.
99. Varāha-6.
106. Meṣa-5.

In a second category, there are some words, *important in the Vedic (and later Sanskrit) language*, which are found in the Avesta in personal names, but which are found in the Rigveda, as *words*, only in late occurences. These are the Avestan *Frāniia*, *Gaṇdərəβā*, *Humāiiā*, *Varšni*, *Vīrāza*, *Xuṇbiia*: Rigvedic *prāṇa*, *gandharva*, *sumāyā*, *vṛṣṇi* (in the sense "manly", apart from its occurrence with the meaning "ram", already referred to above), *virāj/virāṭ*, *kumbha*.

These words *are* found in three hymns in the Early and Middle Books (6, 3, 7, 4, 2):

Book 3:
38. Gandharva-6.
53. Prāṇa-21.

Book 7:
33. Kumbha-13.

But *all three* of these hymns are *late or late redacted* hymns: **III**.38 is one of the six hymns specified in the Aitareya Brāhmaṇa VI.18 as late additions into Book 3 (see earlier on the composer name Ghora), and both **III**.53 and **VII**.33 (both pertaining to the activities of Su-dās) are hymns placed by the western scholars (eg. in Oldenberg's classification of the hymns) among the late or interpolated hymns which do not fit into the numerical principles of arrangement of the hymns in the Family Books.

In the Late Books:

Book 5:
35. Vṛṣṇi-4.

Book 1:
22. Gandharva-14.
66. Prāṇa-1.
88. Sumāyā-1.
116. Kumbha-6.
163. Gandharva-2.
167. Sumāyā-2.
188. Virāṭ-5.

Book 8:
1. Gandharva-11.
3. Vṛṣṇi-10.
6. Vṛṣṇi-6.
7. Vṛṣṇi-23.
77. Gandharva-5.

Book 9:

83. Gandharva-4.
85. Gandharva-12.
86. Gandharva-36.
96. Virāj-18.
113. Gandharva-3.

Book 10:

10. Gandharva-4.
11. Gandharvī-2.
59. Prāṇa-6.
85. Gandharva-40,41.
89. Kumbha-7.
90. Virāj-5, prāṇa-13.
123. Gandharva-4,7.
130. Virāj-5.
136. Gandharva-6.
139. Gandharva-4,6.
159. Virāṭ-3.
166. Virāj-1.
177. Gandharva-2.
189. Prāṇa-2.

In a third category, it may be noted that some of the prefixes and suffixes, already examined, are *late* in themselves as *prefixes* or *suffixes*, not just in personal names, but even in ordinary words: thus the prefix *Priya-* (found in the names Priya-medha and Priya-ratha, already seen) and the prefix *Śruta-* (found in the names Śruta-kakṣa, Śruta-ratha, Śruta-rya, Śruta-rvan, Śruta-vid and Śruta-bandhu, already seen) are *not* found as prefixes at all in the Early and Middle Books. The suffix *–gu* (found in the names Pṛśni-gu, Puṣṭi-gu, Śruṣṭi-gu, Sapta-gu and Andhī-gu, already seen), a form of go-, "cow", is *completely absent* in this form itself in the Early and Middle Books. However, we find them in the Late Books as prefixes and suffix respectively, even in ordinary words:

Book 5:

64. Ruṣad-*gu*-7.

Book 1:

91. *Priya*-stotra-6.
122. *Priya*-ratha-7.
125. Su-*gu*.
140. *Priya*-dhāma-1.

Book 8:

17. Śāci-*gu*-12.
27. *Priya*-kṣatra-19.
62. Bhūri-*gu*-10.
71. *Priya*-jāta-2.
93. *Śruta*-magha-1.

Book 9:

97. *Priya*-sāsa-38.

Book 10:

47. *Śruta*-ṛṣi-3.
150. *Priya*-vrata-3.

To these may be added the Avestan suffix -*sarəda* (Rigvedic -*śardha*): it is not found at all in any personal name in the Rigveda, but it is found as a suffix in ordinary words only in the Late Books:

Book 5:

34. Viśva-*śardhas*-8.

Book 8:

4. Pra-*śardha*-1.

Book 10:

103. Bahu-*śardhin*-3.

And the –*baṇgha* in the Avestan name Pouru.baṇgha, the Vedic word *bhanga*, is found in only one verse in the Rigveda, in **IX.61**.13.

To sum up, the Rigvedic hymns containing name-elements

in common with the Avesta, listed here in Section D, are as follows:

In the Early and Middle Books, only the 5 following hymns, *all classified as late*:

III.36 (Ait. Br.), 38 (Ait. Br.), 53 (Oldenberg).
VII.33 (Oldenberg).
IV.30 (Oldenberg).

In the *Late* Books, 326 hymns:

V.1, 3-6, 9-10, 18-20, 24-27, 30-31, 33-36, 41, 44-49, 52-62, 64, 67-68, 73-75, 79, 81-82 (47 hymns).

I.12-23, 33, 35-52, 61, 66, 83, 88, 100, 105, 112, 114, 116-126, 138-140, 158, 163-164, 167, 188 (58 hymns).

VIII.1-10, 12, 14-15, 19, 21, 23-38, 43-59, 62, 66, 68-71, 74-75, 77, 80, 85-87, 89-90, 92-93, 98-99, 103 (68 hymns).

IX.2, 8, 27-29, 32-36, 41-43, 58, 61, 65, 68, 72, 80-83, 85-86, 94-97, 101-103, 107, 113 (33 hymns).

X.1-8, 10-29, 31, 33, 37, 39, 42-47, 49, 51-52, 54-67, 72-73, 75-78, 80, 85-86, 89-93, 95-99, 101-104, 106, 109, 111-115, 118, 120, 122-123, 128, 130, 132, 134-136, 139, 144, 147-148, 150-152, 154, 157, 159, 163-166, 168, 170, 172, 174-175, 177, 179-180, 186, 188, 191 (120 hymns).

1E.
THREE "BMAC" WORDS IN RIGVEDIC NAMES.

Thus far, we have been examining *only* the evidence of the Avestan names and name-elements in the Rigveda.

In this section, we will see some additional evidence from three words found in the Rigveda and the Avesta, which are *also* found as names or name-elements in the Rigveda, but *not* in the Avesta. The importance of these words is that they appear in the names of four important Rigvedic ṛṣis who are also very important in post-Vedic literature and mythology, and all three words are included by Lubotsky (LUBOTSKY 2000) in a small list of words which are peculiar to Indo-Aryan and Iranian but are not found in any other branch of Indo-

European languages, and which are alleged by Lubotsky to be borrowings into Indo-Iranian from a hypothetical BMAC language in Central Asia.

These words are the Avestan *āθrauuan* (*atharvan*, "fire-priest), *kasiiapa* (*kaśyapa*, "tortoise") and *xšuuaēpa* (*śepa*, "tail"). They are found in the names of the ṛṣis *Atharvan*, *Kaśyapa*, *Śunahśepa* and *Parucchepa*.

In the Rigveda, these words/names are found as follows (the names or patronymics of composers are in brackets):
In the Early and Middle Books:

Book 6:

15. *Atharvan*-17.
16. *Atharvan*-13,14.
47. *Atharvan*-24.

All three of these hymns are placed by the western scholars (eg. in Oldenberg's classification of the hymns) among the late or interpolated hymns which do not fit into the numerical principles of arrangement of the hymns in the Family Books.
In the Late Books:

Book 5:

44. (*Kaśyapa*).

Book 1:

24. Śunah-*śepa*-12,13. (Śunah-*śepa*).
25-30. (Śunah-*śepa*).
80. *Atharvan*-16.
83. *Atharvan*-5.
99. (*Kaśyapa*).
116. *Atharvan*-12.
117. *Atharvan*-22.
127-139. (Paruc-*chepa*).

Book 8:

9. *Atharvan*-7.
27-31. (*Kaśyapa*).

97. (*Kaśyapa*).

Book 9:

3. (Śunah-*śepa*).
5-10. (*Kaśyapa*).
11. *Atharvan*-2. (*Kaśyapa*).
12-24. (*Kaśyapa*).
53-60. (*Kaśyapa*).
63-64. (*Kaśyapa*).
91-92. (*Kaśyapa*).
99-100. (*Kaśyapa*).
111. (Paruc-*chepa*).
112. *śepa*-4.
113. (*Kaśyapa*).
114. *Kaśyapa*-2. (*Kaśyapa*).

Book 10:

14. *Atharvan*-6.
21. *Atharvan*-5.
48. *Atharvan*-2.
85. *śepa*-37.
87. *Atharvan*-12.
92. *Atharvan*-10.
97. (*Atharvan*).
105. *śepa*-2.
106. (*Kaśyapa*).
120. *Atharvan*-9. (*Atharvan*).
163. (*Kaśyapa*).

When this data is added to the data in section D, already seen earlier, we get the following final list of Rigvedic hymns containing names and name-elements in common with the Avesta:

In the Early and Middle Books, *only* the 8 following hymns, *all classified as late*:

VI.15 (Oldenberg), 16 (Oldenberg), 47 (Oldenberg).
III.36 (Ait. Br.), 38 (Ait. Br.), 53 (Oldenberg).

VII.33 (Oldenberg).
IV.30 (Oldenberg).

In the *Late* Books, 386 hymns:

V.1, 3-6, 9-10, 18-20, 24-27, 30-31, 33-36, 41, 44-49, 52-62, 64, 67-68, 73-75, 79, 81-82 (47 hymns).

I.12-30, 33, 35-52, 61, 66, 80, 83, 88, 99-100, 105, 112, 114, 116-140, 158, 163-164, 167, 188 (78 hymns).

VIII.1-10, 12, 14-15, 19, 21, 23-38, 43-59, 62, 66, 68-71, 74-75, 77, 80, 85-87, 89-90, 92-93, 97-99, 103 (69 hymns).

IX.2-3, 5-24, 27-29, 32-36, 41-43, 53-61, 63-65, 68, 72, 80-83, 85-86, 91-92, 94-97, 99-103, 107, 111-114 (69 hymns).

X.1-8, 10-29, 31, 33, 37, 39, 42-49, 51-52, 54-67, 72-73, 75-78, 80, 85-87, 89-93, 95-99, 101-106, 109, 111-115, 118, 120, 122-123, 128, 130, 132, 134-136, 139, 144, 147-148, 150-152, 154, 157, 159, 163-166, 168, 170, 172, 174-175, 177, 179-180, 186, 188, 191 (123 hymns).

We will now examine the importance of this massive evidence in conclusively establishing the relative chronology of the Rigveda and the Avesta.

1F
WHAT THE EVIDENCE SHOWS.

The *massive* evidence of the personal names in the Avesta and the Rigveda is *overwhelmingly and unambiguously* uni-directional: it shows that the development of the common Indo-Iranian culture represented in the two texts, the Rigveda and the Avesta, took place in the period of the Late Books (5, 1, 8-10); and that the period of the Early Books (6, 3, 7) and even the period of the Middle Books (4, 2) *predates* the development of this common culture.

As we saw, the Early Books are characterized mainly by simple names (of single or fused character), and the name-elements shared with the Avesta consist mainly of a few restricted types of compound names with a few prominent prefixes of a basic nature (Su-, Deva-, Puru-, Viśva-), which are found in the names of important historical personalities of the Early Period. However, these name-elements are found in *even* greater profusion in the Late Books.

The significance of this must be noted. The Rigveda and the Avesta are alleged to be books composed by the Iranians and the Vedic Aryans well after they allegedly separated from each other in Central Asia and migrated to their respective historic habitats. If this were true, then common elements should have been found most prominently in the Early Books of the Rigveda, which would then still have retained remnants of the allegedly earlier common Indo-Iranian culture, and *most* or *many* or at least *some* of those elements should consequently have *gone out of vogue* by the time the Late Books were composed. But, in fact, there is no class or category of common name-elements (names, prefixes in names, or suffixes in names) which is found in the Early Books *and* the Avesta, but *missing* in the Late Books.

On the contrary, some important name-elements in the Early Books are already absent *in common* in *both* the Late Books *and* the Avesta: a) the prefix *Diva-* in the name Divo-dāsa, which is found in the Late (and even the Middle) books only in references to the Divo-dāsa of the Early Books, and not in any new name, and b) two words *-mīḷha* and *–hotra* found as secondarily developed suffixes in names in the Early Books. The Early Books, as we saw, had primarily six basic prefixes (*Su-*, *Deva-*, *Diva-*, *Puru-*, *Viśva-*, *Pra-*) + words (one of these words, the word *–śravas* in the name Deva-śravas, as we have seen earlier, later became a common suffix in names, again *in both the Avesta and the Late Books*). However, we find these two words (*mīḷha* and *hotra*) were already developing into suffixes in the Early Books themselves: the word *–mīḷha* in the names Su-mīḷha and Puru-mīḷha, and the word *–hotra* in the name Su-hotra. On the analogy of these names, we find Aja-mīḷha (presumably the brother of Puru-mīḷha, and descendant of Su-hotra; in **IV.44**.6, and in the composer names of **IV**.43-44), and Śuna-hotra (presumably the brother of Su-hotra; in **II**.**18**.6; **41**.4, and in the composer names of **VI**.33-34; **II**.1-3,8-26,30-43.). Both these suffixes, -mīḷha and –hotra, are absent as name-elements *in both the Avesta as well as the Late Books* (*except, in the Late Books, in references to the Puru-mīḷha of the earlier period).*

In sharp contrast to this situation, there is a massive body of name-elements common to the Avesta and the Late Books — elements which are completely missing in the Early and the Middle Books (except, significantly, in a bare handful of historically important hymns specifically characterized by the Aitareya Brāhmaṇa, or by modern western scholars following Oldenberg, as *late* hymns): the very large number of such name-elements, the very large number of Avestan names containing these elements, the very large number of Rigvedic names containing these elements, and the very large number of hymns in the Late Books associated with these names (see Sections D and E, above, for the details), altogether constitutes an overwhelmingly massive body of evidence which is impossible to account for by any hypothesis other than that the Avesta is *contemporaneous* with the Late Books of the Rigveda and *posterior* to the Early and Middle Books, and that the Indo-Iranian culture common to the two texts developed *after* the composition of the hymns of the Early and Middle Books.

That the common names and name-elements are late elements in the Rigveda is obvious: not only are they found exclusively in the Late Books and hymns, but the names continue to be very common in *post*-Rigvedic texts and mythology; and the name-elements are found in *more and more* new names (in the post-Rigvedic Vedic literature, and in the Epics and Purāṇas). A significant example is the suffix *–ayana*, indicating a patronymic. In the Rigveda, we have Ukṣaṇyāyana, Gaupāyana, Yāmāyana, Nārāyaṇa, Kāmāyanī, Vātāyana and Dākṣāyaṇī: *every single one* only in the Late Books. Later, post-Rigveda, we have the Rāṇāyanīya (Sāmaveda) and Maitrāyaṇīya (Yajurveda) Samhitās; the

Śānkhāyana and Śātyāyana Brāhmaṇas; the Mahānārāyaṇa Upaniṣad; the Āśvalāyana, Śānkhāyana, Drāhyāyaṇa, Lāṭhyāyana, Katyāyana and Baudhāyana Sūtras; and, later, Vātsyāyana (Kāma-Sūtra) and Bādarāyaṇa (Brahma-sūtras), apart from Nārāyaṇa as a name for "God". The *total absence* of this suffix, *and all the other names and elements listed in Sections D and E above*, in the Early and Middle Books can only be because the said names and name-elements did not exist at all in those earlier periods.

On the other hand, these elements are *early* elements in the Avesta, present from the very earliest point of composition of the text. All the key words pertaining to the ethos of the *earliest* parts of the Avesta are found only in the *late* parts of the Rigveda: The oldest part of the Avesta consists of the *Gāθās*, composed by *Zaraθuštra* (son of *Pourušāspa*, descendant of *Haēčat.aspa*, clansman of *Dʒjāmāspa* and *Fərašaoštra*, priest of *Vīštāspa*, and enemy to *Arəjaṭ.aspa*) and the oldest period to which the Avesta as a whole harks back is the period of the rule of the mythical first king *Yima* (named in the Gāθās as well) in the mythical land of Airyana *Vaējah*. And the very core of the Avestan religion centres around the fire priests, the *āθrauuans*.

As we have already seen, the name element *Jarat-*, the word *uṣṭra*, the compound name element *–aśva*, the name *Yama*, and the name/word *Atharvan* are all restricted to the Late Books and hymns. In addition, the words *gātha/gāthā* ("song") and *bīja* ("seed") are also found only in the Late Books, as follows:

V. **44**.5; **53**.13.
I. **7**.1; **43**.4; **167**.6; **190**.1.
VIII. **2**.38; **32**.1; **71**.14; **92**.2; **98**.9.
IX. **11**.4; **99**.4.
X. **85**.6,37; **94**.13; **101**.3.

In short: the Early and Middle Books of the Rigveda are *earlier* than the Avesta, and the Late Books of the Rigveda are *contemporaneous* with the Avesta; and the common "Indo-

Iranian" culture visible in the two texts is a product of the *Late* Rigvedic Period. [Some Avestan scholars today deny that the Gāθās were composed by Zaraθuštra, but they nevertheless accept the fact that the Gāθās represent the oldest part of the Avesta. And the fact is that Zaraθuštra (whose name, and those of his colleagues, places him in the period of this common "Indo-Iranian" culture of the Late Books of the Rigveda) is mentioned in the Gāθās along with a few others among the names mentioned above. So if the Gāθās were not composed by him, this means that they are in fact *later* to the period of Żaraθuštra, who is *pre-Gāθā*, which only makes our case stronger].

As we saw, the common names and name-elements, listed in Sections D and E above, are found in 386 hymns in the Late Books and in 8 hymns, classified as late, in the Early and Middle Books. But the contrast between the Early Books and the Late Books becomes even more stark if we consider the names common to the Middle Books and the Avesta, listed in Section C above, of four personalities, named in both the Rigveda and the Avesta, who are *earlier* than the period of Zaraθuštra, the composer of the Gāθās (the *earliest* part of the Avesta). That these personalities are ancestral, in time, to the period of Zaraθuštra, is testified by the Avesta itself in respect of the two most important and most frequently mentioned names, in the Rigveda, of these personalities: Trita (according to Yašt 13.16, θrita is an ancient figure, ancestral to Zaraθuštra's father Pourušāspa) and Gotama (according to Yasna 9.10, Zaraθuštra engaged Nāiδiiā°nha Gaotəma in debate, and defeated him. If Nodhās Gautama, of Book 1, is contemporaneous with Zaraθuštra, the ancestral Gotama and the family name Gautama, of Book 4, are obviously *pre*-Zaraθuštran and *pre*-Avestan). In the Rigveda, these names are completely *absent* in the Early Books (6, 3 and 7, which clearly go back into the remote past), and they first appear in the Middle Books, where the following 60 hymns are associated with these names:

IV. 1-42, 45-58 (56 hymns).

II. 11, 13, 31, 34 (4 hymns).

In the Late Books, the following 63 hymns are associated with these names:

V. 9, 41, 54, 86 (4 hymns).

I. 36, 52, 54, 58-64, 74-93, 105, 112, 116, 155, 163, 183, 187 (37 hymns).

VIII. 7, 12, 41, 47, 52, 88 (6 hymns).

IX. 31-32, 34, 37-38, 77, 86, 93, 95, 102 (10 hymns).

X. 8, 46, 48, 64, 99, 115 (6 hymns).

If these hymns are added to the 386 hymns already listed earlier above (not counting, of course, those of these hymns which are already part of that list), we get the following number of hymns, in each chronological part of the Rigveda, associated with the names listed in sections C, D and E above:

Early Books (6, 3 and 7): 7 hymns (*all 7 classified as Late hymns*) out of 241.

Middle Books (4 and 2): 60 hymns out of 101.

Late Books (5, 1, 8-10): 421 hymns out of 686.

That is: there is a sharp cultural, *and chronological*, dichotomy between the Early Books, *proper*, which do not contain a *single* name of the Rigvedic-Avestan type listed in sections C, D and E above (except in 7 hymns, which are among those specially singled out as late by Oldenberg and the Aitareya Brāhmaṇa), and the Late Books, where 421 hymns out of 686 are associated with these names. Even *these* figures are an understatement, if one notices that these 421 hymns are not associated with only one name each; many of them are associated with more than one such name: **I**.112 actually mentions 13 such names, and **I**.116 mentions 11 names.

[It may be noted that the above figures, of 386 hymns in the Late Books in contrast to only 8 (and Late) hymns in the Early and Middle Books, and 421 hymns in the Late Books in contrast to only 7 (and Late) hymns in the Early Books, do not include the data for words like *gātha/gāthā* ("song") and *bīja* ("seed") mentioned above, since we are concerned in this chapter only with the hymns associated with names and words that directly, and some indirectly, have to do with Avestan and Rigvedic personal names. The words *gātha/gāthā* ("song") and *bīja* ("seed") would add *three* more hymns to the number of hymns in the Late Books (**I**.7, 190; **X**.94). And if we consider a host of other common words in the Rigveda and Avesta, many of them included by Lubotsky and Witzel in their list of alleged "BMAC" words or referred to by Hopkins in his "**Prāgāthikani-I**" (HOPKINS 1896a), like āśā, *gandha/gandhi, kadrū, kṣīra, sūcī, strī, tokman, śanaih, tiṣya, saptarṣi, mūjavat, ambhas, samā and sthūṇa*, we could add even more (**I**.104,162,191; **VIII**.17,91; **IX**.67, **X**.34,82,124,129,146), along with a few more Late (as per Oldenberg) hymns in the Early and Middle Books (**VII**.55,59,104; **IV**.37,57; **II**.32,41). For the purpose of our analysis in this book, however, we will restrict ourselves to the list of 386 hymns in the Late Books in contrast to the 8 (and late) hymns in the Early and Middle Books].

This *flood* of names and words leaves absolutely no scope for any honest and genuine scholar to doubt the evidence. And, as we shall see in the next chapter, this evidence fits in with, and is corroborated by, the evidence of the meters.

1G.
FOOTNOTE: AN "IRANIAN" VASIṢṬHA?

There has been a strange failure, on the part of the scholars examining the evidence, to reach the unavoidable conclusions we have reached in this chapter. The reason for this is of course the fact that they have always viewed the data through the blinkers of the AIT. But the failure runs deeper: there has been a tendency to manufacture evidence and indulge in *fraudulent* scholarship in order to provide substance to their theories which run contrary to the data.

The level of fraudulent and make-believe scholarship which dominates the Aryan debate today can be gauged from the following: Michael Witzel, throughout his various writings, from WITZEL 1995b:334-335 to WITZEL 2005:344, keeps insisting that Vasiṣṭha is an "**Iranian**" or an "**immigrant from Iran**", even a "self-proclaimed" Iranian immigrant. In WITZEL 2005:335, he even refers to "**the origins of the Bharatas and Vasiṣṭha in eastern Iran**".

And this is how he arrives at the conclusion that Vasiṣṭha and the Bharatas are from Iran: he takes up the Rigvedic verse **VII.33**.3, which refers to Sudās' battle with Bheda on the banks of a river. This river is the Yamunā, as per Griffith's footnote to the verse, and as per another direct reference to this incident in another Rigvedic verse **VII.18**.9. But Witzel unilaterally decides that this river is the Indus. Then he further decides that this verse refers, not just to a battle, but to a migratory movement of Vasiṣṭha and the Bharatas across the Indus, the direction being from west to east. Finally, he concludes that the west of the Indus can only mean "eastern Iran". On this basis, Witzel decides that Vasiṣṭha is a "self-proclaimed immigrant" from Iran, and this becomes an article of faith in every Witzelian version of the Aryan invasion or immigration.

[Witzel even produces "linguistic" proof of Vasiṣṭha being an Iranian: "**[...] new grammatical formations such as the absolutives in —*tvā*, -*tvī*, and –*ya* for verbs with preverbs (Tikkanan 1987). Absolutive formation corresponds, among others, to Drav. verbal structure, but absolutives are *not* found in Iranian. Significantly, *Vasiṣṭha*, the self-proclaimed (Iranian?) immigrant author of much of book 7, avoids them**" (WITZEL 2005:344). That is: Vasiṣṭha, being a "self-proclaimed immigrant" from Iran, avoids the use of absolutives since absolutives are lacking in Iranian.

The following is a list of the occurrences of absolutives in the Family Books of the Rigveda:

II. **12**.1; **15**.9; **17**.6; **20**.8; **30**.9-10; **35**.10; **37**.3 (two abs.); **38**.4,6; **43**.1. [Total 12].

III. **21**.1; **26**.1; **32**.1 (two abs.); **34**.9; **35**.6,8; **40**.7; **42**.7; **48**.4 (two abs.); **50**.1; **54**.15; **60**.3. [Total 14].

IV. **4**.12; **18**.12; **26**.6,7; **32**.10; **41**.5. [Total 5].

V. **2**.7; **4**.5; **40**.4; **53**.14 (2 abs). [Total 5].

VI. **40**.1; **50**.5; **59**.6. [Total 3].

VII. **6**.5; **21**.7; **36**.3; **80**.2; **103**.3; **104**.18. [Total 6].

By what statistical logic does Witzel decide that Vasiṣṭha, of Book 7, "avoids" the use of absolutives, presumably in sharp contrast to all the other composers making lavish use of absolutives in their compositions? As we can see, there are *six* occurences of absolutives in Book 7, compared to, for example, only *three* in Book 6, and *five* each in Books 4 and 5. [Book 2, with only around half the number of verses in Book 7, does have *twelve* occurrences; but Book 2, according to Witzel's claims, is the oldest Book in the Rigveda, with the Sarasvatī in this book being the Sarasvatī of Afghanistan, and the Vedic Aryans still "fighting their way" through the mountains of Afghanistan, and therefore, it is presumably closest to the Iranians. So Book 2 should have "avoided" absolutives even more diligently than Book 7. And so should Book 3 (which in fact has *fourteen* occurrences), since according to Witzel, Viśvāmitra was the leader of the proto-Iranian coalition which fought against the Bharatas in the Battle of the Ten Kings. So, in fact, the three Family Books which Witzel's fairy-tales place closest to the Iranians have *more* instances of absolutives than the other three Family Books.]

And yet, on the basis of this *patternless* distribution of absolutive forms in the Rigveda, Witzel concludes that Vasiṣṭha "avoids" the use of absolutives, and that this is proof of his being an immigrant from Iran, where absolutives are unknown. Thus, he produces fake "linguistic" support for his fairy tale, which itself is based on a host of similar false claims and deliberate misinterpretations (see TALAGERI 2000:458-460).

The way in which Witzel arrives at his conclusions is in itself enough to show up his fraudulent scholarship. But what is significant, in the light of our analysis of the Avestan names in this chapter, is that while the Late Books 5, 1 and 8-10 are literally overflowing with compound names of the Avestan type, such names are completely absent in Book 7, the Book of Vasiṣṭha (and also in the Early and Middle Books, 2-4, 6-7, which are the Books associated with the Bharatas. Bharatas are in fact referred to by this name only in the Family Books 2-7: the word Bharata in this sense does not occur even once in the non-family Books). In fact, the *only* Iranian names, of persons and tribes, in the Book of Vasiṣṭha, the "self-proclaimed Iranian", are the names of the *enemies* of Vasiṣṭha and the Bharatas in the Battle of the Ten Kings: Kavi, Kavaṣa, Pṛthus, Parśus, Pakthas, Bhalānas.

Witzel does not brand Viśvāmitra as an Iranian, but he does place Viśvāmitra at the head of the Iranian coalition (of Kavi, Kavaṣa, Pṛthus, Parśus, etc.) ranged against the Bharatas under Sudās and Vasiṣṭha. He arrives at this conclusion on the basis of the fact that the Battle hymns refer to a "Bhṛgu" in the coalition against the Bharatas. On the basis of senseless assertions (see TALAGERI 2000:447-448), Witzel decides that Viśvāmitra is a Bhṛgu, that the "Bhṛgu" referred to in the Battle hymns is Viśvāmitra himself, and that Viśvāmitra therefore actually led the coalition against Sudās. Again, apart from the gratuitous manner in which Witzel arrives at his conclusions, it is significant that Book 3, the Book of Viśvāmitra, is as completely lacking in Avestan-type compound names, or indeed any Iranian names, as Book 7.

At this point, it may be noted that Witzel, like all liars, gets so entangled in his own lies and fairy tales that he loses track of what he is writing: On the one hand, he writes: "**the other tribes began to unite against them** [The Bharatas]**, either due to the intrigues of the ousted Viśvāmitra, or simply because of intratribal resentment. This led to the famous battle of the ten kings which, however, is not mentioned by Book 3, as Viśvāmitra (its author) had by then been displaced by Vasiṣṭha as the *purohita* of Sudās. There is even the possibility that it was Viśvāmitra who — in an act of revenge — forged the alliance against his former chief. Whatever the reason, however, the alliance failed and the**

Pūrus were completely ousted (7.8.4 etc) along with Viśvāmitra (=Bhṛgu, 7.18.6)" (WITZEL 1995b:334). This fairy tale becomes a staple in all of Witzel's versions of the events in subsequent papers and articles.

But, in the *very same* above article, on the previous page, Witzel writes about Book 3: "**This book was composed by Viśvāmitra (and his clan), the *purohita* of Sudās until his ouster by Vasiṣṭha, the reputed author of much of book 7. It praises the dominant position of the Bharata in an area more or less corresponding with the later Kurukṣetra, culminating in an aśvamedha by Sudās to commemorate his triumphs in a late hymn** ([footnote] **i.e. 3.53.11-14)**" (WITZEL 1995b:333). In his critique of my earlier book, Witzel elaborates this further: "**RV 3.53.14 clearly speaks of Kurukṣetra and surroundings, some 750 miles to the west. It refers to the performance of the aśvamedha (3.53.11) after Sudās' victory in the Ten Kings' Battle (7.18: cf. Witzel 1995)**" (WITZEL 2001b:§8).

In other words, according to Witzel's account of the events, Vasiṣṭha ousted Viśvāmitra as the priest of Sudās; and, in revenge, Viśvāmitra led a coalition of tribes in the Ten Kings' Battle against Sudās and Vasiṣṭha, and was "completely" defeated. And, later, the descendants of Viśvāmitra composed a hymn, **III**.53, in "praise" and glorification of the Bharatas, in fond memory of the aśvamedha organized to "commemorate" and celebrate the "triumphs" of Sudās and Vasiṣṭha and the defeat and humiliation of *their own* ancestor Viśvāmitra!

The above instances are not isolated ones: Witzel's writings on the subject of Vedic history are full of baseless fairy tales and cock-and-bull stories; and every word written by Witzel can be contradicted and disproved by other words written by Witzel himself. Yet, there is still no shortage of writers who regularly quote Witzel's pronouncements as if they are some kind of Final Judgement, even when those pronouncements have been repeatedly, completely and conclusively exposed and discredited.

Chapter 2

The Relative Chronology of the Rigveda – I (contd.) The Evidence of the Meters

The hymns, or *sūktas*, of the Rigveda are composed in the form of verses, or *mantras*, set to meters based on the number of syllables in the verse. The most common meter of later times, the *śloka* meter, consists of four lines or *padas* of eight syllables each (8+8+8+8), which is equivalent to the *anuṣṭubh* meter of the Rigveda.

We will examine the evidence of the meters in the Rigveda as follows:

- 2A. The Rigvedic Meters.
  - 2A-1. The Trimeters.
  - 2A-2. The Dimeters.
  - 2A-3. The Mixed Meters.
- 2B. The Chronology of the Dimeters.
  - 2B-1. The Dimeters vis-à-vis the Trimeters.
  - 2B-2. The Internal Chronology of the Dimeters.
- 2C. The Chronology of the Other Meters.
- 2D. The Avestan Meters.

2A. THE RIGVEDIC METERS.

The meters in the Rigveda can be classified into *two* types: simple and mixed. Simple meters are those meters where *every* line of the verse basically has the *same* number of syllables. Mixed meters are those meters where different lines of the verse have different numbers of syllables. Again, simple meters can be classified into two main types: *dimeters* (where every line has basically 7 or 8 syllables), and *trimeters* (where every line has basically 11 or 12 syllables). The two types are called dimeters and trimeters, because the number of syllables, in the two types, is roughly in the ratio of 2:3. The following is a complete listing of the verses composed in the different meters in the ten Books of the Rigveda, under the headings: The Trimeters, the Dimeters and the Mixed Meters.

2A-1. The Trimeters.

Ekapadā Trimeters (Ekapadā Triṣṭubh 11; Ekapadā Virāṭ 10):

IV. **17**.15 (1 verse).
V. **41**.20, **42**.17; **43**.16 (3 verses).
VI. **63**.11 (1 verse).
X. **20**.1 (1 verse).

Dvipadā Trimeters (Dvipadā Triṣṭubh 11+11; Dvipadā Virāṭ 10+10):

I. **65-70** (61 verses).
VI. **10**.7; **17**.15; **47**.25 (3 verses).
VII. **17**; **34**; **56** (39 verses).
IX. **109** (22 verses).
X. **157**.2-5 (4 verses).

Dvipadā Jagatī (12+12):
VIII.**46**.13 (1 verse).

Virāṭ (11+11+11):
I. **120**.9; **149** (6 verses).
III. **25** (5 verses).
VII. **1**; **22**; **31**.10-12; **68**.1-7 (36 verses).
VIII. **9**.11; **46**.16 (2 verses).
IX. **110**.10-12 (3 verses).
X. **20**.9 (1 verse)

Ūrdhvabṛhatī (12+12+12):
IX. **110**.4-9 (6 verses).

Triṣṭubh (11+11+11+11):

I. **24**.1-2,6-15; **27**.13; **30**.16; **31**.8,16,18; **32-33**; **34**.9,12; **35**.2-8,10-11; **51**.14-15; **52**.13,15; **53**.10-11; **54**.6,8-9,11; **58**.6-9; **59-63**; **64**.15; **71-73**; **76-77**; **79**.1-3; **84**.16-18; **85**.5,12; **88**.2-4; **89**.8-10; **91**.1-4,18-23; **92**.5-12; **93**.4-8,12; **94**.15-16; **95-96**; **98-100**; **101**.8-11; **102**.11, **103-104**; **105**.19; **106**.7; **107-109**; **110**.5,9; **111**.5; **112**.24-25; **113**; **114**.10-11; **115-118**; **121**; **122**.1-4,7-15; **123-124**; **125**.1-3,6-7; **126**.1-5; **130**.10; **133**.1; **136**.7; **139**.11; **140**.10,12-13; **141**.12-13; **143**.8; **145**.5; **146-148**; **152-154**; **157**.5-6; **158**.1-5; **161** 14; **162**.1-2,4-5,7-22; **163**; **164**.1-11,13-14,16-22,24-28,30-35,37-40,43-51; **165**; **166**.14-15; **167**.1-9,11; **168**.8-10; **169**.1,3-8; **170**.5; **171**; **173**.1-3,5-13; **174**; **175**.6; **176**.6; **177-178**; **179**.1-4,6; **180-181**; **182**.6-8; **183-186**; **189-190** (734 verses).

II. **3**.1-6,8-11; **4**; **9-10**; **11**.21; **12**; **13**.13; **14-15**; **16**.9; **17**.8-9; **18-19**; **20**.1-2,4-9; **21**.6; **23**.15-19; **24**.12,16; **27-29**; **30**.1-10; **31**.7; **33**; **34**.15; **35**; **38-40**; **42** (209 verses).

III. **1**; **4-7**; **8**.1-2,4-6,8-11; **9**.9; **14-15**; **17-20**; **21**.1; **22**.1-3,5; **23**.15,19; **24**.12,16; **26**.7-9; **28**.4; **29**.2-3,5,7-9,13,16; **30-32**; **33**.1-12; **34-36**; **38-39**; **43**; **46-50**; **51**.4-9; **52**.5,7-8; **53**.1-9,11,14-15,17,19,21,23-24; **54-58**; **60**.1-5; **61**; **62**.1-3 (398 verses).

IV. **1**.4-20; **2-6**; **7**.7-11; **11-14**; **16**; **17**.1-14,16-21; **18-23**; **24**.1-9,11; **25-26**; **27**.1-4; **28-29**; **33-35**; **36**.9; **37**.1-4; **38**; **39**.1-5; **40**.1; **41-44**; **45**.7; **50**.1-9,11; **51**; **54**.6; **55**.1-7; **56**.1-4; **57**.2-3,8; **58**.1-10 (403 verses).

V. **1**; **2**.1-11; **3**.2-12; **4**; **12**; **15**; **27**.1-3; **28**.1,3; **29-33**; **34**.9; **36**.1-2,4-6; **37**; **40**.4,6-8; **41**.1-15,18-19; **42**.1-16,18; **43**.1-15,17; **44**.14-15; **45**.1-8,10-11; **46**.2,8; **47**; **49**; **51**.11-13; **54**.14; **55**.10; **57**.7-8; **58**; **59**.8; **60**.1-6; **62**; **69**; **76-77**; **78**.4; **80**; **83**.1,5-8,10; **85** (283 verses).

VI. **1**; **3-6**; **7**.1-5; **8**.7; **9**; **10**.1-6; **11-13**; **15**.10-14,16,19; **16**.46; **17**.1-14; **18-19**; **20**.1-6,8-13; **21-27**; **28**.1,5-7; **29-30**; **31**.1-3,5; **32-41**; **44**.10-24; **47**.1-18,20-22,26,28-31; **49**.1-14;

50; **51**.1-12; **52**.1-6,13,15-17; **58**.1,3-4; **60**.1-3,13; **61**.14; **62**; **63**.2-10; **64-67**; **68**.1-8,11; **69**; **71**.4-6; **72-74**; **75**.1-5,7-9,11,14,18 (476 verses).

VII. **1**.19-25; **2-13**; **14**.2-3; **18-21**; **22**.9; **23-30**; **33**; **34**.22-25; **35-40**; **41**.2-7; **42-43**; **44**.2-5; **45**; **46**.4; **47-49**; **51-54**; **56**.12-25; **57-58**; **59**.7-8; **60-65**; **67**; **68**.8-9; **69-73**; **75-80**; **84-88**; **90-93**; **95**; **97-101**; **103**.2-10; **104**.8-17,19-20,22,24 (586 verses).

VIII. **1**.33-34; **9**.10; **11**.10; **40**.12; **42**.1-3; **48**.1-4,6-15; **57-58**; **63**.12; **80**.10; **96**.1-3,5-20; **97**.14; **100**.1-5,10-12; **101**.14-16 (62 verses).

IX. **68**.10; **69**.9-10; **70**.10; **71**.9; **74**.8; **81**.5; **82**.5; **85**.11-12; **87-97** (149 verses).

X. **1-8**; **10**.1-12,14; **11**.7-9; **12**; **13**.1-4; **14**.1-12; **15**.1-10,12-14; **16**.1-10; **17**.1-12; **18**.1-10,12; **20**.10; **22**.15; **23**.1,5,7; **27-31**; **32**.6-9; **33**.1; **34**.1-6,8-14; **35**.13-14; **36**.13-14; **37**.10; **39**.14; **42**; **43**.10-11; **44**.1-3,10-11; **45-47**; **48**.7,10-11; **49**.2,11; **50**.3-5; **51-52**; **53**.1-5,8; **54-55**; **56**.1-3,7; **59**.1-7; **61**; **62**.11; **63**.16-17; **64**.12,16-17; **65**.15; **66**.15; **67-68**; **69**.3-12; **70**; **71**.1-8,10-11; **73-74**; **77**.1-4,6-8; **78**.1,3-4,8; **79-80**; **81**.1,3-7; **82**; **83**.2-7; **84**.1-3; **85**.14,19-21,23-24,26,36-37,44; **87**.1-21; **88-89**; **90**.16; **91**.15; **94**.5,7,14; **95**; **96**.12-13; **98-99**; **100**.12; **101**.1-3,7-8,10-11; **102**.2,4-11; **103**.1-12; **104**; **105**.11; **106**; **107**.1-3,5-11; **108**; **109**.1-5; **110-112**; **113**.10; **114**.1-3,5-10; **115**.8; **116**; **117**.3-9; **120-121**; **122**.1,5; **123**; **124**.1-6,8-9; **125**.1,3-8; **126**.8; **128**.1-8; **129**; **130**.2-7; **131**.1-3,5-7; **133**.7; **139**; **142**.3-6; **147**.5; **148-149**; **160**; **161**.1-4; **164**.3; **165**; **168-169**; **177**.2-3; **178**; **179**.2-3; **180-183**; **191**.3 (890 verses).

Jagatī (12+12+12+12):

I. **31**.1-7,9-15,17; **34**.1-8,10-11; **35**.1,9; **51**.1-13; **52**.1-12,14; **53**.1-9; **54**.1-5,7,10; **55-57**; **58**.1-5; **64**.1-14; **82**.6; **83**; **85**.1-4,6-11; **87**; **89**.1-5,7; **92**.1-4; **94**.1-14; **101**.1-7; **102**.1-10; **106**.1-6; **110**.1-4,6-8; **111**.1-4; **112**.1-23; **114**.1-9; **119**;

125.4-5; **140**.1-9,11; **141**.1-11; **143**.1-7; **144**; **145**.1-4; **151**; **155-156**; **157**.1-4; **159-160**; **161**.1-13; **162**.3,6; **164**.12,15,23,29,36,41; **166**.1-13; **168**.1-7; **182**.1-5,7 (353 verses).

II. **1-2**; **3**.7; **13**.1-12; **16**.1-8; **17**.1-7; **21**.1-5; **23**.1-14,16-18; **24**.1-11,13-15; **25-26**; **30**.11; **31**.1-6; **32**.1-5; **34**.1-14; **36-37**; **43**.1,3 (142 verses).

III. **2-3**; **26**.1-6; **28**.5; **29**.6,11,14-15; **51**.1-3; **52**.6; **53**.10,16; **60** (50 verses).

IV. **7**.1; **36**.1-8; **40**.2-5; **45**.1-6; **50**.10; **53**; **54**.1-5; **58**.11 (33 verses).

V. **8**; **11**; **28**.2; **34**.1-8; **36**.3; **44**.1-13; **46**.1,3-7; **48**; **54**.1-13,15; **55**.1-9; **57**.1-66; **59**.1-7; **60**.7-8; **63**; **81**; **83**.2-4 (100 verses).

VI. **7**.6-7; **8**.1-6; **15**.1-2,4-5,7-9; **28**.2-4; **47**.27; **52**.14; **58**.2; **61**.1-3,13; **68**.9-10; **70**; **71**.1-3; **75**.6,10 (38 verses).

VII. **41**.1; **44**.1; **46**.1-3; **50**.1-3; **82-83**; **89**.5; **104**.1-7,18,21,23 (39 verses).

VIII. **9**.12; **46**.17; **48**.5; **59**; **86**; **97**.15; **100**.6 (17 verses).

IX. **68**.1-9; **69**.1-8; **70**.1-9; **71**.1-8; **72-73**; **74**.1-7,9; **75-80**; **81**.1-4; **82**.1-4; **83-84**; **85**.1-10; **86** (166 verses).

X. **11**.1-6; **13**.5; **15**.11; **18**.13; **23**.2-4,6; **32**.1-5; **34**.7; **35**.1-12; **36**.1-12; **37**.1-9,11-12; **38**; **39**.1-13; **40-41**; **43**.1-9; **44**.4-9; **48**.1-6,8-9; **49**.1,3-10; **50**.1-2,6-7; **53**.6-7,9-11; **56**.4-6; **62**.1-4; **63**.1-15; **64**.1-11,13-15; **65**.1-14; **66**.1-14; **69**.1-2; **71**.9; **75-76**; **77**.5; **78**.2,5-7; **83**.1; **84**.4-7; **85**.18,27,43; **91**.1-14; **92**; **94**.1-4,6,8-13; **96**.1-11; **100**.1-11; **101**.9,12; **107**.4; **113**.1-9; **114**.4; **115**.1-7; **117**.1-2; **122**.2-4,6-8; **124**.7; **125**.2; **128**.9; **130**.1; **138**; **142**.1-2; **147**.1-4; **167**; **170**.1-3; **177**.1 (341 verses).

Virāṭ/Virāṭsthānā/ Catuṣpadā Virāṭ (10+10+10+10):

I. **89**.6; **169**.2 (2 verses).

II. **11** (20 verses).

V. **3**.1 (1 verse).

VI. **20**.7; **44**.7-9; **63**.1 (5 verses).

VIII. **96**.4 (1 verse).

X. **10**.13 (1 verse).

Pancapadā Trimeters (Śakvarī/Atijagatī 11+11+11+11+11):
IV. **27**.5 (1 verse).
V. **2**.12; **41**.16-17 (3 verses).
VI. **2**.11; **14**.6; **15**.15; **31**.4; **49**.15 (5 verses).
VII. **50**.4 (1 verse).
X. **115**.9 (1verse).

Atiśakvarī (12+12+12+12+12):
II. **43**.2 (1 verse).
VI. **15**.6 (1 verse).

2A-2. The Dimeters.

Nityadvipadā (8+8):
IX. **67**.16-18 (3 verses).

Gāyatrī (8+8+8):
I. **1-9**; **12-22**; **23**.1-18,21; **24**.3-5; **25-26**; **27**.1-12; **28**.7-9; **30**.1-15,17-22; **37-38**; **41-42**; **43**.1-8; **46**; **50**.1-9; **74-75**; **78**; **79**.7-12; **84**.13-15; **86**; **90**.1-8; **91**.5-16; **93**.9-11; **97**; **120**.1,10-12; **133**.5; **172**; **187**.2,4,8-10; **188** (472 verses).
II. **6-7**; **8**.1-5; **41**.1-15,19-21 (37 verses).
III. **11-12**; **24**.2-5; **27**; **28**.1-2,6; **37**.1-10; **40-42**; **51**.10-12; **52**.1-4; **53**.13; **59**.6-9; **62**.4-18 (104 verses).
IV. **8-9**; **15**; **30**.1-7,9-23; **31-32**; **46**; **49**; **52**; **55**.8-10; **56**.5-7 (113 verses).
V. **5**; **13-14**; **19**.1-2; **26**; **28**.5-6; **51**.1-4; **53**.8,12; **61**.1-4,6-8,10-19; **68**; **70-71**; **82**.2-9 (79 verses).
VI. **16**.1-26,28-45; **45**.1-32; **47**.24; **52**.7-12; **53**.1-7,9-10; **54-55**; **56**.1-5; **57**; **60**.4-12; **61**.4-12 (137 verses).
VII. **15**; **31**.1-9; **55**.1; **59**.9-11; **66**.1-9,17-19; **89**.1-4; **94**.1-11; **96**.4-6; **102** (61 verses).
VIII. **2**.1-27,29-42; **3**.22-23; **5**.1-36; **6-7**; **9**.2-3,20-21;
11.1-9; **14**; **16**; **17**.1-13; **26**.16-19,21,25; **28**.1-3,5; **30**.1; **31**.1-8,10-13; **32**; **33**.16-18; **34**.16-18; **38**; **43-45**; **46**.1-4,6,10,23,29,33; **55**.1-2,4; **56**.1-4; **63**.2-3,6,8-11; **64-65**; **67**; **68**.2-3,5-6,8-9,11-19; **69**.4-6; **71**.1-9; **72-73**; **74**.2-3,5-6,8-

9,11-12; **75-76**; **77**.1-9; **78**.1-9; **79**.1-8; **80**.1-9; **81-85**; **92**.2-33; **93-94**; **101**.3; **102** (738 verses).

IX. **1-4**; **5**.1-7; **6-59**; **60**.1-2,4; **61-65**; **66**.1-17,19-30; **67**.1-15,19-26,28-29; **101**.2-3 (599 verses).

X. **9**.1-7; **19**.6; **20**.3-8; **33**.4-9; **57**; **60**.1-5; **62**.10; **101**.4,6; **105**.1; **118-119**; **127**; **144**.1,3-4; **153**; **156**; **158**.1,3-5; **171**; **175**; **176**.2; **185-189** (108 verses).

Anuṣṭubh (8+8+8+8):

I. **10-11**; **23**.20,22-24; **28**.1-6; **43**.9; **45**; **49**; **50**.10-13; **84**.1-6; **90**.9; **93**.1-3; **126**.6-7; **133**.2-4; **142**; **158**.6; **164**.51; **170**.2-4; **175**.2-5; **176**.1-5; **187**.3,5-7,11; **191**.1-9,14-16 (108 verses).

II. **5**; **8**.6; **32**.6-8; **41**.16-17 (14 verses).

III. **8**.3,7; **13**; **21**.2-3; **22**.4; **24**.1; **29**.1,4,10,12; **33**.13; **37**.11; **53**.12,20,22 (22 verses).

IV. **7**.2-6; **24**.10; **30**.8,24; **37**.5-8; **39**.6; **47-48**; **57**.1,4,6-7 (26 verses).

V. **7**.1-9; **9**.1-4,6; **10**.1-3,5-6; **16**.1-4; **17**.1-4; **18**.1-4; **19**.3-4; **20**.1-33; **21**.1-3; **22**.1-3; **23**.1-3; **25**; **27**.4-6; **28**.4; **35**.1-7; **38**; **39**.1-4; **40**.5,9; **50**.1-4; **51**.14-15; **52**.1-5,7-15; **53**.2; **61**.5; **64**.1-6; **65**.1-5; **66-67**; **73-74**; **78**.5-9; **82**.1; **83**.9; **84**; **86**.1-5 (155 verses).

VI. **2**.1-10; **14**.1-5; **15**.17; **16**.27,47-48; **28**.8; **42**.1-3; **44**.1-6; **45**.33; **47**.23; **48**.22; **51**.16; **53**.8; **56**.6; **59**.7-10; **60**.15; **75**.12-13,15-16,19 (45 verses).

VII. **55**.5-8; **59**.12; **94**.12; **103**.1; **104**.25 (8 verses).

VIII. **2**.28; **3**.21; **5**.39; **8**; **9**.7-9,13,16-19; **10**.3; **22**.8; **24**.30; **26**.20; **30**.4; **31**.9,14; **33**.19; **34**.1-15; **42**.4-6; **46**.8; **55**.3,5; **63**.1,4-5,7; **66**.15; **68**.1,4,7,10; **69**.1,3,7-10,12-15; **70**.14; **74**.1,4,7,10,13-15; **79**.9; **89**.5-6; **91**.3-7; **92**.1; **95**; **100**.7-9; **103**.14 (112 verses).

IX. **5**.8-11; **66**.18; **67**.27,31-32; **98**.1-10,12; **99**.2-8; **100**; **101**.1,4-16 (49 verses).

X. **9**.8-9; **14**.13-14,16; **16**.11-14; **17**.14; **18**.14; **19**.1-5,7-8; **20**.2; **22**.5,7,9; **24**.4-6; **26**.2-3,5-9; **58**; **60**.6-7,10-12; **62**.5,8,9; **72**; **85**.1-13,15-17,22,25,28-33,35,38-42,45-47; **87**.22-25;

90.1-15; **93**.2-3,13; **97**; **103**.13; **109**.6-7; **131**.4; **135-137**; **141**; **142**.7-8; **143**; **145**.1-5; **146**; **151-152**; **154-155**; **159**; **161**.5; **162-163**; **164**.1-2,4; **166**.1-4; **173-174**; **176**.1,3-4; **179**.1; **184**; **190**; **191**.1-2,4 (259 verses).

Pankti (8+8+8+8+8):

I. **29**; **80-81**; **82**.1-5; **84**.10-12; **105**.1-7,9-18 (57 verses).

V. **6**; **7**.10; **9**.5,7; **10**.4,7; **16**.5; **17**.5; **18**.5; **20**.4; **21**.4; **22**.4; **23**.4; **35**.8; **39**.5; **50**.5; **52**.6,16-17; **64**.7; **65**.6; **75**; **79** (49 verses).

VI. **75**.17 (1 verses).

VIII. **19**.37; **31**.15-18; **35**.22,24; **46**.21,24,32; **56**.5; **62**.1-6,10-12; **69**.11,16; **91**.1-2 (24 verses).

IX. **112-114** (19 verses).

X. **59**.8; **60**.8-9; **86**; **134**.7; **145**.6; **164**.5 (29 verses).

Mahāpankti (8+8+8+8+8+8):

I. **191**.10-12 (3 verses).

VIII. **36**.7; **37**.2-7; **39**.1-10; **40**.1,3-11; **41**.1-10 **47**.1-18 (55 verses).

X. **59**.9; **133**.4-6; **134**.1-6; **166**.5 (11 verses).

Śakvarī (8+8+8+8+8+8+8):

VIII. **36**.1-6; **40**.2 (7 verses).

X. **133**.1-3 (3 verses).

2A-3. The Mixed Meters.

Regular Dvipāda Mixed Meters (Dvipadā Virāṭ/Triṣṭubh 8+12 or 12+8):

V. **24** (4 verses).

VII. **32**.3 (1 verse).

VIII. **19**.27; **29**; **43**.30 (12 verses).

IX. **107**.3,16 (2 verses).

X. **157**.1; **172** (5 verses).

Regular Tripadā Mixed Meters (Uṣṇik 8+8+12; Purauṣṇik 12+8+8; Kakubh 8+12+8):

I. **23**.19; **79**.4-6; **84**.7-9; **91**.17; **92**.13-18; **120**.2,6; **150** (19 verses).

III. **10**; **28**.3 (10 verses).

IV. **10**.8; **57**.5 (2 verses).

V. **40**.1-3; **51**.5-10; **53**.1,4-5,10-11,15; **72**; **78**.1-3 (21 verses).

VI. **43**; **48**.13,18; **51**.13-15 (9 verses).

VII. **66**.16 (1 verse).

VIII. **4**.21; **9**.5; **12**.1-33; **13**; **15**; **18**; **19**.34,36; **22**.11; **23**; **24**.1-29; **25**.1-22,24; **26**.1-15,22-24; **28**.4; **30**.2; **46**.5,31; **69**.2; **70**.13,15; **98**.1-12; **103**.8,12 (227 verses).

IX. **60**.3; **67**.30; **102-106** (42 verses).

X. **26**.1,4; **105**.3-6,8-10 (9 verses).

Regular Catuṣpadā Mixed Meters (Bṛhatī 8+8+12+8; Satobṛhatī 12+8+12+8; Prastārapankti 12+12+8+8; Upariṣṭādbṛhatī 8+8+8+12; Āstārapankti 8+8+12+12; Madhyejyotis 12+8+12+12; Upariṣṭājjyotis 12+12+12+8; Sanstārapankti 12+8+8+12; Purastādbṛhatī 12+8+8+8; Viṣṭārapankti 8+12+12+8):

I. **88**.1,6; **139**.5; **164**.42; **170**.1; **179**.5 (6 verses).

II. **41**.18 (1 verse).

III. **9**.1-8; **21**.5; **23**.3; **44-45**; **53**.8 (21 verses).

V. **53**.2,6-7,9,13-14,16; **56**.1-9; **61**.9 (17 verses).

VI. **15**.18; **42**.4; **47**.19; **48**.5,14,19,20; **59**.1-6; **60**.14 (14 verses).

VII. **14**.1; **55**.2-4; **96**.3 (5 verses).

VIII. **1**.5-32; **3**.24; **5**.37-38; **9**.1,4,6,14-15; **10**.1-2,4; **19**.35; **20**.13; **22**.7,12; **30**.3; **33**.1-15; **35**.1-21; **46**.7,9,18-19,22; **62**.7-9; **69**.17-18; **70**.7-11; **78**.10; **89**.7; **97**.1-9,11-12; **101**.4; **103**.1-4,6-7,9,11,13 (118 verses).

IX. **98**.11; **99**.1 (2 verses).

X. **14**.15; **17**.13; **18**.11; **21**; **22**.1-4,6,8,10-14; **24**.1-3; **25**; **93**.1,4-8,10,12,14-15; **101**.5; **102**.1,3,12; **126**.1-7; **132**.2,6; **140**; **144**.2,5-6; **150**.1-5; **170**.4 (74 verses).

Irregular Tripadā and Catuṣpadā Mixed Meters (Purastājjyotis 8+11+11+11; Viraḍrūpā 11+11+11+8 in any order; Padapankti 5+5+5+11; Kāvirāṭ 9+12+9; Naṣṭarūpī 11+11+13; Tanuśirā 11+11+6; Viṣṭārabṛhatī 8+10+10+8; Kṛti 11+11+7; Skandhogrīvī Bṛhatī 7+12+7+8; Anuṣṭuggarbhā Uṣṇik 5+8+8+8; Viṣamapadā 8+10+10+10; Śankumati 5+8+10+8; Uṣṇiggarbhā 5+7+10; Bṛhatī Pipīlīkamadhyā 11+10+6+7; Kakubh Nyankuśirā 10+12+4; Viṣamapadā Bṛhatī 8+8+11+8; Hasīyasī 6+6+7; Pipīlīkamadhyā 11+8+11; Urobṛhatī 9+12+8+8; Akṣarai Pankti 11+7+12+12; Nyankusāriṇī 10+11+8+8; Svarāṭ 10+7+10):

I. **88**.5; **120**.3-5,7-8; **122**.5-6; **167**.10; **173**.4; **175**.1; **187**.1 (12 verses).

II. **20**.3 (1 verse).

III. **21**.4 (1 verse).

IV. **1**.1-4,6-7 (6 verses).

V. **19**.5; **45**.9 (2 verses).

VIII. **25**.23; **46**.14-15,20; **70**.12; **96**.21; **103**.5,10 (8 verses).

IX. **110**.1-3 (3 verses).

X. **81**.2; **85**.34; **93**.9,11; **105**.2,7; **132**.1,3-5; **158**.2 (11 verses).

Pragātha Mixed Meters (Pragātha: Bṛhatī+Satobṛhatī 8+8+12+8 +12+8+12+8; Kakubh Pragatha: Kakubh+Satobṛhatī 8+12+8 +12+8+12+8):

I. **36**; **39-40**; **44**; **47-48**; **84**.19-20 (80 verses).

III. **16** (6 verses).

VI. **46**; **48**.1-4,9-12,16-17 (24 verses).

VII. **16**; **32**.1-2,4-27; **59**.1-6; **66**.10-15; **74**; **81**; **96**.1-2 (64 verses).

VIII. **1**.1-4; **3**.1-20; **4**.1-20; **10**.5-6; **17**.14-15; **19**.1-26,28-33; **20-21**; **22**.1-6,9-10,13-18; **27**; **46**.11-12,25-28; **49-54**; **60**; **61**.1-16; **66**.1-14; **70**.1-6; **71**.10-15; **77**.10-11; **87-88**; **89**.1-4; **90**; **99**; **101**.1-2,4-13 (328 verses).

IX. **107**.1-2,4-15,17-26; **108** (40 verses).

X. **33**.2-3; **62**.6-7 (4 verses).

Complex Mixed Mters (Yavamadhyā Mahābṛhatī 8+8+12+8+8; Atyaṣṭi 12+12+8+8+8+12+8; Atidhṛti 11+16+8+8+7+11+7; Atiśakvarī 8+8+8+8+8+12+8; Aṣṭi 12+12+8+12+12+8; Dhṛti 12+12+8+8+8+12+12; Mahābṛhatī 8+8+8+8+12; Atijagatī 12+12+8+12+8; Mahāpadapankti 5+5+5+5+11; Virāṭpūrvā/Paktyuttarā 10+10+8+8+8; Mahāsatobṛhatī 12+12+8+8+8; Śakvarī 12+12+12+12+8):

I. **105**.8; **127-129**; **130**.1-9; **131-132**; **133**.6-7; **134-135**; **136**.1-6; **137-138**; **139**.1-4,6-10; **191**.13 (93 verses).

II. **22** (4 verses).

IV. **1**.1-3; **10**.5 (4 verses).

V. **86**.6; **87** (10 verses).

VI. **15**.3; **48**.6-8,15,21 (6 verses).

VIII. **35**.23; **37**.1; **97**.10-13 (4 verses).

IX. **111** (3 verses).

X. **59**.10; **132**.7 (2 verses).

The distribution of the different meters in the ten books of the Rigveda is as follows:

The Distribution of the Meters in the Rigveda

	1	2	3	4	5	6	7	8	9	10	Total
Triṣṭubh	734	209	398	403	283	476	586	62	149	890	4190
Jagatī	353	142	50	33	100	38	39	17	166	341	1279
Oth.Trim.	69	21	5	2	7	15	76	4	31	8	238
Total	1156	372	453	438	390	529	701	83	346	1239	5707
Gāyatrī	472	37	104	113	79	137	61	738	599	108	2448
Anuṣṭubh	108	14	22	26	155	45	8	112	49	259	798
Oth.Dim.	60	—	—	—	49	1	—	86	22	43	261
Total	640	51	126	139	283	183	69	936	670	410	3507
Reg.Mixed	25	1	31	2	42	23	7	357	46	88	622
Irreg.Mixed	12	1	1	6	2	—	—	8	3	11	44
Pragātha	80	—	6	—	—	24	64	328	40	4	546
Comp.Mixed	93	4	—	4	10	6	—	4	3	2	126
Total	210	6	38	12	54	53	71	697	92	105	1338
Grand Total	2006	429	617	589	727	765	841	1716	1108	1754	10552

2B.
THE CHRONOLOGY OF THE DIMETERS

From the above chart, we can make a prima facie observation that the trimeters seem to be the oldest form of meters, followed by the dimeters, followed by the mixed meters. This is on the basis of the total number of verses which contain the meters (trimeters 5707, dimeters 3507, mixed meters 1338), as well as the fact that trimeters are found well distributed throughout the Rigveda, while dimeters, other than gāyatrī and anuṣṭubh, are missing in some Books of the Rigveda, and most categories of mixed meters are also missing in one or the other Book.

In this section, we will take a closer look at the chronology of the dimeters:

2B-1. The Dimeters vis-à-vis the Trimeters

As we saw, there are 5707 verses in trimetric meters, and 3507 verses in dimetric verses. On this basis, we can make a prima facie observation that trimeters seem to be older than dimeters. But mere numbers can not be a factor in determining the relative chronology of these meters: it needs to be confirmed by a closer look at the distribution of the dimeters vis-à-vis the trimeters.

Trimeters constitute 54.08 % of the verses in the Rigveda, while dimeters constitute 33.24 %. However, the relative distribution of these meters in the earlier books of the Rigveda is much more skewed:

	Trimeters		Dimeters	
	No. of verses	%-age of total	No. of verses	%-age of total
Book 2	372	86.71	51	11.89
Book 3	453	73.42	126	20.42
Book 4	438	74.36	139	23.60
Book 6	529	69.15	183	23.92
Book 7	701	83.35	69	8.20

Compare the above distribution with the relative distribution of trimeters and dimeters in the Late Books:

	Trimeters		Dimeters	
	No. of verses	%-age of total	No. of verses	%-age of total
Book 5	390	53.46	283	38.92
Book 1	1156	57.63	640	31.90
Book 8	83	4.84	936	54.55
Book 9	346	31.23	670	60.46
Book 10	1239	70.64	410	23.38

It can be seen that, except for a re-emergence of the importance of the trimeters in the latest period of Book 10, there is otherwise a steady increase in the importance of the dimeters in later Books, accompanied by a steady decrease in the relative importance of the trimeters.

The same trend can be seen, even more clearly, if we compare the relative distribution of the trimeters and dimeters in Oldenberg's "ordered" hymns on the one hand, and Oldenberg's "unordered" hymns on the other [as we shall see in detail in the chapter on the Internal Chronology of the Rigveda, Oldenberg, on the basis of earlier studies by other scholars, identified two groups of hymns in each of the Family Books: one, a group of hymns "ordered" on the basis of deity, number of verses, and meter; and two, a group of "unordered" hymns which are out of place in this order of arrangement. Oldenberg, and scholars following him in general, assumed that the "unordered" hymns were *later* than the "ordered" hymns. However, as we will see, the "unordered" hymns, within any Family Book, are generally as early or as late as the "ordered" hymns within that book, but they are generally more likely, than the "ordered" hymns, to have undergone *late redactions*. In either case, the metric composition of the "unordered" hymns is likely to show later trends than the metric composition of the "ordered" hymns].

The following is the distribution of trimeters and dimeters in the "ordered" hymns within each Family Book:

		"Ordered" Trimeters		"Ordered" Dimeters	
Book	No. of "ordered" verses	No. of verses	%-age of total	No. of verses	%-age of total
2	394	360	91.37	28	7.11
3	509	395	77.60	78	15.32
4	456	398	87.28	47	10.31
5	627	376	59.97	219	34.93
6	449	387	86.19	57	12.69
7	642	636	99.06	5	0.78

Compare these figures with the figures for the distribution of trimeters and dimeters in the "unordered" hymns within these same Family Books:

		"Unordered" Trimeters		"Unordered" Dimeters	
Book	No. of "unordered" verses	No. of verses	%-age of total	No. of verses	%-age of total
2	35	12	34.29	23	65.71
3	108	58	53.70	48	44.44
4	133	40	30.08	92	69.17
5	100	14	14	64	64
6	316	142	44.94	126	39.87
7	199	65	32.66	64	32.16

As we can see, in the "ordered" hymns, the trimeters outnumber the dimeters by large margins (except in the case of the Late Book 5, where the margin is not so large). In the "unordered" hymns, on the other hand, the margins are either very small, or the dimeters even outnumber the trimeters (by a large margin in the case of the Late Book 5). Clearly, therefore, either dimeters are relatively later than trimeters, or else their use in the composition of serious ritual verse is relatively later than the use of trimeters.

The second case is more likely. The evidence of the meters in other ancient Indo-European cultures shows that dimeter verse is a common factor in Indo-European poetry.

As Gamkrelidze points out: "**The most archaic meters in the Indo European traditions are characterized by a constant number of syllables in the line. The minimal line consists of seven or eight syllables with a caesura dividing it into 5+3 syllables, 4+4, or 4+3.** [...] **This rhythmic pattern is found in Hittite verse,** [...] **The Rigveda shows identical metrical patterns: an eight-syllabled line divided by a caesura into 4+4, 3+5, or 5+3** [...] **Archaic Greek verse found in Mycenean texts follows the same pattern** [...] **The early Latin Saturnian verses, originally used an eight-syllable line of 4+4** [...] **The most archaic forms of Slavic verse have an eight-syllable line of 3+5 or 5+3 and 4+4** [...] **In Lithuanian folk songs we find, in addition to other line lengths, an extremely archaic type composed of eight syllables with an internal division into 4+4 or 3+5** [...]" (GAMKRELIDZE 1995:738-739).

Therefore, the oldest dimetric meter in the Rigveda, the Gāyatrī, may be as old as the oldest trimetric meter, the Triṣṭubh: the two meters, with 4190 and 2448 verses respectively, together cover 62.91 % of the verses in the Rigveda. But, clearly, the use of trimeters in ritual verses was more normal in the earliest periods than the use of dimeters.

2B-2. The Internal Chronology of the Dimeters

As we saw, the common use of dimeters in ritual verse was slightly later than the use of trimeters. But this was probably more an indication of trend than of the actual age of the type of verse, since, as we saw, dimetric verse is found in all the earliest Indo-European traditions.

However, within themselves, the different dimetric verses show a very distinct chronological pattern. The gāyatrī and anuṣṭubh meters are the oldest, and most common, dimetric meters, since they are found in every single Book of the Rigveda, and cover 92.56 % of the dimetric verses in the Rigveda. However, it is clear that anuṣṭubh is later to the gāyatrī, and in fact developed from the gāyatrī itself (perhaps originally due to the repetition of the last foot or line in the last verse of a hymn, as a kind of refrain, which led to the development of a new 8+8+8+8 verse from the earlier 8+8+8 verse).

An examination of the relative positions of the gāyatrī and anuṣṭubh meters in the Family Books, in the hymns which contain both these meters, shows that, in general, the gāyatrī meter occupies a primary position and the anuṣṭubh occupies a secondary position: in the vast majority of cases, many gāyatrī verses are followed (but in a few cases preceded) by a few or even a single anuṣṭubh verse (there is a slight variation in this pattern only in a few of these hymns):

Book	Gāyatrī	Anuṣṭubh
2	8.1-5 (5 verses) 41.1-15,19-21 (18 verses)	8.6 (1 verse) 41.16-17 (2 verses)
3	24.2-5 (4 verses) 37.2-10 (9 verses)	24.1 (1 verse) 37.11 (1 verses)
4	30.1-7,9-23 (22 verses)	30.8,24 (2 verses)
5	19.1-2 (2 verses) 28.5-6 (2 verses) 51.1-4 (4 verses) 53.8,12 (2 verses) 61.1-4,6-8,10-19 (17 verses) 82.2-9 (8 verses)	19.3-4 (2 verses) 28.4 (1 verse) 51.14-15 (2 verses) 53.2 (1 verse) 61.5 (1 verse) 82.1 (1 verse)
6	16.1-26,28-45 (44 verses) 45.1-32 (32 verses) 47.24 (1 verse) 53.1-7,9-10 (9 verses) 56.1-5 (5 verses) 60.4-12 (9 verses)	16.27,47-48 (2 verses) 45.33 (1 verse) 47.23 (1 verse) 53.8 (1 verse) 56.6 (1 verse) 60.15 (1 verse)
7	59.9-11 (3 verses) 94.1-11 (11 verses)	59.12 (1 verse) 94.12 (1 verse)

In fact, there are only two hymns where the anuṣṭubh verses

outnumber the gāyatrī verses, and both these hymns are included in Oldenberg's list of "unordered" (late redacted) hymns:

Book	Gāyatrī	Anuṣṭubh
3	53.13 (1 verse)	53.12,20,22 (3 verses)
7	55.1 (1 verse)	55.5-8 (4 verses)

That gāyatrī is older than anuṣṭubh, and that anuṣṭubh became more and more important only in the Late Books of the Rigveda becomes clear from the following statistics:

	Gāyatrī		Anuṣṭubh	
Book	No. of Hymns	No. of verses	No. of hymns	No. of verses
2	4	37	4	14
3	14	104	9	22
4	11	113	8	26
6	11	137	17	45
7	9	61	5	8
Total	49	452	43	115

	Gāyatrī		Anuṣṭubh	
Book	No. of Hymns	No. of verses	No. of hymns	No. of verses
5	13	79	34	155

It may be noted:

1. In the Early and Middle Books, the gāyatrī verses far outnumber the anuṣṭubh verses; but in the Late Book 5, the anuṣṭubh verses far outnumber the gāyatrī verses.

2. The number of anuṣṭubh verses in the Late Book 5 are more than the number of anuṣṭubh verses in all the five Early and Middle Books put together.

The development of the anuṣṭubh verse (8+8+8+8) from the gāyatrī verse (8+8+8) is paralleled by the development of the pankti verse (8+8+8+8+8) from the anuṣṭubh verse. In fact, the process is even clearer in this case, as will be seen from the following relative distribution of the two meters in the hymns, in Book 5, which contain both the meters:

Anuṣṭubh	Pankti
7.1-9 (9 verses)	7.10 (1 verse)
9.1-4,6 (5 verses)	9.5,7 (2 verses)
10.1-3,5-6 (5 verses)	10.4,7 (2 verses)
16.1-4 (4 verses)	16.5 (1 verse)
17.1-4 (4 verses)	17.5 (1 verse)
18.1-4 (4 verses)	18.5 (1 verse)
20.1-3 (3 verses)	20.4 (1 verse)
21.1-3 (3 verses)	21.4 (1 verse)
22.1-3 (3 verses)	22 4 (1 verse)
23.1-3 (3 verses)	23.4 (1 verse)
35.1-7 (7 verses)	35.8 (1 verse)
39.1-4 (4 verses)	39.5 (1 verse)
50.1-4 (4 verses)	50.5 (1 verse)
52.1-5,7-15 (14 verses)	52.6,16-17 (3 verses)
64.1-6 (6 verses)	64.7 (1 verse)
65.1-5 (5 verses)	65.6 (1 verse)

Further, as we saw, the following is the distribution of the pankti verses in the Rigveda:

VI. **75**.17 (1 verse)

V. **6**.1-10; **7**.10; **9**.5,7; **10**.4,7; **16**.5; **17**.5; **18**.5; **20**.4; **21**.4; **22**.4; **23**.4; **35**.8; **39**.5; **50**.5; **52**.6,16-17; **64**.7; **65**.6; **75**.1-9; **79**.1-10 (49 verses).

I. **29**.1-7; **80**.1-16; **81**.1-9; **82**.1-5; **84**.10-12; **105**.1-7,9-18 (57 verses).

VIII. **19**.37; **31**.15-18; **35**.22,24; **46**.21,24,32; **56**.5; **62**.1-6,10-12; **69**.11,16; **91**.1-2 (24 verses).

IX. **112**.1-4; **113**.1-11; **114**.1-4 (19 verses).

X. **59**.8; **60**.8-9; **86**.1-23; **134**.7; **145**.6; **164**.5 (29 verses).

While Book 5, the only Late Family Book, *alone* has 49 pankti verses, *all the other* Family Books (which are Early and Middle Books) *together* have only *one* verse: in hymn **VI**.75, the last, and notoriously *latest*, hymn in Book 6, and one marked by Oldenberg as Late.

The next two meters in the order, mahāpankti and (dimeter) śakvarī, are found only in the non-family Books:

Mahāpankti:

I. 191.10-12 (3 verses).

VIII. 36.7; 37.2-7; 39.1-10; 40.1,3-11; 41.1-10; 47.1-18 (55 verses).

X. 59.9; 133.4-6; 134.1-6; 166.5 (11 verses).

(Dimeter) Śakvarī:

VIII. 36.1-6; 40.2 (7 verses).

X. 133.1-3 (3 verses).

As we can see, there are five dimetric meters in the RV:
Gāyatrī: 8+8+8
Anuṣṭubh: 8+8+8+8
Pankti: 8+8+8+8+8
Mahāpankti: 8+8+8+8+8+8
(Dimeter) Śakvarī: 8+8+8+8+8+8+8

And these dimetric meters appear in the Rigveda in three *very clear* chronological stages:

1. *Gāyatrī primary – anuṣṭubh secondary*: The Early and Middle Family Books 2-4, 6-7.
2. *Gāyatrī old – anuṣṭubh primary – pankti new*: The Late Family Book 5.
3. *Gāyatrī, anuṣṭubh & pankti old – mahāpankti & (dimeter) śakvarī new*: The Late non-family Books 1, 8-10.

2C.
THE CHRONOLOGY OF THE OTHER METERS

The mixed meters (i.e., meters which have both dimetric and trimetric lines within the same verse) are clearly the latest forms of meters in the Rigveda. But while noting the distribution of the mixed meters, it is important to note that even the occurrence of dimetric verses and trimetric verses within the same hymn is a relatively late phenomenon.

The following two tables show the number and percentage of a) hymns which are *fully* composed only in dimetric or only in trimetric verses, b) hymns which contain both dimetric and trimetric verses within the same hymn, and c) hymns which contain mixed verses. The first table shows the above data for the "ordered" hymns within each Family Book (Books 2-7), and the second table shows the same data for the "unordered" hymns within each Family Book as well as for Book 8. [Note: the total of the three columns exceeds the total number of hymns in the Book in most cases. This is because some hymns contain both dimetric and trimetric verses *as well as* mixed verses, and these hymns are included in both b) and c). Note that in the "ordered" hymns, there is only one such hymn, **III**.21 in Book 3; while in the "unordered" hymns in the Family Books 2-7, there are, respectively, 0, 2, 1, 3, 4 and 1 of these hymns].

Ordered Hymns		Hymns composed fully in dimeters or fully in trimeters.		Hymns containing both dimetric and trimetric verses.		Hymns containing mixed verses.	
Book	Total no. of hymns	No. of such hymns	%-age of total	No. of such hymns	%-age of total	No. of such hymns	%-age of total
2	39	37	94.87	–	0	2	5.13
3	54	43	79.63	5	9.26	7	12.96
4	47	42	89.36	3	6.38	2	4.26
5	77	70	90.91	1	1.30	6	7.79
6	59	54	91.53	3	5.08	2	3.39
7	87	85	97.70	1	1.15	1	1.15

Unordered Hymns		Hymns composed fully in dimeters or fully in trimeters.		Hymns containing both dimetric and trimetric verses.		Hymns containing mixed verses.	
Book	Total no. of hymns	No. of such hymns	%-age of total	No. of such hymns	%-age of total	No. of such hymns	%-age of total
2	4	2	50	1	25	1	25
3	8	2	25	6	75	2	25
4	11	7	63.64	4	36.36	1	9.09
5	10	3	30	5	50	5	50
6	16	4	25	9	56.35	7	43.75
7	17	6	35.29	4	23.53	8	47.06
8	103	45	43.69	10	9.71	52	50.49

As we can see in the above tables, hymns composed in simple meters of only *one* type (either dimeters or trimeters) constitute the overwhelming majority in the "ordered" hymns in the Family Books, but, in the "unordered" hymns and in the later Book 8, they give way to hymns which contain both dimeters and trimeters and/or mixed meters.

This trend is even more glaring when we compare the actual number of verses in simple meters with the actual number of verses in mixed meters. The contrast between the "ordered" hymns and the "unordered" hymns is striking. It is clear that the mixed meters developed in the period of Book 8 (in which the mixed verses are distributed evenly throughout the Book), at the time when the "unordered" hymns in the Family Books were undergoing their final redaction, and hence we find a greater proportion of mixed verses in these "unordered" hymns. If we divide Book 1 also into two groups, one group being closest to the period of Book 8 (containing hymns 36-50 composed by the Kaṇvas, and hence closest to Book 8 which is the Book of the Kaṇvas, and hymns 127-139 of the Parucchepas, which are among the latest hymns in Book 1 and the only hymns to refer to the camel, otherwise known only to Book 8) and the other group consisting of all the other hymns, we again see a greater concentration of mixed meters in the first group. Likewise, in Book 9, the last and also among the latest hymns in the Book, hymns 102-114, contain the greatest concentration of mixed meters. [Book 10, the last and latest Book of the Rigveda, and a kind of appendix to the rest of the Rigveda, is a very late Book which antedates the complete development of the Rigvedic meters; and it represents a period in which a completely new Atharvavedic ethos prevailed, and yet there was also a trend to imitate old hymns, and hence it shows a revival of the simple meters. Even then, 5.99% of the verses in Book 10 are in mixed meters; and these include various late mixed meters found only in the non-family Books]. The following tables will make this clear:

Books	Verses	Simple Verses	%-age	Mixed Verses	%-age
Ordered 2-7	3076	2986	97.07	90	2.93
1 (1-35,51-126, 140-191)	1728	1688	97.69	40	2.31
9 (1-101)	970	964	99.38	6	0.62
Total	5774	5638	97.64	136	2.36

Books	Verses	Simple Verses	%-age	Mixed Verses	%-age
Unordered 2- 7	892	748	83.86	144	16.14
8	1716	1019	59.38	697	40.62
1 (36-50, 127-139)	278	108	38.85	170	61.15
9 (102-114)	138	52	37.68	86	62.32
Total	3024	1927	63.72	1097	36.28

If we, similarly, examine the distribution of only the complex and pragātha mixed meters (i.e. if we exclude the other, simpler, mixed meters), the contrast is even starker:

Books	Total no. of verses	No. of Complex and Pragātha Mixed verses	%-age
Ordered 2-7	3076	15	0.49
1 (1-35,51-126, 140-191)	1728	4	0.23
9 (1-101)	970	–	0
Total	5774	19	0.33

Books	Total no. of verses	No. of Complex and Pragātha Mixed verses	%-age
Unordered 2-7	892	103	11.55
8	1716	332	19.35
1 (36-50,127-139)	278	169	60.79
9 (102-114)	138	43	31.16
Total	3024	647	21.40

Even the *other* (than Complex and Pragātha) mixed meters clearly originated in the Late Period; perhaps in the period of Book 5, which has 44 verses (out of a total of 727 verses, which is 6.05 %) in such mixed meters while the other five earlier Family Books together have 72 verses (out of 3241, which is 2.22 %).

A look at the distribution of these simpler mixed meters confirms this:

An overwhelming majority of these meters are found only in the non-family Books: āstārapankti, madhyejyotis, upariṣṭājjyotis, sanstārapankti, purastādbṛhatī, viṣṭārapankti, kāvirāṭ, naṣṭarūpī, tanuśirā, viṣṭārabṛhatī, kṛti, skandhogrīvī bṛhatī, anuṣṭuggarbhā uṣṇik, viṣamapadā, śankumati, uṣṇiggarbhā, bṛhatī pipīlīkamadhyā, kakubh nyankuśirā, viṣamapadā bṛhatī, hasīyasī, pipīlīkamadhyā, urobṛhatī, akṣarai pankti, nyankusāriṇī and svarāṭ.

Some others are found only in the non-family Books and in the Late Book 5, and in the *unordered* hymns in the other earlier Family Books (2-4, 6-7): prastārapankti, kakubh, upariṣṭādbṛhatī, purauṣṇik, purastājjyotis and dvipadā virāṭ/triṣṭubh.

The *only* ones found in the ordered hymns in the five earlier Family Books are a few common meters: virāḍrūpā (which is actually just an irregular and aberrant form of triṣṭubh), uṣṇik, bṛhatī and satobṛhatī, and a meter restricted to one hymn in Book 4, padapankti.

Clearly, the few early verses in mixed meters (including the ones in the "ordered" hymns in the Family Books) are the products of redactions in the Late Rigvedic Period.

2D
THE AVESTAN METERS

The first point to be noted is that the Rigveda is composed entirely in metrical verse, and prose sections start appearing only in later Samhitās like the Yajurveda Samhitā. However, the major part of the Avesta is in prose, and it is mainly the *very oldest* portions (the Gāθās) which are in metrical verse.

Of course, this in itself would not constitute clinching evidence for the relative chronology of the Rigveda vis-à-vis the Avesta. That is, this alone does not indicate that the beginnings of the Rigveda are earlier than the beginnings of the Avesta: on just this much evidence, it could just as well be claimed that the Rigveda and the Gāθās were both commenced after the alleged separation of the Iranians and the Vedic Aryans in some pre-Rigvedic period, and it is only that the Iranians later switched over to prose earlier than the Indo-Aryans. After all, we have some "Prakritisms" in the Rigveda itself, and in the Mitanni records (*satta* for *sapta*), but this does not mean that the Rigveda or the Mitanni are contemporaneous with the later age of the Prakrits. These were merely different aberrant "Prakritisms" which arose, in the natural course of development of the language, at earlier points of time in different areas.

But an actual examination of the Avestan meters shows that in this case appearances are not deceptive, and that the Avesta, as a *whole, does* belong to the Late Rigvedic Period:

As we saw, the Gāθās, the oldest part of the Avesta, are in metrical verse. The five Gāθās consisting of 17 hymns composed by Zaraθuštra himself, the oldest and most important among the composers of the Avesta, are included within the Yasna section of the Avesta:

Gāθā Ahunauuaitī (Yasna 28-34).

Gāθā Uštauuaitī (Yasna 43-46).

Gāθā Spəntā.mainiiu (Yasna 47-50).

Gāθā Vohu.xšaθrā (Yasna 51).

Gāθā Vahištōišti (Yasna 53).

Two verses, occurring one before and one after the Gāθās, are also in metrical verses and are attributed to Zaraθuštra:

Yaθā Ahū Vairiiō (Yasna 27.13).

A Airiiɜmā Išiiō (Yasna 54.1).

The meters used in these Gāθās clearly show that they were composed in the Late Rigvedic period, since they contain a range of meters all of which existed only in the Late Period and were absent in the earlier periods:

Gāθā Spəntā.mainiiu, the third Gāθā, is composed in a meter (11+11+11+11) equivalent to the oldest and commonest meter in the Rigveda: the triṣṭubh meter, which is found from the oldest Book 6 (62.22 % of the verses in the Book) to the latest Book 10 (50.74 % of the verses in the Book), and constitutes 39.71 % of the total verses in the Rigveda as a whole.

Gāθā Uštauuaitī, the second Gāθā, is composed in a meter (11+11+11+11+11) equivalent to the Pancapadā trimetric meters śakvarī/atijagatī. These meters are found only in 11 verses in the Rigveda; and all, but one, of these verses are found in predominantly triṣṭubh hymns.

Gāθā Vahištōišti, the fifth Gāθā, and the following Gāθāic formula, A Airiiʒmā Išiiō, are composed in a meter (12+12+7+12+7+12 or 12+12+19+19) which can only be described as equivalent to a Pragātha or a Complex mixed meter; and as we have just seen earlier, these meters are a product of the Late Rigvedic Period, the period of Book 8. In fact, this close relation between the Avesta and Book 8 had been noted long ago by an eminent Zoroastrian scholar, J.C. Tavadia: "**It is the eight Maṇḍala which bears the most striking similarity to the Avesta. There and there only (and of course partly in the related first Maṇḍala) do some common words like *uṣṭra* and the strophic structure called *pragātha* occur … Further research in this direction is sure to be fruitful**" (TAVADIA 1950:3-4). Of course, these meters are not strictly found "there and there only", but, as we have seen, they *are* indeed found overwhelmingly "there" (in Book 8) and in chronologically "related" hymns (the Parucchepa and Kaṇva hymns in Book 1, the last hymns in Book 9, and the redacted "unordered" hymns in the Family Books).

Finally, Gāθā Ahunauuaitī, the first Gāθā, and the preceding Gāθāic formula, Yaθā Ahū Vairiiō, are composed in a dimetric meter (16+16+16), and Gāθa Vohu.xšaθrā, the fourth Gāθā, is composed in a related meter (14+14+14), which are exactly equivalent to a mahāpankti (8+8+8+8+8+8) and a catalectic mahāpankti (7+7+7+7+7+7) respectively. (Note: the combination of two eight-syllabled lines into one sixteen-syllabled line is a common feature in Indo-European metrical traditions like Vedic, Greek and Slavic: GAMKRELIDZE 1995:740). As we have seen, the development of dimetric verse follows a strictly chronological path in the Rigveda: the Early and Middle Family Books know only the gāyatrī (8+8+8) and the anuṣṭubh (8+8+8+8), with the anuṣṭubh clearly in a subordinate position to the gāyatrī, from which in fact the anuṣṭubh is clearly a *development*. In the Late but Family Book 5, a new meter pankti (8+8+8+8+8) develops from the anuṣṭubh. *The mahāpankti (8+8+8+8+8+8), which is totally unknown in the Family Books, appears as a new meter only in the Late non-family Book 8 and later in Book 1 (in the last and latest hymn in the Book) and in Book 10, the last and latest Book in the Rigveda.*

Likewise, when we do find scattered metrical verse-sections sporadically turning up in some other, mainly prose, parts of the Avesta, they are usually in late dimeters: e.g. in Yašt 5, we find lines 23-32 in metrical verse consisting of 8+8+8+8+8, equivalent to a pankti verse. The pankti, as we saw, developed in the Late Rigvedic period, at the time of composition of the hymns in Book 5.

The evidence of the Avestan meters confirms to the hilt the conclusions compelled by the evidence of the Avestan names: namely, that Zaraθuštra, *the first and earliest composer of the Avesta*, is *contemporaneous* with the *Late* Period and Books of the Rigveda (notably with the non-family Books), that the Early and Middle Books of the Rigveda *precede* the period of composition of the Avesta, and that the “Indo-Iranian” culture common to the Rigveda and the Avesta is a product of the *Late* Rigvedic Period.

Chapter 3

The Geography of the RV

As we have seen, in our examination of the relative chronology of the Rigveda vis-à-vis the Avesta, the common development of the joint "Indo-Iranian" culture represented in these two texts took place in the period of the *Late* Books of the Rigveda. The Early and Middle Books of the Rigveda represent periods which are *older* than the period of development of this joint "Indo-Iranian" culture.

This takes us to the question of the geography of these texts: *in which area did this development of the joint "Indo-Iranian" culture take place*? The geographical horizon of the Avesta extends from Afghanistan and southern Central Asia in the west to the Punjab in the east, and that of the Rigveda from (at least) western Uttar Pradesh in the east to eastern and southern Afghanistan in the west. The *common* ground therefore lies in the area stretching from Punjab to Afghanistan.

The next question is: in which area were the *Early* and *Middle* Books of the Rigveda composed; or, in other words, *where* were the Vedic Aryans in the period *before* the development of this joint "Indo-Iranian" culture? As per the AIT, the joint "Indo-Iranian" culture is pre-Rigvedic, and developed in Central Asia before the Vedic Aryans and Iranians separated from each other and migrated into India and Iran respectively. However, as we have seen, the joint "Indo-Iranian culture is in fact *Late* Rigvedic, and took place in an area extending from Punjab to Afghanistan. Now can this fact be incorporated into the AIT by now postulating that the Indo-Iranians, after jointly migrating from Central Asia to a region further south, developed this joint culture before the Vedic Aryans penetrated further into India and the Iranians moved westwards? If so, the geography of the period *before* the development of this joint culture, i.e. the geography of the *Early* and *Middle* Books of the Rigveda, *should point towards Central Asia.*

But an examination of the geographical data in the Early and Middle Books of the Rigveda shows exactly the opposite: it shows that the Vedic Aryans, in the period of the Early and Middle Books of the Rigveda, were inhabitants of an area in the *interior* of India, to the *East* of the Sarasvatī, and were only just expanding into and becoming acquainted with areas further west.

The geographical evidence in the RV is very clear and unambiguous. It has already been detailed in my earlier book (TALAGERI 2000:94-136); but it is necessary to go into it again here, as part of our complete examination of the chronology and geography of the Rigveda as well as to correct minor errors and fill in omissions in our earlier book.

In this chapter, we will examine the geographical data (river names, place names, mountain names, lake names, and animal names) in the Rigveda on the basis of three divisions of the geographical horizon of the Rigveda: *the Eastern Region* (the Sarasvati and areas to its east: mainly present-day Haryana and westernmost Uttar Pradesh), *the Western Region* (the Indus and areas to its west: mainly Afghanistan and contiguous areas of southern Central Asia and northwestern most Pakistan), and *the Central Region* (the Saptasindhu or Punjab between the Indus and the Sarasvati: mainly the northern half of present-day Pakistan, and contiguous parts of Indian Punjab). [The only generally accepted mountain names in the Rigveda are western ones. In the case of animals, Eastern animals are those native, alongwith related species and sub-species, to India, southeast Asia and southern China, but not to Afghanistan and further northwest; Western animals are those native to Afghanistan and further northwest and west. There are no specific Central animals, since the animals from the two other regions spill on to the Central area].

The geographical data pertaining to *the Eastern region* is as follows:

River names: *Sarasvatī, Dṛṣadvatī/Hariyūpīyā/Yavyāvatī, Āpayā, Aśmanvatī, Amśumatī, Yamunā, Gangā, Jahnāvī.*

Place names: *Kīkamṭa, Iḷaspada/Iḷāyāspada* (indirectly *Vara-ā-pṛthivyāh, Nābhā-pṛthivyāh*).

Animal names: *ibha/vāraṇa/hastin/sṛṇi* (elephant), *mahiṣa* (buffalo), *gaura* (Indian bison), *mayūra* (peacock), *pṛṣatī* (chital, spotted deer).

Lake names: *Mānuṣa.*

The geographical data pertaining to *the Western region* is as follows:

River names: *Tṛṣṭāmā, Susartū, Anitabhā, Rasā, Śvetyā, Kubhā, Krumu, Gomatī, Sarayu, Mehatnū, Śvetyāvarī, Suvāstu, Gaurī, Sindhu* (as the Indus river), *Suṣomā, Ārjīkīyā.*

Place names: *Gandhāri.* (indirectly *gandharva*).

Mountain names: *Suṣoma, Ārjīka, Mūjavat.*

Animal names: *uṣṭra* (Bactrian camel), *mathra* (Afghan horses), *chāga* (mountain goat), *meṣa* (mountain sheep), *vṛṣṇi* (ram), *urā* (lamb), *varāha/varāhu* (boar, also found in the Avesta).

Lake names: *Śaryaṇāvat(ī).*

The geographical data pertaining to *the Central region* is as follows:

River names: *Śutudrī , Vipāś, Paruṣṇī, Asiknī, Vitastā, Marudvṛdhā.*

Place names: *Saptasindhavah* (indirectly *sapta+sindhu*).

To get the complete geographical picture of the movements and migrations of the Vedic Aryans, let us examine the geographical data as found in the Books of the Rigveda period-wise, within each geographical area:

3A. The Eastern Region: The Sarasvatī River and east.

3B. The Western region: The Indus River and West.

3C. The Central Region: between the Sarasvatī and the Indus.
3D. Summary of the Data.
3E. Appendix 1: Other Geographical Evidence.
    3E-1. Climate and Topography.
    3E-2. Trees and Wood.
    3E-3. Rice and Wheat.
    3E-4. The Traditional Vedic Attitude towards the Northwest.
3F. Appendix 2. The Topsy-turvy Logic of AIT Geography.
    3F-1. The Sarasvatī.
    3F-2. The Gangā.

3A
THE EASTERN REGION: THE SARASVATĪ RIVER AND EAST

The Eastern region is clearly well known to the whole of the Rigveda: to the Early Books (6, 3, 7), the Middle Books (4, 2), and the Late Books (5, 1, 8-10). The following list of eastern river names, place names, lake names and animal names will make this clear:

The Early Books:

Book 6:

1. Iḷaspada-2.
4. vāraṇa-5.
8. mahiṣa-4.
17. mahiṣa-11.
20. ibha-8.
27. Hariyūpīyā-5, Yavyāvatī-6.
45. Gangā-31.
49. Sarasvatī-7.
50. Sarasvatī-12.
52. Sarasvatī-6.
61. Sarasvatī-1-7,10-11,13-14.

Book 3:

4. Sarasvatī-8.
5. (nābhā-pṛthivyāh-9).
23. Sarasvatī-4, Dṛṣadvatī-4, Āpayā-4, Iḷāyāspada-4, Mānuṣa-4, (vara-ā-pṛthivyāh-4).
26. pṛṣatī-4,6.
29. Iḷāyāspada-4, (nābhā-pṛthivyāh-4).
45. mayūra-1.
46. mahiṣa-2.
53. Kīkaṭa-14, (vara-ā-pṛthivyāh-11).
54. Sarasvatī-13.
58. Jahnāvī-6.

Book 7:

2. Sarasvatī-8.
9. Sarasvatī-5.
18. Yamunā-19.
35. Sarasvatī-11.
36. Sarasvatī-6.
39. Sarasvatī-5.
40. Sarasvatī-3, pṛṣatī-3.
44. mahiṣa-5.
69. gaura-6.
95. Sarasvatī-1-2,4-6.
96. Sarasvatī-1,3-6.
98. gaura-1.

The Middle Books:

Book 4:

4. ibha-1.
16. hastin-14.
18. mahiṣa-11.
21. gaura-8.
58. gaura-2.

Book 2:

1. Sarasvatī-11.

3. Sarasvatī-8, (nābhā-pṛthivyāh-7).
10. Iḷaspada-1.
30. Sarasvatī-8.
32. Sarasvatī-8.
34. pṛṣatī-3,4.
36. pṛṣatī-2.
41. Sarasvatī-16-18.

The Late Books:

Book 5:

5. Sarasvatī-8.
29. mahiṣa-7,8.
42. Sarasvatī-12, pṛṣatī-15.
43. Sarasvatī-11.
46. Sarasvatī-2.
52. Yamunā-17.
55. pṛṣatī-6.
57. pṛṣatī-3.
58. pṛṣatī-6.
60. pṛṣatī-2.

Book 1:

3. Sarasvatī-10-12.
13. Sarasvatī-9.
16. gaura-5.
37. pṛṣatī-2.
39. pṛṣatī-6.
64. mahiṣa-7, hastin-7, pṛṣatī-8.
85. pṛṣatī-4,5.
87. pṛṣatī-4.
89. Sarasvatī-3, pṛṣatī-7.
95. mahiṣa-9.
116. Jahnāvī-19.
121. mahiṣa-2.
128. Iḷaspada-1, Mānuṣa-7.
140. vāraṇa-2.

141. mahiṣa-3.
142. Sarasvatī-9.
143. (nābhā-pṛthivyāh-4).
162. pṛṣatī-21.
164. Sarasvatī-49,52.
186. pṛṣatī-8.
188. Sarasvatī-8.
191. mayūra-14.

Book 8:

1. mayūra-25.
4. gaura-3.
7. pṛṣatī-28.
12. mahiṣa-8.
21. Sarasvatī-17,18.
33. vāraṇa-8.
35. mahiṣa-7-9.
38. Sarasvatī-10.
45. gaura-24.
54. Sarasvatī-4.
69. mahiṣa-15.
77. mahiṣa-10.
96. Amśumatī-13.

Book 9:

5. Sarasvatī-8.
33. mahiṣa-1.
57. ibha-3.
67. Sarasvatī-32.
69. mahiṣa-3.
72. (nābhā-pṛthivyāh-7).
73. mahiṣa-2.
79. (nābhā-pṛthivyāh-4).
81. Sarasvatī-4.
82. (nābhā-pṛthivyāh-3).
86. mahiṣa-40, (nābhā-pṛthivyāh-8).
87. mahiṣa-7.

92. mahiṣa-6.
95. mahiṣa-4.
96. mahiṣa-6,18,19.
97. mahiṣa-41.
113. mahiṣa-3.

Book 10:

1. Iḷaspada-6, (nābhā-pṛthivyāh-6).
8. mahiṣa-1.
17. Sarasvatī-7-9.
28. mahiṣa-10.
30. Sarasvatī-12.
40. vāraṇa-4.
45. mahiṣa-3.
51. gaura-6.
53. Aśmanvatī-8.
60. mahiṣa-3.
64. Sarasvatī-9.
65. Sarasvatī-1,13, mahiṣa-8.
66. Sarasvatī-5, mahiṣa-10.
70. Iḷaspada-1.
75. Sarasvatī-5, Gangā-5, Yamunā-5.
91. Iḷaspada-1, Iḷāyāspada-4.
100. gaura-2.
106. mahiṣa-2, sṛṇi-6.
110. Sarasvatī-8.
123. mahiṣa-4.
128. mahiṣa-8.
131. Sarasvatī-5.
140. mahiṣa-6.
141. Sarasvatī-5.
184. Sarasvatī-2.
189. mahiṣa-2.
191. Iḷaspada-1.

3B
THE WESTERN REGION: THE INDUS RIVER AND WEST

In sharp contrast to the Eastern region, *the Western region is totally unknown to the Early Books and only very newly familiar to the Middle Books*, but quite well known to the Late Books. The western place names (except indirectly, in the form of the word gandharva, in one *late* hymn, as we shall see), animal names, lake names and mountain names are *totally unknown* to both the Early and the Middle Books, and only a *few* (exactly three) western river names appear, and *only* in Book IV, which represents the westernmost thrust of the Vedic Aryans in the Middle period.

The Early Books:

Book 3:

38. (gandharva-6).

[This, *the only word pertaining to the West appearing in the Early Books*, appears in a hymn which, as we have already seen in the course of our analysis of the Avestan names, is one of the six hymns in the Rigveda for which we actually have a categorical mention in the Vedic texts themselves about the hymns concerned being *interpolations or late additions into the text*: i.e. hymns added into the original core Rigveda of the Family Books (II-VII) at the time of inclusion of Books I and VIII into the collection. The Aitareya Brāhmaṇa VI.18 specifies these six hymns: **III**.30-31, 34, 36, 38, 48 — See TALAGERI 2000:73-74, and earlier in this book in the chapter on the Avestan names].

The Middle Books:

Book 4:

30. Sindhu-12, Sarayu-18.
43. Rasā-6.

54. Sindhu-6.
55. Sindhu-3.

The Late Books:

Book 5:

41. Rasā-15.
53. Sarayu-9, Kubhā-9, Krumu-9, Anitabhā-9, Rasā-9, Sindhu-9.

Book 1:

10. vṛṣṇi-2.
22. (gandharva-14).
43. meṣa-6, meṣī-6.
44. Sindhu-12.
51. meṣa-1.
52. meṣa-1.
61. varāha-7.
83. Sindhu-1.
84. Śaryaṇāvat-14.
88. varāhu-5.
112. Rasā-12..
114. varāha-5.
116. meṣa-16.
117. meṣa-17,18.
121. varāhu-11.
122. Sindhu-6.
126. Sindhu-1, Gandhāri-7.
138. uṣṭra-2.
162. chāga-3.
163. (gandharva-2).
164. Gaurī-4.
186. Sindhu-5.

+ in refrain repeated in last verse of **I**.94-96,98,100-103,105-115-Sindhu.

Book 8:

1. (gandharva-11).

2. meṣa-40.
5. uṣṭra-37.
6. Śaryaṇāvat-39, uṣṭra-48.
7. Ārjīka-29, Suṣoma-29, Śaryaṇāvat-29.
12. Sindhu-3.
19. Suvāstu-37.
20. Sindhu-24,25.
24. Gomatī-30.
25. Sindhu-14.
26. Śvetyāvarī-18, Sindhu-18.
34. urā-3.
46. uṣṭra-22,31, mathra-23.
64. Ārjīkīyā-11, Suṣomā-11, Śaryaṇāvat-11.
66. urā-8.
72. Sindhu-7, Rasā-13.
77. varāha-10, (gandharva-5).
97. meṣa-12.

Book 9:

8. meṣa-5.
41. Rasā-6.
65. Śaryaṇāvat-22, Ārjīka-23.
83. (gandharva-4).
85. (gandharva-12).
86. meṣa-47, (gandharva-36).
97. varāha-7, Sindhu-58.
107. meṣa-11.
113. Śaryaṇāvat-1, Arjīka-2, (gandharva-3).

Book 10:

10. (gandharva-4).
11. (gandharva-2).
27. meṣa-17.
28. varāha-4.
34. Mūjavat-1.
35. Śaryaṇāvat-2
64. Sarayu-9, Sindhu-9.

65. Sindhu-13.
66. Sindhu-11.
67. varāha-7.
75. Sindhu-1,3-4,6-9, Ārjīkīyā-5, Suṣomā-5, Gomatī-6, Mehatnū-6, Kubhā-6, Krumu-6, Śvetyā-6, Rasā-6, Susartū-6, Tṛṣṭāmā-6.
85. (gandharva-40-41).
86. varāha-4.
91. meṣa-14.
95. urā-3.
99. varāha-6.
106. meṣa-5.
108. Rasā-1,2.
121. Rasā-4.
123. (gandharva-4,7).
136. (gandharva-6).
139. (gandharva-4,6).
177. (gandharva-2).

3C
THE CENTRAL REGION: BETWEEN THE SARASVATĪ AND THE INDUS

As we have seen in sections A and B, the data pertaining to the Eastern region is known to the *whole* of the Rigveda, while the data pertaining to the Western region (its mountains, places, lakes and animals) is *totally unknown* to the Early and Middle Books, *and even to Book 5, the earliest of the Late Books.*

Three Western *rivers* alone first appear in Book 4 of the Middle Period. In fact, even Book 5, the earliest of the Late Books, practically knows only these *same* three rivers; *all* the new ones are named by a single poet in a single hymn: a poet who also, in other hymns, names the Central Paruṣṇī and the Eastern Yamunā, and, in consequence, even Witzel concedes that all these river names only indicate that the particular poet is widely traveled, and not necessarily that the Vedic people actually occupied the areas of the rivers named: "**all these geographical notes belonging to diverse hymns are attributed to one and the same poet, Śyāvāśva, which is indicative of the poet's travels**" (WITZEL 1995b:317)]

It is obvious that there has been an expansion of the Vedic Aryan territory from the Eastern Region in the Early Period to areas in the Western Region by the Late Period. Logically, therefore, the data pertaining to the Central Region should exhibit a *pattern showing us this expansion from the East to the West in the course of the Early and Middle Periods of the Rigveda.*

And that is precisely what the data pertaining to the Central region shows us in the Rigveda. The Central Region (the Saptasindhavah region or the Greater Punjab region), between the Indus and the Sarasvatī, is usually assumed to be the region where the Rigveda as a whole was composed, and in which the invading/immigrating Vedic Aryans (or Indo-Aryans) were settled at the time of composition of the hymns. However, the data makes it clear that the Vedic Aryans were originally located to the East of this region, and only expanded into this region in the course of the Early Rigvedic Period:

The Early Books:

Book 3:

33. Vipāś-1, Śutudrī-1.

Book 7:

5. Asiknī-3.
18. Paruṣṇī-8,9.

The Middle Books:

Book 4:

22. Paruṣṇī-2.
28. (sapta+sindhu-1).
30. Vipāś-11.

Book 2:

12. (sapta+sindhu-3,12).

The Late Books:

Book 5:

52. Paruṣṇī-9.

Book 1:

32. (sapta+sindhu-12).
35. (sapta+sindhu-8).

Book 8:

20. Asiknī-25.
24. Saptasindhavah-27.
54. (sapta+sindhu-4).
69. (sapta+sindhu-12).
75. Paruṣṇī-15.

Book 9:

66. (sapta+sindhu-6).

Book 10:

43. (sapta+sindhu-3).
67. (sapta+sindhu-12).
75. Vitastā-5, Marudvṛdhā-5, Asiknī-5, Paruṣṇī-5, Śutudrī-5.

The river names of *the Central Region appear in the Early Books* in chronological order from East to West:

1. The chronologically earliest Book, Book 6, is as indifferent to the Central rivers as it is to the Western rivers.

2. The next Book, Book 3, refers to the *two easternmost* of the five rivers of the Punjab, the Vipāś and the Śutudrī, in what was recognized by many Western scholars as a description of an expansionist movement over these two rivers, but wrongly assumed to be an *eastward* movement: Griffith, in his footnote to **III.**33, writes: "**the hymn** [...] **is interesting as a relic of the tradition of the Aryans regarding their progress eastward in the Land of the Five Rivers**".

3. The third oldest Book, Book 7, refers to the *third (from the east)* of the five rivers of the Punjab, the Paruṣṇī, in reference to the greatest historical event recorded in the

Rigveda, the Battle of the Ten Kings, in which the non-Vedic enemies figure as the *western* people of the *fourth* river, the Asiknī.

The place names of the Central Region also appear in chronological order:

1. The Early Books, 6, 3 and 7, are *totally unacquainted* with the phrase sapta+sindhu.

2. The phrase sapta+sindhu *first appears* in the Middle Books.

3. Alongwith the phrase sapta+sindhu, we now also have, in the Late Books, the *only* reference to Saptasindhavah, in the Rigveda, which is generally recognized as referring to the name of a land or region, as in the Avesta.

3D
SUMMARY OF THE DATA

The data is tabulated again, criterion-wise, below, for reference:

Western animals:

I. **10**.2; **43**.6; **51**.1; **52**.1; **61**.7; **88**.5; **114**.5; **116**.16; **117**.17-18; **121**.11; **138**.2; **162**.3.

VIII. **2**.40; **5**.37; **6**.48; **34**.3; **46**.22,23,31; **66**.8; **77**.10; **97**.12.

IX. **8**.5; **86**.47; **97**.7; **107**.11.

X. **27**.17; **28**.4; **67**.7; **86**.4; **91**.14; **95**.3; **99**.6; **106**.5.

Western mountains:

VIII. **7**.29.

IX. **65**.23; **113**.2.

X. **34**.1.

Western lakes:

I. **84**.14.

VIII. **6**.39; **7**.29; **64**.11.

IX. **65**.22; **113**.1.

X. **35**.2.

Western place names:

Direct:

I.126.7.

Indirect:

III. **38**.6 (*Late hymn*).
I. **22**.14; **163**.2.
VIII. **1**.11; **77**.5.
IX. **83**.4; **85**.12; **86**.36; **113**.3.
X. **10**.4; **11**.2; **80**.6; **85**.40,41; **123**.4,7; **136**.6; **139**.4-6; **177**.2.

Western Rivers:

IV. **30**.12,18; **43**.6; **54**.6; **55**.3.
V. **41**.15; **53**.9.
I. **44**.12; **83**.1; **112**.12; **122**.6; **126**.1; **164**.4; **186**.5.
VIII. **7**.29; **12**.3; **19**.37; **20**.24,25; **24**.30; **25**.14; **26**.18; **64**.11; **72**.7,13.
IX. **41**.6; **65**.23; **97**.58.
X. **64**.9; **65**.13; **66**.11; **75**.1,3-9; **108**.1,2; **121**.4.

*Eastern animal*s:

VI. **4**.5; **8**.4; **17**.11; **20**.8.
III. **26**.4,6; **45**.1; **46**.2.
VII. **40**.3; **44**.5; **69**.6; **98**.1;
IV. **4**.1; **16**.14; **18**.11; **21**.8; **58**.2.
II. **34**.3,4; **36**.2.
V. **29**.7,8; **42**.15; **55**.6; **57**.3; **58**.6; **60**.2.
I. **16**.5; **37**.2; **39**.6; **64**.7-8; **85**.4-5; **87**.4; **89**.7; **95**.9; **121**.2; **140**.2; **141**.3; **162**.21; **186**.8; **191**.14.
VIII. **1**.25; **4**.3; **7**.28; **12**.8; **33**.8; **35**.7-9; **45**.24; **69**.15; **77**.10.
IX. **57**.3; **69**.3; **73**.2; **86**.40; **87**.7; **92**.6; **95**.4; **96**.6,18,19; **97**.41; **113**.3.
X. **8**.1; **28**.10; **40**.4; **45**.3; **51**.6; **60**.3; **65**.8; **66**.10; **100**.2; **106**.2,6; **123**.4; **128**.8; **140**.6; **189**.2.

Eastern lakes:

III. **23**.4.

I. **128**.7.

Eastern place names:
Direct:
VI. **1**.2.
III. **23**.4; **29**.4; **53**.14.
II. **10**.1.
I. **128**.1,7.
X. **1**.6; **70**.1; **91**.1; **191**.1

Indirect:
III. **5**.9; **23**.4; **29**.4; **53**.11.
II. **3**.7.
I. **143**.4.
IX. **72**.7; **79**.4; **82**.3; **86**.8.
X. **1**.6.

Eastern Rivers:
VI. **27**.5,6; **45**.31; **49**.7; **50**.12; **52**.6; **61**.1-7,10-11,13-14.
III. **4**.8; **23**.4; **54**.13; **58**.6.
VII. **2**.8; **9**.5; **18**.19; **35**.11; **36**.6; **39**.5; **40**.3; **95**.1-2,4-6; **96**.1,3-6.
II. **1**.11; **3**.8; **30**.8; **32**.8; **41**.16-18.
V. **5**.8; **42**.12; **43**.11; **46**.2; **52**.17.
I. **3**.10-12; **13**.9; **89**.3; **116**.19; **142**.9; **164**.49,52; **188**.8.
VIII. **21**.17,18; **38**.10; **54**.4; **96**.13.
IX. **5**.8; **67**.32; **81**.4.
X. **17**.7-9; **30**.12; **53**.8; **64**.9; **65**.1,13; **66**.5; **75**.5; **110**.8; **131.**5; **141**.5; **184**.2.

Central place names:
Direct:
VIII. **24**.27.

Indirect:
IV. **28**.1.
II. **12**.3,12.
I. **32**.12; **35**.8.

VIII. **54**.4; **69**.12.
IX. **66**.6.
X. **43**.3; **67**.12.

Central Rivers:
III. **33**.1.
VII. **5**.3; **18**.8,9.
IV. **22**.2; **30**.11.
V. **52**.9.
VIII. **20**.75; **75**.15.
X. **75**.5.

As we have seen in the preceding chapters, the joint "Indo-Iranian" culture common to the Avesta and the Rigveda developed during the period of composition of the *Late* Books of the Rigveda.

The joint evidence of the Rigveda and the Avesta shows that the area of development of this joint "Indo-Iranian" culture was the area stretching from the Punjab to Afghanistan. And our analysis of the very unambiguous geographical data in the Rigveda in this chapter makes it very clear that in a period long *before* the development of this common "Indo-Iranian" culture, i.e. at the time of composition of the Early Books of the Rigveda, the Vedic Aryans were inhabitants of areas *far to the East* of the area of development of this joint "Indo-Iranian" culture, *rather than to its North.*. The Vedic Aryans expanded from an Eastern Homeland (East of the Sarasvatī) in the Early Period to areas West of the Indus, *areas totally unknown to them earlier*, by the Late Period.

And the same goes for the proto-Iranians: as we have seen in the chapter on the Evidence of the Avestan names (Kavi, Kavaṣa, Pṛthus, Parśus, Pakthas, etc. as inhabitants of the Central Punjab at the time of the Battle of the Ten Kings), the proto-Iranians were inhabitants of the Central Punjab at the time of composition of the Early Books of the Rigveda, before the development of the joint "Indo-Iranian" culture reflected in the Avesta and the Rigveda, and only expanded westwards in later periods.

3E
APPENDIX 1: OTHER GEOGRAPHICAL EVIDENCE

As we have seen from the evidence of the names of rivers, places, animals, lakes and mountains in the Rigveda, the Vedic Aryans were inhabitants of the areas to the east of the Sarasvatī in the (*pre-Avestan*) Early and Middle periods of the Rigveda with no apparent close familiarity or even acquaintance with areas much further to the west. Some other aspects of the Rigvedic data may also be noted here, which only reaffirm the firmly eastern, and firmly non-western, character of Rigvedic geography:

3E-1. Climate and Topography.

Edward W. Hopkins had long ago noted in some detail, in an article specifically entitled "**The Punjab and the Rigveda**", that "**if the first home of the Aryans can be determined at all by the conditions topographical and meteorological, described in their early hymns, then decidedly the Punjab was not that home. For here there are neither mountains nor monsoon storms to burst, yet storm and mountain belong to the very marrow of the Rigveda**" (HOPKINS 1898:20).

If there is an area which fulfils these conditions, according to Hopkins, it is "**a district** [...] **where monsoon storms and mountain scenery are found, that district, namely, which lies South of Umballa (or Ambālā). It is here, in my opinion, that the Rigveda, taken as a whole, was composed. In every particular, this locality fulfils the physical conditions under which the composition of the hymns was possible, and what is of paramount importance, is the first district east of the Indus that does so**" (HOPKINS 1898:20). Significantly, Hopkins notes that the climate and topography of the Rigveda is decidedly that of a *monsoon land lying to the east of the Punjab*, but, as a concession to the AIT, which he is not out to challenge, he considers the westernmost possible area which could fulfil these climatic conditions.

The climate of the Rigveda is very clearly that of a monsoon land, where the storm-god or thunder-god of the skies, Indra, is the main and most important god. And the monsoon areas of India just stop short of the Punjab. Every western and Indian scholar who has examined the hymns of the Rigveda, *before* the present AIT-vs.-OIT debate rendered caution necessary, has emphasized this monsoon climate nature of the hymns. Even Witzel, in an article written just before our earlier book was published and made a volte face on the matter necessary, writes: "**In general, the books of RV level I (RV 4-6) are thoroughly South Asian and have reference to local climate, trees and animals. We therefore have to take them seriously at their word, and cannot claim that they belong just to Afghanistan**" (WITZEL 2000a:§13).

That this eastern ethos is deeply rooted in the Rigveda (and is not the result of new found acquaintance) is shown not only by the profusion of *references* to eastern geographical references in the early books, in contrast to the *new appearance, in stages,* of western geographical references (completely *absent* in the early books) in later books, but also by the *nature* of these eastern references: the reference to the Gangā in the oldest Book in the Rigveda, in **VI.45**.31, is an idiomatic reference to the wide bushes on the banks of the Gangā which shows traditional familiarity with the scenery descibed. The references to the eastern rivers (Sarasvatī, Āpayā and Dṛṣadvatī), in the second oldest book, in **III.23**.4, speak of the establishment of sacred fires on the banks of these rivers by *ancestors*; and the reference to the Jahnāvī (Gangā), in **III.58**.6, refers to the area of the river as the *ancient and auspicious homeland* of the Vedic gods (the Aśvins).

Likewise, the references to the eastern animals show *traditional familiarity*: the spotted deer (*pṛṣatī*) are the official steeds of the chariots of the Maruts; buffalo (*mahiṣa*) is an epithet applied to various gods signifying power and strength;

gods approaching the sacrifice are likened to thirsty bisons (*gaura*) converging on a watering place in the forest; the outspread plumes of Indra's horses are likened to the outspread plumes of the peacock's (*mayūra*'s) tail; the elephant (*ibha, vāraṇa, hastin, sṛṇi*) is variously described crashing through a forest and uprooting trees in its path, being tracked by hunters, part of the retinue of a mighty king, decked up for ceremonial purposes, and part of a military garrison (TALAGERI 2000:122). All these are "**thoroughly South Asian**" animals, and the descriptions are by "**thoroughly South Asian**" poets.

3E-2. Trees and Wood

As Witzel puts it above, the Rigveda refers to local, "thoroughly South Asian" trees. And it, incidentally, does *not* refer to trees typical of the western areas even within its own broader horizon (i.e. trees of Afghanistan or the mountainous north or northwest) — not even when these tree names are found in the Sanskrit language as a whole in forms cognate to their names in other Indo-European languages outside India: words like *bhūrja* (birch), *pītu* (pine), *parkaṭī/ plakṣa* (oak) (derived from reconstructed PIE roots, with cognate forms in Indo-European languages outside India) are *not* found in the Rigveda, although they are found in later Vedic or Classical Sanskrit vocabulary. [The explanation is clear: these are among many late words which entered Vedic or later Sanskrit as *substrate* words from the dialects of the Anu and Druhyu tribes of the northwest, as the Vedic culture expanded northwestwards and Sanskritized or "Indo-Aryanized" (i.e. Pūru-ized) the remnants of these tribes after the major sections had emigrated from the area].

The Rigveda, however, refers to typically South Asian trees like *kimśuka* (butea frondosa?), *khadira* (acacia catechu), *śalmali* (salmalia malabarica, the silk-cotton tree), *aśvattha* (ficus religiosa, the sacred peepul tree, sacred even in the Rigveda), *śimśapā* (dalbergia sissoo), *parṇa* (butea frondosa?, the holy palāśa tree) and *araṭu* (calosanthes indica). What is more, most of these trees appear in a certain specific context — most of them are mentioned in the context of the material used in the manufacture of chariots: *khadira* and *śimśapā* are woods used in the manufacture of the body of the chariot, *kimśuka* and *śalmali* in the manufacture of the wheels, and *araṭu* in the manufacture of the axle.

This is significant. In the case of the "**Egyptian war chariot**", Tarr points out that "**the timbers in question were not of Egyptian origin but 'came from the north'.** [...] **The timbers used were holm-oak for the axle and the spokes, elm for the pole, ash for the felloes, the chassis and the dashboard, hornbeam for the yoke and birch bark for wrapping and for joining the spokes with the felloes and the hub** [...] **The wooden material of the Egyptian chariots came from the Caucasus**" (TARR 1969:74).

In spite of the fact that the Egyptians are not alleged to have come into Egypt from the Caucasus, they used imported woods from the Caucasus, rather than Egyptian woods, in the manufacture of their chariot. If the Vedic Aryans had immigrated into India from the outside, their chariots should *certainly* also have been manufactured from oak, elm, ash, hornbeam and birch, all of which are trees and woods that are alleged to have been known to them before their alleged immigration into India; but the Vedic Aryans used only *purely Indian* woods in the manufacture of their chariots. This is a very strong argument against the idea that they were immigrants from outside. [This point was first, so far as I know, made by Nicholas Kazanas].

3E-3. Rice and Wheat

Today, rice and wheat are generally the two main cereal grains consumed in India, rice being more typical of the east and south, and wheat comparatively more typical of the north and west. An analysis of the comparative importance of the two, in the Rigveda, brings out some significant points.

Primarily, it would appear that *both* rice *and* wheat are not mentioned in the Rigveda, since both the words *vrīhi* (rice) and *godhūma* (wheat) are missing in the hymns. However, while all the scholars are unanimous in the opinion that the Rigvedic Aryans do not show any acquaintance with wheat, the same can not be said for rice:

The Rigveda mentions three preparations used in rituals, all three of which are known rice-preparations: *apūpa* (a kind of rice-cake), *puroḷā* (a kind of rice-pancake), and *odana* (a brew of rice boiled in milk or water). That they are preparations made from rice is reaffirmed by the fact that the Saraswat brahmins in the south, who have an active tradition of migrating to the south from the area of the Sarasvatī river, and whose language, Konkaṇi, contains many features close to the Vedic language, still prepare the same items: *əppĕ* (a kind of rice-cake), *pŏḷŏ* (a kind of rice-pancake) and *āddəṇə* (boiling rice in water).

The scholars usually translate the words in the Rigveda as the names of barley preparations rather than rice preparations, but this is only because of the assumed absence of reference to rice in the hymns (although it is generally admitted that the word yava in the Rigveda means grain in general, and not barley as it does in later times, and that it could therefore refer to any grain, including rice). However, Griffith, for example, translates *odana* as "**brew of rice**" or "**a brew of rice and milk**"; and points out, in his footnote to the translation of **I.40**.3, that the five-fold offerings to Agni include "**rice-cake**".

Even Witzel, and even as he points out that rice first appears in the Atharvaveda, cautiously notes: "**unless the Ṛgvedic words (brahma-)-udana and puroḷāś mean a certain rice dish, as they do later on**" (WITZEL 1995a:102).

On the other hand, the absence of wheat in the Rigveda is not doubted by any one. Wojtilla, in his detailed study of the Sanskrit word for "wheat", *godhūma*, points out that although "**Kuiper [...] clearly puts it in the group of foreign words**

adopted before the Aryans reached India (Kuiper 1991, p.90), [...] **there are problems** [...]. **The trouble begins with the non-attestation of the word in the Rigveda.** [...] **It is puzzling because this earliest extant text in Sanskrit is supposed to be linked with the earliest Indo-Aryan speakers who entered India. Moreover, the geographical area of the genesis of the Ṛgveda is considered a fertile wheat producing region (cf. Farmers, p.37, Randhawa 1980, p.24)** [...] **As a matter of fact, there is abundant archaeological evidence of wheat remains from the Punjab (Randhawa 1980, p.104)** [...] **from the period before the invasion of Indo-Aryan speakers**" (WOJTILLA 1999:226-227)

Clearly, the main homeland of the Rigvedic Aryans lay to the *east* of the Punjab and/or the Rigvedic ritual traditions developed in northern India *before* the major cultivation and consumption of wheat had taken root in the area (the "**wheat remains** [...] **before the invasion of Indo-Aryan speakers**", referred to above, assumes not only an invasion but also a late date for it).

That wheat was an unfamiliar grain to Vedic traditions, as compared to rice, is indicated by the fact that it was even *defined* in *relation* to rice; and, in contrast to the sacred use of rice in Vedic rituals, wheat is treated with disdain: "**Pāṇini, Arthśā, BṛSam and Vṛkṣ(S) define the word as a type of grain distinct from barley and rice** [...] **Additionally, NāmaMā makes a curious remark: it is a *mlecchabhojya*, 'a food of barbarians'**" (WOJTILLA 1999:228). [Note, in most Brahmin communities, it is not treated as proper "food": when there is death in the family, and members of the family are required to abstain from proper "food" for twelve days, rice is taboo, but not wheat. Just as, in Maharashtrian "fasting", originally foreign food items like sago, potatoes, groundnuts, etc. are allowed during fasting, this could indicate the originally foreign nature of wheat to Vedic tradition]

Again, all this shows the Vedic Aryans to be thoroughly South Asian, and originally unfamiliar with the west beyond the borders of India.

3E-4. The Traditional Vedic Attitude towards the Northwest

A most significant indicator of the insularity of the Rigvedic Aryans within India, and strong evidence of their original unfamiliarity with the northwestern and western areas, is the fact that Vedic traditional attitude towards these areas has always been one of suspicion, disdain or even mild hostility.

Hopkins points out that his interpretation of the climate and topography of the Rigveda as indicating a homeland decidedly east of the Punjab "**is supported even by native traditions. At a very early (Brahmanic) period the 'Northerners' are regarded as a suspicious sort of people, whose religious practices, far from being authoritative, are censured. No tradition associates the ancient literature with the Punjāb. In fact, save for one exception, even the legal manuals do not take cognizance of the Northwest. They have the stanza that defines Āryāvarta, and also the stanzas that extend the geographical boundary still further south; but they ignore the North**" (HOPKINS 1898:20).

Hopkins quotes two verses from Manu: Manu 11.17, which states that *brahmāvarta* or "**the district between the Sarasvatī and Dṛṣadvatī is the home of the Veda**" (HOPKINS 1898:21), and Manu 11.22, which describes the land which is the natural habitat of the blackbuck as the "**district fit for sacrifice**", and points out that "**the Gangetic plain and the country about Kurukṣetra, between Delhi and Umballa and south of the former locality, is still the 'natural habitat' of the blackbuck**" (HOPKINS 1898:23). On both these counts, Hopkins points out that "**Punjab is** [...] **omitted altogether from the list. The most western locality is the place where the Sarasvatī disappears in the north-west, and the Arabian Sea, west of the southern line of the Vindhya**" (HOPKINS 1898:21).

The attitude of all traditional Vedic literature towards peoples and areas further west, including the Punjab, is one of disdain and even mild hostility: the Sūtras (e.g. Baudhāyana Dharmasūtra 1.1.2,14-15), the traditional compendia of Vedic orthodoxy, describe these lands as *mleccha* or barbarian lands, express strong disapproval of their socio-religious practices and customs, and even declare these areas as not fit to be visited by orthodox Brahmins, who are required to undergo purificatory rituals if they do visit these areas. This attitude continues into the Epics: e.g. Mahābhārata VIII.30.35-74.

In fact, it is no coincidence that in the Epics, the villains or the lesser heroes always have a northwestern connection, and the greater heroes have an eastern connection: in the Rāmāyaṇa, the good queen Kauśalyā is from the east, and the bad queen Kaikeyī is from the northwest. In the Mahābhārata, the main good queen Kuntī, mother of the greater Pāṇḍavas, is from the east; the lesser good queen Mādrī, mother of the lesser Pāṇḍavas (depicted, like the Aśvins, the lesser gods of the Rigveda, as twins, and in fact even depicted as the offspring of the Aśvins) is from the west (but she disappears from the scene early on in the story, and her brother, the king of the western Madras, lands up on the side of the bad guys, the Kauravas, in the Great War); and the bad queen Gāndhārī (mother of the Kauravas, the bad guys of the Epic) is from even further west.

In sum, *all* the evidence of Vedic tradition *unanimously* makes it crystal clear that the Vedic culture developed in the areas to the east of the Punjab, and that all the areas to the west, including the Punjab itself, were originally alien, unfamiliar territory to the Vedic Aryans. But this evidence was ignored under the determined assumption that all this represents a *post*-Rigvedic situation, and that the area of composition of the *Rigveda* lay in the Punjab and further west.

This assumption should have been seen as intrinsically absurd at the very outset: Indian tradition in general, and Vedic tradition in particular, has always been particularly orthodox in its extreme reverence for every single place associated with every sacred person and event, real and imaginary. The assumption that the Rigvedic Aryans had *completely* and *absolutely* lost *every single* memory of their alleged extra-Indian associations was bad enough; the further assumption that the post-Rigvedic Aryans had *completely* and *absolutely* lost *every single* memory of the alleged Punjab-and-northwest associations of their oldest and most sacred hymns, which formed the very basis of their religion, to the extent that they actually developed an all-pervading disdain for and hostility towards those areas and the people inhabiting those areas, is *untenable*.

After the evidence examined in the course of this chapter, it becomes clear that the Rigvedic situation was almost exactly the same as the post-Rigvedic situation: the sacred area of the Rigveda (**III**.24), the *vara-ā-pṛthivyāh* (best place on earth) and *nābhā pṛthivyāh* (centre of the earth) of the Rigvedic Aryans, was the same as the *brahmāvarta* of the post-Rigvedic Aryans and the holy *Kurukṣetra* of the Tīrthayātrā Parva of the Mahābhārata (III.81). The Punjab and the northwest, inhabited at the time by the proto-Iranians (the Anus), represented the same unfamiliar western territories that they do in the later texts. The animals, trees, rivers, mountains and lakes to the east of the Punjab were as much home territory to the Rigvedic Aryans, and the animals, trees, rivers, mountains and lakes of the Punjab and beyond as alien to them (gradually becoming more familiar in the Late Rigvedic period), as to the post-Rigvedic Aryans.

3F
THE TOPSY-TURVY LOGIC OF AIT GEOGRAPHY

It is clear that the evidence of the geographical data in the Rigveda, for an originally eastern origin for the Vedic Aryans and for their direction of expansion being from east to west, is too massive and overwhelming, and too unidirectional, to be denied: it simply *can not* be argued against — at least, not on the basis of the geographical data in the Rigveda. In spite of that, AIT scholars have managed to create the impression that the geographical data in the Rigveda provides evidence for the AIT.

Obviously, this can only have been achieved by firmly *ignoring* the actual data in the Rigveda. The Rigvedic geographical case for the AIT is a classic case of circular reasoning: incredible as it may seem, the *entire* case is based *solely and only* on repeated authoritative assertions of subjective impressions, interpretations and conclusions, going sharply contrary to the actual geographical data in the hymns, based on predetermined ideas based on the AIT itself.

This feat has been achieved primarily through the power of suggestion and the power of repetition, and through a total monopoly over the academia and media. A detailed study of the Rigveda is an obscure task few people would care to undertake themselves, and whatever the established scholars have to say becomes the final word on the subject even to people interested in the subject, let alone to the overwhelming majority of the common people who have no interest at all in the truth of the matter.

An analytical examination of just the three following assertions by Michael Witzel provides us with a great many examples of this exercise in deception:

> "**The important clinching factor (Sections 11.6-11.7) to decide the question is that the IAs, as described in the RV, represent something definitely new in the subcontinent. Both their spiritual and much of their material culture are new; these and their language link them to the areas west and northwest of the subcontinent, and to some extent beyond, to the Ural area and to Southern Russia. The obvious conclusion should be that these new elements *somehow* came from the outside**" (WITZEL 2005:343).
>
> "**The world of the Ṛgveda contains the Panjab and its surroundings: eastern Afghanistan, the valley of the Kabul (*Kubhā*, Greek Kophen), Kurram (*Krumu*), Gomal (*Gomatī*), Swat (*Suvāstu*), and** [...] **probably Herat (*Sarayu*, Avestan *Haraiiou*) rivers; also the valley of the rivers of Sistān: the Sarasvatī (*Haraxvaiti/ Harahvaiti*) and the Helmand (*Setumant). In the east, the *Gangā***

> **and the *Yamunā* are already mentioned** [...]" (WITZEL 1995b:317). "**The famous *nadīstuti* of the late book 10** [...] **in this relatively late hymn, the Ṛgvedic territory covers only the area between the Gangā and S.E. Afghanistan (Gomal and Kurram rivers) and between the Himalayas and the northern border of the modern province of Sind. Most of Afghanistan, including Bactria and Herat (Arachosia), is already out of sight**" (WITZEL 1995b:318).

Witzel makes the first assertion in the context of the *absence* of archaeological and anthropological evidence for the AIT [his wording "**clinching factor (Sections 11.6-11.7) to decide the question**" gives the impression that Sections 11.6-11.7 provide this "clinching" evidence for his case. Actually, Sections 11.6-11.7 contain his pleading against this *absence* of archaeological and anthropological evidence!]. He provides no evidence to show how the Rigveda represents something "**definitely *new* in the subcontinent**": the fact that the Rigvedic language links the Vedic people with people all the way west to Europe is beyond question — that is what the whole AIT-vs.-OIT debate is all about — but it does not in itself show that the RV culture is "**new in the subcontinent**" except through circular reasoning based on the AIT itself. That "**both their spiritual and much of their material culture are new**" is only an assertion of faith, given that the spiritual culture of the alleged predecessors of the Rigvedic people, the Harappans, is admittedly still unknown, and the material culture of the Rigvedic people (assuming it to be different from the Harappan culture) is still to be found! And, wholly on the strength of the "**clinching**" nature of this touching assertion of faith, Witzel wants us to believe that the "**obvious conclusion**" is that the Vedic Aryans "***somehow* came from the outside**"!

In the next two assertions, note the subtle and tricky use of the word "**already**": "**In the east, the *Gangā* and the *Yamunā* are already mentioned**" and "**Most of Afghanistan, including Bactria and Herat (Arachosia), is already out of sight**". The impression given is that the *original* area, most of

Afghanistan, is slowly moving *out* of the ken of the Vedic Aryans, and the *new* areas, of the Gangā and the Yamunā, are slowly moving *into* their ken!

The facts, as we have seen, are exactly the opposite: the Gangā and the Yamunā, are mentioned in all *the three oldest* Books of the Rigveda (**VI.45**.31; **III.58**.6; **VII.18**.19), *along with other eastern rivers, lakes, places and animals*; while even the Indus, let alone the rivers, mountains, lakes, places and animals of Afghanistan west of it, is completely *missing* in these books. And far from Afghanistan being "**already out of sight**" in "**the late book 10**", this book not only mentions *all* the rivers of Afghanistan known to the Family Books (i.e. only to Books 4 and 5), but also many *not* known to them (like Gomatī, Mehatnu, Tṛṣṭāmā, Susartu, etc.), apart from the mountains, lakes, places and animals of Afghanistan totally unknown to all the six Family Books!

Note, also, that under the pretext of describing "**the world of the Ṛgveda**" above, Witzel provides a list of the different areas of Afghanistan, only starting with a reference to the Punjab and ending with the suggestive reference to the Gangā and the Yamunā. And the inclusion of "**the valley of the rivers of Sistān**" is based on two names: one, the name Sarasvatī treated (not just as a western "**memory**", see below, but) as a direct reference to the Avestan Harahvaiti, and two, the reconstructed Sanskrit equivalent, **Setumant* (not found in the Rigveda at all!), of the Avestan Haētumant.

Thus there is a regular AIT methodology by which every geographical name or word found in, or missing in, the Rigveda is to be interpreted: every eastern word *found* in the text is to be treated as indicative of a *new* area with which the Rigvedic Aryans are newly becoming familiar, and every eastern word *not* found as indicative of an eastern area not yet known to the immigrating Aryans; every *western* word *found* is to be treated as indicative of an area associated with the early days of the Aryan immigrations, and every western word *not* found as indicative of an area already old and forgotten by the immigrating Aryans.

And when a geographical word in the Rigveda can be associated with both an eastern *and* a western geographical area, the word in the eastern area is to be treated as a later word indicating a "memory" of the earlier western area:

Thus, for example, the Sarasvatī of the east (Haryana, Rajasthan, Kutch) is treated as having been named in "memory" of the western Harahvaiti of Afghanistan. However, see what Erdosy has to say on the subject:

> **"As for Burrow's thesis (Burrow 1973) that some place names reflect the names of geographical features to the west, and thus preserve an ancestral home, they once again rather rely on an assumption of Arya migrations than prove it.** [...] **His cited equivalence of Sanskrit Saraswati and Avestan Haraxvaiti is a case in point. Burrow accepts that it is the latter term that is borrowed, undergoing the usual change of s- > h in the process, but suggests that Saraswati was a proto-Indoaryan term, originally applied to the present Haraxvaiti when the proto-Indoaryans still lived in northeastern Iran, then it was brought into India at the time of the migrations, while its original bearer had its name modified by the speakers of Avestan who assumed control of the areas vacated by proto-Indoaryans. It would be just as plausible to assume that Saraswati was a Sanskrit term indigenous to India and was later imported by the speakers of Avestan into Iran. The fact that the Zend Avesta is aware of areas outside the Iranian plateau while the Rigveda is ignorant of anything west of the Indus basin would certainly support such an assertion"** (ERDOSY 1989:41-42).

Logically, any such common name may have moved from east to west, *or* from west to east; only an analysis of the evidence (if any can be found) can show us the direction of movement. In this case, as we have seen in our analysis of the Rigvedic-Avestan evidence, the *evidence*, on every count, makes it clear that the name of the river migrated from east to west and *not* from west to east: a) the direction of expansion for *both* the Vedic Aryans *as well as* the proto-Iranians was from east to west: the proto-Iranians were settled in the central areas of the Punjab in the Early Period of the Rigveda, and migrated westwards only towards the end of this period, and,

b) *all* the hymns in praise of the eastern Sarasvatī, as well as many of the important references to it, occur in the *Early* Books of the Rigveda; the *oldest* parts of the Avesta, the Gāθās, are contemporaneous with the *Late* Books of the Rigveda; and the western Harahvaiti is found referred to only *once* in the Vendidād, a *late* part of the Avesta.

Incidentally, this picturesque, and purely imaginary, story, of proto-Indo-Aryans moving in, as the advance guard of an Indo-Iranian movement from the north (i.e. from Central Asia into Afghanistan), and being followed by the proto-Iranians, who later occupied the areas in Afghanistan vacated by the southeastward-bound Indo-Aryans, is very popular among AIT theorists. Witzel also tells us: "**It is interesting to note, however, that some of these** [Rigvedic] **names are found in Iranian forms closer to the older, Ṛgvedic home** [Afghanistan!] **of the Vedic tribes** [...] **It seems that the Iranians simply changed the old Indo-Iranian names into their respective Iranian forms when they moved into the area, while the Vedic, Indo-Aryan speakers took some of these names with them eastwards, up to Bihar, in the typical fashion of people on the move**" (WITZEL 1995a:105). Lubotsky provides us with a graphic version of it as part of his BMAC loanwords theory:

"**Starting with the assumption that loanwords reflect change in environment and way of life, we get the following picture of the new country of the Indo-Iranians. The landscape must have been quite similar to that of their original homeland, as there are no new terms for plants or landscape. The new animals like camel, donkey and tortoise show that the new land was situated more to the South** [...] **This picture, which is drawn on exclusively linguistic arguments, is a strong confirmation of the traditional theory that the Indo-Iranians came from the north.** [...] **as we have seen above, there are reasons to believe that the Indo-Aryans formed the vanguard of the Indo-Iranian movement and were the first to come into contact with the**

original inhabitants of the Central Asian towns. […] **the Iranians** […] **were pushing from behind**" (LUBOTSKY 2001:307-308)

Again, see how the predetermined logic of the AIT leads to a round of continuous circular reasoning: a) The AIT requires that the Indo-Iranians came into the Afghanistan region (including its northern frontier areas like Bactria) from the *north*, therefore when animals like the camel or the donkey are first found in Indo-Iranian, it automatically means the Indo-Iranians had just moved into a "**new land** […] **situated more to the South**"; and this, in its turn, then becomes "**a strong confirmation of the traditional theory that the Indo-Iranians came from the north**". b) Again, since the geographical data in the Avesta shows the Iranians as the occupants of this region, at a time when the Indo-Aryans are "**already**" situated further to the east, then the Indo-Aryan contact with this region must have been earlier to that of the Iranians, therefore the Indo-Aryans are to be regarded as the "**vanguard**" of the Indo-Iranian movement, with the Iranians "**pushing from behind**" and later occupying the areas vacated by the Indo-Aryans.

The actual evidence shows us exactly the opposite: a) the camel and the donkey are found named only in the *Late* books and hymns of the Rigveda, and the geography of the *earlier* Books and hymns is exclusively to the east within India, therefore the "**new land**", with camels and donkeys, into which the Indo-Aryans were expanding, was situated more to the *West*. And, b) the camel was actually introduced to the Indo-Aryans by the *Iranians*, to whom it was already a familiar animal (already a part of the name of Zaraθuštra), and it first appears in the Rigveda, in all the three hymns in which it is found in Book 8, as an animal gifted to Vedic ṛṣis by kings with Iranian names (identified as such by western scholars including Michael Witzel). Therefore, it was the *Iranians* who "**formed the vanguard of the Indo-Iranian movement**" from east to west into this "**new land**", with the *Indo-Aryans* "**pushing from behind**".

[Incidentally, another western geographical element in the Rigveda is Soma, which is most probably the name of the ephedra plant (and its juice) native to the mountains of Kashmir, Afghanistan and Central Asia (and not some eastern, Indian, plant as suggested by some OIT writers: Bhagwan Singh, for example, identifies Soma with sugarcane). But this also in no way indicates the direction of movement of the Indo-Aryans: the evidence (see TALAGERI 2000:127-136) clearly shows that Soma (like the camel, but in a much earlier period) was introduced to the Indo-Aryans by the Bhṛgus/ Atharvans, the priests of the Iranians who "**formed the vanguard of the Indo-Iranian movement**" from east to west, who must themselves have been introduced to it by other people to their west].

The analysis of the geographical evidence in the Rigveda, given in our earlier book (TALAGERI 2000), has brought about a sharp turnaround, on many points, in the assertions of Harvard professor Michael Witzel, who has taken on himself the role of a crusader in the holy cause of the AIT, wherever he has realized that many of the logical interpretations and conclusions, based on the Rigvedic data, in his own earlier writings, are now proving to be lethal to the AIT. Here, as an example, we will only examine his assertions on the references to the Sarasvatī and the Gangā in the Rigveda, by seeing what he has to say *after* the publication of our earlier book in contrast to what he had to say *before*:

The names of the rivers in the Rigveda have always been taken as a prime indicator of the geographical horizon of the Rigveda. The general claim has always been that the Rigveda names the Gangā and the Yamunā in the east only a few times, and nothing further to the east or south in the interior of India, while it frequently and familiarly mentions a great many rivers of Afghanistan, every small western tributary of the Indus, apart from all the rivers of the Punjab where AIT scholarship locates the Vedic Aryans at the time of composition of the Rigveda. This is contrasted with the geography of the later

Veda Samhitās, which show a centre in the Āryāvarta region to the east and show acquaintance with areas as far east as Bengal, to conclude that there was a movement of the Vedic Aryans from west to east.

However, our analysis of the geography of the Rigveda (TALAGERI 2000:94-136) completely burst this bubble, and conclusively showed that the geographical habitat of the Rigvedic Aryans lay to the *east* of the Sarasvatī, that they were originally totally *unfamiliar* with western areas, and that their direction of expansion was *from* east to west.

The evidence of the Sarasvatī and the Gangā are particularly important in this respect, since the Sarasvatī is the single most important river in the Rigveda (see TALAGERI 2000:108-110), and the Gangā is the easternmost river named in the hymns:

3F-1. The Sarasvatī.

The importance of the Sarasvatī in Indian historical studies has multiplied manifold since archaeological analyses of the Ghaggar-Hakra river bed, combined with detailed satellite imagery of the course of the ancient (now dried up) river, conclusively showed that it had almost dried up by the mid-second millennium BCE itself, and that, long before that, it was a mighty river, mightier than the Indus, and that an overwhelming majority of the archaeological sites of the Harappan cities are located on the banks of the Sarasvatī rather than of the Indus. This has lethal implications for the AIT, which requires an Aryan invasion around 1500 BCE after the decline of the Harappan civilization, since it shows that the Vedic Aryans, who lived "on both banks" (Rigveda **VII.96**.2) of a mighty Sarasvatī in full powerful flow, must have been inhabitants of the region long before 1500 BCE and in fact may be identical with the indigenous Harappans.

Therefore, there is now a desperate salvage operation on, in powerful leftist and "secularist" political circles in India, to put a *complete full stop* to any further official research on the

Sarasvatī (including archaeological and geological investigations), and to launch an all-out Goebbelsian campaign through a captive media to deny that there ever was a Vedic Sarasvatī river in existence in India: the river named in the Rigveda was either completely mythical, or it was the river in Afghanistan, but it definitely was not identical with the Ghaggar-Hakra!

That the Sarasvatī was identical with the Ghaggar-Hakra has been the near unanimous conclusion of Vedic scholars and archaeologists from day one of commencement of the subject of Vedic studies: even though the compulsions of AIT logistics required that its name be treated as a "memory" of an original Sarasvatī in Afghanistan, there was little doubt in the minds of most scholars that the Sarasvatī referred to, and described with so much reverence, in the Rigveda was the Ghaggar-Hakra of Kurukṣetra. The few scholars who doubted it were the extremist ones who would place the entire geography of the Rigveda in Afghanistan and Central Asia. Any other occasional doubts on the issue (see Griffith's footnote to **VI.61**.2, contrasted with his references to the Sarasvatī throughout the rest of his translations) were based only on the fact that the descriptions of the mighty river in the Rigveda did not seem to fit in with the small present-day stream: *a doubt that has now been cleared by archaeologists and geologists.*

[Thus for example, the early scholar Edward Thomas analyses the geography of the Rigveda, and points out that most of it is centred around Kurukṣetra (Hariyūpīyā and Yavyāvatī, he points out, refer to "**a tirath in Kurukṣetra**"), but he treats the ancient name of the Ghaggar-Hakra as "**an unacknowledged sentiment of a revival of a bygone Sarasvatī on the banks of the Helmand**", and, in a footnote, suggests that the references to a torrentous Sarasvatī represent this sentiment, since "**The Gaggar, Sarasvatī and their tributaries contain but little water except in the rainy season. Their sources being in the outer and lower**

Himalayan range, they are fed by rain only, and not by the melting snows also, as are all the large rivers of Northern India. The collecting ground of these streams, moreover, is, and always must have been very limited. [...] **There is nothing in history to show that these rivers ever contained much more water than they do now**" (THOMAS 1883:364). This has always remained the sentiment among analysts of the Rigveda].

As a crusader in the holy cause of the AIT, who has collaborated closely with many of the eminent leftist historians in anti-OIT campaigns in the Indian media, Witzel contributes his bit to this campaign. In his "review" of TALAGERI 2000, Witzel tries to neutralize the evidence of the Sarasvatī in the Rigveda as follows:

"**The river Sarasvatī found in book 6 (T., p.102) may be discarded** [...]. **In the hymns 6.49, 50, 52, 61, the order of arrangement is disturbed and especially the group 6.49-52 is very suspicious.** [...] **All this points to an addition of materials at an unknown time. Therefore, the Haryana river Sarasvatī (mod. Sarsuti) is not found in the old parts of book 6**" (WITZEL 2000b:§7).

The fact that the hymns in Book 6, which refer to the Sarasvatī, are among Oldenberg's "unordered" hymns does not automatically prove that they are not old hymns and old references: see our analysis of the Internal Chronology of the Rigveda (in appendix 2 of chapter 4, later on in this book). But, apart from that, the Sarasvatī is referred to in many hymns in the three oldest Books of the Rigveda, not only in unordered hymns (**VI**.49, 50, 52, 61: **VII**.96), but also in ordered hymns (**III**.4, 23, 54; **VII**.2, 9, 35, 36, 39, 40, 95), along with other eastern places, lakes and animals (in these or other hymns in these Books), while the western rivers, mountains, lakes, places and animals are completely missing in both the ordered as well as unordered hymns in these Books. The picture is *too large and too consistent* to be "**discarded**" on the basis of Witzel's selective citing of the Sarasvatī-referring hymns in Book 6 alone.

Not content with this, Witzel goes on to make the following juvenile comments: "**Incidentally, it is entirely unclear that the physical river Sarasvatī is meant in some of these spurious hymns: in 6.49.7 the Sarasvatī is a woman and in 50.12 a deity, not necessarily the river (Witzel 1984). (At 52.6, however, it is a river, and in 61.1-7 both a river and a deity — which can be located anywhere from the Arachosian Sarasvatī to the Night time sky, with no clear localization)**" (WITZEL 2000b:§7).

These are clearly not the words of a scholar making serious statements on an academic subject: that the Sarasvatī of **VI.49**.7 "**is a woman**" is ludicrous, to say the least! And if, in any reference, Sarasvatī is the name of a deity or a woman, even an amateur student of the subject could tell Witzel that the circumstance *presupposes* the existence of a river named Sarasvatī, since the word Sarasvatī is clearly originally the name of a *river*: it means "**the one with many ponds**" (WITZEL 1995a:105). The deity came into existence as a riverine deity, and women came to be named Sarasvatī after the name of the river/deity. So, ultimately, all the references show the existence of the river Sarasvatī. And the claim that the Sarasvatī in **VI.52**.6 and **VI.61**.1-7 is a river "**which can be located anywhere from the Arachosian Sarasvatī to the Night time sky, with no clear localization**" is nothing but a piece of *un*scholarly and juvenile arrogance.

All this is sharply contradicted by what Witzel had written in his earlier, pre-crusadorial, writings:

In his paper on Ṛgvedic history written in 1995, Witzel categorically tells us "**Sarasvatī = Sarsuti; Ghaggar-Hakra**" (WITZEL 1995b:318).

He concludes this paper/article with a summary of the "**Geographical Data in the Rigveda**" in detailed charts covering ten pages (WITZEL 1995b:343-352), giving the geographical data classified into columns as per the areas from west to east (West, Northwest, Panjab, Kurukṣetra, East).

In these charts, he specifically locates *every single* reference (*mentioned* by him) to the Sarasvatī in Books 6, 3 and 7 *exclusively* in Kurukṣetra: **VI.61**.3,10 (WITZEL 1995b:343, 349), **III.23**.4 (WITZEL 1995b:343, 347), **VII.36**.6 (WITZEL 1995b:344, 349), **VII.95**.2 (WITZEL 1995b:344, 349) and **VII.96**.1,2 (WITZEL 1995b:344, 349). Further, wherever, in the main body of the article, he gives geographical areas in sequence from west to east in these three Books, the Sarasvatī is inevitably to the east of the Punjab (WITZEL 1995b:318, 320).

He does locate some of the references to the Sarasvatī, in three of the *other* Books, to the West (i.e. Afghanistan): **II.41**.6 (WITZEL 1995b:343, 346), **VIII.21**.17-18 (WITZEL 1995b:344, 350) and **X.64**.9 (WITZEL 1995b:345, 352). In doing so, he creates an uncalled for dual entity in the Rigveda: a Sarasvatī in Kurukṣetra as well as a Sarasvatī in Afghanistan. (Even then, it may be noted that the references to the Sarasvatī in Kurukṣetra appear exclusively in the *earlier* Books, and the alleged references to the Sarasvatī in Afghanistan appear exclusively in the *later* Books!).

Witzel's location of the Sarasvatī in Book 2 in Afghanistan is not an honest one: he does it only because he wants a Rigvedic Book which refers only to western rivers, in order to show the Vedic Aryans "**fighting their way through the NW mountain passes**" (WITZEL 1995b:331) in their alleged movement from west to east, and Book 2 is his only option, since the name of only this one river is mentioned in the whole of this Book, and it is a name which can be manipulated from east to west by creating a dual entity (thanks to the existence of a Sarasvatī, the Avestan Harahvaiti, in Afghanistan) (See TALAGERI 2000:451-460 for more details). But the incorrectness of this location becomes clear from Witzel's *own* writings:

Firstly, he places a doubtful question mark after his location of the Sarasvatī of Book 2 in the West (Afghanistan), in both the places where he locates it there on his charts: "**Sarasvatī? 2.41.6**" (WITZEL 1995b:343, 346); and, in the main text of his article, he uses the word "**probably**" when suggesting that the Sarasvatī of this Book, in **II.3**.8 could refer to "**the Avestan Haraxvaiti rather than** [...] **to the modern Ghaggar-Hakra in the Panjab**" (WITZEL 1995b:331).

Secondly, he vaguely admits, in a footnote, that "**since Gārtsamāda Śaunaka is made a Bhārgava, he could be later than Book 6**" (WITZEL 1995b:316): that is, since Gṛtsamada, the ṛṣi of Book 2, was originally a descendant of Śaunahotra Āngiras of Book 6, Book 2 could be later than Book 6. Since the *earlier* Sarasvatī of Book 6 is placed by Witzel in Kurukṣetra, the *later* Sarasvatī of Book 2 could hardly be the river of Afghanistan, with the Vedic Aryans allegedly still "**fighting their way through the NW mountain passes**". [Incidentally, note the number of ignorant mistakes made by this eminent Vedic and Sanskrit scholar in the name of the ṛṣi of Book 2: he consistently spells Gṛtsa*mada* as Gṛtsa*māda*; he also frequently refers to the eponymous *Gṛtsa*mada, as for example in the above case, as *Gārtsa*māda, "descendant of Gṛtsa*māda*"; and he misunderstands the fact that Gṛtsamada, a ṛṣi of the Śaunahotra Āngiras family, joined the *Śaunaka Bhārgava* family as meaning that a *Śaunaka became* ("**was made**") a *Bhārgava*].

Thirdly, the references to the Sarasvatī in Book 2 are clearly associated with Kurukṣetra and not with Afghanistan: in **II.3**.8, which Witzel, above, suggests could refer to the river of Afghanistan rather than the Ghaggar-Hakra of Kurukṣetra, the Sarasvatī is actually mentioned alongwith the other two great goddesses of Kurukṣetra, Iḷā and Bhāratī, and, the previous verse **II.3**.7 refers to "the three high places" of these three goddesses "at the centre of the earth". And Witzel himself points out, in the course of his description of Kurukṣetra, that it "**became the heartland of the Bharatas well into the Vedic period. It is here that 3.53.11 places the centre of the earth**" (WITZEL 1995b:339).

Likewise, Witzel's location of the Sarasvatī of Book 8 in Afghanistan is neutralized by the fact that he locates the *same* verses, **VIII.21**.17-18, on the *same* page (WITZEL 1995:350), once in Iran (i.e. "eastern Iran" = Afghanistan) and once also in Kurukṣetra. And, for what it is worth, the location in Afghanistan is followed by a speculative question mark, but the location in Kurukṣetra is not.

That leaves only Witzel's speculative location of the reference to the Sarasvatī in Book 10 in Afghanistan. Book 10 is undoubtedly the latest Book in the Rigveda; still, even from a perspective of an east-to-west movement indicated by all the evidence, there is no logical reason why it should be supposed that the Sarasvatī referred to here should be a different one from the Sarasvatī referred to in the rest of the Rigveda.

It is interesting to note that, in spite of the fact that Witzel's article actually only shows that the Sarasvatī of the Rigveda is identical with the Ghaggar-Hakra, other AIT scholars lap up some other spurious and self-contradictory assertions from the article as evidence for the AIT. Hock cites this very article by Witzel, which he claims is "**ignored or denied by Hindu nationalist authors**", as "**evidence which suggests that some of the hymns in which the river Sarasvatī is invoked (or the Goddess for that matter) may go back to a period before the arrival of the āryas in India and to an area outside India, in present-day Afghanistan and eastern Iran; see Appendix A in Witzel 1995b:343 which distinguishes a 'western' Sarasvatī (RV 2:41:6, 10:64:9) and a Sarasvatī in Kurukṣetra (3:24:3 and in book 7)**" (HOCK 1999b:164). Clearly the AIT club is an extremely closed mutual admiration society where one member's unsubstantiated speculative assertions, howsoever absurd, become another member's clinching evidence.

But, in spite of Hock's eagerness in grabbing at the straw of Witzel's suggestion about two different Sarasvatīs in the Rigveda, the *sum* of Witzel's article is that all the references to the Sarasvatī in the *Early* Books refer only to the Sarasvatī of Kurukṣetra: the Ghaggar-Hakra.

Apart from the geographical aspects of Witzel's 1995 article, note what he has to say about the chronology of the case in two different articles written in 1995:

> "[…] **since the Sarasvatī, which dries up progressively after the mid-2nd millennium B.C. (Erdosy 1989), is still described as a mighty stream in the Ṛgveda, the earliest hymns in the latter must have been composed by c.1500 B.C.**" (WITZEL 1995a:98).
>
> "**Prominent in book 7: it flows from the mountains to the sea (7.59.2) — which would put the battle of ten kings prior to 1500 BC or so, due to the now well documented dessication of the Sarasvatī (Yash Pal et al. 1984)** […]. **Two hymns (7.95-96) are composed solely in praise of the Sarasvatī.**" (WITZEL 1995b:335, fn 82).

Here, he not only identifies the Sarasvatī of the Rigveda with the Sarasvatī of Kurukṣetra which dried up progressively after 1500 BCE, but notes that it "**flows from the mountains to the sea**" (a description now often sought to be transferred to the Harahvaiti of Afghanistan, with the Hamun-i-Hilmand being the "sea" described in the verse), and accepts that it shows that the battle of ten kings took place prior to 1500 BCE.

And *nowhere*, in that article or in his charts on the geographical data in the Rigveda, does Witzel talk about women and non-riverine deities, or about Arachosia or the Night time sky, in reference to the word Sarasvatī in these Early Books.

3F-2. The Gangā.

The importance of the Gangā (along with that of the neighbouring Yamunā) lies in the fact that while the Indus and its western tributaries are *completely missing* in the three oldest Books of the Rigveda, the Gangā and the Yamunā and other rivers east of the Sarasvatī, apart from the Sarasvatī itself, are very prominent in these Books.

The Gangā is referred to in the Rigveda by two names: Gangā and Jahnāvī (in later times, Jāhnavī). The verses which refer to the Gangā are **VI.45**.31 and **X.75**.5, and the verses which refer to the Jahnāvī are **III.58**.6 and **I.116**.19 respectively.

Not only is the Gangā, the easternmost river in the Rigveda, found mentioned in the two oldest Books of the Rigveda (6 and 3), but the nature of the references makes it clear that the river is an old familiar feature of the Rigvedic landscape: **VI.45**.31 speaks familiarly about the wide bushes on the banks of the Gangā, and **III.58**.6 refers to the (banks of) the Jahnāvī as the "ancient home" of the Vedic gods.

Witzel, in his "review" of TALAGERI 2000, rejects outright the identity of the Jahnāvī with the Gangā, and tells us: "**Jahnāvī was the wife or a female relation of Jahnu or otherwise connected to him or his clan**", and adds: "**To turn the word Jahnāvī into a name for the Ganges can be done only by retro-fitting the RV evidence to Epic-Purāṇic concepts or to Talagerian conceits of a Gangetic (Uttar Pradesh) homeland of the RV and of the Aryans/Indo-Europeans (T., 1993) In short, Jahnāvī 'Ganges' is not found in the RV**" (WITZEL 2001b:§4). He repeats this in 2005: "**That Jahnāvī refers to a river, the Ganges (Witzel 2001a), is an Epic/Purāṇic conceit. The word can simply be derived from that of the Jahnu clan**" (WITZEL 2005:386, fn 79), and identification of it with the Gangā "**is clearly based on post-Vedic identifications**" (WITZEL 2005:355).

But Jahnāvī is typically a Rigvedic form of the post-Vedic Jāhnavī, and it does not require any "**Epic/Purāṇic concepts**" to recognize it as the name of a river: a river is a geographical feature, not a mythological entity whose identity is based on traditional historical or mythological texts.

On the other hand, *Witzel's* claim that "**Jahnāvī was the wife or a female relation of Jahnu or otherwise connected to him or his clan**" is definitely based on Epic/Purāṇic concepts: *no person named Jahnu is mentioned anywhere in the Rigveda*, and while a clan named Jāhnava appears only in later Vedic texts, Jahnu himself is an Epic/Purāṇic figure probably created (like so many others in the Purāṇas, see Yadu according to SOUTHWORTH 1995:266) in order to provide a mythological explanation for the name of the river and of the clan (who may in fact have been originally named that only because they were the inhabitants of that part of the course of the Gangā which originally bore the name Jahnāvī or Jāhnavī). Not only does Witzel accept this Epic/Purāṇic person as the source of the Rigvedic word Jahnāvī, he even visualizes, in the manner of the Amar Chitrakatha comic books, a mysterious lady named Jahnāvī, "**the wife or a female relation of Jahnu or otherwise connected to him or his clan**", whose very existence is completely unknown to the whole of Vedic and Epic/Purāṇic literature and Indian tradition, but who is apparently so very important in the Rigveda that she is mentioned twice (how many other ladies are mentioned twice in the Rigveda outside of references to people aided by the Aśvins?) in special references, which are worded so peculiarly (what, after all, unless she was a symbol of the motherland, like the present-day Bhāratmātā, has this lady to do with an "ancient home"), that they can be more conveniently and logically translated as references to a river!

One piece of evidence confirming that Jahnāvī is the Gangā, if evidence is necessary, is the fact that the second reference to Jahnāvī, in **I.116**.19, is adjacent to (and forms a continuum with) verse **I.116**.18, which refers to Divodāsa, Bharadvāja and the dolphin, all three of whom are associated with the Gangā (the reference to the Gangā in **VI.45**.31 is in the Divodāsa-Bharadvāja Book 6: "**In book 6 of the Bharadvāja, the Bharatas and their king Divodāsa play a central role**" WITZEL 1995b:332-333).

Witzel, typically, refuses to consider this as evidence: "**T.'s Gangetic dolphin is also found in the Indus river! And RV 1.116.18-19 are not as closely connected as T. wants us to believe; this is part of a long 25-verse list of the miracles of the Āśvins.**" (WITZEL 2001b:§4). But Divodāsa and Bharata are associated with the Gangā, and not with the Indus, and RV **I.116**.18-19 are definitely not unconnected, as Witzel wants us to believe. His objections clearly amount to juvenile quibbling rather than genuine doubts arising from serious examination.

But Witzel's primary ire is directed at the implications of the reference to the Gangā in Book 6, the oldest Book of the Rigveda. In his review of TALAGERI 2000, he tells us: "**One can immediately throw out the reference to the Ganges that appears at RV 6.45.31 (*Gāngya*).** [...] **Applying the principles pioneered by Oldenberg, RV 6.45 can be shown to be a composite hymn built out of tṛcas at an uncertain period. The ordering principle of the old family books clearly points to the addition of all these hymns in mixed meters at the end of an Indra series. Such late additions must not be used as an argument for the age of the bulk of Book 6**" (WITZEL 2001b: §7).

In later writings, he is even more categorical: "**The Ganges is only mentioned twice in the RV, once directly in a late hymn (10.75.5), and once by a derived word, *gāngya* in a late addition (6.45.31). This occurs in a *tṛca* that could be an even later addition to this *additional* hymn, which is too long to fit the order of arrangement of the RV, see Oldenberg 1888**" (WITZEL 2005:386, fn 76).

This is what he writes *after* the publication of TALAGERI 2000, which highlighted the lethal implications, to the AIT, of this reference to the Gangā in the oldest book of the Rigveda.

Now see what he had written *before* TALAGERI 2000:

1. In his 1995 article, he refers to this reference as follows: "**BOOK 6** [...] **mentions even the *Gangā* in an unsuspicious hymn (though in a *tṛca* section)**" (WITZEL 1995b:317). [Just above this, he also notes that "**Book 5** [...] **even knows, in a hymn not suspected as an addition, of the *Yamunā***"].

Although he notes that it is in a "***tṛca* section**", Witzel does not see it as an obstacle to the Gangā being counted as part of the geography of Book 6 proper. He not only notes that this hymn is an "**unsuspicious hymn**", he regularly counts the Gangā among the geographical data in the Rigveda for Book 6 (WITZEL 1995b:318, 320, 343, 345, 348, 352).

2. Two years later, in 1997, Witzel classifies the Rigvedic hymns into six levels of composition. The first two levels, without specifying any particular hymn, he names the "**Indo-Iranian level**" and the "**Pre-Ṛgvedic level**". Thus he takes care of the assumed earlier stages of the Indo-Iranian period when the common Indo-Iranian poetic traditions are assumed to have been first formulated. The next four levels classify the actual Rigvedic hymns into the "**Early Ṛgvedic level**", "**Later Ṛgvedic level**", "**Late Ṛgvedic ritual compositions**" and "**Early Mantra type compositions**". In the last category, he places Books 9 and 10, and in the second-last level, he places most of Book 1. In the third-last level, he places Books 3 and 7.

In the "Early Ṛgvedic level", he names only the following: "**Śamyu Bārhapatasya 6.45.1** [sic]**, some early Kaṇvas (in book 8)**" (WITZEL 1997b:293). Thus, however vaguely and with his usual and typical careless mistakes (Bārhaspatya spelt as Bārhapatasya, etc.), he classifies hymn **VI**.45 in the "Early Ṛgvedic level".

3. By 2000, Witzel is *even more* categorical, and *much more* systematic and specific in his classification. At around the time of publication of TALAGERI 2000 itself, Witzel writes as follows:

> **"Even now, however, three RV periods can be established, as follows:**
> **1. *early Ṛgvedic period:* c.1700-1450 BCE: RV books 4, 5, 6.**
> **2. *middle, main Ṛgvedic period:* c.1450-1300 BCE: books 3, 7, 8.1-47, 8.60-66 and 1.51-191, most probably also 2; prominent: Pūru chieftain Trasadasyu and Bharata chieftain Sudās and their ancestors, and**
> **3. *late Ṛgvedic period:* c.1300-1200 BCE: books 1.1-50, 8.48-59 (the late Vālakhilya hymns), 8.67-103, large sections of 9, and finally 10.1-84, 10.85-191; emergence of the Kuru tribe, fully developed by the time of Parīkṣit a descendant of Trasadasyu."** (WITZEL 2000a:§6).

Witzel not only provides us with tentative dates for the different periods, but he systematically places Book 6 *distinctly and categorically before* at least Books 1-3 and 7-10.

Is hymn **VI**.45 excluded from this classification? Far from it, in his footnote to the "**early Ṛgvedic period: c.1700-1450 BCE**", he writes: "**With Indo-Aryan settlement mainly in Gandhāra/Panjab, but occasionally extending upto *Yamunā/Gangā*, e.g. Atri poem 5.52.17; the relatively old poem 6.45.13** [sic] **has *gāngya*** [...]" (WITZEL 2000a:§6).

Later, he reiterates: "**Even the oldest books of the RV (4-6) contain data covering all of the Greater Panjab: note the rivers *Sindhu* 4.54.6, 4.55.3, 5.53.9 'Indus'; *Asiknī* 4.17.5 'Chenab'; *Paruṣṇī* 4.22.3. 5.52.9 'Ravi'; *Vipāś* 4.30.11 (Vibali) 'Beas'; *Yamunā* 5.52.17; *Gangā* 6.45.31 with *gāngya* 'belonging to the Ganges'** [...]."(WITZEL 2000a:§6).

Finally, he leaves no room for any doubt as to what he is saying: "**G. van Driem and A. Parpola (1999) believe that these oldest hymns were still composed in Afghanistan** [...]. **This is, however, not the case as these books contain references to the major rivers of the Panjab, even the Ganges (see above).**" (WITZEL 2000a:§6).

Note what Witzel is writing shortly before reading TALAGERI 2000: he repeatedly refers not only to Book 6 in general, not only to hymn **VI**.45 in general, but specifically to the verse in that hymn which refers to the Gangā, as pertaining to the "**early Ṛgvedic period**" and as constituting part of the geographical data of "**the oldest books**" and "**the oldest hymns**", and he even takes up issue with other western scholars who think otherwise!

He categorically places the reference to the Gangā in **VI.45**.31 (as well as the reference to the Yamunā in **V.52**.17) *before* Books 1-3 and 7-10: i.e. *before* the Battle of the Ten Kings on the Paruṣṇī (in **VII**.18, 83), *before* the crossing of the Vipāś and the Śutudrī (in **III**.33), and *before* the establishment of the sacred fire at "the centre of the earth" in Kurukṣetra by the ancestors of Sudās (in **III**.23); and naturally *long* before the introduction of camels to Vedic ṛṣis by kings with proto-Iranian names (in **VIII**.5, 6, 46).

But immediately after reading the analysis of the Rigveda in TALAGERI 2000, there is a magical transformation in Witzel's attitude: suddenly, he realizes that this reference "**occurs in a tṛca that could be an even later addition to this additional hymn**" and finds this revelation so compelling that he has no alternative except to "**immediately throw out the reference to the Ganges that appears at RV 6.45.31 (Gāngya)**"!

The fact is that writing in historical subjects has become a front for pursuing political agendas or personal ego-trips. Before the year 2000, also, Witzel was an AIT writer; but this was not his main battlefront. It had genuinely never occurred to him, any more than it could have occurred to any other AIT writer, that there could be a serious and fundamental threat to the AIT model on which the analysis of the ancient history of South Asia, and of the Vedic texts, had so far been based. Therefore, they could indulge in academic quibbling on other minor points within the AIT framework. Witzel was, since quite a few years before the year 2000, engaged in debate with other western academicians on the question of the linguistic identity of the Harappan language: Witzel's contention was that the Vedic language contained a strong Munda substratum acquired in the area of the Harappan civilization, and that the language, or indeed one of the two languages, of the Harappan civilization was a Kol-Munda language. In the course of this debate, with Witzel's contentions being challenged or opposed by other western scholars, it became necessary, for various reasons (see, for example, WITZEL 2000a:§10), for Witzel to demonstrate that the Vedic Aryans had penetrated considerably far into the interior of northern India in a considerably early period of composition of the Rigveda. Hence, all the pre-2000 assertions and conclusions about the Gangā!

But, after the publication of TALAGERI 2000, priorities changed rapidly: it became necessary to close AIT ranks in a holy crusade against the new case and the new evidence for the OIT. The identity of the Harappan language could wait — or could be pursued separately in different articles; after all, Witzel has a limitless capacity for writing mutually contradictory things, sometimes on the very same page, without causing the slightest dent in the faith and loyalty of his admirers — what was important now was to rapidly drag the Vedic Aryans of the early period all the way back from the area of the Gangā to the safety of Afghanistan. Hence, all the post-2000 assertions and conclusions about the Gangā!

Clearly, such writing can not be called scholarly writing under any circumstance, and one must be very, very careful indeed before placing the slightest credence in the views, interpretations and conclusions of such writers, howsoever high a position they may hold in the academic world.

In conclusion, we can only repeat: the evidence of the geographical data in the Rigveda, for an originally eastern origin for the Vedic Aryans and for their direction of expansion being from east to west, is too massive and overwhelming, and too unidirectional, to be denied: it simply *can not* be argued against.

Chapter 4

The Internal Chronology of the Rigveda

In our analysis of the Relative Chronology (vis-à-vis the Avesta) and Geography of the Rigveda, we have seen that the data falls into clear categories showing a clear distinction between the Early Books of the Rigveda, the Middle Books of the Rigveda, and the Late Books of the Rigveda. In this chapter, we will go more deeply into the question of this Internal Chronology of the Rigveda.

In my earlier book on the Rigveda, I examined the Rigvedic data in detail, and showed that the chronological order of the ten Books of the RV is: 6,3,7,4,2,5,8,9,10, with different parts of Book 1 covering the periods of all but the three earliest Books. I also showed in systematic detail that Family Books 6, 3 and 7 belong to the Early period, Family Books 4 and 2 to the Middle period, and the rest (Book 5 among the Family Books, and all the other, ie. *non*-family, Books, 8, 9 and 10, and most of Book 1) belong to the Late period (for details, see TALAGERI 2000:35-93). That chronological order is *irrefutable*.

But, after the publication of my book, fraudulent scholars like Michael Witzel preferred to ignore the *vital significance and importance* of this internal chronology in unraveling the history of the Vedic, and indeed the Indo-European, period; and chose instead to quibble and obfuscate the issues, and, in general, to derail serious discussion, by diverting the discussion into totally *irrelevant* issues such as the date of the amplified Anukramaṇī texts. His fraudulent pretensions have been conclusively exposed, and his fraudulent objections conclusively refuted, in my reply to his "review" of my book (see TALAGERI 2001).

As we have just seen in our analysis of the Avestan evidence, this internal chronology of the Rigveda is *absolutely indispensable* in our study of Indo-Iranian history. We can, therefore, expect renewed, and desperate, attempts by academic shysters like Witzel to try to discredit this chronology. Therefore, we need to examine the issue once more in detail, trying, as far as possible, to give less scope for these shysters to play their diversionary games.

Therefore, in the main body of this chapter, we will examine this issue purely on the basis of the consensus among western scholars, and see how our analysis of the relative chronology and the geography of the Rigveda, in the preceding chapters, stands conclusively established on *that* basis alone. In two appendix-sections, we will go more deeply into the internal chronology, taking all other factors into account, with the clear understanding that *any quibbling by critics can be possible only in respect of the matter in these appendices*, and that our conclusions regarding the relative chronology and the geography of the Rigveda stand *unaffected* by this quibbling.

We will examine the subject under the following heads:

4A. The Late Books as per the Western Scholars Themselves.

4B. Can This Evidence be Refuted?

4C. Appendix 1: The Internal Order of the Early and Middle books.

- 4C-1. The Early vis-à-vis the Middle Books.
- 4C-2. The Early Books.
- 4C-3. The Middle Books.

4D. Appendix 2: "Late" Hymns.

- 4D-1. Facts.
- 4D-2. Testimony.
- 4D-3. Deductions.
- 4D-4. Speculations.

4A
THE LATE BOOKS AS PER THE WESTERN SCHOLARS THEMSELVES

Firstly, let us examine what constitute the Late Books of the Rigveda, *as per the Western scholars.*

1. In his 1995 papers in the volume edited by Erdosy, Witzel tells us: "**The structure of the text has been more extensively studied, already by Bergaigne (1878-83) and Oldenberg in the 19th century. From the latter's *Prolegomena* (Oldenberg 1888), it appears that the Ṛgveda was composed and assembled in the following stages, beginning 'at the centre' with books 2-7**" (WITZEL 1995b:309). Witzel even provides a graph on the page, vividly showing this order of *composition and assembly*, with Books 2-7 as the earliest core of the text, parts of 1 and 8 forming the second layer, the rest of 1 and 8 forming the third layer, followed by Book 9, and finally by "the great appendix to the Ṛgveda" (WITZEL 1995b:310), Book 10.

More recently, Theodore Proferes (frequently quoted by Witzel to promote his own trickling-in theory) puts it as follows: "**The formation of the Ṛksamhita** [...] **appears to have been carried out in three stages. First, the 'clan books' 2-7 were collected and ordered** [...] **At a later stage, Books 1 and 8 were added to the case like book ends. It was likely at this stage that Book 9 was added as well. Lastly, the heterogenous material in Book 10 was appended to the entire collection**" (PROFERES 1999:10).

In short, the first basic fact, generally accepted by all the scholars, is that the Family or "clan" books (2-7) represent an *earlier* stage of composition and compilation and the non-family books (1, 8-10) represent a *later* stage of composition and compilation.

2. But there is a further point noted by the scholars, distinguishing one of the six Family books from the other five, and clubbing it with the non-family books:

Edward Hopkins, as long ago as 1896, wrote a long and detailed article ("**Prāgāthikāni-I**", in JAOS, the Journal of the American Oriental Society, 1896) about the late chronological position of Book 8. In this article, he refers to **"the intermediate character of v, between viii and the other family books"** (HOPKINS 1896a:88), and repeatedly points out *with detailed evidence* (see HOPKINS 1896a:29-30 fn, 88-89) that there are a great many **"evidences of special rapport between viii and v"** (HOPKINS 1896a:89). Further, he emphasizes that

> **"the vocabulary of the Kaṇva maṇḍala often coincides with that of the Atri maṇḍala when it shows no correspondence with that of other family books. This subject deserves special treatment"** (HOPKINS 1896a:29).

More recently, Proferes, after pointing out, in his Harvard thesis above, that the Family Books 2-7 are earlier than the non-family Books 1, 8-10, repeatedly singles out Book 5 as having a close relationship with Books 1 and 8, the two Books which he earlier tells us were appended to the collection of the Family books **"at a later stage"**:

> **We need not rely exclusively on the Anukramaṇī to affirm that there were important interactions between the priestly groups represented in Books 1, 5 and 8. As Oldenberg [1888b:213-215] has shown, evidence from the hymns themselves supports this conclusion** (PROFERES 1999:75).

> "**the *pavamāna* collection consists primarily of late authors, those from Books 1, 5, 8 and in a limited number of cases, 10**" (PROFERES 1999:69).

In a more recent paper, Proferes repeats the above point:

> **"the clan book composers, except those from Book 5, are not well represented among the *pavamāna* composers of Book 9"** (PROFERES 2003:12).

> "**These circles are represented by the Kāṇva, Ātreya and Āngirasa authors from Books 1, 5 and 8, as well as by descendants of these authors**" (PROFERES 2003:16).

> **"the breakdown of the strict separation of the ritual poetry of different clans and the preservation of that poetry together in a single collection began with the Kāṇva, Ātreya and Āngirasa poets of Books 1, 5 and 8"** (PROFERES 2003:18).
>
> [Most significantly]: **"The connections of Book 5 with Books 1 and 8 and not with the other clan books (2-4, 6-7) is interesting, since it seems to belong to the core RV collection (Oldenberg [1888a]; Witzel [1997])"** (PROFERES 2003:16, fn)..

In short, the second basic fact, clear from the writings of the scholars, is that, from among the Family or "clan" books (2-7), *Book 5 is classifiable with the non-family Books (1, 8-10) rather than with the other Family Books*, and stands chronologically between the other Family Books (2-4, 6-7) and the non-family Books (1, 8-10).

Thus, even without going into the details of the internal chronological order *within* the group of other Family Books (2-4, 6-7), we already have the following three chronological stages:

1. Books 2-4, 6-7.
2. Book 5.
3. Books 1, 8-10.

These chronological stages are also confirmed by the evidence of the meters, as we saw in Chapter 2, where Book 5 represents the period of development of the pankti meter.

What is important, at this point, is to make it very, very clear, at the outset itself, that *this* level of chronological information, simply classifying the Books into "earlier" (2-4, 6-7), and "later" (5, 1, 8-10), *officially accepted by the western scholars themselves*, is sufficient (without going into further chronological details) to *irrefutably establish* the two conclusions that we arrived at in our chapters on the Relative Chronology and Geography of the Rigveda, chiefly:

1. That the Avesta is contemporaneous with the period of the "later" Books 5, 1, 8-10, and *posterior* to the period of the "earlier" Books 2-4, 6-7.

2. That the Vedic Aryans expanded from the East in the "earlier" periods to the (earlier totally unknown) West in the "later" periods.

It is clear, therefore, that Witzel's fraudulent diversions on the subject of the Anukramaṇīs, in his criticism (in WITZEL 2001) of the chronology elaborated in my earlier book (TALAGERI 2000), were just that: fraudulent diversions to derail serious analysis and discussion.

4B.
CAN THIS EVIDENCE BE REFUTED?

But first, a basic question arises: can our two conclusions, above, be dismissed or refuted?

The answer is clearly in the negative: the above conclusions are indeed irrefutable, since the evidence is too sweeping and overwhelming to be avoided; and the *only* way to "refute" them is to simply *refuse* to consider the evidence at all, and to concentrate on carrying out political propaganda campaigns against the evidence and derisive smear campaigns against those who recognize it. This is something at which the likes of Witzel and Farmer are past masters.

An alternate tactic (a *tactic*, rather than an honest academic procedure) is to attack the correctness of the evidence. Witzel tries to do it by refusing to accept some of the eastern geographical data as geographical data at all (*Jahnāvī, ibha,* etc), and even transferring, for example, many of the references to eastern rivers from the earth to the "night time sky" by converting the earthly rivers into celestial phenomena.

But this, besides being seemingly "possible" (by straining the credulity of even the most credulous and partisan reader to the utmost limit) only in respect of a very few names, would *not* help in explaining the *almost complete absence* of Western geographical data in the Early Books. Therefore, Witzel also tries to transfer *eastern* geographical data to the west, directly (eg. identifying *Yavyāvati* with the Afghan *Zhob*, although he had himself, in an earlier article, WITZEL 1987:193, admitted that the actual location would seem to be in the Kurukshetra region), or by creating dual entities (eg. an Eastern Haryana-Sarasvatī, as well as a Western Afghan-Sarasvatī, *both* referred to in the Rigveda, with Witzel being the only person possessing the key to distinguish which Sarasvatī is being referred to in which verse. Even when Witzel, here, flatly contradicts his own earlier writings, where he had clearly placed in Haryana many verse-references which he now places in Afghanistan, we still have supposedly honest scholars like Hock, in HOCK 1999b:163-166, enthusiastically citing Witzel's dubious right-about-turn *claims* as clinching *evidence*).

But even these tactics, apart from being desperate and obvious ploys, do not change the picture presented by the data one bit. For one thing, these tactics cannot actually *transfer* unambiguous geographical words from one part (book/hymn) of the Rigveda to another. And nothing can be done about the unambiguous evidence of the Avestan names and name-elements examined by us in Chapter 1.

So, if the evidence has to be rejected, it can only be done on three grounds, each of which would involve a *very desperate* level of special pleading, and would create more problems than it "solves":

1. The only way to really account for the *almost complete absence* of Western geographical data in the earlier group of Books (i.e. *complete* absence in Books 6, 3, 7; and in Book 2. Book 4 alone, as we saw, names three Western *rivers* in four hymns, two of which, ironically, have been classified by Oldenberg as late hymns in this Book), as well as the complete absence of Avestan name-elements in these books, is to allege that all such references were systematically *extrapolated* from the hymns in these Books at a point of time before the RV attained its extant form. Perhaps by those arch villains, (to put it in Witzel's words:) the "**redactors active at the Sanskritizing court of Videha** [who] **often skewed the historical evidence found in the original RV**"? (WITZEL 2001b:§1)?

2. A more "scholarly" and time-tested way to try to avoid the inevitable is to introduce a significant element of scholarly ambiguity in the chronological framework, and then use this to cause confusion and obfuscate all the issues. Thus Witzel, in his review of my book, protests: "**the composition of the RV occurred in complex layers — not in the tidy sequential patterns imagined by Talageri**" (WITZEL 2001b:§1). The word "complex" is a handy tool to deliberately complicate matters. There are two ways in which the chronological order of the Books may be claimed to have exceptions:

a) *Early Books may contain late hymns, or early hymns may contain late verses*: Proferes, after giving his account of the formation of the Rigveda in his Harvard thesis, writes: "**At intermediate points along the way, individual verses and entire hymns were inserted into the RV collection**" (PROFERES 1999:10).

b) *Late Books may contain early hymns*: In an earlier paper, Witzel, after explaining the formation of the RV, suggests: "**It must be noted that the arrangement in these books does not always mean that a particular hymn is older and younger than some others** [...] **some may have been composed early but entered the corpus at a comparatively late date** [...] **Some in book 8, sometimes even in books 1 and 10 can be as early as those in the 'family books'**" (WITZEL 1995b:310).

The first claim by Proferes has a grain of truth in it, while the second one by Witzel is more dubious; but, in any case, it must be remembered that these claims refer to a *few exceptions to the rule — exceptions which require to be specified and satisfactorily explained in each individual case*. However, in arguing with the OIT school, Witzel sees no need for these niceties, and behaves as if the rule were the exception and the exception the rule, and as if it were up to us to specify and justify each point even when it actually *fits in* with the basic arrangement accepted by Oldenberg, Proferes and himself.

In the present case, however, the overwhelming mass of evidence simply does not allow for such obfuscatory tactics:

As we saw, there are 386 hymns in the *Late* Books which are associated with the Avestan name-elements:

V.1, 3-6, 9-10, 18-20, 24-27, 30-31, 33-36, 41, 44-49, 52-62, 64, 67-68, 73-75, 79, 81-82 (47 hymns).

I.12-30, 33, 35-52, 61, 66, 80, 83, 88, 99-100, 105, 112, 114, 116-140, 158, 163-164, 167, 188 (78 hymns).

VIII.1-10, 12, 14-15, 19, 21, 23-38, 43-59, 62, 66, 68-71, 74-75, 77, 80, 85-87, 89-90, 92-93, 97-99, 103 (69 hymns).

IX.2-3, 5-24, 27-29, 32-36, 41-43, 53-61, 63-65, 68, 72, 80-83, 85-86, 91-92, 94-97, 99-103, 107, 111-114 (69 hymns).

X.1-8, 10-29, 31, 33, 37, 39, 42-49, 51-52, 54-67, 72-73, 75-78, 80, 85-87, 89-93, 95-99, 101-106, 109, 111-115, 118, 120, 122-123, 128, 130, 132, 134-136, 139, 144, 147-148, 150-152, 154, 157, 159, 163-166, 168, 170, 172, 174-175, 177, 179-180, 186, 188, 191 (123 hymns)

And there are eight hymns, all of which are classified as Late, in the Early and Middle Books, which contain these elements:

VI.15 (Oldenberg), 16 (Oldenberg), 47 (Oldenberg).

III.36 (Ait. Br.), 38 (Ait. Br.), 53 (Oldenberg).

VII.33 (Oldenberg).

IV.30 (Oldenberg).

In order to explain the *complete* absence of these elements in the Early and Middle Books (except in the eight hymns classified as *Late*), in contrast to the profusion of these elements in 386 hymns in the *Late* Books, *even while continuing to maintain that the Avestan elements in the Rigveda represent pre-Rigvedic remnants*, we would have to postulate that the *entire* mass of 386 hymns in the Late Books "**may have been composed early but entered the corpus at a comparatively late date**" and "**can be as early as those in the 'family books'**". Or, actually, *earlier* than them since these "pre-Rigvedic" elements are *absent* in the Family Books.

Likewise, there are 92 hymns, in the *Late* Books, which mention Western geographical words:

V. 41, 53 (2 hymns).

I. 10, 22, 43-44, 51-52, 61, 83-84, 88, 94-96, 98, 100-103, 105-117, 121-122, 126, 138, 162-164, 186 (39 hymns).

VIII. 1-2, 5-7, 12, 19-20, 24-26, 34, 46, 64, 66, 72, 77, 97 (18 hymns).

IX. 8, 41, 65, 83, 85-86, 97, 107, 113 (9 hymns).

X. 10-11, 27-28, 34-35, 64-67, 75, 80, 85-86, 91, 95, 99, 106, 108, 121, 123, 136, 139, 177 (24 hymns).

But there are only five hymns, in two of the Early and Middle Books, which mention Western geographical words, three of which are classified as *Late*:

III. 38 (Ait. Br.).

IV. 30 (Oldenberg), 43, 54, 55 (Oldenberg).

As we saw, *only* Book 4 really mentions three Western rivers (but *not yet* Western places, mountains, lakes or animals), and this is in line with the direction of geographical expansion of the Vedic Aryans in the three Early Books: Book 6 knows only the Sarasvatī and rivers east; Book 3 first mentions the *first two easternmost* rivers of the Punjab, the Śutudrī and the Vipāś, in the context of a *historical military crossing*; Book 7 mentions *the next two from the east*, the Paruṣṇī and the Asiknī, in the context of a battle being fought on the *third* river, Paruṣṇī, with the enemies being the inhabitants of the region of the *fourth* river, Asiknī; Book 4 finally takes the geographical horizon of the Rigveda to the Indus and beyond, including the battle beyond the Sarayu *west* of the Indus.

Contrast this with the wealth of Eastern geographical words (including every significant Eastern word in the Rigveda), in 45 hymns, in the Early and Middle Books:

VI. 1, 4, 8, 17, 20, 27, 45, 49-50, 52, 61 (11 hymns).

III. 4-5, 23, 26, 29, 45-46, 53-54, 58 (10 hymns).

VII. 2, 9, 18, 35-36, 39-40, 44, 69, 95-96 (11 hymns).

IV. 4, 16, 18, 21, 58 (5 hymns).

II. 1, 3, 10, 30, 32, 34, 36, 41 (8 hymns).

In order to explain the *complete* absence of *Western* geographical words in the Early and Middle Books (except some river names in Book 4), in contrast to the profusion of these words in 92 hymns in the Late Books, and also in contrast with the *profusion* of *Eastern* geographical words in 45 hymns in *these* very Early and Middle Books, *even while continuing to maintain that the Vedic Aryans expanded from the West in earlier times to the East in later times*, we would have to postulate that *all* these 92 hymns in the Late Books, which have Western geographical words, "**may have been composed early but entered the corpus at a comparatively late date**" and "**can be as early as those in the 'family books'**". Or, actually, *earlier* than them since these Western geographical words are almost completely *absent* in the Early and Middle Books. And also that *all* the 45 hymns in the Early and Middle Books, which have Eastern geographical words, are hymns which "**at intermediate points along the way** [...] **were inserted into the RV collection**".

Clearly, all this would amount to *extreme* special pleading.

3. The third way in which all the evidence could be overturned is simply by deciding that the scholars and linguists were *wrong* all the time in placing the Family Books before the non-family Books, and that it is actually *the other way round*: the non-family Books (1, 8-10) are the oldest books of the RV, Book 5 comes next, followed by Book 4, and that the bulk of the other Family Books (2-3, 6-7 — *except* the very hymns in these books singled out by Oldenberg as *late*, which are, in fact, now to be taken as actually being *earlier* than the rest of the hymns in these Books) constitute the *latest* parts of the RV, by which time the incoming Vedic Aryans had lost all contact with the Western areas through which they had immigrated into India, and all the Avestan type names and name-elements had gone *completely* out of fashion, which is why there are no references to those areas, and no names of the Avestan type, in these Books.

[Of course, in the post-Rigvedic texts, and all later traditions, those names and name-elements mysteriously came back into fashion with a vengeance!].

While no scholar would dare to try to overturn two hundred years of scholarship so completely in this direct, and extreme, way merely in order to try to counter the OIT, many scholars do indeed try to suggest, in more subtle and "complex" ways, that the non-family Books and Book 5 actually represent an earlier age, even if they were merely "compiled" and "included in the collection" at a date later to the rest of the corpus of the Family Books. The creation of that other *dual entity*, the two waves of Aryan invaders, is useful in attempting to perform these juggling acts with the facts and figures.

Thus, Parpola puts it as follows: **"although the 'youngest' hymns of the Ṛgveda are most recent from the point of view of the *textual history*, ie. the time of their composition and inclusion in the text collection, from the point of view of *dialect formation* involving the entry of Indo-Aryan speakers in South Asia at different times they reflect an earlier layer"** (PARPOLA 2002:57). He clarifies this further by telling us that, although it is **"generally agreed that the original core, the oldest part of the Ṛgveda-Samhita consists in the 'family books', RV 2-7, each composed by a particular family of poets"**, nevertheless in his **"opinion it is the hymns of these poet families (including the hymns assigned to them in books 1 [the latter half], 9 and 10) that represent the Pūru-Bharata tribes of the 'second wave'"** (PARPOLA 2002:57); and that **"the earliest wave** [is] **of the Yadu and Turvaśa tribes identified here with the poetic tradition of the Kaṇvas"** (PARPOLA 2002:66).

Rather a funny way of putting it: from the point of view of "**dialect formation**", ie. from the point of view of the linguistic stage, the language of the non-family Books is in actual fact even more emphatically *later* than that of the Family Books. But Parpola tells us that it is precisely from *this* point of view that they "**reflect an earlier layer**". He even seems to concede that they were not just "**included**", *but even* "**composed**" later, and yet insists they belong to an "earlier wave".

But Witzel also picks up the refrain, and regularly talks, in his articles, of two "waves" of Aryan invaders (or immigrants or tricklers-in), of which the Pūru-Bharata tribes were the latest wave (the period of Sudas, Books 3 and 7, being a particularly "late period" in Rigvedic history.), and the Yadus, Turvaśas and Kaṇvas represent the earlier wave. The Rsis of the *later* (second-wave) Pūru-Bharata immigrants apparently first composed the *original* core of the RV (i.e. most of the Family Books), and *later* included the *earlier* (than their own) compositions (i.e. the non-family Books) of the *earlier* (first-wave) immigrants (but in an *even later* form of Rigvedic dialect) into the corpus!

Again, this amounts to *extreme* special pleading _besides, again, failing to explain the mysterious *disappearance* of crucial geographical words (including the names of several common western animals), technological words (like spokes), and Avestan names and name-elements (including the names of several important Vedic personalities), in the compositions of the so-called "second wave", and their even more mysterious *reappearance* in all later texts, *especially since, in all these speculations, it is the "second wave" which is supposed to be linguistically closer to the Iranians.*

In short, the data in the Rigveda gives us a very *consistent picture* of its internal chronology and of the geography of its different periods. The facts cannot be challenged, except through such desperate and untenable pleas.

And the unchallengeable evidence clearly shows that the Vedic Aryans expanded from the East in the pre-Rigvedic period towards the northwest by the Late period, and that the various Iranian groups were emigrants from India in this Late period.

4C.
APPENDIX 1: THE INTERNAL ORDER OF THE EARLY AND MIDDLE BOOKS

As we saw, western scholars officially accept the following three stages in the composition and compilation of the ten Books of the Rigveda:

1. Books 2-4, 6-7.
2. Book 5.

3. Books 1, 8-10.

Book 5 shares affinities with the first group of Books, both *in the sense that it was already a part of the first core collection of the Rigveda*, consisting of (as numbered at present) Books 2-7; and also in its *geography*: i.e. in the fact that it is as ignorant, as the earlier Books, of the Western place names, mountain names, lake names and animal names, so well known to the later Books, and is, for all practical purposes, acquainted only with the three Western rivers known to the earlier Book 4, which saw the westernmost thrust of expansion in the Middle Period. However, in respect of the *meters*, as we saw, it stands exactly in between the first and the third group of Books.

But *in every other respect*, as we saw in our chapters on The Relative Chronology of the Rigveda, and as we shall see in the course of the discussion in this chapter, *it falls together along with the later Books, in a category that we have classified as the Late Books.*

One more point of divide between the earlier Books (2-4,6-7) and the Late Books is that the earlier Books attribute hymns to the eponymous ṛṣi (except in special cases) even when the hymns are clearly composed by different descendant ṛṣis of the family, while the Late Books generally attribute hymns to the actual composers themselves. [Thus, 59 out of 75 hymns in Book 6, 46 out of 62 hymns in Book 3, 101 out of 104 hymns in Book 7, 56 out of 58 hymns in Book 4, and 36 out of 43 hymns in Book 2, are attributed to the eponymous ṛṣi of the respective Books. However, only 14 out of 87 hymns in Book 5 are attributed to the eponymous ṛṣi of the Book. Book 5 names at least 42 ṛṣis as composers for its 87 hymns, while all the five earlier Books put together name only around 26 ṛṣis as composers for their 342 hymns (see TALAGERI 2000:52-53)].

About the other Late Books (Books 1, 8-10), we need not go too deeply into their exact internal chronology: firstly, because the chronological order is practically the same as their serial order; secondly, because this fact is officially accepted by the Western scholars (see WITZEL 1995b:309-310 and PROFERES 1999:10, quoted at the very beginning of Section A above); and thirdly because the precise internal chronological order of the Late Books is, in any case, not so vital to our analysis: that they are Late Books is sufficient. Book 1, as we have shown in detail (TALAGERI 2000:37-72), consists of a collection of small family mini-books, and their period of composition is spread out over a long time from the post-Early to the very Late periods; but even these distinctions are not *very* relevant to our analysis, since all these mini-books received their *final* shape in the Late period.

However, a more detailed examination of the internal chronological order of the earlier Books (Books 2-4, 6-7) is *absolutely vital* for a *more* detailed understanding of Vedic, Indo-Iranian, and Indo-European history. As shown in our earlier book, these five Books fall into *two* groups in the following chronological order: the Early Books 6, 3, 7; and the Middle Books 4, 2.

We will examine, firstly, the evidence for classifying Books 6, 3 and 7 as Early Books while classifying 4 and 2 as Middle Books. Then we will examine the evidence for the internal order within each of the two groups.

4C-1. The Early vis-à-vis the Middle Books

Books 6, 3 and 7 represent an earlier period than Books 4 and 2:

1. The Early Books are *pure* Family Books, in the sense that *every single hymn* in these three Books has a ṛṣi-composer belonging to the particular family, or branch of a family, to which that Family Book belongs: thus, every single hymn in Book 6 has a composer from the Bharadvāja branch of the Angiras family, every single hymn in Book 3 has a composer from the Viśvāmitra family, and every single hymn in Book 7 has a composer from the Vaṣiṣṭha family.

The Middle Books are slightly *less pure* Family Books: Book 4 (which belongs to the Gotama branch of the Angiras family) has two hymns, **IV.**43-44, wholly composed by ṛṣis belonging to the Bharadvāja branch of the Angiras family; and Book 2 (which belongs to the Gṛtsamada or Kevala Bhṛgu family) has four hymns, **II**.4-7, wholly composed by a ṛṣi belonging to the Bhṛgu family. But, in both the cases, the outsider ṛṣi-composers belong to groups *related* to the family or branch of the respective Book.

The Late Books, on the contrary, are multi-family books, having hymns composed by ṛṣis belonging to diverse and unrelated families. Book 5, although a Family Book of the Atri family, has six hymns, **V**.15, 24, 33-36, wholly composed by non-Atris: by ṛṣis belonging to the Vasiṣṭha, Viśvāmitra, Angiras and Agastya families; and one hymn, **V**.44, primarily by ṛṣis belonging to the Kaśyapa family.

2. The Early Books do not have a *single* hymn composed by descendants of any ṛṣi-composer from any other Book.

The Middle Books, on the other hand, have hymns composed by descendants of ṛṣi-composers from Book 6: in Book 4, hymns **IV**.43-44 are jointly composed by Purumīḷha Sauhotra and Ajamīḷha Sauhotra, descendants of Suhotra Bhāradvāja (composer of **VI**.31-32); and, in Book 2, Gṛtsamada Śaunahotra himself, the eponymous ṛṣi of the Book, is a descendant of Śunahotra Bhāradvāja (composer of **VI**.33-34). In fact, it would even appear that the eponymous ṛṣi of Book 4, Vāmadeva Gautama, is a descendant of a ṛṣi-composer from Book 1: the mini-book **I**.74-93 is attributed to Gotama Rāhūgaṇa. [In this case, though, what we actually have is three related groups of hymns: the hymns in Book 4 by ṛṣis of the Vāmadeva Gautama group, hymns **I**.58-64 by the Nodhās Gautama group, and hymns **I**.74-93 by Gotama ṛṣis other than these two groups].

The Late Books, needless to say, are loaded with hymns composed by descendants of ṛṣi-composers from the earlier Books (see TALAGERI 2000:38-50).

3. The Early Books 6 and 3 do *not refer*, within their hymns, to *any* composer from any other Book. Book 7 refers in **VII.96**.3 to Jamadagni, a composer from Book 3. It also refers to three *contemporary* ṛṣis, all three of whom have mini-books

composed by their *descendants* in Book 1: Agastya (**VII.33**.10,13), the brother of Vasiṣṭha; Parāśara (**VII.18**.21), a grandson of Vasiṣṭha; and Kutsa (**VII.25**.5), a colleague of Vasiṣṭha.

The Middle Book 4, on the other hand, refers to two ṛṣi-composers from mini-books in Book 1: Māmateya (=Dīrghatamas) in **IV.4**.13, and Kakṣīvān in **IV.26**.1 (see TALAGERI 2000:55).

The Late Books and mini-books, of course, are loaded with references to composers from other Books (see TALAGERI 2000:56-58).

4. The Early Books belong to the period of the early Bharata kings: the ancestral Bharata himself is referred to only once in the Rigveda, in the oldest Book 6, though already an ancestral figure, and the two most important Bharata kings, Divodāsa and Sudās, are contemporaneous with these Books.

The Middle Books are contemporaneous with the descendants of Sudās, Sahadeva and Somaka, both of whom are contemporaneous with Book 4. Divodāsa is once referred to in Book 2 as a figure from the past.

To the Late Books, of course, Divodāsa, referred to in Books 1, 8 and 9, and Sudās, referred to in Book 1, are figures from the past, the stuff of traditional memory and legend.

5. As we already saw in the case of the Avestan name-elements in the Rigveda, four eminent Rigvedic personalities (Turvīti, Gotama, Trita, and Kṛśānu — in the Avesta, the pre-Zoroastrian Tauruuaēti, Gaotəma, θrita and Kərəsāni) are *completely unknown* to the Early Books 6, 3 and 7; *first mentioned* in the Middle Books 4 and 2; and *commonly known* to the Late Books 5, 1, 8-10.

4C-2. The Early Books

The Early Books are clearly in the chronological order 6, 3, 7:

1. Book 6 is the *purest* Family Book, since *every single hymn and verse* in the Book is composed by a ṛṣi belonging to the Bharadvāja branch of the Angiras family.

Book 3 has ṛśis belonging to the Viśvāmitra family as composers in every single hymn, but two hymns also have a *few verses* composed by other ṛṣis: hymn 36 has one verse (out of eleven), **III.36**.10, by an Angiras ṛṣi; and hymn 62 has three verses (out of eighteen), **III.62**.16-18, jointly by a Bhṛgu ṛṣi and a Viśvāmitra ṛṣi. But these other composers are still, within those hymns, *junior* partners of the Viśvāmitra ṛṣi-composers.

Book 7 also has ṛṣis belonging to the Vasiṣṭha family as composers in every single hymn, but now we have *two whole hymns*, 101 and 102, jointly composed, as *equal* partners, by an Angiras ṛṣi and a Vasiṣṭha ṛṣi.

2. Book 6 covers the period of Divodāsa, and is therefore decidedly earlier to Books 3 and 7. Books 3 and 7, more contemporaneous, cover the period of his descendant Sudās. But, within a contemporaneous period, the core of Book 3 is slightly earlier than the core of Book 7, since it is generally accepted that the period of Viśvāmitra as the priest of Sudās *preceded* the period of Vasiṣṭha as the priest of Sudās. Besides, as we already saw, Book 3 (like Book 6) does not refer to any composer from any other Book, while Book 7 refers to Jamadagni from Book 3.

4C-3. The Middle Books

Of the two Middle Books, Book 4 is earlier than Book 2 (although, in this case, it makes little difference to our analysis, since Book 2 is a very neutral Book, which does not refer to ṛṣi-composers from any other Book, and whose ṛṣi-composers are not referred to in any other Book, and which, in fact does not even refer to any river other than the Sarasvatī):

1. Book 4 is still a relatively pure Family Book like the three Early Books, since the outsider ṛṣi-composers in Book 4 belong merely to a different branch of the same family: both the Bharadvājas and the Gotamas share one āprī-sūkta, **I**.142. The aprī-sūkta is the defining element of a family in the Rigveda.

On the other hand, the outsider ṛṣi-composers in Book 2, the Bhṛgus, though a related group, have a different āprī-sūkta,

X.110, from the āprī-sūkta, **II**.3, of the Gṛtsamadas or Kevala Bhṛgus of Book 2.

2. Even more significantly, Book 4 shows a cultural continuity with the Early Books. The first four Books (6, 3, 7, 4) seem to represent the Bharata period proper of the Vedic Age: They represent the periods of Divodāsa (6), Sudās (3, 7), and Sahadeva/Somaka (4). The first prominent Bharata king after the eponymous Bharata, named in the Rigveda, is Devavāta, and he is mentioned only in these four Books. Sṛñjaya, his son, is likewise mentioned only in Books 6 and 4.

[The Bharata period is clearly the Early period of the Rigveda: a) the Bharatas themselves are mentioned in all the Family Books, but in none of the non-family Books; and b) (see TALAGERI 2000:149) there is a pattern in the references, in the āprī-sūktas, to the goddess Bhāratī (family deity of the Bharatas): five families (Angiras, Bhṛgu, Viśvāmitra, Vasiṣṭha and Agastya), which originated in the Early period, mention Bhāratī as the first of the Three Goddesses; two families (Gṛtsamada and Kaśyapa), which originated in the later Middle period, shift the position of Bhāratī back in the enumeration of the Goddesses; and three families (Atri, Kaṇva and Parucchepa), which originated in the Late period, do not mention Bhāratī by name at all.]

The neutral Book 2 seems to represent a peaceful interregnum period between the Books of the Bharata period, and the Books of the general Pūru period.

All these factors confirm that Books 6, 3 and 7, *in that order*, are the Early Books, and that Books 4 and 2, *in that order*, are the Middle Books. Understanding this helps us in understanding the chronological development of Vedic history and culture. Any nitpicking objections (about the Anukramaṇīs, etc) can only be diversions, and it must again be noted that they will only result in obfuscating a more detailed understanding of the chronological development of Vedic history and culture. But *not* in obfuscating the two vital conclusions that we have noted at the conclusion of section B above, which are based on a chronological division into "earlier" and "later" Books officially recognized by Western scholars.

4D
APPENDIX 2: "LATE" HYMNS

The subject of the internal chronology of the Rigveda cannot be completed without a close examination of what constitutes "late" hymns within any Book.

As we saw above, Witzel makes the sour claim that "**the composition of the RV occurred in complex layers — not in the tidy sequential patterns imagined by Talageri**" (WITZEL 2001b:§1). Unfortunately for Witzel, the pattern of occurrence of different categories of words (Avestan name-elements, geographically distinctive words, technological terms, etc.) indeed shows that the composition of the Rigveda *did* take place in **"tidy sequential patterns"**, rather than as the **"complex"**, hopelessly jumbled, mess that the Rigveda seems to represent in Witzel's own confused analyses in different papers and articles, and that Witzel (particularly when choosing to question the logical analyses of his opponents) seems to *demand* from the data almost as his *birthright*.

Thus, in a nutshell, the Books of the Rigveda lie in "tidy sequential patterns" in the following order: *Early* 6, 3, 7, *Middle* 4, 2, *Late* 5, 8, 9, 10 (with 1, though ultimately belonging to the *Late* level, consisting of a collection of mini-books ranging, in their beginnings, across the periods of 4, 2, 5, 8, 9, 10).

But there is now the question of *Late hymns* within each Book: hymns that seem to be *later* than the general period of the particular Book to which they belong. What exactly is the position of these Late hymns? There are also verses within various hymns, which seem to be *later* than the rest of the verses in the hymn. What exactly is the position of these Late verses? And, more importantly, how do these Late hymns and verses affect our historical analysis of the Rigveda?

The fact, as we shall see, is that *they do not affect our historic analysis of the Rigveda at all*, for the simple reason that almost all the late elements have to do with rituals and religious matters, or else with purely linguistic redactions of old hymns with no historic implications. The *only* historically significant personalities whose names were interpolated into older hymns are Purukutsa and Trasadasyu (see TALAGERI 2000:66-72), but, as we saw, *these* also did not affect the analysis of the relative chronology and geography of the Rigveda that we undertook in the earlier chapters.

Nevertheless, for the record, let us see what information we get on the relative chronology of hymns within the different Books, on the basis of four criteria on a descending level of solidity: Facts, Testimony, Deductions, and Speculations:

4D-1. Facts

The *first* factual situation is that we have the ten books of the extant Rigveda, which, as we saw, can be chronologically arranged as follows: 6, 3, 7, 4, 2, 5, 8, 9, 10 (1 spread across the periods of 4, 2, 5, 8, 9, 10). The western scholars, as we have seen, are officially agreed on the fact that 6, 3, 7, 4, 2 are *earlier* than 5, 1, 8, 9, 10 (though not agreed on the above internal chronological order within the first group). The number of hymns and verses in the ten books are as follows:

Book	Number of Hymns	Number of Verses
6	75	765
3	62	617
7	104	841
4	58	589
2	43	429
5	87	727
1	191	2006
8	103	1716
9	114	1108
10	191	1754
Total	1028	10552

The *second* factual situation is that the Rigvedic tradition itself contains awareness that eleven of the hymns included in Book 8 are later additions into the Book: these are hymns **VIII.**49-59 (80 verses), which are separately known as the Vālakhilya hymns. Some Western scholars (like Griffith) go so far as to place these hymns at the end of the Book, and to change the numbering of the following hymns in the Book from 60-103 to 49-92. But these hymns are additions made *within* the period of the ten books; and do not have any direct relevance to our historical analysis, since *both* Book VIII *as well as* the additions belong to the Late period. All the hymns are characterized by late words and grammatical features.

The *third* factual situation is that there seem to be some verses which were added to the Rigveda even after the whole text was given its final form: **VII.59**.12, as well as a few verses in Book 10 (**X.20**.1; **121**.10; **190**.1-3), *found in the extant Rigveda, but missing in Śākalya's padapātha.* Again, we are not concerned with the verses in Book 10; but **VII.59**.12 (which is characterized by late words, unknown to the rest of the Rigveda, like *tryambaka*) is in an Early Book. However, this does not affect our historical analysis of the Rigveda in any way, other than to necessitate a revision of the number of original verses in Book 7 from 841, above, to 840.

4D-2. Testimony

We actually have direct testimony in the Aitareya Brāhmaṇa VI.18, to the effect that six hymns in Book 3 are late compositions, which were added into the Book at a late date as a solution to a dispute between the Viśvāmitras and the Vāmadevas. These six hymns are **III**.30-31, 34, 36, 38, 48 (See TALAGERI 2000:73-74).

In my above book, I had erroneously given the hymn numbers as 21, 30, 34, 36, 38-39 (and consequently calculated the wrong number of verses), for which I faced sharp criticism from Witzel. However, while Witzel's criticism was perfectly *valid* so far as it concerns my gross carelessness in giving the wrong hymn numbers (and the consequent wrong calculations), it was *invalid* insofar as it affected the chronological point I was making about the late provenance of these six hymns. Witzel rejects the testimony of the Aitareya Brāhmaṇa, or what he claims is *my* interpretation of it, on the ground that these hymns are *not* listed in Oldenberg's list of late hymns, which violate the order of arrangement of the hymns in the Family Books.

However, Witzel's protests are totally untenable, since a) the account in the Aitareya Brāhmaṇa does not allow for any other logical interpretation, and b) the testimony of the Aitareya Brāhmaṇa provides the solution to the otherwise insoluble mystery as to why the six Family Books, 2-7, were arranged in that particular serial order (which is clearly not the same as their chronological order of composition, unlike the serial order of the non-family Books which coincides with their chronological order of composition). When the number of verses in these six hymns is deducted from the verse count of Book 3, we get the following original number of verses in the Family Books 2-7, in serial order: 429, 536, 589, 727, 765, 840 (omitting **VII.59**.12, above). The six Family Books were clearly arranged according to increasing number of verses.

Further, the testimony of the Aitareya Brāhmaṇa stands confirmed by our analysis of the relative chronology and geography of the Rigveda in the earlier chapters. As we saw, of the *only eight hymns* in the Early and Middle Books, which are associated with the late names and name-elements common to the Rigveda and the Avesta, *six* are late as per Oldenberg, and the *other two* are late as per the Aitareya Brāhmaṇa. And the *only* hymn (of these eight) which mentions a Western geographical word is a hymn which is late as per the Aitareya Brāhmaṇa.

4D-3. Deductions

Oldenberg, in his writings (notably his *Prolegomena*) has identified certain principles in the arrangement of most of the hymns in the Family Books 2-7: each Family Book begins with a group of hymns to Agni, followed by a group of hymns to Indra, followed by groups of hymns to various other deities, arranged according to decreasing number of hymns per deity; within each deity-group, the hymns are again arranged according to decreasing number of verses. Within this arrangement, hymns with the same number of verses are arranged according to meter, starting with *jagatī* and *triṣṭubh*, and followed by *anuṣṭubh* and *gāyatrī*.

That Oldenberg and his predecessors identified a very important set of principles in the arrangement of the Rigvedic hymns is beyond doubt. But what followed this identification is more important: Oldenberg identified hymns, in each Family Book, which seemed to violate these principles of arrangement by either being too short or too long, or having different deities or meters, and concluded that these "unordered" hymns were late hymns as compared to the other, "ordered", hymns in the Books. The list of "ordered" and "unordered" hymns in each Book is as follows:

"Ordered" Hymns	"Unordered" Hymns
II. 1-31, 33-40 (39 hymns).	**II**. 32, 41-43 (4 hymns).
III. 1-25, 30-50, 54-61 (54 hymns)	**III**. 26-29, 51-53, 62 (8 hymns)
IV. 1-14, 16-29, 33-36, 38-47, 49, 51-54 (47 hymns).	**IV**. 15, 30-32, 37, 48, 50, 55-58 (11 hymns).
V. 1-24, 29-39, 41-50, 52-60, 62-77, 79-81, 83-86 (77 hymns).	**V**.25-28, 40, 51, 61, 78, 82, 87 (10 hymns).
VI. 1-14, 17-43, 53-58, 62-73 (59 hymns).	**VI**. 15-16, 44-52, 59-61, 74-75 (16 hymns).
VII. 1-14, 18-30, 34-54, 56-58, 60-65, 67-73, 75-80, 82-93, 95, 97-100 (87 hymns).	**VII**. 15-17, 31-33, 55, 59, 66, 74, 81, 94, 96, 101-104 (17 hymns).

As we saw, there is logic behind the identification of the principles of arrangement of (the majority of) the hymns in the Family Books; and the consequent identification of two groups of hymns in each book. But there is absolutely *no* evidence that the hymns classified by Oldenberg as "unordered" are chronologically *later* than the hymns classified by him as hymns which are "ordered" according to the principles of arrangement of the hymns:

1. E.V.Arnold, for example, points out: "**Position in the collections is not a safe guide. Several hymns for which there is good evidence of late date** [...] **appear in their right place in the collections of books i-ix; others which are out of place** [...] **not only shew no other signs of lateness, but have many of the marks of early date**" (ARNOLD 1897: 211-213).

A linguistic study of the hymns shows that this is right: for example, in Book 6, hymn 45, with 33 verses, contains the archaic word *sīm* (found 50 times in the first nine Books of the Rigveda, but only once in the last Book 10, and not even once in the Atharvaveda); and does not contain a *single* word of late date. On the other hand, hymn 28, with only 8 verses, has no particular mark of early date, but abounds in late words like *khila*, *riś*, *bhakṣ*, *kṛś* and *taskara*. Yet, hymn 45 is included in Oldenberg's list of "unordered" hymns, and hymn 28 (counted by Arnold as one of only *four* "late hymns" in Book 6, along with hymns 47, 74 and 75) is included in Oldenberg's list of "ordered" hymns.

2. As we saw earlier, there is no doubt whatsoever that the six hymns (**III**.30-31, 34, 36, 38, 48), specified by the Aitareya Brāhmaṇa to be interpolations or later additions into Book 3, *are* indeed definitely late hymns in the book. And yet, *every single one of them* appears in its proper place in the Book, and consequently all of them are included in Oldenberg's list of "ordered" hymns. Obviously, therefore, Oldenberg's criterion is grossly inadequate in identifying late hymns in opposition to earlier ones.

3. Further, the identification of the six above hymns in Book 3 as late additions, as we saw, provides the solution to the mystery of the order of arrangement of the Family Books 2-7. They were originally arranged in order of *increasing number of verses*: 429, 536, 589, 727, 765, 840. However, if we go by

Oldenberg's list of "ordered" hymns, the following is the original number of hymns in Books 2-7, in serial order: 39, 54, 47, 77, 59, 87. And the following is the original number of verses, in serial order: 394, 509, 456, 627, 449, 641. As we can see, there is now no logical pattern at all in the order of arrangement of the Family Books: just the kind of "complex" mess so dear to Witzel's heart.

4. The two groups of hymns, in each Family Book, identified by Oldenberg, show *perfect conformity* with each other in their historical topics. Thus, for example, Book 6 deals with the period of Divodāsa, and he is mentioned in *six* hymns. Of these, *three* hymns, 26, 31 and 43, are included in Oldenberg's list of "ordered" hymns, and *three*, 16, 47, and 61, in his list of "unordered" hymns. Likewise, Books 3 and 7 deal with the period of Sudās. Of the *two* hymns in Book 3, which deal with Sudās' activities, *one*, hymn 33, is included in Oldenberg's "ordered" list, and *one*, hymn 53, in his "unordered" list. And in Book 7, of the *ten* hymns which refer to Sudās, *eight*, 18-20, 25, 53, 60, 64 and 83, are included in his "ordered" list, and *two*, 32 and 33, in his "unordered" list. Clearly, *both* the groups of hymns, within any particular Family Book, share historical concerns of the *same* period.

5. It may be argued that the above may simply be due to the fact that composers of the *same* family or clan, even in *different later* periods, continued to be concerned only with the historical events associated with their illustrious ancestors. However, the geographical references cannot be similarly explained away, since it is *extremely* presumptuous to assume that all later composers within any Book would restrict the geographical references in their own compositions to the geographical areas known to their ancestors and mentioned by these ancestors in earlier compositions in that Book — after all, the cornerstone of AIT dogma is that the Vedic poets were so geographically self-centred in their outlook that they had already forgotten, or discarded in their compositions, the alleged extra-Indian associations of their ancestors. So the following facts give the lie to the idea that Oldenberg's "ordered" hymns and "unordered" hymns belong to different periods:

In the Early and Middle Family Books (Book 5 is, in any case, a *Late* Book as a whole), references to *Western* geographical words are *missing* in *both*: the "ordered" hymns as well as the "unordered" hymns in Books 6, 7, and 2. In Book 4 (with its Western thrust), these references are *found* in *both*: the "ordered" hymns, 43 and 54, *as well as* the "unordered" hymns 30 and 55. (In Book 3, the *single* hymn with a Western geographical reference, hymn 38, is included in Oldenberg's "ordered" list, but is a *late* addition according to the Aitareya Brāhmaṇa.).

At the same time, the references to *Eastern* geographical words are *found* in *both* the "ordered" hymns *as well as* the "unordered" hymns:

"Ordered" Hymns.	"Unordered" Hymns.
II. 1, 3, 10, 30, 34, 36. **III**. 4-5, 23, 45-46, 54, 58. **IV**. 4, 16, 18, 21. **VI**. 1, 4, 8, 17, 20, 27. **VII**. 2, 9, 18, 35-36, 39-40, . 44, 69, 95	**II**. 32, 41. **III**. 26, 29, 53. **IV**. 58. **VI**. 45, 49, 50, 52, 61. **VII**. 96.

The long and short of it is that *both* the "ordered" *as well as* the "unordered" hymns in any Family Book share the *same* geographical frontiers.

6. The common provenance, of Oldenberg's "ordered" and "unordered" hymns within any Family Book, is *conclusively* proved by the distribution of the late Avestan name-elements.

These elements (very common in the *post*-Rigvedic Vedic literature, and *later* in the Epics and Purāṇas) are found in profusion in the *Late* Books: in 47 out of 87 hymns in Book 5; in 78 out of 191 hymns in Book 1; in 69 out of 103 hymns in Book 8; in 69 out of 113 hymns in Book 9; and in 123 out of 191 hymns in Book 10. But in the *Early* and *Middle* Books (which, as we saw, are "earlier" than the Late Books even according to the official Western classification) they are found in only 8 out of 342 hymns, *all* 8 of which are classified as Late. This *conclusively* proves the validity of the basic chronological distinction between the earlier (i.e. the Early and Middle) Books on the one hand and the Late Books on the other.

But, it *does not prove*, and in fact it conclusively *disproves*, the validity of the *alleged* chronological distinction between Oldenberg's "ordered" hymns and his "unordered" hymns *within* the Family Books: of the 8 late hymns in the earlier Books, where these elements are found, six hymns, **VI**.15,16,47, **III**.53, **VII**.33, and **IV**.30, are "unordered" hymns according to Oldenberg, and two hymns, **III**.36 and 38, are "ordered" hymns according to Oldenberg (but late according to the Aitareya Brāhmaṇa). In keeping with this, in Book 5, the only Late Family Book, 42 out of 77 "ordered" hymns, and 5 out of 10 "unordered" hymns have these elements. The distribution, or absence, of these elements, in *both* the groups ("ordered" and "unordered"), is roughly proportionate.

To sum up, the Original Rigveda, consisting of the six Family Books, 2-7, when it was compiled into one collection, and before *even the composition* of the overwhelming bulk of the hymns in the non-family Books, *already* included both the groups: Oldenberg's "ordered" hymns (except for the six hymns **III**.30-31, 34, 36, 38, 48) as well as Oldenberg's "unordered" hymns (except **VII**.59.12). And the six Books consisted *more or less* of the following number of verses, in serial order: 429, 536, 589, 727, 765, 840.

Furthermore, as the evidence of the Avestan name-elements (as well as the evidence of the late pankti meter, which is found in 19 "ordered" hymns in Book 5) shows, the five earlier Family Books (6, 3, 7, 4, 2), *both the "ordered" as well as the "unordered" hymns within them*, were *already* composed and compiled, before *even the composition of even the "ordered" hymns* in Book 5. At the same time, the compilation of the six Family Books into *one* single collection took place in the Late Period, *after* the composition and compilation of Book 5, but *before* the composition and compilation of the overwhelming bulk of the other Books (1, 8-10).

Therefore, while the validity and vital importance of Oldenberg's classification of the hymns in the Family books into two groups cannot be denied, the interpretation of this division as representing chronologically "early" and "late" hymns is clearly untenable: they should, rather, simply be interpreted as "ordered" and "unordered" hymns.

But then, what is the logic behind the fact that the hymns in each Family Book *can*, indeed, be classified into "ordered" and "unordered" hymns? What could be the genesis of this division?

The answer could lie in the fact that the basic purpose of the Rigveda was liturgical. The compulsions of the ritual needs of the times must have led to the classification of the hymns in the corpus of each Family Book collection into two groups: *one* group of hymns regularly used in the liturgical procedures devised and employed at the time, which were regularly arranged according to certain principles of arrangement based on deity, number of hymns and verses, meter, etc.; and a *second* group, consisting of all the other hymns in the Family collections, which were placed separately at the end of each collection.

But, *later*, when the canonical text was expanded with the addition of new Books, by which time the liturgical priorities had probably changed, the two groups of hymns were combined by placing the hymns of the unordered group *within* the hymns of the ordered group. Why the compilers placed them in positions where they stood out as violating the principles of arrangement of the ordered hymns is anybody's guess, but the facts show that they *were* placed in such positions, perhaps deliberately; and Oldenberg's guess, as to the exact logic behind their doing so, would be as good as ours.

Our guess (based on the fact that, in every Family Book, the "unordered" hymns *always* include one or more of the serially *last* hymns in the Book) is as follows: the present group of "unordered" hymns include *early* or *original* hymns (which existed in the original collection of each Family Book) as well as certain *late* hymns which were added to the family Books at the last moment (i.e. at the time of adding the non-family Books to the corpus). This would therefore give us *four sets of hymns* in the present version of each Book: original "ordered hymns", original "unordered" hymns, late "ordered" hymns, and late "unordered" hymns:

Stage 1: The original hymns in each book (i.e. the original "ordered" hymns + the original "unordered" hymns), when each Book was composed and compiled in its time (the Bharadvāja, Viśvāmitra and Vasiṣṭha books in the Early Period, the Vāmadeva and Gṛtsamada Books in the Middle Period, and the Atri Book in the Late Period) were as follows (the numbers of the Books and hymns given below, obviously, are their *present* Book and hymn numbers):

II. 1-31, 33-40 + 32 (40 hymns, 402 verses).

III. 1-25, 32-33, 35, 37, 39-47, 49-50, 54-61 + 26-29, 51-53 (55 hymns, 518 verses).

IV. 1-14, 16-29, 33-36, 38-47, 49, 51-54 + 15, 30-32, 37, 48, 50 (54 hymns, 553 verses).

V. 1-24, 29-39, 41-50, 52-60, 62-77, 79-81, 83-86 + 25-28, 40, 51, 61, 78, 82 (86 hymns, 718 verses).

VI. 1-14, 17-43, 53-58, 62-73 + 15-16, 44-52, 59-61 (73 hymns, 742 verses).

VII. 1-14, 18-30, 34-54, 56-58, 60-65, 67-73, 75-80, 82-93, 95, 97-100 + 15-17, 31-33, 55, 59, 66, 74, 81, 94, 96 (100 hymns, 796 verses).

In the first stage of formation of the Rigveda, these six Books were arranged in this above order, according to increasing number of verses, and combined into one text.

Stage 2a: At the time of expansion of the text, with the addition of Books 1 and 8, a few new hymns, composed in the Late Period, were added to, *and placed at the end of,* each Family Book. They were the following hymns, which we may call the late "unordered" hymns:

II. 41-43 (27 verses. Now totally: 43 hymns, 429 verses).

III. 62 (18 verses. Now totally: 56 hymns, 536 verses).

IV. 55-58 (36 verses. Now totally: 58 hymns, 589 verses).

V. 87 (9 verses. Now totally: 87 hymns, 727 verses).

VI. 74-75 (23 verses. Now totally: 75 hymns, 765 verses).

VII. 101-104 (44 verses. Now totally: 104 hymns, 840 verses).

To *distinguish* the other, original, "unordered" hymns (which, as we saw, were also originally just placed *after* the "ordered" set at the end of each Family Book) from these new or late "unordered" hymns, the original "unordered" hymns were *inserted in between* the "ordered" hymns, but *in positions where they stood out as violating the principles of arrangement* of the "ordered" hymns, while the new late "unordered" hymns alone were now placed *at the end* of each Family Book. Thus, all three sets were now distinguishable. [This principle is in evidence in another case: when the non-family Books were added, one by one, to the corpus of the six Family Books, they were generally simply placed after the Family Books: first the Kaṇva Book (Book 8), then the Soma Book (Book 9), and, finally, Book 10. But Book 1, although added perhaps at the same time as Book 8, was placed *before* the Family Books, to distinguish it from the other three Books which were Late *in toto*, since Book 1 contained many mini-books which, either as a whole or in their beginnings, were actually *earlier* than some of the Family Books (like Book 5, and some even than Books 4 and 2) (see TALAGERI 2000:39-45) Thus, here also, the three sets of Books were distinguishable: 1, 2-7, 8-10].

Stage 2b: But, at the same time, now, the six *new* hymns which had been composed by the Viśvāmitras, as compensation for the original ones appropriated by the Vāmadevas (see TALAGERI 2000:73-74, and the Aitareya Brāhmaṇa VI.18), were also added to the corpus of the Viśvāmitra Book: hymns **III**.30-31, 34, 36, 38, 48. But they were deliberately inserted within the set of ordered hymns *in their correct positions* according to the principles of arrangement of the "ordered" hymns, since the purpose was that they were *not to be distinguished* from the original "ordered" hymns. These hymns may be called the late "ordered" hymns.

Thus we now finally have the Six Family Books, arranged and numbered as at present (with Book 3 now having 62 hymns and 617 verses), except for one verse **VII.59**.12, added after Śākalya's padapātha.

And now for the other side of the story: the distribution of the historical topics, the geographical references, and the late Avestan name-elements, in the Family Books, shows that the "ordered" hymns and the "unordered" hymns *within* any one Book belong to the *same early* (or, in the case of Book 5, *same late*) chronological period. Thus, while Book 2, for example, does *not* have any late Avestan name element in a *single* hymn, "ordered" *or* "unordered", Book 5 has these elements in 42 out of 77 "ordered" hymns, and 5 out of 10 "unordered" hymns. Nevertheless, it cannot be ignored that when these elements *do* appear in the rare hymn in the Early and Middle Books, Oldenberg's classification has a role to play in the matter: while *two* of the hymns which have these elements are testified as *Late* hymns by the Aitareya Brāhmaṇa, the *other six* are testified as "late" by Oldenberg on the basis of the fact that they are "unordered" hymns. Clearly, when a rare *late* word appears just once or so in the earlier Books, it is *generally more likely* to appear in an early "unordered" hymn than in an early "ordered" hymn. What is the explanation for this?

The answer is obvious: the "ordered" hymns were, *at least at the time of original division of the hymns into these two groups*, more sacred and important in the liturgical procedures of the time, and hence were preserved more faithfully and carefully; while the "unordered" hymns were more of the popular type, and hence may have been *constantly linguistically updated* in recitation and practice, until, at some point of time in the Late Period (*first*, after the composition and compilation of Book 5, when the six Family Books were combined into one text, and *finally*, later on, after the composition and compilation of Book 8 and the inclusion of Books 1 and 8 into the corpus of the Rigveda), they were given their final canonical form. Therefore, the "unordered" hymns are *not* "late" hymns, but they are *more generally likely*, than the "ordered" hymns, to be "late redacted" hymns.

Of the six "unordered" hymns, which have late Avestan name-elements, two, **III**.53 **and VII**.33, pertain to the activities of Sudās (like the "ordered" hymns **III**.33**, and VII**.18, 83), and hence it is clear that they are early hymns pertaining to the Early Period, probably much recited as ballads before an audience, and hence constantly linguistically updated. In linguistically updating such hymns, the redactors obviously did not care, *or perhaps were not even aware of the fact*, that some of the words and grammatical forms used by them, or some of the new meters to which they redacted their hymns, were new ones which probably did not exist at the time of composition of the original hymns. Thus, while these two hymns *do not* interpose later historical persons (with *late* Avestan type elements in their names) or events, or later geographical locations, or later technological innovations (spoked wheels, domesticated camels, etc.), into their narratives about the exploits of Sudās, they *do* use new words: *prāṇa* (breath: **III.53**.21), *kumbha* (pitcher: **VII.33**.13), and *Yama* (originally a proto-Iranian king, but already, in the Late Books of the Rigveda, the God of the Realm of the Dead: **VII.33**.9,12) in their recitals. More such instances of isolated late words in the "unordered" hymns will be noticed if we examine further aspects of the late vocabulary of the Rigveda.

But, again, while this is the *general trend*, exceptions (i.e. unordered hymns which do not use new words, as opposed to ordered hymns which *do*) also occur: we have already pointed out, earlier, the example of hymn **VI**.45, which, within its 33 verses, does not contain a *single* late word, but *does* contain archaic words like *sīm*, and yet it is an "unordered" hymn; while hymn **VI**.28, within only 8 verses, contains many late words (and is consequently considered by Arnold as one of the *only four* late hymns in Book 6), but is included in the "ordered" list. This may be because *all* the hymns in the "ordered" list may not have been *equally* important in the liturgical procedures, or some may not have continued to *remain* important throughout the time interval, from the point of time when they were included in the "ordered" group in the Early Period to the point of time when they were finally frozen into a fixed form in the Late Period, and may consequently have continued to sporadically evolve linguistically in this interval. In any case, this is the only explanation for the late linguistic or metrical elements that occasionally crop up in otherwise undoubtedly early "ordered" hymns. Meanwhile, some hymns in the "unordered" group, from *not* being used in popular recitation, may *not* have linguistically evolved and may have remained frozen in form from the beginning.

4D-4. Speculations

Thus far, we examined the question of "late" hymns and verses, in the Family Books, *on the basis of clues in the basic data: first,* the factual position of the hymns and verses in the extant Rigveda and in the *padapāṭha*; *second*, the testimony of the Aitareya Brāhmaṇa; and *third*, the distribution of the hymns in three groups: the early "ordered" hymns, the early "unordered" hymns *inserted* into the "ordered" group, and the late "unordered" hymns placed *after* the "ordered" group at the end of each Book.

But, would we have been able to know that verse **VII.59**.12 was perhaps the absolutely last verse composed in the corpus of the Family Books, if the padapāṭha had not made this clear? Would we have guessed that the six hymns, **III**.30-31, 34, 36, 38, 48, were late additions to Book 3, skillfully inserted into their correct positions in the Book, if the Aitareya Brāhmaṇa had not testified to this fact? Would we have known about the distinction between the three groups of hymns, if the principles of arrangement had been indiscernible? We would certainly have continued to remain at a loss to explain why the six Family Books were arranged in their existing serial order; or to account for the only two "ordered" hymns (**III**.36, 38) associated with late Avestan name-elements in the Early Books.

So we must assume that there may be other minor cases of hymns or verses, which are *actually late* in the Family Books, but which have *left us no clues* about their late provenance. These hymns and verses must be very few in number: certainly, as we saw, they did not create any problems in our analysis of the relative chronology and geography of the Rigveda. But, they can always crop up in our analysis, and in these cases, rational speculation, based on logical premises and our knowledge of the general trends of the evidence (to which these rare cases will appear to pose exceptions), can be our only guide.

The case of the references to Purukutsa in **VI.20**.10, and his son Trasadasyu in **VII.19**.3; **IV.38**.1; **42**.8-9, is one such case. These references did not disturb our analyses of the relative chronology or the geography of the Rigveda, but they pose one (and the major one) such anomaly in the data in the Rigveda. These kings definitely belong to the Late Period, since they are contemporary to Books 5 and 8, where they figure as patrons of the ṛṣis in **V.27**.3; **33**.8; **VIII.19**.32,36; hence references to them in the Early and Middle Books are definitely out of place. The only logical explanation is that these must be interpolations; and *extraordinary* interpolations at that, since we see that the deliberate interpolated introduction of the names of later historical persons, places or events, into earlier hymns, is *never* a part of the redaction in *any* other case in the Rigveda.

The nature of the references to Trasadasyu, in particular, also testifies to their extraordinariness: in **VII.19**.3, the praise of Trasadasyu is almost on parallel lines to the praise of Sudās (unquestionably *the* hero of Book VII) in the same verse; in **IV**.38, one of three hymns to Dadhikrās, a deified form of the war-horse, the first verse praises Trasadasyu in special terms as the god-sent saviour of the Pūrus (the Vedic Aryans); and in **IV.42**.8-9, Trasadasyu is twice referred to as *ardhadeva*, "demi-god", a term used nowhere else in the Rigveda, and the circumstance of his birth is glorified, again in a manner unparalleled in the Rigveda (but which we see in later times in respect of great or religiously important persons all over the world). These references stand out in sharp contrast to the references in the Late Books to these two kings, where they are normal gift-giving patrons of the composers (in **V.27**.3; **33**.8; **VIII.19**.32,36) or normally mentioned like various other kings and heroes (in **I.112**.14; **VIII.36**.7; **37**.7; **49**.10; **X.33**.4; **150**.5).

As I have pointed out in detail in my earlier book (TALAGERI 2000:66-72), the references to Purukutsa and Trasadasyu in the four above hymns, in the Early and Middle Books, are *extraordinary* interpolations, by composers of the *Late* Period belonging to the two families most closely, and continuously, associated with the Bharatas (the branch of the Pūrus to whom the Early and Middle Periods and Books of the Rigveda belong), i.e. by the Angirases and the Vasiṣṭhas, into their early Family Books. These interpolations were made in order to express their special gratitude for some extraordinary aid rendered to the Pūrus by these two Tṛkṣi kings (extraordinary aid to the Pūrus *categorically referred to* in **IV.38**.1, and also in **VII.19**.3).

Therefore, it is clear that these references are *late interpolations*; and the *only* reason the fact does not stand out at once is because these extraordinary interpolations are in "ordered" hymns.

But a closer examination gives us other clues:

a) In respect of **IV.42**.8-9, Griffith, in his footnote to the translation of the hymn, informs us that "**Grassmann banishes stanzas 8, 9 and 10 to the appendix as late additions to the hymn**".

b) **VI.20**.10 is the *only* verse, in the Early and Middle Books, singled out by Prof. Hopkins (HOPKINS 1896a:72-73), in the "Final Note" to his path-breaking article "**Prāgāthikāni-I**", as a verse which seems to have "**interesting marks of lateness**", in spite of the fact that hymn **VI**.20 is *not* a late hymn as per the principles of arrangement of the hymns. He notes not only that Purukutsa, named in the verse, "**is known only to** [Book] **i and to the late *dānastuti* of iv.42**"; but also that the verse contains the late phrase *purah śāradīh*, also "**found elsewhere only in** [Book] **i**"; and, most significantly, the phrase *pra stu-*, which is "**a very important word in the liturgical sense; and it is one of the commonest of words in late literature**". It is found commonly in the Brāhmaṇas and the Upaniṣads, five times in the Atharvaveda, and, interestingly, commonly in the Avesta as *fra stu-, but only this once* in the Early and Middle Books; otherwise *only* in the Late Books as follows:

   V. **33**.6.
   I. **153**.2; **154**.2; **159**.1.
   VIII. **16**.1; **22**.6; **35**.11; **81**.5.
   X. **67**.3; **105**.6.

c) **VII**.19 is not specifically noted by any scholar as a late or interpolated hymn in the Book, or verse 3 as a late or interpolated verse in the hymn. But, while the core of

Book 7 pertains to the period of Sudās, this particular hymn is noted by Griffith, in his footnotes to the translation of the hymn, as one composed long after the period of Sudās: "**who must have lived long before the composition of this hymn, as the favour bestowed on him is referred to as old in stanza 6**".

d) Finally, the fourth hymn, **IV**.38, is also not noted by any scholar, so far as I know, as late or interpolated; but verse **IV**.**38**.1 is definitely *totally out of place* in the hymn. Hymns 38-40 are hymns in praise of Dadhikrās, the deified war-horse, and this one verse, out of the 21 verses in the three hymns, is the only verse which differs from the other 20 verses in deifying Trasadasyu (who is not mentioned at all in the other verses) rather than Dadhikrās. This, added to the force of the rest of the evidence, and also the fact that Book 4 is unique in seeming to have interpolated verses at the *beginning* of hymns [the very first three verses in the Book, **IV**.**1**.1-3, may well be interpolated verses, since they are composed in complex mixed meters, which are found in 126 verses in the Rigveda, of which 112 verses are in the Late Books, and 6 verses in "unordered" hymns in Book 6. Only 8 verses in the Middle Books are ambiguous: **II**.**22**.1-4 (the entire hymn) and **IV**.**1**.1-3; **10**.5, which must also, therefore, logically, all be interpolated verses], would suggest that **IV**.**38**.1 is an interpolated verse.

In this context, it is also possible that **IV**.**30**.18, *the only verse in the whole of the Early and Middle Books to name a person with late Avestan name-elements in his name*, is also an interpolated verse. The hymn itself, in any case, is an "unordered" hymn.

Chapter 5

The Relative Chronology of the Rigveda – II
The Mitanni Evidence

The evidence of the personal names in the Avesta, as we saw earlier, shows that the Early and Middle Books of the Rigveda are *earlier* than the Avesta, and the Late Books of the Rigveda are *contemporaneous* with the Avesta; and that the common "Indo-Iranian" culture visible in the two texts is a product of the Late Rigvedic Period, when *the proto-Iranians were still living to the northwest of India and had not expanded far beyond its borders.*

An examination of the evidence of the Mitanni names, as we shall see in this chapter, shows the same situation regarding the Mitanni IA (Indo-Aryan) language of West Asia: *it shows that the Mitanni IAs were emigrants from India in the Late Rigvedic Period.*

In this chapter we will examine only the aspect of relative chronology of the Mitanni IA evidence vis-à-vis the Rigvedic evidence: i.e. whether the Mitanni IA data represents a pre-Rigvedic period as alleged by Michael Witzel (and as generally assumed in academic circles), or whether it represents a Late Rigvedic period.

The evidence has to be examined from two angles:

5A. Witzel's Fraudulent Arguments.
5B. The Actual Evidence.
5C. Footnote: Edward W. Hopkins.

5A
WITZEL'S FRAUDULENT ARGUMENTS

In a recent paper (WITZEL 2005), Witzel argues, in some

detail, a point frequently made by him earlier: that the Indo-Aryan elements in Mitanni indicate a *pre*-Rigvedic language, with linguistic features which necessarily rule out any idea that the Mitanni could have emigrated from India — that the Mitanni were in fact an offshoot of the pre-Rigvedic Indo-Aryans as yet on their way *towards* India.

Witzel notes that the Mitanni IA language "**is attested by a number of OIA loan words (Mayrhofer 1979, EWA III 569 sqq.) in the non-IE Hurrite language of the Mit. realm of northern Iraq/Syria (c.1460-1330 BCE). The loans cover the semantic fields of horses, their colors, horse racing, and chariots, some important 'Vedic' gods, and a large array of personal names adopted by the ruling class**" (WITZEL 2005:361).

[About the Kassites: "**The Kassite conquerors of Mesopotamia (c.1677-1152 BCE) have a sun god *Šuriiaš*, perhaps also the *Marut* and maybe even *Bhaga* (*Bugaš*?), as well as the personal name *Abirat(t)aš (Abhiratha)*; but otherwise the vocabulary of their largely unknown language hardly shows any IA influence, not even in their many designations for the horse and horse names (Balkan 1954)**" (WITZEL 2005:362).]

After this brief and *reasonably accurate* summary of the Mitanni (and Kassite) evidence, Witzel gives his arguments, about the pre-Rigvedic character of Mitanni, as follows:

1. "**absence of typical Indian features and grammatical innovations in Mit. IA** [...] **the Mitanni documents do not show any typical *South Asian* influence** [...] **absence of retroflexion**" (WITZEL 2005:361).

"**the vocabulary does not yet show signs of typical *South Asian* influence: for example, there is no retroflexation in *mani-nnu*** [...] **But retroflexation is precisely what is found once OIA enters South Asia: RV *maṇi* 'jewel'**" (WITZEL 2005:361-2).

"**without any of the local South Asian innovations (no retroflex in *mani-*, etc) that are already found in the RV**" (WITZEL 2005:363).

2. "**Mit. IA also does not have typical South Asian loan words such as *āṇi* 'lynch pin'**" (WITZEL 2005:362).

"***without* any particularly local Indian words (lion, tiger, peacock, lotus, lynch pin *āṇi*)**" (WITZEL 2005:363).

3. "**These remnants of IA in Mit, belong to an early, pre-Ṛgvedic stage of IA, seen in the preservation of IIr *–zdh-* > Ved. *–edh-*, IIr. *ai* > Ved. *e*"** (WITZEL 2005:361).

"**the Ṛgvedic dialect features (*ai* > *e*, *zdh* > *edh*) *not yet* in place**" (WITZEL 2005:363).

"***sazd-* > *sed*** [...] **post-Mitanni, which keeps the sequence *azd*. In other words, Ṛgvedic is younger than the Mitanni words preserved at *c.*1450-1350 BCE**" (WITZEL 2005:364).

"**note *–zd-* in *Priyamazdha* (*Bi-ir-ia-ma-as-da*)** [...] **retention of IIr *ai* > Ved. *e* (*aika: eka in aikavartana*)** [...] **retention of *j'h* > Ved. *h* in *vasana(s)saya* of 'the race track' = [*vazhanasya*] cf. Ved. *vahana-***" (WITZEL 2005:389, note 112).

This — three basic points, repeated again and again — constitutes the sum total of Witzel's arguments in support of his claim that the Mitanni IA language is pre-Rigvedic. And *all three points* are misleading or fraudulent:

1. The argument about "retroflexation" is clearly fraudulent, since it is clearly impossible to know whether the Mitanni IA language had cerebral (retroflex) sounds or not. But, in either case, whether they had them or not, it constitutes no objection to their emigration from Rigvedic India:

Witzel himself admits, in the opposite direction, that languages moving *into* India *acquire* retroflex sounds: "**retroflexion affects all those moving into the East Iranian borderland, the Indus plain and the subcontinent**" (WITZEL 2005:364). [Contrarily, he writes: "**Interestingly, the c.1000-year-old Indian Parsi pronunciation and recitation in Zoroastrian ritual of Avest., while clearly Indianizing as in *xšaθra* > [*kṣatra*], still has not developed retroflexes**" (WITZEL 2005:390, note 130). This is clearly an attempt to obfuscate the issues: obviously, sounds like *xš* and *θ* were not found in Indian languages, and therefore they were simply converted *in pronunciation* into their equivalent Indian sounds *kṣ* and *th* in the process of "Indianization". However, both dental and retroflex sounds were, and are, found in Indian languages, so there is no reason why "Indianization" should have resulted in the conversion of Avestan dentals into retroflexes, or in the splitting of the existing Avestan dentals, *recorded in writing*, into dentals and retroflexes. Incidentally, what Witzel, in his ivory tower armchair, "does not know" is that the Parsi dialect of Gujarati is actually more cerebralized than the normal Gujarati dialects, and Parsis tend to pronounce many words (which have no retroflexes) with retroflexion (a trait they share with the dialect of the Shia Muslim Dawoodi Bohra community)].

Likewise, languages moving *out* of India tend to *lose* retroflex sounds: The Romany or Gypsies emigrated from *deeper* within India at a *later* point of time when retroflex sounds were even *more* intrinsic a part of the Indo-Aryan phonetic system, yet they did not retain the retroflex sounds. Observe also the speech of many post-second generation NRIs when they speak their ancestral Indo-Aryan languages.

But we need not necessarily assume that the Mitanni IA language had no retroflex sounds in order to refute Witzel's argument. In fact, it is perfectly likely, and very logical, that they did have those sounds, but that those sounds are not recorded in the written form:

It must be remembered — a fact that Witzel himself points out above, but ignores in the course of his arguments — that *there is no such thing as a recorded Mitanni IA language:* we have only a few handfuls of words (and many more personal names in dynastic lists and historical records) recorded as **"loan-words"** in the **"non-IE Hurrite language"** of **"c.1460-1330 BCE"**.

Now, even Witzel will agree that there was no written alphabet — much less an alphabet with distinct representation of dental and retroflex sounds — among the IAs (in India, or wherever the IAs were located at that point of time according to him) at the time the Mitanni IAs separated from the other IAs, which was long before they appeared in West Asia and established their kingdom in 1460 BCE. And *even modern Indians*, who speak languages loaded with words having retroflex sounds phonemically distinct from dental sounds, and who use alphabets which have distinct letters for dental sounds and retroflex sounds, *never bother* (except, *but not always*, in some very particular categories of academic scholarly works) to distinguish between dental and retroflex sounds while writing Indian language words in the Roman alphabet.

So is there any logic and common sense in the argument that the "non-IE Hurrite" language speakers using a *few handfuls* of *loanwords*, from a language *then probably already a dead language*, would have *invented special letters* in their writing system, to represent strange retroflex sounds *occurring only in one or two of those loanwords*, if the original Mitanni IA language had those sounds? What does one conclude about the intellectual level of a "scholar par excellence" who repeatedly cites the non-representation of those sounds in the record as clinching evidence that the original Mitanni IA language did not possess those sounds?

Note, moreover, how Witzel denies the more logical contention that the Mitanni IA language already showed a few signs of "Prakritization" or "Middle-IA"ization in the forms of a few words like *satta* ("seven", for *sapta*) (a circumstance which need not necessarily show that it was chronologically close to the Prakrit period, as argued by some OIT writers — the RV language itself also contains a few "Prakritizations", and the emigrating Mitanni could have developed a few others around the same time during their migrations):

Witzel argues that claims about "Prakritization" are "**misguided as this form is due to the peculiarities of the cuneiform writing system**" (WITZEL 2005:362) (although, a few lines later, he admits that "**sapta could easily be written in**

cuneiform"), and he even makes the *incredible* claim (also made by Hock in an earlier article) that the word *sapta* "**has been influenced by Hurrite *šinti* 'seven'**" (WITZEL 2005:362), to produce the *exact* Prakritic form *satta*, and repeats and elaborates this claim in his note (WITZEL 2005:389, note 121). But it does not seem to strike him that the non-representation of retroflex sounds in the Hurrite texts could *much more* logically "**be due to the exigencies of cuneiform writing and Hurrite pronunciation in the Mit. Realm**" (WITZEL 2005:362).

Significantly, the *very word* cited by Witzel in his arguments about "retroflexation", the word *maṇi* "jewel", proves the Late Rigvedic provenance of the Mitanni IA language (see later).

2. Witzel's second argument, about the absence of "typical South Asian loan words" and "local Indian words" in the Mitanni IA language is in the same fraudulent vein. The only Mitanni IA words in the record are the names of a handful of Vedic Gods, some numerals, some words connected with horses (their colours, chariots, racing, etc), a handful of other words (eg. *mani*), and, as Witzel aptly puts it, "**a large array of personal names adopted by the ruling class**". Beyond this *very* limited wordlist, nothing is known about the Mitanni language *at all*. The limited *available* Mitanni IA wordlist can certainly be analysed, but how on earth can anyone presume to make categorical declarations about which words were *absent* in the Mitanni IA language? Is Witzel in possession of rare manuscripts or documents unseen by, and unknown to, other mortal men: as, for example, a complete dictionary of the Mitanni IA language — a dictionary, moreover, *so* complete that a word missing in that dictionary is automatically a word absent in the Mitanni IA language?

3. Witzel's third argument is that the Mitanni words seem to preserve certain sounds which had been transformed into other sounds already in the RV language: the RV has *edh*, *e* and *h* where the reconstructed pre-RV forms (also in Iranian)

were *azd*, *ai* and *jh* respectively, while the Mitanni IA words seem to preserve the original sounds.

This argument is not necessarily fraudulent in its essence, but it is nevertheless as baseless and misleading as the others. Obviously, the Mitanni IA *words* (recorded in *non-IE* language West Asian documents in the 15th century BCE) were *remnants* and *residual elements* from a *much older* living language spoken a few centuries *earlier* (see the chapter on the Absolute Chronology of the Rigveda), whose speakers must have emigrated from India *even earlier*, and they have preserved a phonetic stage current in India in the early second millennium BCE, *or earlier*; while the Rigvedic hymns, although composed *much earlier*, were repeatedly *phonetically redacted* till they attained their final phonetic form in 1400 BCE (and, if Witzel is to be believed, 1200 BCE, and even 500 BCE.), and have therefore preserved a *later* evolved *phonetic form*.

And *my* word need not be taken on this point; see what some western scholars themselves have to say:

According to P. Thieme: "**The fact that proto-Aryan *ai* and *au* are replaced in Indo-Aryan by *e* and *o*, while in Iranian they are preserved as *ai* and *au* and that *ai* and *au* regularly appear on the Anatolian documents (eg. Kikkuli's *aika*), is unfortunately inconclusive. It is quite possible that at the time of our oldest records (the hymns of the Rigveda) the actual pronunciation of the sounds developed for *ai* and *au* spoken and written by the tradition as *e* and *o*, was still *ai* and *au*. The *e* and *o* can be a secondarily introduced change under the influence of the spoken language or the scholastic recitation**" (THIEME 1960:301-2).

According to Madhav Deshpande: "**While The Mitanni documents, the Old Persian documents and the Aśokan edicts, coming from inscriptions as they do, are frozen in time, that is not the case with the Ṛgveda or the Avestan texts. These have been subject to a long oral tradition**

before they were codified, and the texts available to us represent a state of affairs at the end of this long oral transmission, rather than at the starting point of their creation" (DESHPANDE 1995:68). [Deshpande, in this article, even suggests that the cerebral/retroflex sounds in the Vedic language may not have existed at the time of actual composition of the hymns, and retroflexion must have been a later phonetic development which influenced the pronunciation of pre-retroflex hymns as well: "**the time gap between the composers of the hymns and the collectors, editors and collators was quite large. This gap must have been quite enough to lead to a kind of homogenisation.**" (DESHPANDE 1995:69)].

Witzel himself, in many of his articles, points out that, as in "**an ancient inscription**", the words of the RV "**have not changed since the composition of these hymns c.1500 BCE, as the RV has been transmitted almost without any change**", but in certain "**limited cases certain sounds — but not words, tonal accents, sentences — have changed**" (WITZEL 2000a:§1). Witzel, of course, usually refers to phonetic changes in "**minor details such as the pronunciation of svar instead of suvar, etc**", but (as in Deshpande, above) changes from *azd* to *edh* or *ai/au* to *e/o* could very logically have been among the changes affected in the phonetic redactions.

As Witzel makes very clear, the final redactions resulted in changes in the *sounds* in the original hymns, but *not* changes in the *words*. So any comparison of the Vedic and Mitanni IA data should be on the basis of *words* and not *sounds*.

5B
THE ACTUAL EVIDENCE

The wordlist, consisting of the names of Vedic Gods, numerals, and words connected with the horse, is not particularly useful in placing the Mitanni IAs in their exact place in the chronological scheme vis-à-vis the RV, since all the words are more or less Rigvedic. The only point that has been made by some scholars is that the four RV Gods named in the Mitanni treaty are found named together in the RV in that same order only in one verse, **X.125**.1. This verse happens to be found in a hymn in the chronologically *latest* Book of the RV, a fact that would not be very significant in *itself.*

One of the not-even-a-handful of Mitanni IA words known, not belonging to the above categories, and one frequently cited by Witzel, is the word *mani*, "jewel". Significantly, "**as has been known for the past 130 years**" (to use one of Witzel's favourite phrases, WITZEL 2005:351, the kind of phrase which, in his review of my book, WITZEL 2001, was always accompanied by some juvenile sentence like "**but not** [known] **to Talageri**"), this is one of the RV words which has been classified as a *late* word since it is found only in the *latest* parts of the RV, but is a common word in *post*-RV times: the word *mani* is very frequently used in the Atharvaveda, and is a very common word in later times, but it is *completely unknown* to the Early and Middle Books of the RV, and even in the Late Books is found only *twice*, in **I.33**.8 and **122**.14.

However, the bulk of the Mitanni evidence is in the "large array of personal names adopted by the ruling class". The names are clearly IA names, containing certain common suffixes and prefixes. The following is a generally accepted list of such Mitanni names:

1. *-aṭithi*: Biriatti, Mittaratti, Asuratti, Mariatti, Suriatti, Dewatti, Intaratti, Paratti, Suatti.
2. *-aśva*: Biriassuva, Bartassuva, Biridasva.
3. *-ratha*: Tusratta.
4. *-medha*: Biriamasda.
5. *-sena*: Biriasena.
6. *-bandhu*: Subandu.
7. *-uta*: Indarota, Yamiuta.

8. *vasu-*: Wasdata, Waskanni.
9. *ṛta-*: Artasumara, Artatama, Artamna.
10. *priya-*: Biria, Biriasauma, Biriasura, Biriawaza (also above: Biriatti, Biriassuva, Biriamasda, Biriasena).

Also, the *only known* Kassite IA name:

3. *-ratha*: Abirattas.

[There are many more Mitanni names in the records of West Asia, and some more suggested prefixes like kṣema-, karma-, asu-, sapta-, yami-, mati-, uru-; and suffixes like –asura/śūra, -smara, -vāja, -taraṇa/tarṇa, -mna, -sama/sāma, -jana, -dīti, -jina, -data/dāta, -gama, etc., but there is no consensus, known to me, on these suffixes and prefixes. And it will be seen that all these suggested prefixes and suffixes are either post-Rigvedic, or, again, found only in the Late Books and/or the Avesta. Also, there are a few suggested names like Aitara, Vāyava, Puruṣa, about which also, the same is the case so far as their use as personal names is concerned].

Names with the above suffixes and prefixes, which we will, in short, refer to as MT (Mitanni Type) names, are found in the RV as well. The following is a list of such names found in the RV and, in brackets, *other* MT names found among the composers of the RV:

1. *-atithi*: Medhātithi, Nīpātithi, Mitrātithi, Medhyātithi (Devātithi, Brahmātithi).
2. *-aśva*: Aśva, Aghāśva, Iṣṭāśva, Ṛjrāśva, Ninditāśva, Marutāśva, Vyaśva, Vidadaśva, Śyāvāśva (Bhṛmyaśva, Yuvanaśva).
3. *-ratha*: Citraratha, Priyaratha, Bṛhadratha, Śrutaratha, Svanadratha, Śucadratha (Pratiratha, Apratiratha).
4. *-medha*: Aśvamedha, Priyamedha, Nṛmedha, Sumedha (Purumedha).
5. *-sena*: Ṛṣṭiṣeṇa.
6. *-bandhu*: Subandhu (Śrutabandhu, Viprabandhu).

7. *-uta*: Indrota.
8. *vasu-*: Vasurocis (Vasuśruta, Vasūyus, Vasukra, Vasukṛta, Vasukarṇa, Vasumanas).
9. *rta-*: Ṛtastubh.
10. *priya-*: Priyamedha, Priyaratha.

There are common names in the two above lists: Mittaratti (Mitrātithi), Dewatti (Devātithi), Subandu (Subandhu), Indarota (Indrota) and Biriamasda (Priyamedha).

We have already seen the evidence of the Avestan names and name-elements. The evidence of the Mitanni names is exactly the same: observe the chronological position of MT names in the RV (almost all of which can be referred to in the lists given in Chapter 1, except Indrota):

Not a single MT name is found in the Early Books (6,3,7).

Only one MT name is found in the Middle Books (4,2): Citraratha in **IV.30**.18. And it is significant that hymn **IV**.30 is one of the hymns classified by Oldenberg as a late hymn in Book 4.

All the other MT names are found *only* in the hymns of the Late Books:

V. **27**.4-6; **33**.9; **36**.6; **52**.1; **61**.5,10; **79**.2; **81**.5.

I. **36**.10,11,17-18; **45**.3-4; **100**.16-17; **112**.10,15,20; **116**.6,16; **117**.17-18; **122**.7,13; **139**.9.

VIII. **1**.30,32; **2**.37,40; **3**.16; **4**.20; **5**.25; **6**.45; **8**.18,20; **9**.10; **23**.16,23-24; **24**.14,22-23,28-29; **26**.9,11; **32**.30; **33**.4; **34**.16; **35**.19-21; **36**.7; **37**.7; **38**.8; **46**.21,23; **49**.9; **51**.1; **68**.15-16; **69**.8,18; **87**.3.

IX. **43**.3; **65**.7.

X. **33**.7; **49**.6; **59**.8; **60**.7,10; **61**.26; **73**.11; **80**.3; **98**.5-6,8; **132**.7.

Further, while not a *single* hymn in the Early Books (6,3,7) *or* the Middle Books (4,2) is attributed to a composer with a MT name, the following hymns, every single one found *only* in the Late Books (5,1,8-10), have composers with MT names:

V. 3-6, 24-26, 47, 52-61, 81-82 (20 hymns).

I. 12-23, 100 (13 hymns).

VIII. 1-5, 23-26, 32-38, 46, 68-69, 87, 89-90, 98-99 (24 hymns).

IX. 2, 27-29, 32, 41-43, 97 (9 hymns).

X. 20-29, 37, 57-60, 65-66, 75, 102-103, 132, 134, 179 (23 hymns).

Further, *as has been known for the past 110 years* at least, the *commonest* prefix in the above list of MT names, *priya-* is *completely absent* as a prefix in the Early and Middle Books, not only in names but even in ordinary compound words: Prof. Edward Hopkins pointed out long ago that "***priya* compounds** [fn. **That is, with *priya* as the first member of the compound] are a formation common in Smṛti** [...] **Epic** [...] **In AV, VS, and Brāhmaṇa** [...] **but known in RV only to books viii, i, ix, x**" (HOPKINS 1896a:66). The same goes for the commonest suffix in the above list of MT names, *-atithi*, as a suffix in ordinary compound words.

To recapitulate the evidence regarding the relative chronology of the Rigveda: we find a large array of elements in personal names shared by the Rigveda — but only and exclusively by the *Late* Books of the Rigveda, and a handful of avowedly *Late* hymns in the earlier Books — in common with the Avesta, the Mitanni, and the Kassites:

The suffix –ratha is common to all the four groups: the Late Rigveda, the Avesta, the Mitanni and the Kassites.

The suffixes –atithi, -aśva and –medha, the prefixes vasu-, ratha- and priya-, and the element bandhu, are common to the Late Rigveda, the Avesta and the Mitanni.

The suffixes –sena and -uta are common to the Late Rigveda and the Mitanni.

And a very large array of other prefixes, suffixes and names are common to the Late Rigveda and the Avesta, as we have seen in Chapter 1.

The *Late* Rigveda, the Avesta, the Mitanni and the Kassites share *a common culture*, with common names and name-elements fundamentally important in *all* these four groups *and* in later Vedic and Iranian traditions; and the *Early* and *Middle* Books stand *isolated* from this common culture, and clearly represent a period *earlier* to the period of development of this common culture.

It would take *very, very, very* special pleading indeed to ignore all this massive and uni-directional evidence and claim that the Mitanni IAs represented a *pre-RV* stock of IAs. Very clearly, the proto-Mitanni IAs were a group of emigrants from RV India in the Late Rigvedic Period in which they shared a common culture with the proto-Iranians and the proto-Kassites (*if* these proto-Kassites were different from the proto-Mitanni).

5C
FOOTNOTE: EDWARD W. HOPKINS

It will not be right to close this chapter on the Relative Chronology of the Rigveda without paying tribute to a great Vedic scholar from the past, who had anticipated this state of relative chronology of the Rigveda (*at least in respect of the Avesta*) in his writings as early as the late nineteenth century. However, as the facts did not accord with the logic and logistics of the then unquestioned Aryan Invasion theory, blindly accepted as sacrosanct, he unfortunately did not pursue the point to its logical conclusion. I refer to Prof. Edward W. Hopkins, in his article "**Prāgāthikāni, I**" (HOPKINS 1896a) published in the "Journal of the American Oriental Society", 1896.

Writing primarily on the late chronological position of Book 8 of the Rigveda vis-à-vis the Family Books 2-7 (in HOPKINS 1896a as well as in a separate article, HOPKINS 1896b, entitled "**Numerical Formulae in the Veda**"), Hopkins also frequently refers to the relative chronological position of the Zend Avesta vis-à-vis the Books of the Rigveda, as per his study of various aspects of the vocabulary and grammar of the two texts, as follows (by General Books, Hopkins refers below to Books, 1, 9-10):

"[...] **viii with the General Books and post-Rik literature agrees with Avestan as against the early family books**" (HOPKINS 1896a:73).

"[...] **viii joins the later Avesta to post-Rik literature and the other General Books**" (HOPKINS 1896a:74).

Further, he examines at length the suggestion that common features between Book 8 and the Avesta, *missing* in the Family Books, indicate that Book 8 (alongwith the Avesta) is older than the Family Books, and *dismisses it categorically.* He points out that all these common features are very common to the non-family (or General) Books *as well as to post-Rigvedic literature*, and accepting them as early features would lead to a distorted and illogical hypothesis where one would have to assume a *middle* period where a large body of words and features, very common in both the assumed *earlier* period as well as the assumed *later* period, were *totally unknown or unused.* He therefore concludes that Books 2-7 belong to a period *earlier to both Book 8 as well as the Avesta:*

> "[...] **to point to the list of words common to the Avesta and viii with its group, and say that here is proof positive that there is closer relationship with the Avesta, and that, therefore, viii after all is older than the books which have not preserved these words, some of which are of great significance, would be a first thought. But this explanation is barred out by the fact that most of these Avestan words preserved in viii, withal those of the most importance, are common words in the literature posterior to the Rik. Hence to make the above claim would be tantamount to saying that these words have held their own through the period to which viii (assuming it to be older than ii-vii) is assigned, have thereupon disappeared, and then come into vogue again after the interval to which the maker of this assumption would assign ii-vii. This, despite all deprecation of negative evidence, is not credible.**
>
> **Take, for instance, *udara* or *uṣṭra* or *meṣa*, the first is found only in viii., i., x.; the second in viii., i.; the last in viii., i., ix., x. Is it probable**

> **that words so common both early and late should have passed through an assumedly intermediate period (of ii.-vii.) without leaving a trace? Or, again: is a like assumption credible in the case of *kṣīra*, which appears in the Iranian *khshīra*; in RV. viii., i., ix., x.; disappears in the assumedly later group ii.-vii.; and reappears in the AV. and later literature as a common word? Evidently, the facts are not explained on the hypothesis that the Avesta and RV. viii. are older than RV. ii.-vii.**
> **We must, I think, suppose that the Avesta and RV. viii. are younger than RV. ii.-vii.; or else that the poets of viii. were geographically nearer to the Avestan people, and so took from them certain words, which may or may not have been old with their Iranian users, but were not received into the body of Vedic literature until a time posterior to the composition of ii.-vii.**" (HOPKINS 1896a:80-1).

The truth that Hopkins realized, on the basis of his analysis of some important words and grammatical features common to the Avesta and parts of the Rigveda (as well as all post-Rigvedic literature), but could not pursue to its logical end because no then-prevalent theory of Indo-European origins could explain it, has been elaborated by us on the basis of a complete analysis of personal names. [Hopkins, for the sake of completeness, throws in the alternative suggestion that the common elements, in Book 8 and the other non-family Books on the one hand and the Avesta on the other, could be either because "**the Avesta and RV. viii. are younger than RV. ii.-vii.**" *or* because "**the poets of viii. were geographically nearer to the Avestan people, and so took from them certain words**". But the second alternative is obviously not correct since these words are shared by the Atharvaveda and later texts, which were geographically much further to the east and therefore geographically much further from the Avestan people. The common factor is *late date*, and not *close geographical location*].

As we saw, there is a large class of personal names and name-elements *common* to the *Late* Books and hymns of the

Rigveda (386 hymns in the *Late* Books of the Rigveda and 8 *Late* hymns in the earlier Books), and to the Avesta (the *bulk* of the names, right from the name of the *first* composer of the Avesta, and the names of his closest associates), the Mitanni (including *every* common name element known), and the Kassites (the *only* known name). These names and name-elements are *fundamental* to all four groups, but completely *absent* in the Early and Middle Books of the Rigveda (apart from the 8 *Late* hymns mentioned earlier). And all these names and name-elements are very *common in post-Rigvedic texts*.

As Hopkins pointed out as early as 1896, this means that the Books of the Rigveda, in which this common vocabulary or nomenclature are *completely missing*, i.e. Books 2-4 and 6-7, *predate* the other Books of the Rigveda and the other sources (the Avestan texts, and the Mitanni and Kassite references in inscriptions and documents) which share this common vocabulary or nomenclature in abundance.

Chapter 6

The Absolute Chronology of the Rigveda

The absolute chronology of the Rigveda is a crucial issue that I have not categorically touched in my earlier books, although my (till then) tentative, and intuitive, estimate was that the composition of the earliest hymns of the text must have commenced sometime in the fourth millennium BCE, and that the text was given its final form in the mid-second millennium BCE, somewhere around the period of the Mahābhārata events.

I was aware that this clashed with the views of most OIT scholars, who would generally have the Rigveda more or less *completed* by 3100 BCE, *their* date for the Mahābhārata events, as well as with the views of AIT scholars, who would have the composition of the Rigveda *commencing* after 1500 BCE, *their* date for the assumed Aryan entry into India. I felt, at the time, that any estimate of absolute chronology, *in the absence of concrete, recorded dateable evidence*, could only be a subjective estimate based on the personal opinions and prejudices of the scholar making the estimate; and that while I too had my own estimate, it was just as pointless as any of the others *until such evidence turned up*. [But, as we shall see in this chapter, such evidence was *already there all the time.*].

Therefore, in my earlier book, I wrote that I was "**concerned with the chronological sequence of the different parts of the Rigveda, and not with the exact century BC to which a particular part belongs**", and that I therefore intended to "**leave the subject for the present to other scholars**" (TALAGERI 2000:77). Likewise, when, shortly after the publication of the book, I was repeatedly urged by Steve Farmer (during our group e-mail debate) to state my "estimated range of dates" for the composition of the Rigveda,

I replied that I did not wish "**to be so naïve as to join in the game of making speculative assignments of specific 'hard dates' to Maṇḍalas, hymns and verses without hard proof (such as an archaeologically dateable and decipherable inscription commemorating some Rigvedic personality or event)**" (email dated 11/7/2000).

But, even though not committing myself absolutely, I did not conceal my views: I only made it clear that, at that point, they were more *views* than *conclusions*. After the above disclaimer, I suggested in my book that "**by a conservative estimate, the total period of composition of the Rigveda must have covered a period of at least two millenniums**" (TALAGERI 2000:78). Since I had always maintained that the Rigveda was completed around the period of the Mahābhārata events, which I had dated to the mid-second millenniums BCE, my estimated dating (mid-fourth to mid-second millennium BCE) was implicit, and I made it clear in specific words to Farmer in my email dated 15/7/2000. *Farmer and his crony Witzel responded by publicizing the dates on their internet site to the accompaniment of derisive remarks and comments.*

However, it appears that I will be having the last laugh: as we will be seeing in this chapter, there actually is concrete, recorded, dateable evidence to date the Rigveda, or at least parts of the Rigveda; and this evidence is present *not* in our Indian records, but in the academically well-established records of the civilizations of West Asia: in short, in the records pertaining to the Mitanni and Kassite people of West Asia. And this evidence gives us, on the strength of recorded and dated inscriptions in West Asia, a sheet-anchor for absolute dating of parts of the Rigveda; and, in the process, also a sheet-anchor, more than a millennium earlier to the currently accepted sheet-anchor of the Aśokan inscriptions, for the dating of Indian history.

Now, before proceeding to point out the implications of the Mitanni evidence, let me state my *final* dates (which I will *still* call a *conservative* estimate) *as of now*:

Early Period — Books 6, 3, 7, early 1: 3400-2600 BCE.
Middle Period — Books 4, 2, middle 1: 2600-2200 BCE.
Late Period — Books 5, 8, 9, 10, rest of 1: 2200-1400 BCE.

We will examine the evidence under the following heads:

6A. The Mitanni Evidence.
6B. The Additional Chronological Evidence.
6C. The Implications.

6A
THE MITANNI EVIDENCE

The Mitanni evidence is crucial in providing us with a sheet-anchor for fixing the absolute chronology of the Rigveda, *and also of Indian history* to a point more than a millennium earlier than the presently accepted sheet-anchor of the Aśokan inscriptions.

The evidence basically consists of **"a number of OIA loan words (Mayrhofer 1979, EWA III 569 sqq.) in the non-IE Hurrite language of the Mit. realm of northern Iraq/Syria (c.1460-1330 BCE)."**(WITZEL 2005:361).

1. To begin with, it has to be noted that there was *no* Mitanni *IA language* present in northern Iraq/Syria in 1460-1330 BCE. There was only the *non*-Indo-European Hurrite or Hurrian language (belonging, as Witzel informs us, "**to the North (Eastern) Caucasian group of languages**"), the language of the Mitanni kingdom, which contained a number of *loan words* from the Mitanni IA language; and the ruling class of this kingdom bore Mitanni IA *names*, indicating perhaps that the ruling class was descended from Mitanni IA stock: "**Other evidence, from Mitanni and neo-Hittite sources, indicates that the names of Mitanni kings were traditionally Indo-Aryan, even though the Mitanni belonged to the Hurrian-speaking peoples. We therefore surmise that the Mitanni once lived close to an early Indo-Aryan group, that had perhaps taken a dominant position over the pre-Mitanni**

population, and then became quickly acculturated as Hurrian speakers" (WITZEL 1995a:110).

Witzel (WITZEL 2005:361) refers to these words as the "**remnants**" of IA in the Hurrite language of the Mitanni, and Mallory, see below, refers to them as "**the residue of a dead language in Hurrian**".

J.P.Mallory puts the case as follows: "**Our dating of the Indo-Aryan element in the Mitanni texts is based purely and simply on written documents offering datable contexts. While we cannot with certainty push these dates prior to the fifteenth century BC, it should not be forgotten that the Indic elements seem to be little more than the residue of a dead language in Hurrian, and that the symbiosis that produced the Mitanni may have taken place centuries earlier**" (MALLORY 1997:?)

In other words, the *actual* Mitanni *IA language* must have been present in the area as a living language, influential enough to influence its neighbouring languages, only *centuries before* 1460 BCE.

How many centuries earlier? Fortunately we do not have to depend entirely on speculation: there is evidence which pushes the date back by *at least* two centuries *to begin with*: the Kassite IA evidence.

The Kassites, exactly like the Mitanni, were speakers of a *non*-Indo-European language: as Witzel tells us, "**the Kassite language belongs to an altogether unknown language group**" (WITZEL 2005:380, fn.12), and, apart from the names of three (/four?) gods (the sun-god, *Šuriaš*, the war god *Maruttaš*, and another god, *Bugaš: perhaps also an Inda-Bugaš?*), and one personal name *Abirattaš*, "**the vocabulary of their largely unknown language hardly shows any IA influence, not even in their many designations for the horse and horse names**" (WITZEL 2005:362).

But the words referred to above are definitely IA words, and have been identified as such by a consensus among the scholars. And one of these few words, the *only known* Kassite

IA personal name on record, as we saw, is *a MT name with the suffix –ratha.*

Therefore the Kassites (whose conquest of Mesopotamia is dated by Witzel to 1677 BCE, though earlier dates have been suggested) probably acquired their few IA words some time earlier from the original Mitanni IA language which was probably already a dying language by the time the Kassites conquered Mesopotamia around 1677 BCE, and must have been an influential living language in parts of West Asia well before the seventeenth century BCE at the very latest.

As we have seen, the MT names represent a common culture with the Rigvedic Aryans (and the Avestan Iranians) which originated, or came into vogue, in the period of the Late Books of the Rigveda. These Vedic Aryans of the Late Books are the same people as the Vedic Aryans of the Early and Middle Books of the Rigveda, who, as we have seen, lived in a period *prior* to the development of this common culture, and in areas *further east within India.*

Therefore the culture of the speakers of the original proto-Mitanni IA language, which became the Mitanni IA language in West Asia, was a culture which developed in northwestern India in the period of the Late Books of the Rigveda; and these proto-Mitanni speakers must have migrated *from* India *well* after the development of this common culture at some time in the Late Rigvedic Period. Since they are *already* established in West Asia by the eighteenth century BCE, they must have *set out* on their migration from India at least *a few centuries earlier*, by the beginning of the second millennium BCE, or the end of the third millennium BCE, *at the latest.*

This puts the period of the Late Books of the Rigveda already into the third millennium BCE, and the *beginnings* of this Late period *well back* into the third millennium. And it takes the periods of the Early and Middle Books of the Rigveda (which are totally lacking in MT names) *even further back* into the third millennium BCE *or earlier.*

In the *earliest* period, the Vedic Aryans, as shown by the geographical data in the RV, were totally ignorant of areas to the *West* of the Indus, and were only then expanding from the areas to the East of the Sarasvati to areas to its West.

6B
THE ADDITIONAL CHRONOLOGICAL EVIDENCE

In my 1993 book, I had dealt with the Mitanni evidence, but only superficially, since I did not realize that the data, although so meager, could be so potent. In any case, I had not yet analyzed the internal chronology and geography of the RV, or even suspected that I would be doing so in future.

It was Witzel's taunts in his review of my *second* book which first provoked me enough to think of going into the matter once more: "**The dates provided by the Old Indo-Aryan words in the Mitanni documents of c.1400 BCE are not mentioned in Talageri's book; the forms are slightly *older* than the corresponding forms in the RV (ma-ash-da [mazd[h]a] for medhA, vaj'hana > vashana- [vazhhana] for vAhana. They certainly do not support the 'hoary' chronology developed in Talageri's book**." (WITZEL 2001b:§5). The fraudulent arguments in the Bryant-Patton volume (WITZEL 2005), quoted earlier in the chapter on the Relative Chronology of the Rigveda-II, were the last straw.

But the pointer to the absolute chronology of the Rigveda provided by the Mitanni evidence does not stand isolated (if such a *mass* of *uni-directional* evidence can be described as "isolated"). It stands supported by a number of other pieces of evidence. And in respect of all this *other* evidence as well, it is Witzel and his crony Farmer who, through their misguided claims, unwittingly showed the direction:

1. *Spoked wheels*: In the year 2000, shortly after the publication of my second book, I was drawn into an e-mail debate between Farmer (joined later by Witzel) and some OIT protagonists on the subject of references to spoked wheels. It was the claim of Farmer and Witzel that the references to spoked wheels *throughout* the RV showed that the traditionalist OIT claim that the RV was *completed* by the

fourth millennium BCE was *wrong*, and the AIT claim that the RV *as a whole* was composed in the late second millennium BCE was *right*, since spoked wheels were invented in the *late* third millennium BCE.

The OIT side of the debate was unable to provide any coherent reply, and their main argument was that spoked wheels probably existed earlier, and only remained to be found in the archaeological record. However, appealing to *faith* against *facts* has never been my line, and I decided to examine the distribution of the references to spokes in the RV. I was confident they would be found *only* in the Late Books, and not "throughout" the RV. And, surely enough, that indeed was the exact case. The following are the *only* verses in the RV which refer to spokes:

V. **13**.6; **58**.5.
I. **32**.15; **141**.9; **164**.11-13,48.
VIII. **20**.14; **77**.3.
X. **78**.4.

It was then Farmer and Witzel who were reduced to appealing to faith against facts: quoting poetic references in the Rigveda to the "swift" motion of vehicles as evidence of the existence of spokes (as if references, in the RV, to vehicles "moving through the sky" were evidence of aeroplanes, and references to the destruction of mountains by Indra's weapon are evidence of atomic weapons or explosives.). In fact, Witzel indulges in his compulsive lying and fraudulent behaviour in the recent Bryant-Patton volume, where he writes: **"There have been efforts, of course always on the internet, to push back the dates of chariots and spoked wheels (also implied by Talageri's 2000 years composition period for the RV, see Witzel 2001a,b)"** (WITZEL 2005:393, note 159). When, in fact, far from **"pushing back the dates**" of spoked-wheeled chariots, I placed those dates *exactly* where Farmer and Witzel placed them, and only pointed out that the total ignorance of spokes in the books of the Early and Middle periods "pushed back" the dates of those *books* to periods before the invention of spokes.

In short, the Early and Middle Books of the Rigveda hark back to a period in the third millennium BCE or earlier, when spoked wheels were yet unknown or uninvented.

2. *Ruined cities*: Witzel frequently refers to the references to *armaka*, "ruins", in the RV, as evidence that the RV is later to the desolation of the Indus cities; for example: "**The RV also does not know of large cities such as that of the Indus civilization but only of ruins (*armaka*, Falk 1981)** [...] **Therefore, it must be later than the disintegration of the Indus cities in the Panjab at circa 1900 BCE**" (WITZEL 2005:342). It is difficult to decide the validity of the identification of the word *armaka* as referring to ruined cities, and yet the argument that the Brāhmaṇas frequently refer to the collection of bricks from *armakas*(?) for the purpose of building ritual altars, and these could be the ruins of the Indus cities, is not unreasonable. [Witzel, of course, in his opportunistic way, has no compunctions in quoting the opposing opinions of different scholars, in different contexts, when it is convenient to him; and in this same volume, a few pages later, he gives a completely *different*, and *opposite*, interpretation of the term to explain the absence of archaeological remains of the "pastoral" and "nomadic" Indo-Aryans: "**the constantly shifting river courses in the Panjab may have obscured many of the shallow remnants of the IA settlements: temporary, rather rickety resting places (*armaka*, Rau 1983)**" (WITZEL 2005:346). So, *armakas* are *both* the "ruins" of the "large cities" of "the Indus civilization", *as well as* "the shallow remnants of the IA settlements". And yet, the large cities of the Indus civilization are totally unrelated to the IA settlements!].

In any case, the word *armaka*, so frequently referred to in the post-RV literature, is found in the RV only in one *late* hymn in a Late Book: in **I.133**.3. The Early and Middle Books, and even much of the Late Books, are totally ignorant about these ruins, and therefore these Books must go back much further in time than 1900 BCE.

3. *Bactria-Margiana words*: A pet obsession with Witzel is the theory about "Bactria-Margiana Archaeological Complex (BMAC) words" in "Indo-Iranian". In his review of my book, he wrote about "**the substrate words common to both Indo-Aryan and Iranian (Witzel 1999a, Lubotsky forthc.)** [...] **such common non-Indo-Iranian words differ from the typical Rgvedic and post-Rgvedic substrate and indicate that both the proto-Indo-Aryans and proto-Iranians, perhaps even the speakers of proto-Indo-Iranian, entered a Central Asian/ Afghan territory that was also occupied by a previous population speaking non-Indo-European language(s) (pace J.Nichols!) — most probably the language(s) of the Bactria-Margiana Archaeological Complex (BMAC)**" (WITZEL 2001b:§7). "**The evidence suggests the various Indo-Iranian tribes entered a non-Indo-European speaking area, Bactria-Margiana, and brought new local loan-words taken over there with them into Iran and the Greater Punjab**" (WITZEL 2001b:§9)

So, according to Witzel, both the Iranian and Indo-Aryan branches, *before* they entered their earliest known historical territories, borrowed certain words from the BMAC language in Central Asia, and brought them into Afghanistan-Iran and India respectively.

Witzel, in his EJVS article "Substrate Languages in Old Indo-Aryan" (WITZEL 1999:54-55), gives a list of 18 such words.

[Incidentally, Witzel is very fond of the word "substrate" in his discussions on the AIT. How a list of a few handfuls of *non-basic* loan words allegedly borrowed *en route* from the hypothetical BMAC language, by languages allegedly passing through the area, can make that hypothetical language an alleged *substrate* rather than an alleged *adstrate* language is a mystery. The same goes for the alleged "substrate" languages in India that allegedly gave loanwords to Vedic, and to "Indo-Aryan" in general — the actual or alleged loan words are almost all of them non-basic words which indicate an *adstrate*, rather than a "substrate": a substrate would be indicated mainly by basic words seeping upwards into a language which has superimposed itself upon the speakers of another earlier existing language. Which is why Witzel is so obsessed with *superimposing* this word onto the discussion, and, master-politician that he is, and aware that attack is the best form of defence, he objects to the use of the word "adstrate" in this context, and refers to "adstrate" as "**the favoured position by those autochthonists who recognize that they actually have a problem**" (WITZEL 2005:344). *By Witzel's logic, Latin and French, and countless other languages of the world, are "substrate" languages in England, and English is a "substrate" in other languages in almost every corner of the world.* Incidentally, and interestingly, Lubotsky, Witzel's authority for his list of words, is more diplomatic in his use of the word "substrate", since he tells us: "**I use the term 'substratum' for any donor language, without implying sociological difference in its status, so that 'substratum' may refer to an adstratum or even superstratum**" (LUBOTSKY 2000:302)].

However, as I pointed out in my reply to his review, *all* these 18 words are late words in the Vedic or Sanskrit language as a whole. If these words were *pre-RV* loan words in the language of the Vedic Aryans, they would already have been found *throughout* the Rigveda. However, while all these are *very common* words in later texts, *seven* (*iṣṭi, godhūma, ṣaṇa, sasarpa, khaḍga, vīṇā* and *khara*) of these *eighteen* words are post-Rigvedic words, not found in the RV at all (and the same is the case with another word, *linga*, named by him in another article). *Another ten* (*uṣṭra, kadrū, kapota, kaśyapa, parṣa, pṛdāku, bīja, bhanga, yavya* and *sthūṇā*) are found *only* in the Late Books, as follows:

V. **45**.2; **53**.13; **62**.7.

I. **30**.4; **59**.1; **138**.2, **173**.12.

VIII. **5**.37; **6**.48; **17**.14-15; **45**.26; **46**.22,31; **98**.8.

IX. **61**.13; **114**.2.

X. **18**.13; **48**.7; **85**.37; **94**.13; **101**.3; **165**.1-5.

The *only* word in his list, which *does* occasionally occur in the earlier Books, is the word *bhiṣaj*, found 40 times in the Late Books, and in *four* hymns in the Early and Middle Books, *which could well be classified as late or late redacted hymns* within those Books. [However, we find the word *Yavyāvatī* as an alternative name of the *Hariyūpīyā* in an early hymn].

An examination of the "evidence" in this case (significant *only* in the sense that these are words common to Indo-Aryan and Iranian but absent in other IE branches) therefore confirms our chronological hypothesis, but it in *no* way supports the Lubotsky-Witzel theory that these are "BMAC" words: the BMAC language is *totally* unknown, and direct claims about particular words being from that unknown language are typical of Witzel's presumptuous and insolent style of writing — see also WITZEL 1999 (his EJVS article "Substrate Languages in Old Indo-Aryan", EJVS 5-1, 1999), where he confidently produces, and even discusses in detail, not *one* but *two* distinct Harappan languages. How, for example, does one decide that geographically neutral words like *bhiṣaj,* "medicine", or *kapota*, "pigeon", or *bīja*, "seed", originated in the totally unrecorded and unknown BMAC language: is there any evidence, or even the faintest indication, that either the science of medicine itself, or pigeons, or seeds, originated in the BMAC, or that the reddish-brown colour, *kadrū*, was unknown outside the BMAC?

The only logic behind these claims is that words which seem, or can be alleged, *not* to have clear IE or IIr (Indo-Iranian) etymologies or forms, and seem to be found *only* in Indo-Aryan and Iranian but not in other IE languages, must have been borrowed *after* the separation of "Indo-Iranian" from other IE branches but *before* the separation of Indo-Aryan and Iranian from each other; and, in any AIT scenario, this separation could only have taken place in Central Asia. A circular argument, where the presumption proves the conclusion! However, the only thing the actual distribution of the list of words shows is that these words were jointly formed (if IIr) or borrowed (if non-IIr) in the *Late* Rigvedic Period, after the Vedic Aryans had moved westwards, and the place where this took place was in and around northwest India (present-day Pakistan).

[In a later, and more detailed, article (WITZEL 2006), Witzel becomes even bolder: he sweepingly classifies important and basic RV words like *amśu* (soma plant), *yātu* (magic), *atharvan* (priest), *ṛṣi* (seer), *uśij* (sacrificing priest), *śarva* (a name of Rudra), *Indra* (the primary Vedic god) and *gandharva* (demi-god or demon) as BMAC words, and boldly admits: "**All these words are at the center of much of Vedic and also (pre-) Zoroastrian religion, but have not been considered as being non-IIr (non-IE) so far**" (WITZEL 2006:95). Incidentally, it is interesting that an allegedly *Central Asian* word from this recklessly insolent list, *Indra*, should be found not only "at the center of much of Vedic" religion, and not even just in the Mitanni IA language, but *even in Hittite*: the only known Indo-European myth found in Hittite mythology is about the Hittite god *Inar* who slays the Great Serpent who is placing obstacles in the activity of the Hittite rain-god (see LAROUSSE 1959:85). So, according to Witzel, the Hittites also passed through Bactria-Margiana on their way to Anatolia].

The words, taken as a whole, *neither* necessarily have anything to do with the BMAC, *nor* actually give any clues to their age in terms of absolute chronology, except *two* words, and even Witzel cannot wholly ignore this fact: "**However, some words that can be reasonably well plotted both in time and place, that is, *ustr 'camel', *khar 'donkey', and *ist 'brick', point to the areas along the northern rims of Greater Iran (BMAC, for short) [...] We know that, in this civilization, the domesticated camel was used, that it continued the largescale use of unburnt bricks, and that the donkey was introduced from the Near East at the time.**

These three *leitfossils* also provide a time-frame, the speakers of IIr will hardly have moved into this complex earlier than the introduction of donkeys" (WITZEL 2006:84).

Witzel names *three* words, but the word **ist* "brick" is totally *absent* in the RV, and clearly has to do with the bricks of the Indus sites, the *armaka*, from where, in the later Vedic texts, *iṣṭikā* "bricks" were collected for constructing altars. The other two words, for the domesticated camel and donkey, however, definitely *do* **"point to the areas along the northern rims of greater Iran (BMAC for short)"** and to a period *later* **"than the introduction of donkeys"**, as claimed by Witzel. As he points out, "**The Bactrian camel was domesticated in Central Asia in the late 3rd mill. BCE and introduced in the BMAC area late in the 3rd mill./ 2000 BCE (Meadow 1983, Masson 1992: 39 sq 229, 233). It is also found on a few Indus copper plates. Its Mesopotamian designation, found in middle and new Akkad. *udru* 'Bactrian camel', is a loan from Iran (EWA I 238, KEWA III.652 cf. Diakonoff in JAOS 105, 1985, 600)** [...] **The case of the donkey is of similar nature, though the source of the word seems to be** [...] **Akkadian** [...] ***hārum***" (WITZEL 2006:88).

But the conclusion to which the two words point is starkly in the *opposite* direction to that suggested by Witzel: the word *khara* is totally absent in the RV, and is a *post*-Rigvedic word, but another word for the donkey, *gardabha*, is found twice in the *Late* Books, **I.29**.5; **VIII.56**.3, and once in a hymn in the Early Books, classified by Oldenberg as a *late, or late redacted*, hymn, and notorious for its late words: **III.53**.23. [Again, a piece of irony: this second word, another name for an animal introduced in Central Asia only at the end of the third millennium BCE, is found in the Tocharian language in a clearly related form, *kercapo*, suggesting a *common proto-form* "**before the falling together of *-o, *-a, and *-e, in Indic**" (MALLORY 1997:33)].

The word for the domesticated camel settles the issue conclusively: the word is *not* only found *only* in the Late Books (**I.138**.2; **VIII.5**.37; **6**.48; **46**.22,31, already included in the earlier list above), but in *all* the three hymns in Book 8, the camel, as we have already seen in chapter 1, is known only by virtue of being an animal gifted to the Ṛṣis of the hymns by certain royal patrons, who, *in each of the three hymns*, have been identified by various scholars, *including Witzel himself*, as having *Iranian* names: Kaśu Caidya (hymn 5), Tirindira Parśava (hymn 6) and Pṛthuśravas Kānīta (hymn 46).

In short, coupled with the other evidence (*one*: the fact cited by Witzel above, that the West Asian word for the Bactrian camel is borrowed from Iranian, and *two*: the fact that the composer of the Gāθās, the very *earliest* core of the Avesta, Zaraθuštra, already has the camel as a part of his name), indicates that the Iranians were the ones who introduced the Bactrian camel to everyone else, including the Vedic Aryans.

Therefore the words indicate that the speakers of Indo-Aryan, or Vedic, never passed through the BMAC area at any point of time: the camel, as well as its BMAC name, were introduced to the Vedic Aryans by the *Iranians*, who occupied the BMAC areas, or the areas between the BMAC and the Vedic Aryans, in the late 3rd , or early 2nd, millennium BCE — which was also the Late period of the RV, when the Vedic Aryans had expanded westwards from their East-of-the-Sarasvati homeland.

And, again, all this indicates that the Early and Middle Books of the Rigveda go back into the third millennium BCE and beyond.

4. *The Sintashta-Arkaim Evidence*: Whenever Witzel introduces dated elements, even *dubious* ones, into the discussion, they inevitably end up giving the same chronological implications. In his article, "The Home of the Aryans", Witzel takes his picture of the Proto-Indo-Iranian culture (in AIT terms) even further back in time, and further

west in space, than the BMAC: to the Sintashta-Arkaim culture on the W. Siberian plains east of the Urals, "**dated to c.2200/2100-1700/1600 BC**", where he tells us we find "**the earliest attested traces of Aryan material culture — and even of Aryan belief**". There we find: "**remnants of horse sacrifices (*aśvamedha*) and primitive horse drawn chariots (ratha, *raθa*) with spoked wheels** [...] **a real *tripura*** [...] **adobe bricks (**išt*)** [...] **frame houses (which reminds of Rgvedic *kula* 'hollow, family'** [...]) [...] **Most tellingly, perhaps, at the site of Potapovka (N. Krasnayarsk Dt., near Kybyshev on the N. Volga steppe), a unique burial has been found. It contains a human skeleton whose head has been replaced by a horse head, a human head lies near his feet, along with a bone pipe, and a cow's head is placed near his knees. This looks like an archaeological illustration of the Rgvedic myth of Dadhyanc, whose head was cut off by Indra and replaced by that of a horse. The bone pipe reminds, as the excavator has noted, of the RV sentence referring to the playing of pipes in Yama's realm, the world of the ancestors (Gening 1977)**"(WITZEL 2000b:283-5).

Note the *very consistent* provenance of all the Rigvedic connections drawn up by Witzel:

a. Spoked wheels, we have already seen, are known only to the Late Books.
b. The word *tripura* (not to mention (**išt*) is a post-Rigvedic term, unknown to the RV, but very common later.
c. The word *kula* is a late word, very common later, but found in the Rigveda only in the very Late Books: **I.161**.1; **X.179**.2.
d. Everything connected with the horse sacrifice is found only in the Late Books: hymns **I.**162-163 describe the horse sacrifice, **X.157**.1-3 were the verses recited at the sacrifice, and the word *Aśvamedha* (though only as a personal name) is found only in **VIII.68**.15-16.

e. *Dadhyanc* is named almost exclusively in the very Late Books: in **I.80**.16; **84**.13; **116**.12; **117**.22; **119**.9; **139**.9; **IX.108**.4; **X.48**.2; and in one hymn in an Early Book classified by Oldenberg as a *late or late redacted* hymn, notorious for its late words: **VI.16**.14. And the myth of his head being replaced by that of a horse is known only to the late references in Book I.

f. *Yama*, the ruler of the realm of the ancestors, a very prominent figure in later Hindu mythology and ritual, is almost unknown to the Early and Middle Books of the RV, being mentioned in only one hymn, classified by Oldenberg as a *late or late redacted* hymn, notorious for its late words: **VII.33**.9. He is, otherwise, exclusively referred to in the very Late Books: **I.35**.6; **38**.5; **83**.5; **116**.2; **163**.2; **164**.46; **X.10**.7,9,13; **12**.6; **13**.4; **14**.1-5,7-15; **15**.8; **16**.9; **17**.1; **21**.5; **51**.3; **52**.3; **58**.1; **60**.10; **64**.3; **92**.11; **97**.16; **123**.6; **135**.1,7; **154**.4,5; **165**.4.

For all these Rigvedic elements, developed only in the Late Rigvedic period (and absent in the Books of the Early and Middle Rigvedic periods), to have travelled all the way to the Sintashta-Arkaim culture on the W. Siberian plains east of the Urals, "**dated to c.2200/2100-1700/1600 BC**", the Late Rigvedic period must definitely go back deep into the third millennium BCE and beyond.

Exactly how *much* evidence can you sweep under the carpet? Note that all the different types of evidence we have examined point to the very same scenario: *all* the references to Western geographical terms, and *all* the references to elements which, in terms of absolute chronology, originated at the end of the third millennium BCE, are found almost exclusively, or *only*, in the Late Books 5,1,8-10 (late according to Oldenberg as well as according to our analysis), and, when they do rarely appear in the earlier Books 2-4,6-7, it is specifically in hymns which have been classified as *Late* (by Oldenberg or by the Aitareya Brāhmaṇa).

6C.
THE IMPLICATIONS

To sum up, *the evidence, as we have seen, shows that, somewhere towards the end of the third millennium BCE at the latest, the culture of the Late Rigvedic Period (the common elements of which are found in the Late Books 5, 1, and 8-10, in the Zend Avesta, and, already as dead residual elements of a proto-Mitanni past, in the records of the Mitanni and Kassite people in West Asia as early as 1677 BCE) was already fully developed.* Before this was the Middle Period, and before this the Early Period, *both of which periods preceded the development of this common culture.*

For the correctness of my dating of *the fully developed culture* of the *Late* Period to the late third millennium BCE *at the latest*, we have the evidence of the Mitanni and Kassite records, supported by the late references to spoked wheels, *armaka*, and camels and donkeys in the Rigveda. For my dating of the *Early* and *Middle* Periods, we still do not have any recorded evidence, but it is clear that *these periods preceded the development of this common culture;* and the totally different culture of those periods, as evident from the totally different culture of the Early and Middle Books, cannot have been transformed in a day to the culture of the Late Period (with its spoked wheels, camels, Avestan/Mitanni type names, broader geographical horizon, etc.). Therefore, even at the *most* conservative, the Early Period must go *deeply back* into the third millennium BCE or earlier.

In this Early Period, *long* before the late third millennium BCE, we have the Vedic Aryans located to the East of the Sarasvatī, totally *unacquainted* (as we see from the evidence of the geographical references in the Early Books) with the

Indus and areas to its West, and only *just* becoming acquainted with the Land of the Seven Rivers to the West of the Sarasvatī.

How can this scenario be reconciled with the "Aryan invasion/immigration/trickling-in" theory?

The answer is: *it simply can not.*

The AIT is built up on a number of extra-Indian factors, which necessarily require that the Vedic Aryans should be brought into India *no earlier than 1500 BCE.* In fact, as we saw in our earlier book, some extremist writers go so far as to place the Vedic Aryans in the peripheral areas even then; and some, like Victor H. Mair (MAIR 1998:853), go so far as to portray the undivided Indo-Iranians still located to the north and west of the Caspian Sea in 1500 BCE (see TALAGERI 2000:232-235).

But, as we saw, the evidence not only locates the Vedic Aryans, *many* centuries before the late third millennium BCE, in a region to the East of the Saptasindhu area, totally unacquainted with the West, but even the proto-Iranians, the *ancestors* of all the Iranian groups known to history, including the composers of the Avesta, are also located in the same area, although slightly to the West of the Vedic Aryans, in the same period. [Note also the fact that this places the joint Indo-Iranians squarely in the area of the Indus Valley Civilization in its heyday.]

All this is *impossible* to reconcile with any theory which locates the original homeland of the Indo-European family of languages *anywhere* outside India.

Section II

The Indo-European Homeland in India.

Chapter 7

The Evidence of the Isoglosses

The linguistic case *for the AIT* consists almost entirely of circular arguments and invasionist dogmas; and the corollary linguistic case *against the OIT*, likewise, is nothing but a case against certain *other* dogmas, held by certain sections of proponents of the OIT, such as that: a) The Rigveda was composed by around 3100 BCE, and b) the Vedic language is the ancestor of the other Indo-European languages.

But these dogmas have never formed any part of the OIT hypothesis presented in our two earlier books, where we have placed the completion of the Rigveda at around the mid-second millennium BCE, treated the Vedic language as a normal language constantly undergoing changes with the passage of time (even *within* the period of composition of any one text), and very emphatically rejected the idea that the Vedic language was the ancestor even of the languages known today as the Indo-Aryan languages, let alone of all the Indo-European languages. Hence none of the linguistic arguments against the OIT are effective, *or even relevant*, against the case presented by us (as we will see, in short, in the appendix to this chapter).

The eminent linguist, Hans H. Hock, for one, accepts that the OIT case has two distinct versions: the one which treats Sanskrit itself as the original ancestral language, and the one which accepts the linguistic hypothesis of a Proto-Indo-European language (as much ancestral to Vedic as to the other ancient Indo-European languages) but places the geographical location of that ancestral language in India.

> **"The claim that the āryas are indigenous to India can therefore be reconciled with the relationship of Indo-Aryan to the rest of Indo-**

European only under one of two hypotheses: Either the other Indo-European languages are descended from the earliest Indo-Aryan, identical or at least close to Vedic Sanskrit, or Proto-Indo-European (PIE), the ancestor of all the Indo-European languages, was spoken in India and (the speakers of) all the Indo-European languages other than Sanskrit/Indo-Aryan migrated out of India. For convenience, let us call the first alternative the 'Sanskrit-origin' hypothesis, and the second one, the 'PIE-in-India' hypothesis" (HOCK 1999a:1).

And he further accepts the fact that the first version is easily refutable on linguistic grounds, *but that the second one is not:*

"...**the 'Sanskrit-origin' hypothesis runs into insurmountable difficulties, due to the irreversible nature of relevant linguistic changes [...but...] the likelihood of the 'PIE-in-India' hypothesis cannot be assessed on the basis of similar robust evidence"** (HOCK 1999a:2).

"The 'PIE-in-India' hypothesis is not as easily refuted as the 'Sanskrit-origin' hypothesis, since it is not based on 'hard-core' linguistic evidence, such as sound changes, which can be subjected to critical and definitive analysis. Its cogency can be assessed only in terms of circumstantial arguments, especially arguments based on plausibility and simplicity" (HOCK 1999a:12).

But Hock, naturally, does not accept the "PIE-in-India" hypothesis. Assessing it "in terms of circumstantial arguments, especially arguments based on plausibility and simplicity", he presents *two* "severe difficulties" allegedly faced by this hypothesis: one non-linguistic (the "equine argument") and one linguistic (the evidence of the isoglosses).

Hock puts forward the "equine argument" as follows:

"While disagreeing on minor details, those familiar with Indo-European linguistic paleontology and with the archeological evidence in Eurasia agree that the use of the domesticated horse spread out of the steppes of the Ukraine, and so did the horse-drawn two-wheeled battle chariot, as well as the great significance of the horse in early Indo-European culture and religion. Indo-Europeanists and specialists in general Eurasian archeology are

> **therefore convinced, too, that these features spread into India along with the migration of Indo-Aryan speakers. [...] The question whether the archeological evidence supports the view that domesticated horses were a feature of the Harappan civilization is still being debated; see the summary of arguments in CHENGAPPA, 1998. Significantly, however, to my knowledge no archeological evidence from Harappan India has been presented that would indicate anything comparable to the cultural and religious significance of the horse or the important role of the horse-drawn two-wheeled chariot which can be observed in the traditions of the early Indo-European peoples, including the Vedic āryas. On balance, then, the 'equine' evidence at this point is more compatible with migration into India than with outward migration**" (HOCK 1999a:12-13).

The "equine argument" is one of the most *hypocritical* arguments in the AIT armory, since the crux of the argument seems to be as follows: "the equine archaeological data does not provide material evidence for an OIT, therefore the OIT stands automatically disqualified. The equine archaeological data does not provide any material evidence whatsoever for an AIT either; but this does not disqualify the AIT, as the AIT does not require this evidence since the AIT is beyond doubt or question".

Hock, above, does not even deny outright that "**domesticated horses were a feature of the Harappan civilization**", since he admits that "**the question is still being debated**". He denies that the Harappans could have been Indo-Europeans simply because there is "**no archeological evidence**" that would indicate "**anything comparable to the cultural and religious significance of the horse or the important role of the horse-drawn two-wheeled battle chariot which can be observed in the traditions of the early Indo-European peoples, including the Vedic āryas**". In short, even if horses were a feature of the Harappan civilization, there is no archaeological evidence indicating that this feature was on the *scale* indicated by the Indo-European and Vedic Aryan evidence; so the Harappans *can not* be Indo-Europeans or Vedic Aryans.

But *nor* is there any archaeological evidence whatsoever to indicate "**anything comparable to the cultural and religious significance of the horse or the important role of the horse-drawn two-wheeled battle chariot which can be observed in the traditions of the early Indo-European peoples, including the Vedic āryas**" *anywhere* on any archaeological trail leading from South Russia to Central Asia, or in archaeological sites within Central Asia (e.g. in the BMAC sites, touted by Witzel and some others as the Central Asian sites occupied by the immigrating Indo-Iranians), or on any archaeological trail leading from Central Asia into northwestern India, or on any archaeological trail leading from the northwestern parts of India into deeper areas in the interior of India, within *any* of the time-frames mooted for the alleged immigrations of the Indo-Aryans into India. Nor has any archaeological site, *anywhere* in India, been identified as a *Vedic Aryan* site indicating "**anything comparable to the cultural and religious significance of the horse or the important role of the horse-drawn two-wheeled battle chariot which can be observed in the traditions of the early Indo-European peoples, including the Vedic āryas**". Yet Hock seems to have no problems in assuming that such Vedic Indo-Aryans did exist in India, in the periods and areas postulated for them by AIT scholars, and that they did immigrate across all the trails, and in all the time-frames, postulated by the AIT scholars for their migrations.

The mere fact that the domesticated horse is supposed to have originated in some particular area does not make it necessary that the Indo-Europeans (because of the "cultural and religious significance of the horse" in their traditions) should also have migrated from that area, any more than the "cultural and religious significance" of *sābūdāṇā khicḍī* (a preparation consisting of sago, potatoes, chilies and groundnuts) in the diet of Maharashtrians (who commonly eat this dish whenever they do religious fasting) indicates that Maharashtrians migrated from America (original home to all the ingredients in this preparation). All that the evidence suggests is that the domesticated horse, *whatever* its geographical origins, had probably become known to the Indo-Europeans at a time when their unity had not yet broken up completely.

In fact, if the actual "equine evidence" is "assessed in terms of circumstantial arguments, especially arguments based on plausibility and simplicity", we find that it militates strongly *against* the view that horses were brought into India somewhere around 1500 BCE by immigrating Aryans:

1. To begin with, as Hock himself puts it, "the question whether the archeological evidence supports the view that domesticated horses were a feature of the Harappan civilization is still being debated". If horses were present in the Harappan civilization in the third millennium BCE or earlier (and the archaeological evidence for this is at least as strong for the Harappan sites as for any other areas in the Indian subcontinent, and on its borders, postulated as part of the AIT scenario), this itself deals a death blow to any "equine argument".

2. The idea that Indo-Europeans domesticated the wild horse "on the steppes of the Ukraine" is totally inconsistent with the linguistic evidence: the common reconstructed PIE word for the domesticated horse, **ekwo*, has no accepted Indo-European etymology; and the word, moreover, specifically refers to the domesticated horse, and there is no common Indo-European word for the wild horse. Therefore, far from suggesting that the Indo-European homeland is to be located in the area of domestication of the horse, the linguistic evidence suggests exactly the opposite: "**The Indo-European homeland has to be localized at the area where the wild horse did not live**" (BLAŽEK 1998:29).

3. The idea that invading Indo-Aryans entered India, bringing the horse with them, and introduced the animal into India, is also totally inconsistent with the linguistic evidence, as pointed out in my first book: "**Sanskrit has many words for the horse: *aśva*, *arvant* or *arvvā*, *haya*, *vājin*, *sapti*, *turanga*, *kilvī*, *pracelaka* and *ghoṭaka*, to name the most prominent**

among them. And yet, the Dravidian languages show no trace of having borrowed any of these words; they have their own words *kudirai*, *parī* and *mā* [...] The Santali and Mundari languages, however, have preserved the original Kol-Munda word *sādom*. Not only has no linguist ever claimed that the Dravidian and Kol-Munda words for 'horse' are borrowed from 'Aryan' words, but in fact some linguists have even sought to establish that Sanskrit ghoṭaka, from which all modern Indo-Aryan words are derived, is borrowed from the Kol-Munda languages" (TALAGERI 1993:160). [Note also what the Encyclopaedia Britannica, 15th edition, Vol. 9, p.348, has to say in the course of a description of Indian archaeology: "**Curiously, however, it is precisely in those regions that used iron, and were associated with the horse, that the Indo-Aryan languages did not spread. Even today, these are the regions of the Dravidian language group**"].

The above point is "echoed" by none other than Michael Witzel: "**Dravidian and Indo-Aryan (IE) words for domesticated animals are quite different from each other, for example, Drav. DEDR 500 Tam. *ivuḷi*, Brah. (*h*)*ullī*, 1711 Tam. *kutirai*, etc. DEDR 3963 Tam. *pari* 'runner', 4870 Tam. *mā* 'animal' (horse, elephant), Tel. *māvu* 'horse', cf. Nahali *māv* 'horse'** [...]**; they have no relation with IA *aśva* 'horse' and various words for 'runner' (*arvant, vājin,* etc.)**." (WITZEL 2000a:§15).

In fact, far from suggesting that the earliest (archaeologically fully attested) horses in India were associated with the Aryans, Witzel here associates them with *Dravidians*: "**perhaps it was they who made horses statues at Pirak (1700 BCE), and not the IA (?) Bhalānas. Obviously, use of horses is not linked to speakers of an IA language**" (WITZEL 2000a: §15).

[There is also the independent question of whether the IE word **ekwo* originally referred to the horse or to some other equid. Some Indian OIT writers have suggested that the word may originally have referred to some other equid known to the

IEs, such as the onager (equus hemionus), before the horse was introduced among the IE speakers and became the dominant equid of their acquaintance and association. Witzel, with his characteristic contempt for Indians, refers to this suggestion as a "**truly asinine proposition**" (WITZEL 2005:393). However, it is significant that a western academic scholar makes a similar suggestion in respect of the Dravidian word for "horse" found in both Tamil and Brahui and therefore presumably an Old Dravidian word: "**Burrow (1972) notes the existence of a word for the horse which is found only in Tamil and Brahui (DED 500: Tamil *ivuḷi*, Brahui (*h*)*ullī*) and which therefore must have existed in the earliest Dravidian [...] McAlpin suggests that this early Dravidian word probably referred to the Asian wild ass, *Equus Hemionus*, which is native to South Asia, rather than to the domesticated horse, *Equus Caballus*"** (SOUTHWORTH 1995:268, fn 13).

And note the following suggestion: "**The lack of a clear Proto-Indo-European word for 'donkey', given the presence of domesticated donkeys throughout most of the territory where horses were domesticated and where the Indo-European tribes must have lived, can be explained by assuming that *ek^{h}wos was originally used with the meaning 'donkey' as well as 'wild horse; horse'**" (GAMKRELIDZE 1995:482). What is significant is that Gamkrelidze offers this suggestion to explain the lack of a clear PIE word for the donkey, found in the same areas as the wild horse for which also there is no separate PIE word. But the real explanation for both is different: there is no clear PIE word for the donkey, *as* there is no word for the wild horse, since the PIE speakers lived in an area "**where the wild horse did not live**" (BLAŽEK 1998:29), and nor did the domesticated donkey, i.e. they lived in "**Central and Eastern Asia, where paleozoological data show that the domesticated donkey is a recent introduction**" (GAMKRELIDZE 1995:482).].

In short, the relevance of the "equine argument", in any debate on the AIT and OIT, is absolutely *zero*; and it will continue to remain a *big zero* until someone produces evidence to show an archaeological trail of horse finds, in archaeological sites independently and conclusively identified as associated with immigrating Indo-Aryans, leading from the Ukraine (or wherever) into Central Asia, and thence into the northwestern parts of India, and then further into the interior of India, in the time frames attributed to the alleged Aryan immigrations. Till then, any serious OIT writer will be justified in dismissing any "equine argument" as so much hot air. The only reason why the subject is being touched upon here at all is because Hock presents it, along with his main linguistic argument, as one of the two most serious objections to the OIT.

To recapitulate, Hock accepts that while the "**hard core**" linguistic arguments against the OIT (Out of India Theory) are very effective in refuting any "Sanskrit-origin" hypothesis (as put forward by most other OIT writers), they are not really valid against any "'PIE-in-India' hypothesis" (such as put forward, though not noted by Hock, in TALAGERI 1993 and TALAGERI 2000). However, a strong linguistic case *can*, according to Hock, be made against the "'PIE-in-India' hypothesis" if it is "**assessed only in terms of circumstantial arguments, especially arguments based on plausibility and simplicity**": in this context, Hock presents his case based on *the Evidence of the Isoglosses*. However, Hock's case is made up of flawed arguments, and an examination of the *actual* Evidence of the Isoglosses, in fact, shows, as we will see in this chapter, that the "'PIE-in-India' hypothesis" is the only hypothesis which explains all the isoglosses and all the existing facts and evidence in the AIT-vs.-OIT debate.

We will examine Hock's case, the actual Evidence of the Isoglosses, and other related linguistic and other issues, under the following heads:

7A. Hock's Linguistic Case.
7B. Hock's Case Examined.
7C. The Evidence of the Isoglosses.

7A
HOCK'S LINGUISTIC CASE

Hock's *main*, or *only*, supposedly conclusive linguistic case against the "PIE-in-India" version of the OIT (Out-of-India Theory) is allegedly based on the Evidence of the Isoglosses.

An isogloss is a special linguistic feature which develops in any one language and then spreads to other languages and dialects over a contiguous area. Thus, the distinction between dental sounds and cerebral sounds (i.e. between *t*, *d* and *n* as opposed to *ṭ*, *ḍ* and *ṇ*) is an isogloss peculiar to the Indian area: it is found in all kinds of languages not genetically related to each other: Indo-Aryan, Dravidian, Austric (Kol-Munda) and Burushaski. Likewise, within the parameters of this isogloss, we find another isogloss restricted to a *part* of the Indian area: a distinction between a dental *l* and a cerebral *ḷ*, found in the Dravidian languages of South India but only in certain Indo-Aryan languages found closest to the Dravidian area: Konkani, Marathi and Gujarati on the west and Oriya on the east. There is another isogloss restricted to an even smaller part of *this* area: a distinction between a hard c sound before certain vowels (e.g. ci) and a soft ts-like c sound (ç) before certain other vowels (e.g. çā, çu), found in Konkani, Marathi, Telugu, and some contiguous dialects of Kannada.

From all this, it is clear that an isogloss is an indicator of geographical proximity, rather than of genetic relationship, in respect of dialects and languages sharing that isogloss. Likewise, when, in some cases, some of the dialects or languages sharing the isogloss move geographically away from each other (into non-contiguous areas), and continue to retain the linguistic feature, that linguistic feature is a testimony to their geographical proximity in the past.

A linguistic examination of the different extant or recorded branches of the Indo-European language family shows different linguistic features found as isoglosses linking different branches to each other. The branches sharing any particular isogloss are not necessarily spoken in contiguous areas at present, and many are not on record as having been spoken in contiguous areas even in historical times; the *only* conclusion that can be drawn is therefore that these branches, in the form of the respective ancestral dialects of Proto-Indo-European, were spoken in *contiguous* areas in the original Indo-European homeland, before they separated from each other or at various points and stages during the process of their separation.

Hock's main contention is that the pattern of distribution of these isoglosses among the different branches conclusively disproves the Out-of-India theory "in terms of circumstantial arguments, especially arguments based on plausibility and simplicity".

In this context, Hock first sets out the main background of his argument:

> **"As is also well known, the early Indo-European languages exhibit linguistic alignments which cannot be captured by a tree diagram, but which require a dialectological approach that maps out a set of intersecting 'isoglosses' which define areas with shared features, along the lines of Figure 2. While there may be disagreements on some of the details, Indo-Europeanists agree that these relationships reflect a stage at which the different Indo-European languages were still just dialects of the ancestral language and as such interacted with each other in the same way as the dialects of modern languages"** (HOCK 1999a:13).

Then he proceeds to list out some major isoglosses uniting various Proto-Indo-European dialects (ancestral forms of the latter-day Indo-European branches), and then presents, in the "Figure 2" which he refers to above (Figure 1 in our present chapter), a "dialectological arrangement" of the various Indo-European dialects in the relative geographical position (to each other) that they would have to assume in order to be able to explain every single one of these isoglosses as being the result of contiguous proximity of the dialects which share that isogloss. Hock's main contention is that there is a:

> **"close correspondence between the dialectological arrangement in Figure 2 (based on the evidence of shared innovations) and the actual geographical arrangement of the Indo-European languages in their earliest attested stages. [...] True the dialectological arrangement is relative and could a priori be turned around or flipped in many different directions. However, the relative positions of the dialects can be mapped straightforwardly into the actual geographical arrangement if we assume that there have been no major realignments and that the relative positions were generally maintained as the languages fanned out over larger territory. Any other original arrangement of the dialect map of Proto-Indo-European would require the assumption of a major realignment in later times, which curiously would leave the relative position of the dialects unchanged. A hypothesis which would postulate such an alternate scenario would have to be justified by compelling empirical evidence; but such evidence does not seem to exist at this point."** (HOCK 1999a:16).

In other words: Hock's Figure 2 (Figure 1 in our present chapter) shows the various Indo-European dialects *arranged in the relative positions to each other in which they are found in their "earliest attested stages*": i.e. Indo-Aryan is to the extreme south-east, Iranian is to its west, Armenian to the (north-)west of Iranian, and Greek to the (north-)west of Iranian and Armenian; Germanic is to the extreme north-west, Celtic to its (south-)west, Italic to the south of Germanic and Celtic, Baltic to the east of Germanic, and Slavic to the south(-east) of Baltic. On this arrangement, Hock purports to show that *every single isogloss can be mapped out showing all the dialects which share that isogloss lying in a contiguous area*, without any intrusions of any dialect which does not share that particular isogloss. This shows that the dialects, when they were together with each other in the Original Homeland at the time the isoglosses were formed, lay in the *same* relative geographical positions to each other as they were in their earliest attested stages after separating from each other. Further, this, according to Hock, conclusively disproves the OIT, since it is logically extremely *unlikely* that the different Indo-European dialects (which developed into the various branches) could have lain in a particular geographical arrangement in relation to each other (A to the east of B, B to the north of C, etc) in an original homeland *within* India, then moved out one by one through the bottleneck passes of the northwest into the outer world, and then again, in that larger geographical world testified in their "earliest attested stages", fallen in place once more in exactly the *same* pattern of geographical arrangement in relation to each other:

> **"To be able to account for these dialectological relationships, the 'Out-of-India' approach would have to assume, first, that these relationships reflect a stage of dialectal diversity in a Proto-Indo-European ancestor language within India. While this assumption is not in itself improbable, it has consequences which, to put it mildly, border on the improbable and certainly would violate basic principles of simplicity. What would have to be assumed is that the various Indo-European languages moved out of India in such a manner that they maintained their relative position to each other during and after the migration. However, given the bottle-neck nature of the route(s) out of India, it would be extremely difficult to do so. Rather, one would expect either sequential movement of different groups, with loss of dialectological alignment, or merger and amalgamation of the groups, with loss of dialectal distinctiveness. Alternatively, one would have to assume that after moving out of India, the non-Indo-Aryan speakers of Indo-**

European languages realigned in a pattern that was substantially the same as their dialectological alignment prior to migration a scenario which at best is unnecessarily complex and, at worst, unbelievable. The 'PIE-in-India' hypothesis thus runs into severe difficulties as regards plausibility and simplicity. By contrast, there is no problem if we accept the view that Proto-Indo-European was spoken somewhere within a vast area 'from East Central Europe to Eastern Russia' (HOCK & JOSEPH 1996:523). As suggested earlier, all we need to assume is that the Indo-European languages by and large maintained their relative positions to each other as they fanned out from the homeland. In that case, however, the speakers of Indo-Aryan must have migrated out of an original Eurasian homeland and into India." (HOCK 1999a:16-17).

Figure 1. Hock's Dialectological Arrangement

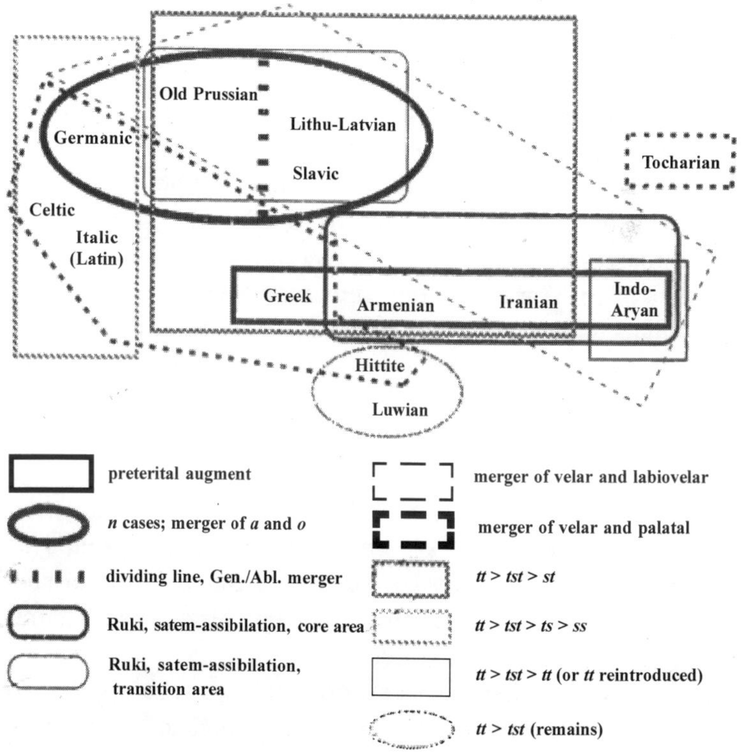

Old Prussian
Lithu-Latvian
Germanic
Slavic
Tocharian
Celtic
Italic (Latin)
Greek
Armenian
Iranian
Indo-Aryan
Hittite
Luwian

preterital augment
n cases; merger of *a* and *o*
dividing line, Gen./Abl. merger
Ruki, satem-assibilation, core area
Ruki, satem-assibilation, transition area
merger of velar and labiovelar
merger of velar and palatal
tt > *tst* > *st*
tt > *tst* > *ts* > *ss*
tt > *tst* > *tt* (or *tt* reintroduced)
tt > *tst* (remains)

7B
HOCK'S CASE EXAMINED

Hock's case appears quite logical, until one submits it to a closer examination.

1. To begin with, he makes certain fundamental assumptions about the "PIE-in-India" hypothesis which help him to show that hypothesis to be "at best unnecessarily complex, and, at worst, unbelievable", *but these assumptions have no basis whatsoever in any logical "PIE-in-India" hypothesis:* for example, Hock's criticism of the Indian homeland scenario unwarrantedly assumes that the "PIE-in-India" hypothesis postulates the formation and differentiation of the different IE dialects to have taken place *within* the Indian mainland, and then has the different dialects all trooping out, isoglosses fully in place, one by one, through the Khyber pass.

But I have pointed out right from my first book that Indian tradition *begins* the accounts of *pre*-Rigvedic history with the *Druhyus* and *Anus*, as yet *not* fully differentiated internally into very distinct groups, *already* on the periphery of the subcontinent and beyond: the *Pūrus* (the Vedic Aryans) are to the east of the Sarasvatī, the *Anus* (ancestors of the Iranian, Armenian, Greek and Albanian branches) are already in the present-day Pakistan area and beyond, and the *Druhyus* (ancestors of the other Indo-European branches) are already in Afghanistan and Central Asia. A preliminary analysis of the isoglosses (TALAGERI 2000:266-282) already points out that the differentiation of the different IE dialects, and the formation of the isoglosses covering different groups of dialects, took place *not in the interior of India* but in an area covering northwest India, Pakistan, Afghanistan, and Central Asia and some areas to its north.

[Incidentally, Hock's above objection can be applied to some extent even to the AIT hypothesis presented by Hock himself:

Hock, for example, is quite right when he points out that "given the bottle-neck nature of the route(s) out of India" it would be extremely unlikely "to assume that after moving out of India, the non-Indo-Aryan speakers of Indo-European languages realigned in a pattern that was substantially the same as their dialectological alignment prior to migration" (*if*, that is, the formation of the isoglosses were to be assumed to have taken place *within* India).

However, the scenario assumed by him, "that the Indo-European languages by and large maintained their relative positions to each other as they fanned out from the homeland" which was situated in a central location "from East Central Europe to Eastern Russia", is not as free from this problem of realignment as Hock assumes it to be. The fact is that the Eurasian world outside India and its northwestern mountain passes is not a flat piece of paper, as it is in Hock's figure 2: *it* is also full of mountain ranges and passes, rivers and other physical barriers. The last branches in the homeland, Greek, Armenian, Iranian and Indo-Aryan, would certainly require some dexterity to have spread out from a central location "from East Central Europe to Eastern Russia" in such a manner as to land up in their widely spread out earliest attested areas, south of the Eurasian mountain ranges, *still* in the same relative alignment to each other (and to the other branches) as in the homeland. The joint Indo-Iranians, for example, in his scenario, throughout their journey, sometimes eastwards and sometimes southwards, from East Central Europe to Central Asia, must certainly have been quite determined to maintain the position of the Indo-Aryans to the east and the Iranians to the west].

2. Hock also puts forward the plea that "**it would be considerably simpler to envisage only one migration into India (of Indo-Aryan) rather than a whole series of migrations out of India (of all the other languages)**" (Hock 1999a:16).

This is an example of the kind of simplistic arguments made by western AIT writers in the smug confidence that no-one is likely to question their logic. The question here can not be one of "one migration into India" versus "a whole series of migrations out of India", since this would apply *equally* to *any* other proposed homeland theory: *every one* of the Indo-European branches has its own earliest attested area, and *every* proposed homeland theory must necessarily place the proposed homeland in the territory of any *one* particular branch, and, consequently, *any* homeland theory will *necessarily* postulate "a whole series of migrations" out of that area of all the Indo-European branches other than the branch attested in that area.

In fact, on the basis of the evidence of the isoglosses, linguists have postulated a general order in which the various branches of Indo-European languages emigrated out of the original homeland, *wherever* the homeland is to be postulated. According to this order, the *last* branches left in the homeland were the "Indo-Iranian", Armenian and Greek branches: "**After the dispersals of the early PIE dialects** [...] **there were still those who remained** [...] **Among them were the ancestors of the Greeks and Indo-Iranians** [...] **also shared by Armenian; all these languages it seems, existed in an area of mutual interaction.**" (WINN 1995:323-324). Hock does not propose the location of the original homeland in the "earliest attested" geographical areas of any of these *last* languages, as would be the natural case, but somewhere in an area from "East Central Europe to Eastern Russia". Therefore his theory, in fact, requires that *every single* dialect, not even excepting *one*, emigrated out from the original homeland, and then one of the earlier emigrant dialects (in whose earliest attested area Hock would place the location of the original homeland) actually immigrated back into that area. To paraphrase Hock, "it would be considerably simpler to envisage a whole series of connected migrations out of India, in broadly one direction, of *all, but one*, branches rather than a whole series of independent migrations of *every single* Indo-European branch, in every conceivable direction, from a homeland somewhere in the area from East Central Europe to Eastern Russia, followed by a re-immigration, later, of one of the earlier emigrating branches".

3. But most fatal to Hock's case is the fact that the evidence of the isoglosses, as presented by him, is *deliberately* partial and selective: not only does Hock fail to take into account many important isoglosses linking together different branches, but he even pointedly excludes from his arrangement one crucial branch, Tocharian, on the plea that "**it is difficult to find dialectal affiliation**" (HOCK 1999a:16) for it.

Tocharian is important because it shares certain important isoglosses with the Anatolian (Hittite) branch and the Italic branch. Now, the Tocharian branch is found at the *north-eastern* corner of the Indo-European world and Italic at the *opposite south-western* corner. Hittite is at the *south-central* edge, but separated from Italic (even if we treat the landscape as a flat piece of paper) by the Greek and Albanian branches; and, in any case, since neither Italic, nor Hittite, is alleged to have immigrated into its earliest attested areas from south-eastern Europe, the paths of the two branches are obviously divergent. In *no* reasonable dialectological arrangement of Indo-European dialects can these three dialects (Hittite, Tocharian and Italic) be shown to be sharing these important isoglosses with each other in *contiguous* areas and then "**maintaining their relative positions to each other as they fanned out from the homeland**" to their respective earliest attested areas. So Hock simply ignores the concerned isoglosses, and excludes Tocharian from his arrangement, and crosses his fingers in the hope that no-one notices.

It is therefore clear that the actual evidence of the isoglosses in fact shows quite *the opposite* of what Hock claims for it: it in fact shows that the Indo-European homeland simply cannot be situated in any central area (such as the area from "East Central Europe to Eastern Russia") with the different dialects simply "maintaining their relative positions to each other as they fanned out from the homeland" to their respective earliest attested areas.

Hittite, Tocharian and Italic are the dialects which, in any generally accepted schedule of migrations, were the first, second and third, respectively, to migrate from the original homeland; and the fact that they share a few isoglosses almost exclusively with each other (in spite of being found at opposite corners of the earliest attested dialectological arrangement), makes it likely that these isoglosses were formed due to interaction between these three dialects in an area near a *common exit point* from this original homeland as they moved away from that homeland. [The idea of the existence of a *common exit point* is also necessitated by the linguistic isolation of Hittite from all the other branches. According to all the suggested migration schedules, Hittite was the first branch to separate *completely* from the rest, and all the other branches *together* developed certain *fundamental* features in common which are missing in Hittite. Any isoglosses shared by Hittite with *some, but not all,* of these other branches, are formed only *after* this initial separation, and could therefore only have been formed outside this common exit point when those particular branches were also moving out of the common homeland].

The homeland, in fact, must therefore be situated in an area either to the *north* (the Arctic Homeland?) or to the *south* (the Indian Homeland, or the Anatolian Homeland) of the general Indo-European world: the exit point, *leading away from the other dialects*, led into the Eurasian zone, from where the three dialects migrated or expanded into their earliest attested areas.

But this *cannot* be an area to the *north*, since the last dialects in the homeland (see earlier), Indo-Aryan, Iranian, Armenian, Greek, and also Albanian as we shall see, are all found, in their earliest attested stages, as the *southernmost* dialects of Indo-European.

The Anatolian Homeland theory, likewise, fails to explain the isoglosses shared by the last branches in the Homeland: Winn points out that the Anatolian theory fails to explain "**the Indo-Iranian problem.** [...] **Greek and Indic are thus separated by millenniums of linguistic change — despite the**

close grammatical correspondences between them (as we saw in Chapter 12, these correspondences probably represent shared innovations from the last stage of PIE)" (WINN 1995:341-342).

As Mallory and Adams make clear: "**Any homeland solution must account for the dispersal of *all* the IE stocks**" (MALLORY 1997:297). The Indian Homeland theory, backed by the evidence of Vedic literature and Indian historical traditions, is the *only* theory which fully explains the isoglosses and accounts for the dispersal of all the Indo-European branches, as we shall now proceed to see.

7C
THE EVIDENCE OF THE ISOGLOSSES

The Indo-European family of languages, for all practical purposes of examination of the isoglosses, contains the following twelve branches: Anatolian (mainly Hittite), Tocharian, Italic, Celtic, Germanic, Baltic, Slavic, Greek, Albanian, Thraco-Phrygian (Armenian), Iranian, and Indo-Aryan.

According to Indian historical tradition, among the original inhabitants of northern India were three tribal conglomerates, Druhyus, Anus and Pūrus, along with some others to their south and east (Yadus, Turvasus, etc.). By pre-Rigvedic times, the Druhyus, originally inhabitants of the present-day areas of Pakistan, had expanded westwards into the areas of Afghanistan and Central Asia. The Anus, originally inhabitants of Kashmir, had expanded southwards into the present-day areas of Pakistan, later to expand into ever larger territories westward and northwestward. The Pūrus were primarily inhabitants of the Haryana-Western U.P. area (and later expanded eastwards, into the areas of the other tribal conglomerates).

As we have shown in our earlier books (TALAGERI 1993 and TALAGERI 2000), and we will see again later on in this chapter, the Vedic Aryans are clearly identifiable *only* with that section, of the ancient Indian populace, known as the Pūrus. But these Pūrus were one of many related ethnic groups. Therefore, we have *two* paradigms: The Indo-Aryans as one of many linguistic groups related to each other, and the Vedic Aryans as one of many ethnic (tribal conglomerate) groups related to each other. The two paradigms can be coordinated with each other only if the other linguistic groups in the first paradigm turn out to be identifiable with the other ethnic groups in the second paradigm. And, as we have seen in our earlier books, and will see again later on in this chapter, *the Iranians are clearly identifiable as part of that tribal conglomerate known as the Anus.*

As per our theory, the original homeland of the Indo-European family of languages was in India, and all the above twelve dialects were spoken by different groups of people who were referred to in Indian tradition as people belonging to the above three tribal conglomerates: the *Druhyus* (Hittite, Tocharian, Italic, Celtic, Germanic, Baltic, Slavic), the *Anus* (Greek, Albanian, Armenian, Iranian) and the *Pūrus* (Indo-Aryan).

The expansions and migrations of the different Indo-European branches took place in different stages, and the different isoglosses were formed in the course of these expansions and migrations as the Druhyus expanded northwards and westwards and the Anus expanded westwards. The migration schedules explain the presence of the different branches in their earliest attested areas in a more logical manner, taking almost every relevant factor into consideration, than any other homeland theory and migration schedule could do.

[Certain isoglosses, linking together two or three branches which have been geographically *together* from their earliest attested stages, have *not* been counted in the analysis, since these isoglosses could have been formed at *any* time in their pre-historical periods in their earliest attested areas, or earlier during the journey from any proposed original homeland to these areas (unless there is any particular reason to believe that this journey was not made together): for example, isoglosses linking together Indo-Aryan with Iranian; or Baltic and Slavic with each other or with Germanic; or Italic and Celtic with each other or with Germanic. Some of the isoglosses mentioned by Hock belong to this category: e.g. "***m*-cases, merger of *a* and *o***", and "**genitive/ablative merger**" (HOCK 1999a:14-15): such isoglosses do not help us in any way in locating the original homeland].

The isoglosses can be explained very logically as having been formed during different stages in the expansions and migrations of the Indo-European branches, as they moved out of the homeland area in two major waves of movement: the Druhyu dialects (Hittite, Tocharian, Italic, Celtic, Germanic, Baltic and Slavic) in a slow movement northwards from Afghanistan, and the Anu dialects (Albanian, Greek, Armenian/Phrygian and Iranian) in a slow movement westwards and northwestwards from present-day Pakistan.

The movements, naturally occurring slowly over long periods, are frozen here in six stages (Figures 2 to 7) [Note: the references cited below, GAMKRELIDZE, etc., are only for the isoglosses identified and not for their OIT implications]

Stage One (Figure 2): In the first stage, the Anatolian (Hittite) dialect had moved out northwards into the Central Asian zone. In this stage, *all the dialects, other than Anatolian*, developed the following linguistic features in common:

1. Feminines in *ā, *ī, *ū. (GAMKRELIDZE 1995:35).
2. Instrumental plural masculine *-ōis (GAMKRELIDZE 1995:345).
3. Independent (deictic) demonstrative pronouns *so, *sa, $t^{h}o$ (pl.th) (GAMKRELIDZE 1995:345).

At the same time, *the Italic and Celtic dialects in the west, and the Armenian/Phrygian, Iranian, and Indo-Aryan dialects in the east*, jointly developed a common priestly system with some common religious elements (WINN 1995:102) in the northern mountainous parts of Afghanistan, Pakistan, and adjoining parts of present-day India.

Figure 2. Stage 1 of the Indo-European Migrations.

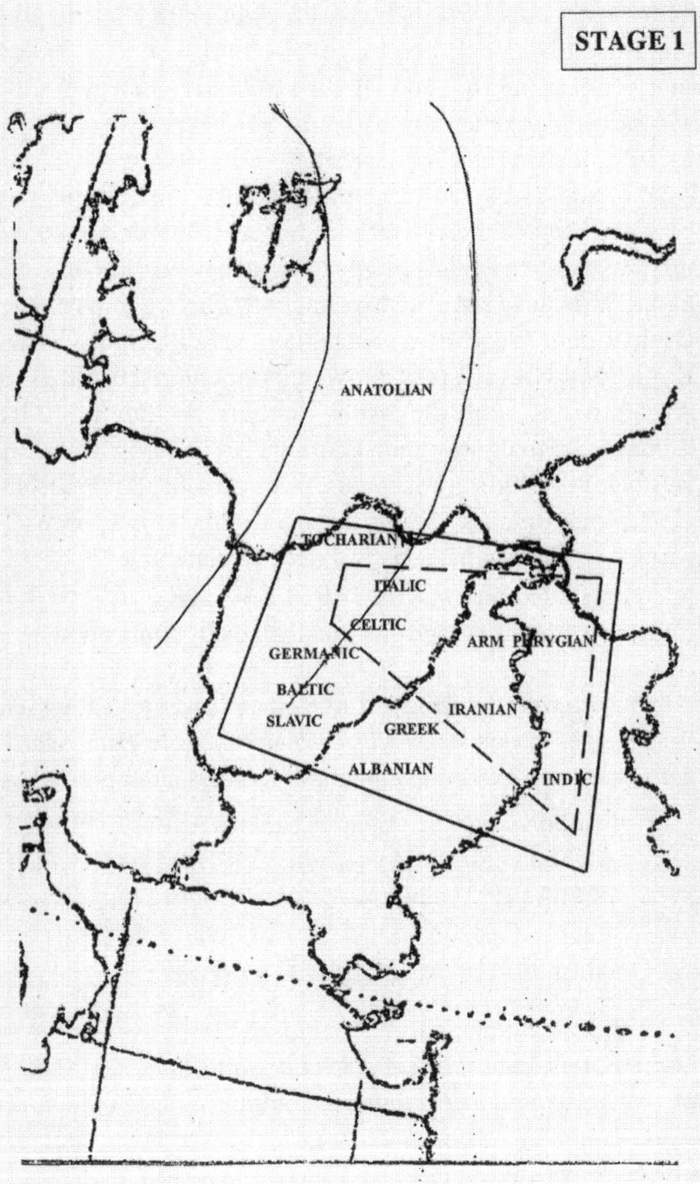

Stage Two (Figure 3): In the second stage, the Tocharian dialect had also moved out northwards into the Central Asian zone (while the Anatolian dialect moved out westwards towards the Caspian Sea, where it remained settled for a considerable period of time), while the other Druhyu dialects correspondingly expanded northwards. In this stage, certain religious and cultural features developed in common between *the Italic, Celtic, Germanic, Baltic and Slavic speakers in the west, and the Iranians in the east*, for example religious and/or cultural traditions and myths involving otters and beavers (GAMKRELIDZE 1995:447-449).

Stage Three (Figure 4): In the third stage, the Italic and Celtic dialects had also moved out into the Central Asian zone (the Tocharian branch having moved out eastwards, where, like the Anatolian branch to the west, it remained settled for a considerable period of time), while the other Druhyu dialects to the south correspondingly expanded northwards. In this stage, different innovations took place in the northern parts as well as in the southern parts:

In the north, *the Anatolian, Tocharian and Italic dialects* developed one isogloss in common: the relative pronoun *khois (GAMKRELIDZE 1995:345).

The Tocharian, Italic and Celtic dialects developed the following two isoglosses in common:

1. Genitive singular *-ī (GAMKRELIDZE 1995:345).
2. Subjunctives in *-ā, *-ē (GAMKRELIDZE 1995:345).

The Anatolian, Tocharian, Italic and Celtic dialects, partly along with Armenian/Phrygian (the northernmost of the southern dialects), developed one isogloss in common: Middles in *-r (GAMKRELIDZE 1995:345).

In the south, *the Germanic, Baltic and Slavic dialects in the west, along with the Albanian, Greek, Armenian/Phrygian, Iranian and Indo-Aryan dialects in the east*, jointly developed Middles in *-oi/*-moi (GAMKRELIDZE 1995:345).

Figure 3. Stage 2 of the Indo-European Migrations.

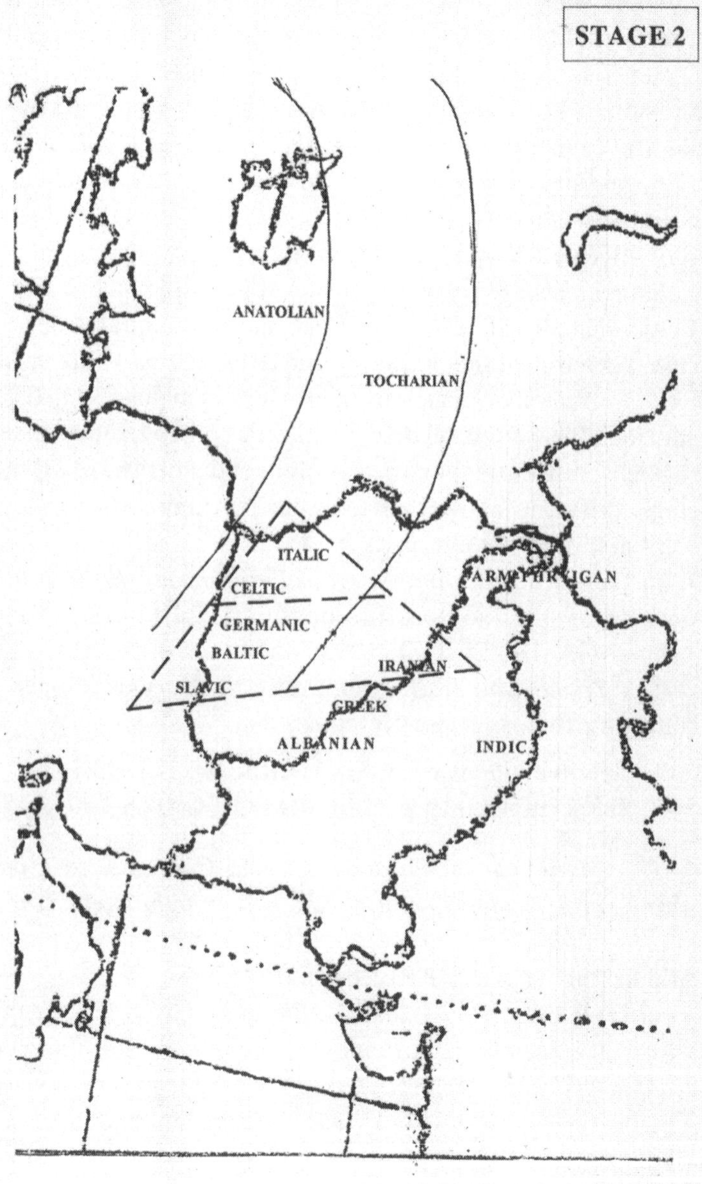

Figure 4. Stage 3 of the Indo-European Migrations.

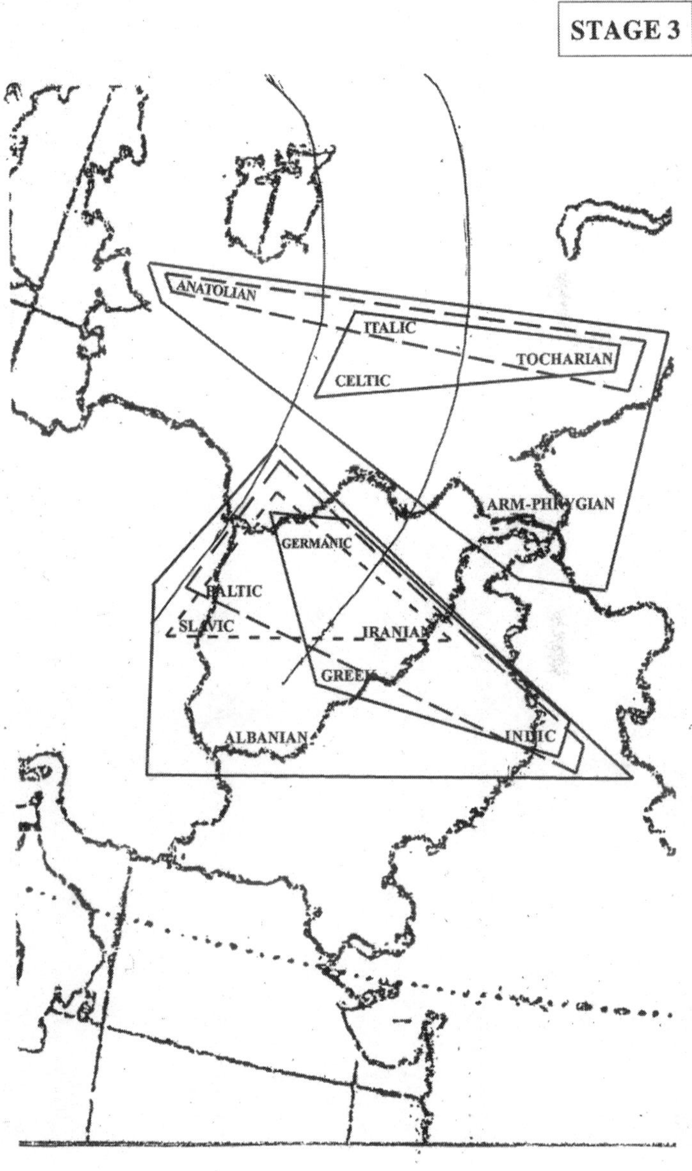

Figure 5. Stage 4 of the Indo-European Migrations.

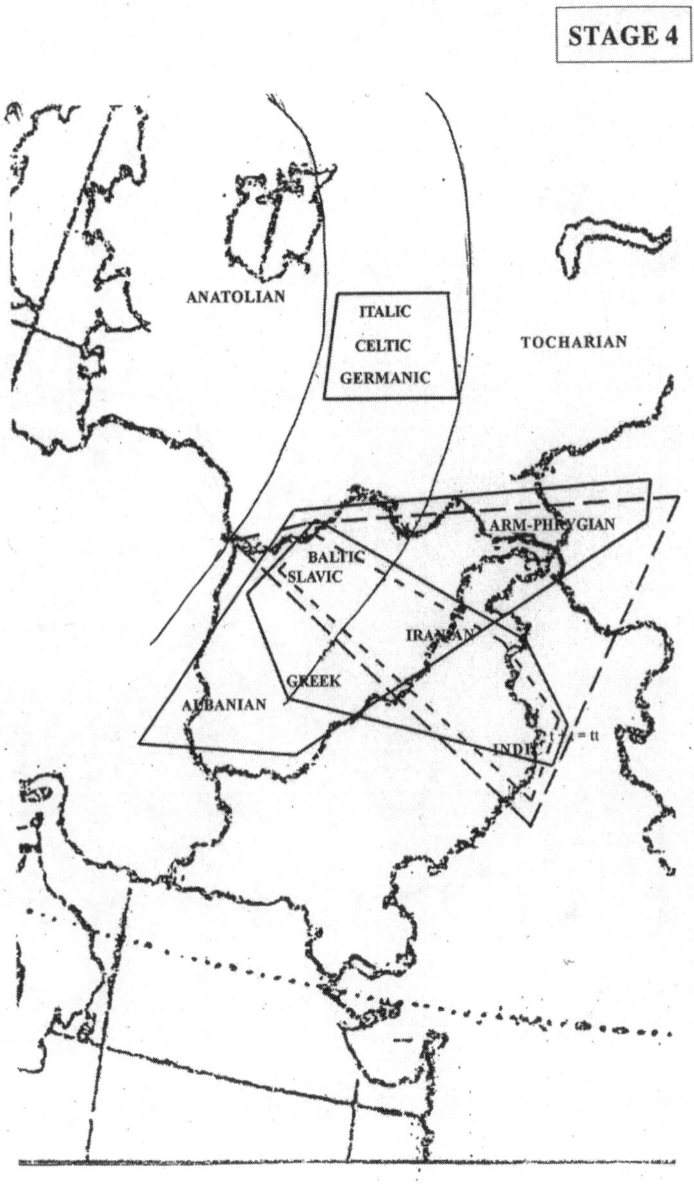

The Germanic dialect in the west, along with the Greek, Iranian and Indo-Aryan dialects in the east, developed one isogloss in common: the comparison of adjectives in *-t^{h}ero and *-is-t^{h}o (GAMKRELIDZE 1995:345).

The Germanic, Baltic and Slavic dialects in the west, along with the Iranian dialect in the east, lost the aspiration in voiced aspirated stops (LUBOTSKY 2001:302).

The Germanic and Baltic dialects in the west, along with the Iranian and Indo-Aryan dialects in the east, developed one isogloss in common: the instrumental singular masculine *-ō (GAMKRELIDZE 1995:345).

Stage Four (Figure 5): In the fourth stage, the Germanic dialect had also moved out northwards into the Central Asian zone, while the other Druhyu dialects to the south (Baltic and Slavic) correspondingly expanded northwards. Likewise, the Albanian and Greek dialects in the east slowly shifted westwards into the void left by the northwards expanding Druhyu dialects. Several isoglosses developed in this stage:

In the north, the Italic, Celtic and Germanic dialects jointly developed one isogloss in common: the original Proto-Indo-European *tt changed to ss. However, *in Anatolian*, it changed to tst. *In the south*, it changed to ss *in the Baltic, Slavic, Greek, Albanian and Iranian dialects*, while it remained tt *in Indo-Aryan* (HOCK 1999a:15-16; according to whom all these changes took place after an initial change in PIE itself from *tt to *tst, which was retained in Anatolian, while Indo-Aryan tt is a result of a change back again from tst to tt, "**either by regular sound change or through some kind of analogical reintroduction**").

In the south, certain other innovations took place in a core area excluding the west-expanding Greeks further south, mainly in *the Iranian, Indo-Aryan and Armenian/Phrygian dialects in the east, with a transition area in the Baltic and Slavic dialects to the west:*

1. Satem assibilation: palatals > assibilated stops (> sibilants) (HOCK 1999a:14-15).

Figure 6. Stage 5 of the Indo-European Migrations.

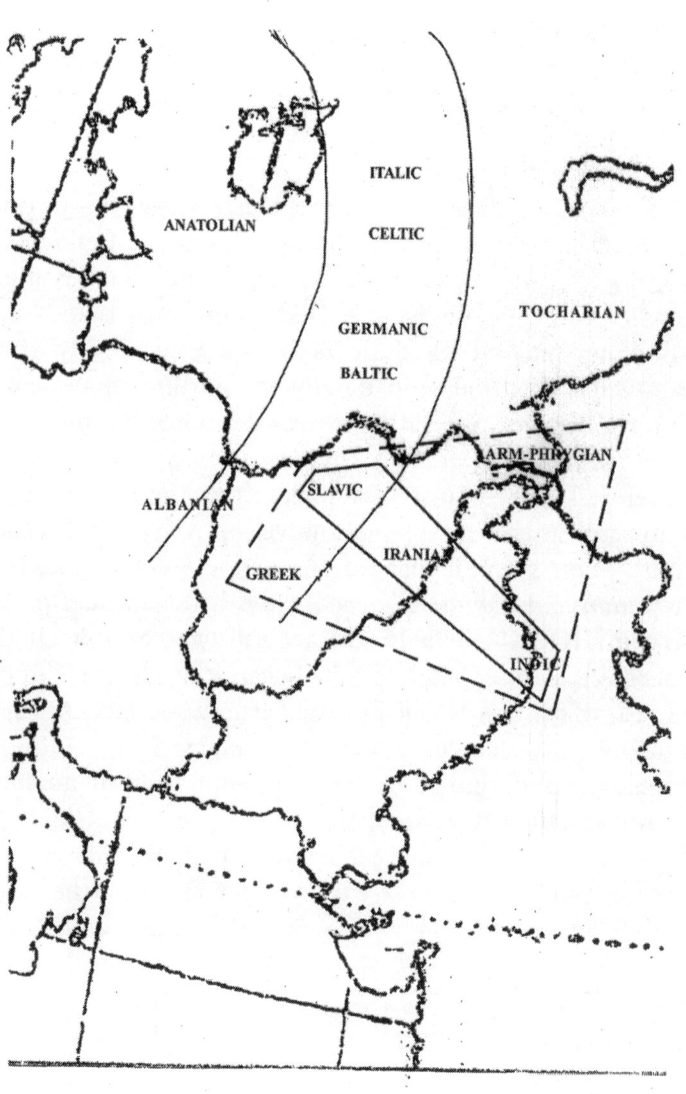

2. "Ruki" rule (HOCK 1999a:14-15).

In practically the same area, *the Baltic and Slavic dialects, along with the Iranian and Indo-Aryan dialects, with a transition area in the Armenian/Phrygian dialect to the north,* merged the original PIE velars and labio-velars (while a merger of the original velars and palatals took place in all the other Indo-European dialects) (HOCK 1999a:15).

One more joint innovation took place in the south, in *the Baltic, Slavic, Greek, Iranian and Indo-Aryan dialects:* the Locative *-s-u/*-s-i (GAMKRELIDZE 1995:345).

Stage Five (Figure 6): In the fifth stage, the Baltic dialect had also moved out northwards into the Central Asian zone. The Albanian and Greek dialects also shifted further westwards. The Slavic dialect was the last of the Druhyu dialects to remain in the south, and developed certain isoglosses in common with the other dialects in the south:

The Slavic dialect, along with the Greek, Armenian/ Phrygian, Iranian and Indo-Aryan dialects, developed the relative pronoun *yos (GAMKRELIDZE 1995:345).

The Slavic dialect remained in particularly close contact with the Iranian and Indo-Aryan dialects for some time, and developed some things in common:

1. Genitive-locative dual *-os (GAMKRELIDZE 1995:345).
2. First person singular pronoun: nominative, genitive and accusative (GAMKRELIDZE 1995:345).

Stage Six (Figure 7): In the sixth and final stage, the Slavic dialect had also moved out into the Central Asian zone, while the Italic and Celtic dialects had already moved out to the north of, and beyond, this zone. In the south, the Albanian, Greek and Iranian branches had also moved out westwards to fully occupy the area formerly occupied by the Druhyu branches. Many important features developed in this stage:

The Germanic, Baltic and Slavic branches in the north developed one isogloss in common: Oblique cases in *-m-

Figure 7. Stage 6 of the Indo-European Migrations.

STAGE 6

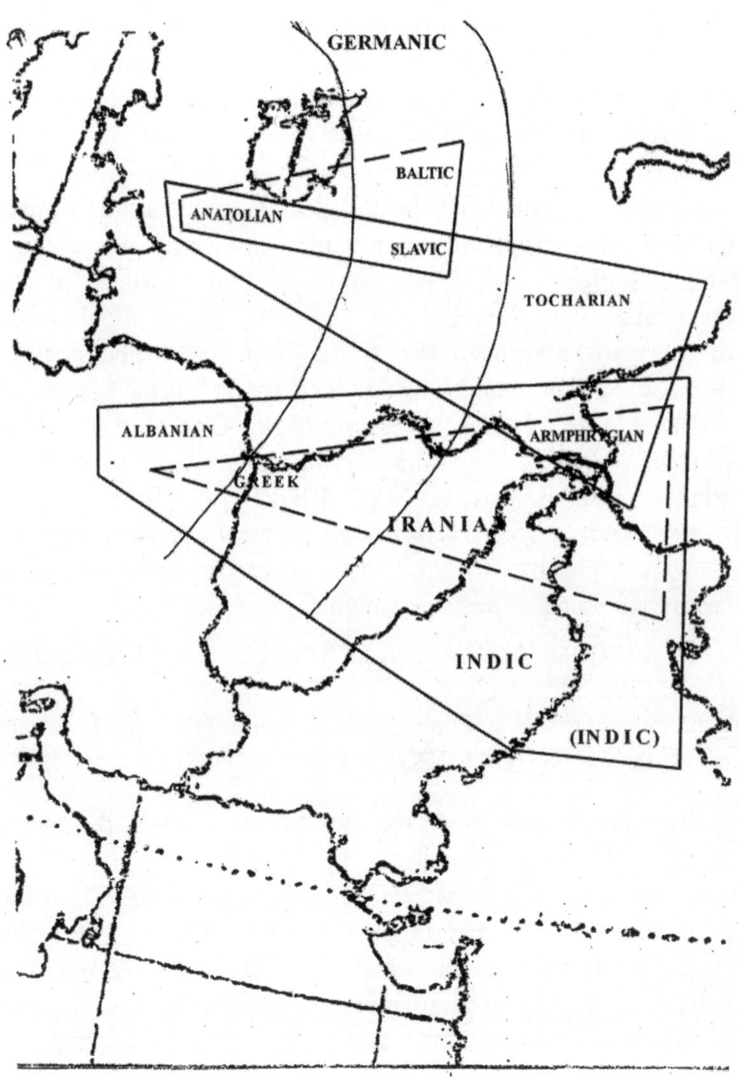

(GAMKRELIDZE 1995:345), while, *in the south, the Albanian, Greek, Armenian/Phrygian, Iranian and Indo-Aryan dialects* developed Oblique cases in *-b^{h}i- (GAMKRELIDZE 1995:345).

In the north, the Anatolian dialect, along with the Baltic and Slavic dialects, developed the Middle present participle in *-mo- (GAMKRELIDZE 1995:345).

The Anatolian and Tocharian dialects, along with the Slavic dialect, with a transition area in the Armenian/Phrygian dialect (the northernmost of the southern dialects), developed Modal forms in *-l- (GAMKRELIDZE 1995:345).

In the south, there was a "**complete restructuring of the entire inherited verbal system**" (GAMKRELIDZE 1995:340-341,345), in *the Albanian, Greek, Armenian/Phrygian, Iranian and Indo-Aryan dialects*, with the formation of athematic and thematic aorists, augmented forms and reduplicated presents.

The Greek, Armenian/Phrygian and Iranian dialects underwent another innovation: *s > h from initial *s before a vowel, from intervocalic *s, and from some occurrences of *s before and after sonants, while *s remained before and after a stop (MEILLET 1908/1967:113).

As we saw, *all* the isoglosses can be explained logically in the above scenario. This scenario is fully based on what Hock calls "**arguments based on plausibility and simplicity**" (HOCK 1999a:12), and represents "**a scenario of migrations that would account for the dialectological relationships between the early Indo-European languages**" (HOCK 1999a:13) more plausibly and simply, *and completely*, than any other scenario could do. The scenario is so logical that almost any other genuine isogloss that may be discovered, among the different IE dialects, can be similarly adjusted into it. [Note again: certain isoglosses, among dialects which were spoken in contiguous areas in more than one stage, may have been formed during stages other than those postulated above:

for example, the separate formation of Oblique cases in *-m- and in *-b^hi- in two different groups of dialects, assumed to be in Stage Six above (only because the five dialects in the south, which jointly developed Oblique cases in *-b^hi-, also developed some other isoglosses together in the last stage), may actually have been formed in Stage Three (when the same two groups of dialects were in separate contiguous areas to the west and the east, respectively, in the south)].

And this scenario is placed in a specific geographical area, and in specific historical contexts supported by literary evidence, *as well as by other linguistic and logistic evidence*, as we shall see presently.

7D
THE EVIDENCE IN PERSPECTIVE

The scenario of expansions and migrations, outlined above, can be examined in detail in the context of the three groups of dialects which emerge in any discussion on the Indo-European migrations:

1. *The Early Dialects*: Anatolian (Hittite), Tocharian.
2. *The European dialects*: Italic, Celtic, Germanic, Baltic, Slavic.
3. *The Last Dialects*: Albanian, Greek, Armenian/ Phrygian, Iranian, Indo-Aryan.

7D-1. The Early Dialects

The Early Dialects, Anatolian and Tocharian, can be best explained only on the basis of the scenario outlined above:

1. The above scenario requires *minimum movement* from the Original Homeland to their earliest attested areas:

Tocharian, in any case, lands almost directly into its earliest historically attested area after it moves out northwards from Afghanistan into Central Asia. This area, eastwards, is the very area attested by the archaeological discoveries of Tocharian documents and by all the suggested literary references to the Tocharian people in other ancient texts.

Anatolian (Hittite), likewise, after a northwestward movement from Afghanistan into Central Asia, lands up near the eastern shores of the Caspian Sea. A natural expansion along the shores of the Caspian Sea would naturally lead to the northeastern borders of Anatolia; and it is from the northeastern borders of Anatolia that the Hittites made their entry into their earliest attested areas in West Asia.

Nichols (quoting Dyen) points out, "**As defined by Dyen (1956), a homeland is a continuous area and a migration is any movement causing that area to become non-continuous (while a movement that simply changes its shape or area is an expansion or expansive intrusion)** [...] ***Homelands are to be reconstructed in such a way as to minimize the number of migrations, and the number of migrating daughter branches, required to get from them to attested distributions*** **(Dyen 1956:613)**" (NICHOLS 1997:134). The scenario outlined by us above requires no migrations for the two Early Dialects (*as also for the Last Dialects*), as they were simply expansions into adjacent territories, which in later times became "**remnants of formerly continuous distributions. They were stranded by subsequent expansions of other language families, chiefly Turkic, in historical times**" (NICHOLS 1997:136).

On the other hand, as pointed out in our earlier book, the "**theories which place the original homeland in South Russia postulate a great number of separate emigrations of individual branches in different directions: Hittite and Tocharian would be the earliest emigrants in two different and opposite directions, and Indo-Iranian, Armenian and Greek would be the last emigrants, again, in three different and opposite directions**" (TALAGERI 2000:287).

About Tocharian, Childe had accepted long ago that "**the simplest explanation of the presence of a Centum language in Central Asia would be to regard it as the last survivor of an original Asiatic Aryan stock. To identify a wandering of Aryans across Turkestan from Europe in a**

relatively late historical period is frankly difficult" (CHILDE 1926:95-996).

Therefore, on grounds of "plausibility and simplicity", the migration scenario from the Indian homeland, outlined by us above, is more feasible than any other scenario, since it postulates the *least* movements for the two Early Dialects as compared to any migration scenario from any other suggested homeland.

2. There would also appear to be some kind of literary references to the existence of the Tocharian and Anatolian (Hittite) branches to the north of the Himalayan ranges; although it must be admitted that this is speculative, and can only be considered in conjunction with all the other evidence given in this chapter:

The traditional texts sometimes refer to two great tribes or peoples living to the north of the Himalayas, referred to as the *Uttara-Madra* and the *Uttara-Kuru*. While the exact location (and identity) of these two peoples has been the subject of much speculation — the suggested locations ranging from Himachal Pradesh to Tibet to Central Asia — many writers, Indians in particular, have identified the Uttara-Kurus with the Tokharians; and this is supported by the similarity of the name *Uttara-Kuru* with the name Tocharian (*Twγry* in an Uighur text, and *Tou-ch'u-lo* or *Tu-huo-lo* in ancient Chinese Buddhist texts) suggesting that *Uttara-Kuru* may be a Sanskritization of the native appellation of the Tocharians (preserving, as closely as possible, what Henning calls "**the consonantal skeleton (dental + velar + r) and the old *u*-sonant** [which] **appears in every specimen of the name**" (HENNING 1978:225)).

It is further possible that, since the eastern of the two great tribes to the north were called the Uttara-Kuru, the western were called the Uttara-Madra on the analogy of the actual Kurus and the Madras to the south being to the east and the west respectively; and the term Uttara-Madra may therefore refer to the Anatolians (Hittites).

That the Hittites may have had some contact with the Indo-Aryans is suggested by the presence, in Hittite mythology, of *Indra*, who is so completely unknown to all the other Indo-European mythologies and traditions (except of course, the Avesta, where he has been demonized) that Lubotsky and Witzel (see WITZEL 2006:95) feel emboldened to classify it as a word borrowed by "Indo-Iranian" from a hypothetical BMAC language *in Northern-Afghanistan/Central-Asia:*

The Larousse Encyclopaedia of Mythology records, as the *only* Indo-European myth still extant among the Hittites, the myth of the Great Serpent who had dared to attack the weather-god (name unknown) and who was subsequently killed by *Inar*. This is clearly a version of the killing of Vṛtra by Indra in the Rigveda. The Larousse Encyclopaedia actually describes Inar as "**Inar, a God who had come from India with the Indo-European Hittites**" (LAROUSSE 1959:85).

3. Finally, incredible as it may seem, we actually have some kind of racial evidence (though nothing to do with any "Aryan race") indicating that the Hittites immigrated into West Asia from Central Asia rather than from the West:

While the existence of the Hittites as a prominent historical tribe in West Asia has been known on the basis of detailed historical records since early times (they are very prominent in the Old Testament of the Bible as well), it was only in the beginning of the twentieth century that their language was discovered and studied in detail and they were conclusively identified linguistically as Indo-Europeans. Shortly after this, a paper in the Journal of the American Oriental Society makes the following incidental observations: "**While the reading of the inscriptions by Hrozny and other scholars has almost conclusively shown that they spoke an Indo-European language, their physical type is clearly Mongoloid, as is shown by their representations both on their own sculptures and on Egyptian monuments. They had high cheek-bones and retreating foreheads.**" (CARNOY 1919:117).

The Early Dialects, thus, can be explained more convincingly on the basis of the Indian Homeland scenario outlined in this chapter than on the basis of any other homeland scenario.

7D-2. The European Dialects

In respect of the European dialects (Italic, Celtic, Germanic, Baltic and Slavic), we get the only clear case of migration, as opposed to expansion followed by a break with the parent area. The European dialects moved northwards from Afghanistan into Central Asia, and then, *in the same above order*, appear to have gradually migrated by a northwest path into Europe, and continued right up to Western Europe, where the Italic and Celtic branches expanded to occupy southwestern and central-western Europe respectively, the Germanic branch occupied the northwestern areas, and the Baltic and Slavic branches occupied the northeastern and eastern areas of Europe respectively. There is plenty of evidence forthcoming for this scenario:

1. The Indo-European dialects, as we saw, can be divided into three groups, the Early Dialects, the European dialects, and the Last Dialects. It is significant that the Early Dialects and the Last Dialects, and, more particularly, the Early Dialects and "Indo-Iranian", do not share any isoglosses with each other. As Gamkrelidze points out: "**It is significant that the Anatolian languages give no evidence of contact with Indo-Iranian and vice versa. This is evidence of an early break between Anatolian and Aryan dialects within Indo-European and their early movement in different directions with no subsequent contact between them**" (GAMKRELIDZE 1995:807-808). The same may be said for Tocharian vis-à-vis the "Aryan" dialects (Indo-Aryan and Iranian): "**There are words demonstrating the affinity of Tocharian with some or all of the ancient European languages but not with Indo-Iranian (see Benveniste 1936:234-237 [1959:100-101], Van Windekens 1976:614-617; see also I.7.5.9 above).**" (GAMKRELIDZE:1995:831). [Of course, we see from stray words like Indra/Inar, or *gardabha/kercapo*, that there *were* contacts, but these contacts

were late contacts and not contacts between dialects developing common isoglosses at an early date].

On the other hand, as we have seen, the European dialects developed isoglosses with both the Early Dialects *as well as* with the Last Dialects.

Now, let us see how this reconciles with Hock's scenario in which the original homeland was located in the area from "**East Central Europe to Eastern Russia**" with the different dialects simply "**maintaining their relative positions to each other as they fanned out from the homeland**":

From any homeland located in this area, the Early Dialects would have had to migrate *eastwards* and *southwards* in order to reach their earliest attested historical habitats. After them, the European Dialects would have had to migrate *westwards* in order to reach their earliest attested historical habitats. In the last stage, the speakers of "Indo-Iranian" would again have had to migrate *eastwards* and *southwards* to reach their earliest attested historical habitats. And since they would have been "**maintaining their relative positions to each other as they fanned out from the homeland**", it is to be assumed that their original relative positions in the homeland would also be as follows: the European dialects in the *western parts* of the homeland,; and in the *eastern* parts, Tocharian to the *northeast*, Indo-Aryan and Iranian to the *southeast*, and Hittite to the *south*.

In these circumstances, it is extremely strange that the Early dialects did *not* develop any isoglosses with "Indo-Iranian", either in the original homeland itself, where they were both located in the eastern parts of the homeland, *or* later when the "Indo-Iranians" migrated eastwards and should have come into close contact again with the Early Dialects which preceded them there (or at least with Tocharian in or around Central Asia). But, at the same time, both, the Early Dialects *as well as* "Indo-Iranian", separately, developed several isoglosses in common with the European dialects that were located in the western parts of the homeland and later migrated further west! Clearly, looked at from the point of view of "**plausibility and simplicity**", any homeland located in any area "from East Central Europe to Eastern Russia" would run into very "**severe difficulties**" indeed.

On the other hand, the isoglosses are explained logically in the Indian homeland scenario outlined in this chapter: the Early Dialects (Hittite and Tocharian) first migrated from Afghanistan into the Central Asian zone and remained settled on the outskirts there for a long period of time. Indo-Aryan and Iranian remained to the south of this zone till historical times, and therefore never developed any isoglosses in common with the Early Dialects. The various European Dialects, on the other hand, developed isoglosses in common, separately, with both the Last dialects as well as the Early Dialects, since they expanded from the southern zone (where the Indo-Aryan and Iranian dialects were located) to the northern zone (where the Early Dialects were located) before they set out on the migratory route which ultimately took them to Europe. *From the point of view of "plausibility and simplicity", this homeland scenario definitely fits the bill.*

Of course, long-winded arguments *could* be concocted, both in support of the "East Central Europe to Eastern Russia" scenario and against the Indian homeland scenario, in order to disprove the points made above; but they would really involve a tremendous amount of special pleading and an equally prodigious determination to ignore facts, and would certainly not fit into any criteria of "plausibility and simplicity".

2. Johanna Nichols, in a *very detailed linguistic study*, appropriately entitled "**The Epicentre of the Indo-European Linguistic Spread**", examines loan-words from West Asia (Semitic and Sumerian) found in Indo-European and also in other families like Caucasian (separately Kartvelian, Abkhaz-Circassian and Nakh-Daghestanian), and the mode and form of transmission of these loan-words into the Indo-European family as a whole as well as into particular branches, and combines this with the evidence of the spread of Uralic and its connections with Indo-European. All this diverse evidence of

loan-words is combined with several kinds of other linguistic evidence (see below), and she arrives at the conclusion that the locus or epicenter of the spread of the Indo-European languages lay in **"ancient Bactria-Sogdiana"**: i.e. in the very area outside the exit point from Afghanistan into Central Asia indicated by the evidence of the isoglosses as shown by us above:

> **"Several kinds of evidence for the PIE locus have been presented here. Ancient loanwords point to a locus along the desert trajectory, not particularly close to Mesopotamia and probably far out in the eastern hinterlands. The structure of the family tree, the accumulation of genetic diversity at the western periphery of the range, the location of Tocharian and its implications for early dialect geography, the early attestation of Anatolian in Asia Minor, and the geography of the *centum-satem* split all point in the same direction: a locus in western central Asia. Evidence presented in Volume II supports the same conclusion: the long-standing westward trajectories of languages point to an eastward locus, and the spread of IE along all three trajectories points to a locus well to the east of the Caspian Sea. The *satem* shift also spread from a locus to the south-east of the Caspian, with *satem* languages showing up as later entrants along all three trajectory terminals. (The *satem* shift is a post-PIE but very early IE development). The locus of the IE spread was therefore somewhere in the vicinity of ancient Bactria-Sogdiana."** (NICHOLS 1997:137).

Without going into the details of this linguistic study, which covers two volumes of detailed analysis, we may only note how Nichols' description of the dispersal of the Indo-European languages (in effect, the European Dialects) westwards, from this locus in Bactria-Sogdiana, fits in with our scenario above. According to Nichols:

> **"The vast interior of Eurasia is a linguistic spread zone** [...] **where** [...] **a single language or language family spreads out over a broad territorial range"** (NICHOLS 1997:122).
>
> **"The central Eurasian spread zone (Figure 8.4), as described in Volume II, was part of a standing pattern whereby languages were drawn into the spread zone, spread westward, and were eventually**

> **succeeded by the next spreading family. The dispersal for each entering family occurred after entry into the spread zone. The point of dispersal for each family is the locus of its proto-homeland, and this locus eventually is engulfed by the next entering language** [...] **the locus is one of the earliest points to be overtaken by the next spread**" (NICHOLS 1997:137).

Further, she notes that the locus is "**a theoretical point representing a linguistic epicenter**" (from where the languages spread out westwards into Eurasia) and:

> "**not a literal place of ethnic or linguistic origin, so the ultimate origin of PIE need not be in the same place as the locus. There are several linguistically plausible possibilities for the origin of pre-PIE. It could have spread eastward from the Black Sea steppe (as proposed by Mallory 1989 and by Anthony 1991, 1995), so that the locus formed only after this spread but still early in the history of disintegrating PIE** [...] **It could have come into the spread zone from the east** [...] **Or it could have been a language of the early urban oases of southern central Asia**" (NICHOLS 1997:138-139).

Nichols, without being an advocate of the OIT (she talks, elsewhere, about the Aryans "**spreading into northern India**" (NICHOLS 1997:135), even though a movement in this direction of any Indo-European group is not testified by her linguistic analysis) presents a clear-cut and unambiguous linguistic case for the origin of the westward spread of the European Dialects from an original epicenter at the exit point from Afghanistan into Central Asia.

3. Independently of the diverse linguistic evidence analyzed by Nichols above (which pertains to linguistic contacts of the European dialects with languages *to the west and southwest* of Central Asia), there is other linguistic evidence (pertaining to contacts with the languages *to the east and north* of Central Asia as well), indicating that the European Dialects had migrated to Europe after a long sojourn in Central Asia.

A western academic scholar of Chinese origin, Tsung-tung Chang, shows, on the basis of a study of the relationship between the vocabulary of Old Chinese (as reconstructed by Bernard Karlgren, *Grammata Serica*, 1940, etc.) and the etymological roots of Proto-Indo-European vocabulary (as reconstructed by Julius Pokorny, *Indogermanisches Etymologisches Wörterbuch*, 1959) that there was a very strong Indo-European influence on the formative vocabulary of Old Chinese:

> "**In the last four years, I have traced out about 1500 cognate words, which would constitute roughly two-thirds of the basic vocabulary in Old Chinese. The common words are to be found in all spheres of life including kinship, animals, plants, hydrography, landscape, parts of the body, actions, emotional expressions, politics and religion, and even function words such as pronouns and prepositions, as partly shown in the lists of this paper.**" (CHANG 1988:32).

And the particular Indo-European dialects or branches that show these common words are not Indo-Aryan or Iranian, but the European dialects, and especially Germanic: "**Among Indo-European dialects, Germanic languages seem to have been mostly akin to Old Chinese**" (CHANG 1988:32); and Chang points out that these connections indicate that "**Indo-Europeans had coexisted for thousands of years in Central Asia** [...] (before) **they emigrated into Europe**" (CHANG 1988:33).

The presence of Germanic, as well as Celtic, in ancient Central Asia is confirmed by Gamkrelidze and Ivanov as well, who deal with this point at length in section 12.7 in their book, entitled "**The separation of the Ancient European dialects from Proto-Indo-European and the migration of Indo-European tribes across Central Asia**" (GAMKRELIDZE 1995:831-847), where they trace the movement of the European Dialects from Central Asia to Europe on the basis of a trail of linguistic contacts between the European Dialects and various other language families on the route. This evidence includes (apart from borrowings from the European Dialects into Old Chinese, already discussed above) borrowings from the Yeneseian and Altaic languages into the European Dialects and vice versa.

What is significant is that Gamkrelidze and Ivanov advocate an original homeland in Anatolia (Turkey) in West Asia. But the linguistic evidence for contacts between the European Dialects and the eastern languages in and around Central Asia is so undeniable that they are compelled to suggest a *roundabout route* for the European dialects (map in GAMKRELIDZE 1995:850-851), bringing them eastwards all the way from Anatolia to Central Asia, and then turning them around again and taking them to Europe via the migratory route from Central Asia to Europe indicated in our scenario in this chapter.

4. There is also literary evidence for this migration of the European Dialects from India to Central Asia. As we have seen, the traditional texts speak of three main tribal conglomerates residing in northernmost and northwestern India: the Pūrus, the Anus and the Druhyus; and the Pūrus alone are identifiable with the Vedic Aryans, and the Anus are identifiable with the Iranians (and also the Armenians/ Phrygians, Greeks and Albanians, as we shall see). In this scenario, the term Druhyus logically must refer to the other dialects to the north and west: i.e. the European dialects.

And in the case of the Druhyus, *and in their case alone*, the traditional histories record distinct memories of their migration to the northwest *and beyond*. The three tribal conglomerates are originally placed as follows: the Pūrus in the heart of north India (in the Delhi-Haryana-Western U.P area), with the Anus to their north (in the Himalayan areas of Himachal Pradesh and Kashmir), and the Druhyus to their west (in the northern half of present-day Pakistan). Traditional history then records upheavals in which wars attributed to the Druhyus (depicted somewhat like the Huns of mediaeval times) led to a united front of the other tribes; at the end of which the Anus had expanded southwards to occupy the areas, in the northern half of Pakistan, originally occupied by the Druhyus, and the Druhyus had been pushed far to the west, into Afghanistan: "**the next Druhyu king Gandhāra retired to the northwest and gave his name to the Gandhāra country**" (PARGITER 1962:262).

All the scholars who have translated or studied the traditional historical literature have noted the significance of the Purāṇic traditions which relate that, several generations later (i.e. gradually, in the course of time), the Druhyus slowly migrated to the north from this area (i.e. from Afghanistan), and established settlements in the northern areas:

> "**Indian tradition distinctly asserts that there was an Aila outflow of the Druhyus through the northwest into the countries beyond, where they founded various kingdoms**" (PARGITER 1962:298).
>
> "**Five Purāṇas add that Pracetas' descendants spread out into the *mleccha* countries to the north beyond India and founded kingdoms there**" (BHARGAVA 1956/1971:99).
>
> "**After a time, being overpopulated, the Druhyus crossed the borders of India and founded many principalities in the Mleccha territories in the north, and probably carried the Aryan culture beyond the frontiers of India**" (MAJUMDAR 1951/1996:283).

Of the three tribes, the Pūrus had the Angirases as their priests, and the Anus had the Bhṛgus or Atharvans as their priests (see our earlier books, and further on in this chapter), but any name for the corresponding priests of the Druhyus is not discernible from the references in the Rigveda or the traditional historical texts. However, a closer examination indicates that Druhyu was itself the name of the priestly class, and *the name* "Druhyu" as a name *for the entire spectrum of tribes to the west and north of the Anus* would appear to be based on a generalized use of the name of their priestly class:

The *only* important historical references to the Druhyus in the Rigveda are found in the Dāśarājña battle hymn **VII**.18, where they are referred to thrice out of a total of six references to them in the whole of the Rigveda (the other three references being merely listings of the name in directional enumerations of different tribes); and the nature of these three references must be noted: in **VII.18**.14, the reference is to the two tribal conglomerates (Anu and Druhyu), in **VII.18**.12, the reference is to the kings or leaders of these tribes in the battle (Kavaṣa and the Druhyu), and in **VII.18**.6, the reference is to the priests (Bhṛgu and Druhyu) of the two tribal conglomerates. The general use of the word Druhyu as an appellation for the tribe, the king *and* the priests shows that the Druhyus were already a minor and distant tribe at the time of this battle, and the remnants of the tribe, who joined the Anus as allies in this battle fought on Anu territory, were looked on by the Pūrus already as an amorphous entity.

Of the three uses of the word, it is clear that the word originally referred to the *priests*:

Firstly, the Vedic hymns were composed by priests, and it is logical that the name of the priestly class of the distant tribal conglomerate would be more likely to be used by them to coin a generalized name for that tribal conglomerate (especially, if that tribal conglomerate were already too diverse to have a common name of its own for itself).

Secondly, the Avesta makes it clear that *Druhyu* was an appellation for a class of rival or enemy priests: the priests of the Iranians were the *Āθravans* (*Atharvans* or *Bhṛgus*), and the terms *Angra* (*Angiras*) and *Druj* (*Druhyu*) are regularly used in the Avesta in reference to the demon enemies of Ahura Mazda and Zaraθuštra, and in Vendidad 19, it is an *Angra* and a *Druj* who try to tempt Zaraθuštra away from the path of Ahura Mazda.

Thirdly, the third known class of priests among the Indo-Europeans are the *Drui* (genitive druad, hence *Druid*), the priestly class among the Celtic people. Like the Vedic and Zoroastrian priests, the main curriculum of the "**Celtic Druids** […] **involved years of instruction and the memorization of innumerable verses, as the sacred tradition was an oral one**" (WINN 1995:54). After noting, in some detail, the similarities in their priestly systems, rituals, and religious and legal terminology, Winn concludes that the "**Celts, Romans, and Indo-Iranians shared a religious heritage dating to an early Indo-European period**" (WINN 1995:103).

[The *Bhṛgus* or *Atharvans* are indirectly remembered in Celtic traditions, as they are remembered in Vedic traditions (see TALAGERI 2000:172-174), as the earliest ṛṣis or teachers: two of the three Great Goddesses of the Celts were named *Anu* and *Brigit*, and while all the Goddesses in general were associated with fertility cults, "**Brigit, however, had additional functions as a tutelary deity of learning, culture and skills**" (LAROUSSE 1959:239). Most significantly, *Brigit is primarily associated with the maintenance of eternal fires*, like the eternal fires of the Iranian priests, and this was the central feature of her main temple at Kildare in Ireland, where eternal flames were maintained by priestesses.

They are also remembered in Germanic tradition: the Norse god of poetry and wisdom is *Bragi*, and although he is not directly associated with fire rituals, a suggested etymology of his name, often rejected simply because he is not known to be associated with fire or fire rituals, is from the word *braga*, "to shine": i.e. his name is also derived from the same IE root as the name of the *Bhṛgus*, the originators of the Vedic fire-rituals, and the *Phleguai*, the Greek fire-priests].

Further, while the word *Druhyu* and its cognates (*Druh, Drugh, drogha, droha*) in the Rigveda, *as well as* the word *Druj* in the Avesta, refer to demons or enemies; cognate forms have the opposite meaning in the European languages: while *Drui* is the name for the priests of the Celts, the word means "friend" in the Baltic and Slavonic languages (e.g. Lithuanian *draugas* and Russian *drug*. "Friend" may have been a symbolic word for priest: the Rigvedic reference to the two priestly classes of Sudas' enemies is as follows, Griffith's translation: "**The Bhṛgus and the Druhyus quickly listened: friend rescued friend mid the two distant peoples**"), and something like "soldier" in the Germanic languages (Gothic ga-*drauhts*, Old Norse *drōtt*, Old English *dryht*, Old German *truht*).

Therefore, it is clear that the term Druhyu was used in the Rigveda, and subsequent texts, as a term for the tribal conglomerate comprising primarily the proto-speakers of the European Dialects, and the traditional histories relate the emigration of these Druhyus from Afghanistan into the north and beyond.

5. Of all the extant Indo-European groups, it is the European Dialects for whom we have the clearest archaeological evidence regarding their movement into their historical habitats (i.e. most of Europe). As Winn points out:

> "**A 'common European horizon' developed after 3000 BC, at about the time of the Pit Grave expansion (Kurgan Wave #3). Because of the particular style of ceramics produced, it is usually known as the Corded Ware Horizon.** [...] **The expansion of the Corded Ware cultural variants throughout central, eastern and northern Europe has been construed as the most likely scenario for the origin of PIE (Proto-Indo-European) language and culture.** [...] **the territory inhabited by the Corded ware/Battle Axe culture, after its expansions, geographically qualifies it to be the ancestor of the Western or European language branches: Germanic, Baltic, Slavic, Celtic and Italic**" (WINN 1995:343, 349-350).

This archaeological phenomenon "**does not** [...] **explain the presence of Indo-Europeans in Asia, Greece and Anatolia**" (WINN 1995:343), but it explains the presence of the European branches, and *their expansion from Eastern Europe to the northern and western parts of Europe.*

The origins of the Corded Ware culture has been traced further east: to the Kurgan Culture of the South Russian Steppes, to the north of the Caucasus and south of the Urals. And more recently, the earliest origins of many of the elements of the Kurgan Culture have been traced to Central Asia.

The movement of the European Dialects from Central Asia to Europe is thus corroborated by the evidence of linguistics and archaeology; and the earlier movement from Afghanistan to Central Asia is recorded in Indian historical traditions.

7D-3. The Last Dialects

The evidence for the origin of the Last Dialects in India is overwhelming:

1. The evidence of the isoglosses, as we have seen, shows that the Last Dialects were indeed the last dialects to remain in the homeland after all the others had departed ["**After the dispersals of the early PIE dialects** [...] **there were still those who remained** [...] **Among them were the ancestors of the Greeks and Indo-Iranians** [...] **also shared by Armenian; all these languages it seems, existed in an area of mutual interaction.**" (WINN 1995:323-324)]. Therefore the logical conclusion can only be that the original homeland lay in the earliest attested historical area of one of these Last Dialects.

Of these Last Dialects, however, it is clear that the original homeland did not lie in the earliest attested historical areas of Albanian (Albania), Greek (Greece) or Armenian (Armenia), since these areas have never figured as candidates in any serious hypotheses about the original homeland; and the place-names in these areas are quite conclusive in this regard: as B.K.Ghosh points out, quoting Eduard Meyer, "**among the numerous personal and place-names handed down to us from Armenia up to the end of the Assyrian age, there is absolutely nothing Indo-European**" (MAJUMDAR ed.1951/ 1996:209-210); and S.M.M. Winn tells us, "**numerous place-names** [...] **show that Indo-European did not originate in Greece. The same can be said for Italy and Anatolia.**" (WINN 1995:326).

The same is the case with the Iranians *with regard to the land known today as Iran*: the earliest references to Iranians in Iran do not occur till after the beginning of the first millennium BCE:

> **"We find no evidence of the future 'Iranians' previous to the ninth century BC. The first allusion to the Parsua or Persians, then localized in the mountains of Kurdistan, and to the Madai or medes,**

already established on the plain, occurs in 837 BC in connection with the expedition of the Assyrian king Shalmaneser III. About a hundred years afterwards, the Medes invaded the plateau which we call Persia (or Iran) driving back or assimilating populations of whom there is no written record" (LAROUSSE 1959:321).

"**By the mid-ninth century BC two major groups of Iranians appear in cuneiform sources: the Medes and the Persians.** [...] **What is reasonably clear from the cuneiform sources is that the Medes and Persians (and no doubt other Iranian peoples not identified by name) were moving into western Iran from the east**" (Encyclopaedia Britannica, 1974, Vol.9, 832).

"**'Persians' are first mentioned in the 9th century BC Assyrian annals: on one campaign, in 835 BC, Shalmaneser (858-824) is said to have received tributes from 27 kings of Paršuwaš; the Medes are mentioned under Tiglath-Pileser III (744-727 BC)** [...] **There are no literary sources for Iranians in Central Asia before the Old Persian inscriptions (Darius's Bisotun inscription, 521-519 BC, ed. Schmitt) these show that by the mid-1st millennium BC tribes called Sakas by the Persians and Scythians by the Greeks were spread throughout Central Asia, from the westernmost edges (north and northwest of the Black Sea) to its easternmost borders**" (SKJÆRVØ 1995:156).

Therefore, the records show that the *earliest* evidence for the Iranians, outside the Avesta, does not place them in Iran and Central Asia before the first millennium BCE. As SkjÊrvì points out, the Avesta alone provides evidence for their earlier history: "**In view of the dearth of historical sources it is of paramount importance that one should evaluate the evidence of the Avesta, the holy book of the Zoroastrians, parts at least of which antedate the Old Persian inscriptions by several centuries**" (SKJÆRVØ 1995:156).

The geography of the Avesta is almost entirely centered around Afghanistan and the areas of present-day northern Pakistan (see SKJÆRVØ 1995, WITZEL 2000b, GNOLI 1980, etc.), i.e. to the *east* of Iran and Central Asia, in a period *earlier* to their recorded presence in Iran and Central Asia.

As we saw in Section I of this present book, the Avesta belongs to the Late Rigvedic Period (i.e. the period of the Late

Books of the Rigveda), and was composed somewhere in the second millennium BCE.

But (as we saw in the chapter on the Absolute Chronology of the Rigveda) in an *even earlier* period, in the earlier half of the third millennium BCE *or earlier*, the Early books of the Rigveda record that the proto-Iranians were residents of the Saptasindhu area in northern Pakistan at the time of the battle of the Ten Kings, in which a coalition of ten Anu tribes, including the Iranian *Parśu* (Persian), *Pṛthu* (Parthian), *Paktha* (Pakhtoon) and *Bhalāna* (Baluchi) tribes, led by a king with the Iranian name *Kavaṣa* and a priest with the Iranian name *Kavi*, fought the Bharata king Sudās in their own Anu territory on the banks of the Paruṣṇī (Ravi). [Other records testify to the *Madra* (Medes) as one more of the Anu tribes in that area].

Therefore, it is clear that the evidence of the Rigveda testifies to the presence *not only of the Indo-Aryans, but of the proto-Iranians as well*, in the northwestern parts of India in the early third millennium BCE or earlier, long before their recorded presence (*or the recorded presence of any other Indo-European group*) anywhere else in the world.

This, in itself, even in the absence of any other evidence, would make a strong case for India being the original homeland of the Indo-European languages.

2. The evidence of the isoglosses, even without our analysis in Section I of this book, makes a strong case for the presence of the other Last Dialects in northwestern India:

The Last Dialects, as we saw, share a great many isoglosses which could only have developed in the original homeland after the migration of the other Indo-European dialects from that homeland, including oblique cases in *-b^{h}i-, and a "**complete restructuring of the entire inherited verbal system**" (GAMKRELIDZE 1995:340-341,345), in *the Albanian, Greek, Armenian/Phrygian, Iranian and Indo-Aryan dialects*, with the formation of athematic and thematic aorists, augmented forms and reduplicated presents.

But there is also the strange phenomenon that *Iranian shares certain isoglosses with Armenian/Phrygian and Greek, which it does not share with Indo-Aryan*: the change of *s > h from initial *s before a vowel, from intervocalic *s, and from some occurrences of *s before and after sonants, while *s remained before and after a stop (MEILLET 1908/1967:113), as also the change of the original Proto-Indo-European *tt to ss (while it remained tt in Indo-Aryan) (HOCK 1999a:15-16).

Though AIT scholars would prefer to ignore the implications of these isoglosses, these implications are very clear: Iranian, Armenian/Phrygian and Greek developed these isoglosses in common, and were therefore dialects in close and contiguous contact with each other at the time. As per the AIT, Indo-Aryan and Iranian parted company with the other IE dialects in the original homeland (somewhere in the area from "East Central Europe to Eastern Russia"), so these isoglosses must have developed in that original homeland itself. This means that Indo-Aryan and Iranian were already *completely distinct* dialects from each other in that area itself, long before they parted company with the other dialects and traveled together all the way from the area "East Central Europe to Eastern Russia" to Central Asia.

That Indo-Aryan and Iranian are two distinct dialects is accepted by the more objective among the scholars. As Winn points out, there are:

> **"ten 'living branches'** [...] **Two branches, Indic (Indo-Aryan) and Iranian dominate the eastern cluster. Because of the close links between their classical forms — Sanskrit and Avestan respectively — these languages are often grouped together as a single Indo-Iranian branch.** [...] **a period of close contact between the Indic and Iranian people brought about linguistic convergence, thus making the two languages misleadingly similar**" (WINN 1995:37, 385).

Meillet had pointed out long ago that:

> **"It remains quite clear, however, that Indic and Iranian developed from different Indo-European dialects, whose period of common development was not long enough to effect total fusion**" (MEILLET 1908/1967:44).

On the other hand, the connection "between their classical

forms — Sanskrit and Avestan respectively" is indeed very close: Witzel, for example, insists that the two are derived from one original parent IE dialect which "**can be reconstructed by comparative linguistics, and large parts of the IIr spiritual and material culture as well, by *carefully* using the method of linguistic paleontology**" (WITZEL 2005:353).

[In the process, in his typical fraudulent style, Witzel even makes *the blatantly and incredibly false allegation* that "**Talageri 2000, against all linguistic evidence, even denies close relationship of both groups**" (WITZEL 2001a:45), an allegation repeated again later: "**Talageri (2000) even refuses the link of Vedic with Iranian**" (WITZEL 2005:384). Apparently, Witzel cannot distinguish between the claim that Indo-Aryan and Iranian are two distinct, but closely evolved, branches (a claim made not just by me, but even by Winn and Meillet above), and the claim that there is no "close relationship" or "link" at all between them.].

Thus, there are *two* factual circumstances: *one*, that Iranian, already as an IE dialect separate from Indo-Aryan, developed certain isoglosses in common with Armenian/Phrygian and Greek when the three dialects were in close and contiguous areas; and, two, that the Avestan and Rigvedic languages and cultures are very close to each other. The two facts are *very difficult* to reconcile with each other if one takes the AIT stand that the first circumstance took place in a far off area from "East Central Europe to Eastern Russia", and the *second* took place after a long journey by the "Indo-Iranians" from East Central Europe and Eastern Russia to Central Asia, followed by a separation and migration in two different directions, followed by the separate composition of the Avesta and the Rigveda. [And they become actually *impossible* to reconcile with each other when we see (see Section I of this present book) that the Avesta was composed in the Late Rigvedic period, which followed certain *earlier* periods in which both the Iranians and the Indo-Aryans were settled in the areas of present day northern Pakistan and adjacent areas of present north India, respectively, with no knowledge of areas further west].

Witzel's partner in his BMAC theory, A. Lubotsky, clearly sees the contradiction in the two circumstances, but seems to feel that a mere confident assertion of the two contradictions in a single invasionist statement is enough to reconcile them:

> **"In the case of Indo-Iranian, there may have been early differentiation between the Indo-Aryan and Iranian branches, especially if we assume that the Iranian loss of aspiration in voiced aspirated stops was a dialectal feature which Iranian shared with Balto-Slavic and Germanic (cf. Kortlandt 1978:115). Nevertheless, Proto-Indo-Iranian for a long time remained a dialectal unity, possibly even up to the moment when the Indo-Aryans crossed the Hindu Kush mountain range and lost contact with the Iranians"** (LUBOTSKY 2001:302).

The only way, on grounds of maximum "plausibility and simplicity", the two facts can be reconciled with each other is if the first circumstance took place *not* in any area "East Central Europe to Eastern Russia" but in areas adjacent to the areas of composition of the Avesta and the Rigveda: i.e., in and around present day Pakistan and Afghanistan.

3. There is, in fact, literary evidence for the presence of the three other Last Dialects (Albanian, Greek and Armenian) in the vicinity of the "Indo-Iranians" in the Early Rigvedic Period.

As we already saw, the hymns describing the Battle of the Ten Kings, in the Early Rigvedic Period, name various Iranian tribes in the Anu-Druhyu coalition against the Bharata king Sudās: the Pṛthu (Parthians), the Parśu (Persians), the Paktha (Pakhtoons), the Bhalāna (Baluchis), etc. Three other tribes named are the *Alina* (*Hellene* = Greeks), the *Bhṛgu* (Armenians/*Phrygians*) and the *Śimyu* (*Sirmio* = Albanians). We have identified these three tribes with these three Indo-European branches in both our earlier books (TALAGERI 1993:369, TALAGERI 2000:262). There has, of course, been criticism on the ground that the names do not correspond exactly. *Obviously* they do not: the names *Alina, Bhṛgu* and *Śimyu* are the versions found in hymns referring to incidents which took place in the early third millennium BCE or earlier, in the area of present-day Pakistan, recorded in the language of the Indo-Aryan dialect of that time. The names *Hellene, Phryge* and *Sirmio* are self-appellations in the languages or ethnic groups concerned, in the first millennium BCE or later, in areas far to the west (i.e. in the earliest attested historical areas of the respective groups).

It would be a strange coincidence indeed that a list of names of ten tribes described in the course of one historical battle recorded in the Rigveda should, *by mere and sheer chance*, so closely resemble the names of so many tribal and ethnic groups from among the speakers of the earliest historically recorded forms of the Last Dialects.

What is more, these names have left a clear trail in the names of historically attested tribes found on the migration/expansion route, from northwestern India to southeast Europe, by which the speakers of the Last dialects must have migrated westwards (see figure 8, already shown in TALAGERI 2000:opp. 264): the *Śimyu*, the *Alina* and the *Bhṛgu* expanded or migrated westwards from the present day areas of northern Pakistan in the Early Rigvedic Period. They expanded through the northern parts of present day Iran, and northwards into the Caucasus region between the Caspian and the Black Seas, where they must have settled down for a period. While the *Bhṛgu* settled down mainly in the southernmost part of this region (as the Proto-Armenians) and one group among them migrated westwards from the south of the Black Sea across Anatolia to western Turkey (the *Phrygians*), the other two tribes, the *Śimyu* and the *Alina*, settled down to the north and northeast of the Black Sea (as the *Sarmatians* and the *Alans*), and later further expanded westwards and into southeast Europe (as the *Sirmios* = Proto-Albanians and the *Hellenes* = Proto-Greeks). [The Sarmatians and the Alans became almost completely Iranianized, and the Armenians reasonably so, in the course of the historical Iranian expansions (just as the residual Anu groups in northwestern India, the Madras, Kekayas, etc., became almost completely Indo-Aryanized in historical times)].

Some evidence for the movement of the Greeks through this region may be found recorded by Gamkrelidze, in a section entitled "**The Greek migration to mainland Greece from the east. Greek-Kartvelian lexical ties and the myth of the Argonauts**" (GAMKRELIDZE 1995:799-804), even though only as part of his theory that the Indo-European homeland lay in Anatolia.

The evidence for the expansion of the Last Dialects from an Indian Homeland is clearly too strong to be denied.

The *last* of these Last Dialects to remain in the greater Indian area were the Iranian dialect, which remained India's western neighbour into historical times and to the present day (starting with the Pashtu and Baluchi languages to the west, and the Dardic or Pishacha languages to the north), and the "Indo-Aryan" dialect which remained within India. We will now examine the close relationship between these two dialects, and these two Indo-European groups, in greater detail, for further evidence.

7E
THE LAST TWO OF THE LAST DIALECTS

"Indo-Aryan" and Iranian were the *last* of the Last Dialects to remain in close contact with each other till historical times, and the "Indo-Aryans" and Iranians have been neighbours to this day, separate from all the other branches of Indo-European languages. In fact, they were so close that even the historical religions developed by them, Vedic Hinduism and Zoroastrianism, share a great many features in common: the two oldest texts of these two religions, the Rigveda and the ("Zend") Avesta, seem to reflect two sides of the same religious coin, and, as we saw in the first two chapters of this book, share such a close socio-culturo-historical heritage in common that our present book has had to be entitled "The Rigveda and the Avesta".

An examination of the joint Indo-Iranian evidence sets the seal on the problem of the original Indo-European homeland: we saw, in Section I of this book, that the Iranians were inhabitants of the areas of present-day northern Pakistan (and migrated westwards only later) in the Early Rigvedic period which — on the basis of the *extremely and vitally important* Mitanni evidence, which provides us with a securely dated chronological sheet-anchor for Indian history (going far beyond the hitherto accepted sheet-anchor of the securely dated Aśoka pillars and the historical Greek accounts of India in the first millennium BCE) — we can now securely date to at least (on a *conservative* estimate) the early third millennium BCE and earlier.

There is a great deal of other evidence which helps us to place this history, and the relationship between the Iranians and the Vedic Aryans, *in India*, in *greater* perspective and *deeper* into the past. We have already examined this evidence (particularly the textual aspects of it) in detail in our earlier books. We will, here, examine once more *some* of this evidence, both textual and linguistic, with some *more* details.

7E-1. The Textual Evidence

The Rigveda and the Avesta share a close relationship, and have a religious and socio-culturo-historical heritage in common; but there is one peculiar aspect of this relationship which has struck most scholars examining this heritage: the two traditions, Vedic and Avestan, seem to represent two entities sharing a common tradition, *but as rival entities within this common tradition*. And echoes of this rivalry persist down to the later forms of these two traditions, Purāṇic Hinduism and Pahlavī Zoroastrianism: e.g. in the Epic-Purāṇic mythological traditions of the battles between the devas (gods) and the *asuras* (demons). In the Avesta and in later Zoroastrianism, *Ahura* stands for god, and Daēva for demon.

Helmut Humbach, the eminent Avestan scholar, makes the following very pertinent observations: "**It must be emphasized that the process of polarization of relations between the Ahuras and the Daēvas is already complete in the Gāthās, whereas, in the Rigveda, the reverse process of polarization between the Devas and the Asuras, which does not begin before the later parts of the Rigveda, develops as it were before our very eyes, and is not completed until the later Vedic period. Thus, it is not at all likely that the origins of the polarization are to be sought in the prehistorical, the proto-Aryan period.** [...] **All this suggests a synchrony between the later Vedic period and Zarathuštra's reform in Iran.**" (HUMBACH 1991:23).

We have already examined the evidence for the early history of the joint "Indo-Iranians" in India, in our earlier books (TALAGERI 1993:179-182, 271-279, 344-367, etc.; TALAGERI 2000:137-231, etc.). Here we will examine once more the evidence for the identity of the Vedic Aryans with the Pūrus and the Iranians with the Anus in Indian historical traditions, and for the expansions of the Iranians:

1. *The Pūrus as the Vedic Aryans*: Indian historical traditions speak of five "lunar" tribes or races (races not in the eyes-hair-and-cranium sense) in ancient India (apart from the "solar" tribe or race, the Ikṣvākus = the Rigvedic Tṛkṣis): the Druhyu, the Anu and the Pūru in the north, and the Yadu and Turvasu (Turvaśa in the Rigveda) more in the interior.

Of these, the Pūrus are clearly identifiable with the Vedic Aryans. The historical traditions place the Pūrus in the central region, in and around Brahmāvarta or Kurukṣetra, the holiest of holy lands of the later Vedic texts, which, as we have seen, was the "centre of the earth" for the Vedic Aryans in the Rigveda as well. The Books of the Rigveda, as we have repeatedly seen, can be divided into Early, Middle and Late; and the evidence (TALAGERI 2000:137-160) unanimously shows that in the Early Books (6, 3 and 7), and the Middle Books (4 and 2), the Bharatas (a branch of the Pūrus) were the

People of the Book, and, in the Late Books (5, 1, 8-10), the Vedic culture had become more widespread or cosmopolitan, but it was still a text of the Pūrus alone:

a) The nature of the references to the five tribes makes it clear that the Pūrus *alone* are the People of the Book in the Rigveda: all the five tribes are named in one verse (**I.108**.8), and one or more are named in four other verses: Yadus, Turvaśas, Druhyus and Anus (in **VIII.10**.5); Druhyus, Pūrus (and Tṛkṣis) (in **VI.46**.8); Anus and Turvaśas (in **VIII.4**.1); and Turvaṣas alone (in **I.47**.7). All these are directional references, in which the names of the tribes are merely used as pointers or in enumerations of tribes. *Apart from these directional references*, the following are the references to the different tribes:

The Druhyus are named in only *one* hymn, where they figure as *the enemies* in the hymn: in **VII.18**.6,12,14 (in reference to the Battle of the Ten kings).

The Anus are named in *four* hymns: in *two* of them, **VI.62**.9 and **VII.18**.13,14, they figure as *the enemies* in the hymns. [In the other two hymns, they are mentioned in two different contexts; and although these are not hostile references, they again help us in identifying the Anus with the Iranians, as we will see presently].

The Yadus and Turvaśas are mentioned in many more hymns: 19 in all, but the references make it clear that they are different from the People of the Book. *Firstly*, as Witzel puts it, they are "**at times friends and at times enemies of the Pūru-Bharatas**" (WITZEL 1995b:328), i.e. of the People of the Book (Witzel subconsciously realizes that people depicted as friends or enemies of the composers in any hymn are, automatically, actually the friends or enemies of "**the Pūru-Bharatas**"). *Secondly*, they are "**regularly paired**" (WITZEL 1995b:313); i.e. they are overwhelmingly more often than not (i.e. in 15 of the 19 hymns which refer to them) named *together* by the composers of the hymns, as if they were one entity, or at any rate a pair difficult to distinguish from each other, which is always a sign of unfamiliarity or distance. And, *thirdly*, the verses (most of which actually seem to refer to two particular historical incidents where the Yadus and Turvaṣas came to the aid of the Pūrus) also regularly refer to them as coming "from afar" (**I.36**.18; **VI.45**.1), from "the further bank" (**V.31**.8) across flooded rivers (**I.174**.9; **IV.30**.17), and "over the sea" (**VI.20**.12).

On the other hand, the references to the Bharatas and the Pūrus are very much in a *first-person sense*, and make it very clear that the Pūrus are *the People of the Book* in the Rigveda:

All the Vedic Gods are identified as the *Gods of the Pūrus: Agni* is described as a "fountain" to the Pūrus (**X.4**.1), a "priest" who drives away the sins of the Pūrus (**I.129**.5), the Hero who is worshipped by the Pūrus (**I.59**.6), the protector of the sacrifices of the Pūrus (**V.17**.1), and the destroyer of enemy castles for the Pūrus (**VII.5**.3). *Mitra* and *Varuṇa* are described as affording special aid in battle and war to the Pūrus, in the form of powerful allies and steeds (**IV.38**.1,3; **39**.2). *Indra* is described as the God to whom the Pūrus sacrifice in order to gain new favours (**VI.20**.10) and for whom the Pūrus shed Soma (**VIII.64**.10). Indra gives freedom to the Pūrus by slaying Vṛtra or the enemy (**IV.21**.10), helps the Pūrus in battle (**VII.19**.3), and breaks down enemy castles for the Pūrus (**I.63**.7; **130**.7; **131**.4). He even addresses the Pūrus, and asks them to sacrifice to him alone, promising in return his friendship, protection and generosity (**X.48**.5), in a manner reminiscent of the Biblical God's "covenant" with the People of the Book.

The *only two* unfriendly references to the Pūrus, in this case clearly to sections of *non-Bharata* Pūrus who entered into conflict with the Bharata clan or sub-tribe, are in **VII.8**.4 (which talks about "Bharata's Agni" conquering the Pūrus) and **VII.18**.3 (which talks about conquering "in sacrifice" the scornful Pūrus who failed to come to the aid of the Bharatas in the Battle of the Ten Kings). The Bharatas are undoubtedly the unqualified heroes of the hymns in the Family Books 2-7 (*all* *but one* of the references to the Bharatas appear only in the Family Books: **I**.**96**.3; **II**.**7**.1,5; **36**.2; **III**.**23**.2; **33**.11,12; **53**.12,24; **IV**.**25**.4; **V**.**11**.1; **54**.14; **VI**.**16**.19,45; **VII**.**8**.4; **33**.6): in many of these verses even the Gods are referred to as Bharatas: Agni in **I**.**96**.3, **II**.**7**.1,5; **IV**.**25**.4 and **VI**.**16**.9, and the Maruts in **II**.**36**.2. In other verses, Agni is described as belonging to the Bharatas: **III**.**23**.2; **V**.**11**.1; **VI**.**16**.45 and **VII**.**8**.4. There is not a single reference even faintly hostile to the Bharatas.

[Witzel, in his 1995 papers, recognizes that it is "**the Pūru, to whom (and to** [...] **the Bharata) the Ṛgveda really belongs**" (WITZEL 1995b:313), and that the Rigveda was "**composed primarily by the Pūrus and Bharatas**" (WITZEL 1995b:328), and even that the Bharatas were "**a subtribe**" (WITZEL 1995b:339) of the Pūrus. But he convinces himself that, while Divodāsa and Sudās were Bharatas, *Purukutsa and Trasadasyu* were Pūrus; and hence confuses every reference to Pūrus (i.e. to the Bharatas) as a reference to those *non*-Pūru *Tṛkṣi* kings, whom, moreover, he somehow identifies as the *enemies* of Sudās and the Bharatas in the Battle of the Ten Kings. Altogether, therefore, he ends up with a thoroughly chaotic and confused picture of Rigvedic history, for which he blames "**conflicting glimpses**" and "**inconsistencies**" in the hymns: "**Although book 7 is strongly pro-Bharata, it provides several, conflicting, glimpses of the Pūru** [...**in**] **7.5.3, Vasiṣṭha himself praises Agni for vanquishing the 'black' enemies of the Pūrus — this really ought to have been composed for the Bharatas. Inconsistencies also appear in hymn 7.19.3, which looks back on the ten kings' battle but mentions Indra's help for both Sudās and Trasadasyu, the son of Purukutsa, and also refers to the Pūrus' winning of land** [...]" (WITZEL 1995b:331)!]

b) The area of the Sarasvatī river was the heartland of the Vedic Aryans. It was so important that it is the only river to have three whole hymns (apart from many other references) in its praise: **VI.**61; **VII.**95 and 96. Sarasvatī is also one of the three Great Goddesses praised in the *āprī sūktas* (family hymns) of all the ten families of composers of the Ṛgveda.

As per the evidence of the Rigveda, the Sarasvatī was a purely *Pūru* river, running through *Pūru* territory, with *Pūrus* dwelling on *both* sides of the river: "**the Pūrus dwell, Beauteous One, on thy two grassy banks**" (**VIII.96**.2). Significantly, another one of the three Great Goddesses is Bhāratī, the deity of the Bharata clan or subtribe of the Pūrus.

c) The identity of the Pūrus with the Vedic Aryans is so unmistakable, that the line between "Pūru" and "man" is distinctly blurred in the Rigveda: Griffith, for example, sees fit to translate the word as "man" in at least five verses: **I.129**.5; **131**.4; **IV.21**.10; **V.171**.1 and **X.4**.1. In one verse (**VIII.64**.10), the *Rigveda itself* identifies the Pūrus with "mankind": "**Pūrave** [...] **mānave jane**". Finally, the Rigveda actually coins a word *pūruṣa/puruṣa* (descendant of *Pūru*), on the analogy of the word *manuṣa* (descendant of *Manu*), for "man".

The identity of the Pūrus with the Vedic Aryans is impossible to miss: as we saw, even Witzel, with his confused and chaotic understanding of the Vedic situation and Vedic history, points out that it is "**the Pūru, to whom (and to their dominant successors, the Bharata) the Ṛgveda really belongs**" (WITZEL 2005b:313), and that the Rigveda was "**composed primarily by the Pūrus and Bharatas**" (WITZEL 1995b:328). And Southworth (SOUTHWORTH 1995:266) even identifies the Vedic Aryans *linguistically* and *archaeologically* with the Pūrus (see section 8B-1 of the next chapter).

2. *The Anus as the Proto-Iranians*: with the identity of the Pūrus as the Vedic Aryans beyond doubt, it is clear that the Iranians must be found among one of the other four tribes. But the Yadus and the Turvasus are to the south/east of the Pūru, in the interior of India, and the Druhyus are far to the west beyond the Anus. Therefore, it is clear that it is the Anus or (Ānavas) who represent the proto-Iranians, the western neighbours of the Vedic Aryans:

a. The Anus are depicted as inhabitants of the area of the Paruṣṇī river in the centre of the Punjab (or the Land of the Seven Rivers) in the early Books of the Rigveda: in the Battle of the Ten Kings, fought on the banks of the Paruṣṇī, the *Anus* are the inhabitants of the area of this river who form a coalition to fight the imperialist expansion of Sudās and the Bharatas, and it is the land and possessions of the *Anus* (VII.18.13) which are taken over by the Bharatas after their victory in the battle. This point is also noted by P L Bhargava: "**The fact that Indra is said to have given the possessions of the Anu king to the Tṛtsus in the battle of Paruṣṇī shows that that the Anus dwelt on the banks of the Paruṣṇī**" (BHARGAVA 1956/1971:130). The area, nevertheless, continues even after this to be the area of the Anus, who are again shown as inhabitants of the area even in the Late Books: "**The Anu live on the Paruṣṇī in 8.74.15**" (WITZEL 1995b:328, fn 51), and even in later historical times, where it is the area of the *Madras* and the *Kekayas*, who were Anus.

The Avesta (Vd. I) mentions the Haptahəndu (Saptasindhavah) as one of the sixteen *Iranian* lands, past and contemporary.

b) The Anu tribes who fought Sudās in the Battle of the Ten Kings include at least the *Parśu* or *Parśava* (The Persians), the *Pṛthu* or *Pārthava* (Parthians), the *Paktha* (Pakhtoons) and the *Bhalāna* (Baluchis): all names of historical Iranian peoples in later times. The king of the Anu coalition is *Kavi* (Avestan name *Kauui*, name of the dynasty which included Vīštāspa, contemporary and patron of Zaraθuštra) Cāyamāna, and the priest is *Kavaṣa* (an Avestan name, *Kaoša*). The two most prominent Anu tribes in later texts are the *Madra* (the *Madai* or *Medes*) and the *Kekaya* (a typical Iranian sounding name).

c) In later historical times, the name *Anu* is prominently found at both the southern and northern ends of the area described in the Avesta: Greek texts (e.g. *Stathmoi Parthikoi*, 16, of Isidore of Charax) refer to the area and the people immediately north of the Hāmūn-ī Hilmand in southern Afghanistan as the *anauon* or *anauoi*; and *Anau* is the name of a prominent proto-Iranian or Iranian archaeological site in Central Asia (Turkmenistan).

d) The conflict between the *devas* (gods) and the *asuras* (demons), which is a central theme in Purāṇic mythology, is recognized (e.g. HUMBACH 1991, etc.) as a mythologization of an earlier historical conflict between the Vedic Aryans and the Iranians. There is also a priestly angle to this conflict: the Epics and the Purāṇas depict the priest of the *devas* as an Angiras (Bṛhaspati), and the priest of the *asuras* as a Bhṛgu (*Kavi Uśanā* or *Uśanas Kāvya*, also popularly known as *Uśanas Śukra* or *Śukrācārya*).

Robert P. Goldman, in a detailed study entitled "**Gods, Priests and Warriors: the Bhṛgus of the Mahābhārata**", points out that the depiction of the Bhṛgus in the Epics and Purāṇas "**may shed some light on some of the most basic problems of early Indian and even early Indo-Iranian religion**" (GOLDMAN 1977:146), and that the Bhṛgus may originally have been the priests of the Iranians, and that certain elements in the myths about the "**ultimate disillusionment with the demons** [of one branch of the Bhṛgus] **and their going over to the side of the gods may also be viewed as suggestive of a process of absorption of this branch of the Bhṛgus into the ranks of the orthodox** [i.e. Vedic] **brahmins**" (GOLDMAN 1977:146).

An examination of the evidence shows the close connection between the Anus and the Bhṛgus on the one hand, and the Iranians and the Bhṛgus on the other:

The Anus and the Bhṛgus: the Anus are referred to in only *four* hymns, apart from the neutral directional references, and these four hymns fall into two categories: the hostile references (in **VI**.62 and **VII**.18) and the neutral references (in **V**.**31**.4 and **VIII**.**74**.4). The close connection between the Anus and the Bhṛgus is clear from both the categories of references:

The *hostile* references, which treat the Anus as enemies, are in **VI**.62 and **VII**.18, and in **VII**.18, verse 14 refers to the *Anus* and Druhyus, while verse 6 refers to the *Bhṛgus* and Druhyus, thus making it clear that the Anus are somehow equivalent to the Bhṛgus (actually the latter as the priests, and a subtribe, of the former). The *neutral* references are in **V**.31 and **VIII**.74, and **V.31**.4 describes the Anus as manufacturing a chariot for Indra. In **IV.16**.20, it is *Bhṛgus* who are described as manufacturing a chariot for Indra, thus again reiterating the equivalence. [In the other neutral reference, in **VIII.74**.4, which refers to the sacrificial fire of the Anus, the reference is to an Anu king named *Śrutarvan Ārkṣa* (son of *Ṛkṣa*). Both the prefix Śruta- and the name Ṛkṣa are found in the Avesta (Srūta- and ə rəxša), and, in this case, the king could be a proto-Iranian king (although the Avestan connection of the names, in itself, could also be due to the common culture of the Late Rigvedic period)].

[It is significant that the two neutral references appear in the more cosmopolitan Late Books, in which the conflicts of the earlier period have become a thing of the past, and the composers occasionally have some nice things to say even about the Dāsas (the non-Pūrus). Significantly, of the three hymns which have nice things to say about Dāsas, **VIII**.5, 46 and 51, the first two are hymns which have *camel-gifting kings with proto-Iranian names.*].

Griffith has the following to say about the above reference to the Anus in **V.31**.4, in his footnote to the verse: "***Anus*: probably meaning Bhṛgus who belonged to that tribe**".

The Iranians and the Bhṛgus: The Bhṛgus are also known as the *atharvans* in the Rigveda, and, in later mythology, Atharvan is the name of the son of the eponymous Bhṛgu. The priest of the *asuras* or demons in later mythology is the Rigvedic *Kavi Uśanā* or *Uśanas Kāvya* (Uśanas, son of Kavi), also more popularly known as Śukrācārya, who is nevertheless treated with great respect in both the Rigveda and the later texts, and often treated in the later mythology as even superior (in, for example, his knowledge of the *sanjīvanī mantra*, which could bring the dead back to life) to *Bṛhaspati*, the priest of the *devas* or gods.

The priests of the Iranians were (and are, till today) known as the *āθrauuans* in the Avesta, and *Usan*, son of *Kauui*, is an ancient mythical ancestral figure in the Avesta.

Goldman (see above) writes about one branch of the Iranian priests "**going over to the side of the gods**" and about the "**absorption of this branch of the Bhṛgus into the ranks of the orthodox** [i.e. Vedic] **brahmins**" (GOLDMAN 1977:146). This refers to a branch led by Jamadagni, who, in later Indian tradition, is treated as the patriarch of the Bhṛgu *gotras* among Vedic brahmins, and consequently, often even referred to as "Bhṛgu". As we have seen in detail in our earlier book (see TALAGERI 2000:164-180), the Bhṛgus are treated with disdain in the earlier parts of the Rigveda, and it is only in the later parts of the Rigveda that they are accepted into the Vedic mainstream; and later on, in post-Rigvedic Hinduism, the Bhṛgus actually go on to become the *single most important* family of Vedic *ṛṣis*.

An examination of the names of the Bhṛgu composers in the Rigveda shows that most of them contain name-elements in common with the Avesta, but as this is a feature found in a large number of names (*whatever* the family of the ṛṣis) in the Late Books (where almost all the hymns composed by Bhṛgus are found), this does not signify much. But the same can not be said for the names of the first Bhṛgu ṛṣi of the Rigveda, Jamadagni (who belongs to the Early period), and of his son Rāma:

The name Jamadagni is clearly a proto-Iranian name: *not* a name containing a name-element common to both the Rigveda and the Avesta, but a name which is linguistically *Iranian* rather than "*Indo-Aryan*". (This is in spite of the fact that the word *agni* for "fire" is found in the Vedic but not in the Avestan language: in opposition to this is the fact that we find the suffix *-agni* as a name-element in *another* name only in the Avesta: the name *Dāštāγni*): "**Iranian simply lacks the many innovations that characterize Ved.**" (WITZEL 2005:367). One of these innovations is "**the Ṛgvedic normalization in**

g*- of the present stems beginning in *j/g [...] **Avest. *jasaiti*:: Vedic *gacchati*. Note that j is retained only in traditional names such as *Jamad-agni* and in the perfect *ja-gām-a*, etc.**" (WITZEL 2005:392:149). Witzel assumes that the initial *j*-, instead of *g*-, in the name *Jamadagni* is an exception to the rule because it is a "traditional" name; but *actually the initial j- is found in the name Jamadagni because it is a proto-Iranian name.*

The name of Jamadagni's son is Rāma: he is called Rāma Jāmadagnya as the composer of **X**.110. However, he is also known as *Parśu*–Rāma in later times; and, consequently, Epic-Purāṇic mythology, in the belief that the word *parśu* means "axe" or "battle-axe", creates an enduring range of mythical tales centred around the idea of an axe-wielding Parśurāma. However, the word *parśu* in the sense of "axe" (*paraśu*) is not found in the Rigveda at all: it is a much later word. The original sense of the word *parśu* as an appellation in the name of Rāma Jāmadagnya was in respect of his identity as a member of the Anu (Iranian) tribe of the *Parśu*.

3. *The Iranian Expansions*: The earliest expansions of the Anus = Iranians are recorded in traditional Indian historical accounts:

a) The earliest locations of the five tribes, as recorded in the Purāṇas, are: the Pūru in the central region (Haryana, Delhi, western U.P.), *the Anu to their north (i.e. in the mountainous regions to the north of the Haryana-Delhi-western U.P area)*, the Druhyu to their west (in the northern half of present-day Pakistan), and the Yadu and Turvasu to the west and east, respectively, in the interior of India to the south of the Pūru.

Significantly, Iranian traditions record the earliest homeland of the Iranians as *Airyana Vaējah*, a land characterized by extreme cold. Gnoli, one of the greatest Avestan scholars, suggests that this land, mentioned in the list of the sixteen Iranian lands in the Avesta in Vendidād I, should be "**left out**" of the discussion since "**the country is characterized, in the Vd.I context, by an advanced state of mythicization**"

(GNOLI 1980:63). However, it is clear that the list of sixteen Iranian lands is arranged in rough geographical order, in an anti-clockwise direction which leads back close to the starting point; and the fact that the sixteen evils created by Angra Mainyu in the sixteen lands created by Ahura Mazda start out with "**severe winter**" in the first land *Airyana Vaējah*, move through a variety of other evils (including various sinful proclivities, obnoxious insects, evil spirits and physical ailments), and end again with "**severe winter**" in the sixteenth land, *Raŋhā*, shows that the sixteenth land is close to the first one. And since Gnoli identifies the sixteenth land, *Raŋhā*, as an "**eastern mountainous area, Indian or Indo-Iranian, hit by intense cold in winter**" (GNOLI 1980:53), it is clear that *Airyana Vaējah* is also likely to be an eastern, mountainous, Indian area.

b) The first major movement of the Anus took place in a tumultuous era of conflicts recorded in traditional history: the Druhyus started conquering eastwards and southwards, and their conquests brought them into conflict with all the other tribes and peoples. This led to a concerted effort by the other tribes to drive them out, and the result was that they were driven out not only from the east but also from their homeland in the northern half of present-day Pakistan. This area was occupied by the Anus who moved southwards and westwards: "**One branch, headed by Uśīnara established several kingdoms on the eastern border of the Punjab** [...] **his famous son Śivi originated the Śivis** [footnote: **called Śivas in Rigveda VII.18.7**] **in Śivapura, and extending his conquests westwards** [...] **occupying the whole of the Punjab except the northwestern corner**" (PARGITER 1962:264). *Thus, the Anus now became inhabitants also of the areas in present-day northern Pakistan originally occupied by the Druhyus*, and the Druhyus were pushed out further west (from where, as we have already seen, they later moved out northwards, and subsequently migrated to distant lands).

There is significant evidence in the Avesta for the early Iranian occupation of the Punjab:

i) Vendidād-I names *Haptahəndu*, the Punjab, as one of the sixteen Iranian lands.

ii) *Uśīnara*, the initial Purāṇic conqueror of the eastern Punjab (whose son extended the conquests *west*wards), has an Iranian name found in the Avesta as well: *Aošnara*.

iii) That the Iranians, earlier, lived in the Punjab to the west of the Kurukṣetra region is testified also by the reference in the Avesta to Manuša (the lake Mānuṣa referred to in the Rigveda, **III.23**.4, as being located at the vara ā pṛthivyāh, "the best place on earth", in Kurukṣetra. Witzel also identifies it as "**Manuṣa, a location 'in the back' (west) of Kurukṣetra**": WITZEL 1995b:335). Darmetester translates the verse, Yašt 19.1, as follows: "**The first mountain that rose up out of the earth, O Spitama Zarathuštra! was the Haraiti Barez. That mountain stretches all along the shores of the land washed by waters towards the east. The second mountain was Mountain Zeredhō outside mount Manusha: this mountain too stretches all along the shores of the land washed by waters towards the east**". Note that the "**first**" mountains that rose up out of the earth, for the Avesta, (i.e. the earliest lands known to the Iranians), are "**towards the east**". Darmetester interprets the word *Manusha* as the name of a mountain, but the verse specifies that it is talking only about the "first" and the "second" mountains, close to "**land washed by waters**", so the reference is definitely to lake Mānuṣa.

iv) In the Avesta, the king of Airyana Vaējah, Yima, creates a *vara* ("enclosure"?) as protection against the "severe winters" of the kingdom. This *vara* is at "the centre of the earth". This could be a reference to the

Iranian sojourn in the region to the west of Kurukṣetra, described in the Rigveda as *vara ā pṛthivyāh* "the best place on earth" or *nābhā pṛthivyāh* "the centre of the earth".

There is evidence in the Rigveda as well:

i) In the early part of the Early Period, the Rigveda (**VI**.27) records a battle on the banks of the Harīyūpīyā and Yavyāvatī (the Dṛṣadvatī) in Kurukṣetra, where the Bharatas are aligned with a king Abhyāvartin Cāyamāna, who is described as a Parthian (Pārthava).
ii) Later, by the late part of the Early period, the Parthians (**VII.83**.1) are now among the enemies of the Bharatas in a coalition led by a king Kavi Cāyamāna (**VII.18**.12), clearly a descendant of the earlier Abhyāvartin. This is the Battle of the Ten Kings, in which the Anu-Druhyu coalition fighting against the Bharatas, in the centre of the Punjab, includes (as we have already seen in detail) various proto-historical Iranian tribes led by a king and a priest with Iranian names. The Iranians were, thus, inhabitants of the areas to the west of Kurukṣetra (i.e. the Punjab) in the Early Rigvedic Period.
c) The Battle of the Ten Kings led to the beginnings of major expansions of the Anus = Iranians to the west. The Middle Rigvedic Period, which followed, saw the commencement of the common development of the "Indo-Iranian" culture represented in Vedic Hinduism and Zoroastrianism, and this common development of culture continued even more prominently into the Late Rigvedic period, and possibly later as well. The Late Rigvedic Period also saw the Zoroastrian "reforms" in the Iranian religion to the west, and the formulation of a distinctly Iranian religion which sought (not always successfully) to shake off some of the perceived religious cobwebs of the past.

   Anus continued to be the inhabitants of the Punjab in the Late Period (**VIII**.74); and also in later historical times (the Madras, Kekayas, etc.), but these were increasingly Vedicized or Sanskritized or "Indo-Aryanized" Anus. The bulk of the proto-Iranians had expanded to the west, into Afghanistan.

The consensus among western scholars (e.g. GNOLI 1980, SKJÆRVØ 1995, WITZEL 2000b, etc.) is that the geographical horizon of the Avesta is centered in and around Afghanistan.

d) In later historical times, we find the Iranians expanding into their historical areas in Iran and Central Asia; and later, even *further*: at its height, the Iranian expansions went right up to Europe (the Croats of the Balkan areas are believed to be of Iranian origin).

7E-2. The Uralic Evidence.

There is a linguistic factor which is generally, and thoughtlessly, interpreted as evidence of the movement of the Indo-Aryans and Iranians from west to east through Eurasia on their way to Central Asia (and thence to India and Iran): the evidence of close contacts between the "Indo-Iranian" and the Uralic languages. But, as we will see, this is, in fact, strong evidence *against* the above proposition.

A large number of words found in the Uralic — specifically the Finno-Ugric branch of the Uralic languages, and not the Samoyedic branch — are very clearly borrowed from Indo-Aryan or Iranian, and have been *very correctly* taken as evidence of close contacts between Finno-Ugrians and "Indo-Iranians":

> **"The earliest layer of Indo-Iranian borrowing consists of common Indo-Iranian, Proto-Indo-Aryan and Proto-Iranian words relating to three cultural spheres: economic production, social relations and religious beliefs. Economic terms comprise words for domestic animals (sheep, ram, Bactrian camel, stallion, colt, piglet, calf), pastoral processes and products (udder, skin, wool, cloth, spinner), farming (grain, awn, beer, sickle), tools (awl, whip, horn, hammer or mace), metal (ore) and, probably, ladder (or bridge). A large group of loanwords reflects social relations (man, sister, orphan, name) and includes such important Indo-Iranian terms like *dāsa***

> **'non-Aryan, alien, slave' and *asura* 'god, master, hero'. Finally a considerable number of the borrowed words reflect religious beliefs and practices: heaven, below (the nether world), god/ happiness, *vajra*/'Indra's weapon', dead/mortal, kidney (organ of the body used in the Aryan burial ceremony). There are also terms related to ecstatic drinks used by Indo-Iranian priests as well as Finno-Ugric shamans: honey, hemp and fly-agaric**" (KUZMINA 2001:290-291).

These borrowings must have taken place close to the homeland of the Uralic languages. Various different viewpoints have been put forward, and hotly debated, about the location of the Uralic homeland, and about the exact dating of various chronological levels of the "Indo-Iranian" borrowings. Kuzmina favours a "**west Siberian homeland of the Uralic tribes** [...] **a west Siberian Uralic homeland on the eastern side of the Ural mountains**", although he points out that "**romantic primary homelands**" have been postulated "**in the early days of research, which located the Uralic homeland in the Altai mountains, or in the territory of the Central Asian oasis cultures in Khorezm or even further in the east**" (KUZMINA 2001:323).

However, strictly speaking, none of these issues are really relevant to our discussion here. The main point is that at *some* point or points in the prehistoric past, there were contacts between Uralic speakers and "Indo-Iranian" speakers *somewhere* between East Europe and Central Asia. The exact when and where of it are *less* important than the fact that *all* these borrowings are in *only one* direction: from "Indo-Iranian" to Uralic. There is not a *single* accepted example of a borrowing in the opposite direction.

The *utter impossibility*, or at least *the extreme unlikelihood*, of the proposition, that speakers of two languages could have been *so closely* in contact with each other that one of the two languages borrowed *such a wide range of words* from the other, but that the other did not borrow a *single word* from the first, should have alerted the scholars to the fact that there was something wrong with the theory that these close contacts were between the "Indo-Iranian" of the south and the Uralic speakers. Especially when the *other* in this case is supposed to be "Indo-Iranian", which (or at least the Indo-Aryan half of which), according to the scholars, has been in the habit of borrowing words from every X, Y and Z of a language with which it came into contact!

The inevitable logical conclusion should have been that there *must* have been equally large numbers of Uralic words borrowed by the Indo-Aryan and Iranian speakers from whom Uralic borrowed all the above words. But no such words are found in the historical Indo-Aryan and Iranian languages of South Asia and greater Iran. Therefore, these words can not have been borrowed by Indo-Aryans and Iranians allegedly moving *from Eastern Europe to Central Asia* (and later further south), but by Indo-Aryans and Iranians moving *from Central Asia to Eastern Europe*. The Indo-Aryan and Iranian speakers, whose speech contained all these Uralic borrowings, were emigrants moving *away* from the main body of Indo-Aryan and Iranian speakers in the south, never to come into contact with them again, so these Uralic words never reached the Indo-Aryan and Iranian languages of the south (South Asia and Iran). The west migrating Indo-Aryans and Iranians are, unfortunately, lost to history, but their existence is vouched for by the borrowed words in the Uralic languages.

The fact that the words were borrowed by Uralic speakers from Indo-Aryans and Iranians moving *from Central Asia to East Europe* is also corroborated by the nature of the words borrowed. It is, to begin with, unlikely, *even from the point of view of the AIT*, that the language of the "Indo-Iranians", when still allegedly on their way towards Central Asia from the west, could have been so culturally rich as to possess such a rich stock of words pertaining to so many different spheres. But what sets the seal on the direction of movement is the fact that the borrowed words include words for peculiarly Central Asian things like Bactrian camels: "**The name and cult of the Bactrian camel were borrowed by the Finno-Ugric speakers from the Indo-Iranians in ancient times (Kuzmina 1963)**" (KUZMINA 2001:296).

Lubotsky also raises this problem, and is obviously not able to answer it from the point of view of the AIT: "**Another problem is how to account for Indo-Iranian isolates which have been borrowed into Uralic** [...which form part of...] **the new vocabulary, which most probably was acquired by the Indo-Iranians in Central Asia** [...]" (LUBOTSKY 2001:309). The answer is: these words were acquired from Indo-Aryan and Iranian groups moving out from Central Asia to Eastern Europe. [Incidentally, another aspect of the Indo-Aryan words in Uralic is that many of them are late words which appear only in the Late Books of the Rigveda or only in later Vedic texts].

The Uralic evidence thus shows that there were Indo-Aryan and Iranian groups, *now lost to history*, with a fully developed historical Indo-Iranian vocabulary formed in the southern parts of Asia, who migrated through Central Asia to the west in the ancient past. It also pointedly shows that the main body of Indo-Aryans and Iranians in the south did *not* themselves pass through Eurasia.

It thus reinforces *other* linguistic evidence that we have seen earlier in this chapter: the evidence of contacts between the European Dialects of Indo-European and *various non-Indo-European languages of Eurasia*, which shows that the European Dialects had passed through Central Asia and Eurasia in the past. In that case also, evidence of contacts between "Indo-Iranian" and those various non-Indo-European languages of Eurasia was conspicuously missing. Likewise, while all the European and Anatolian Dialects share isoglosses with Tocharian, Indo-Aryan and Iranian do not.

In sum: the evidence shows that there is *no* linguistic ground for any assumed movement of the main body of Indo-

Aryans and Iranians *of the south* through Eurasia in any direction at any time in the past.

7F
THE LINGUISTIC ROOTS IN INDIA

After examining the evidence concerning the Early Dialects, the European Dialects and the Last Dialects as a whole, as well as that concerning the last two of the Last Dialects (i.e. Indo-Aryan and Iranian), we finally come to the Last of the Last Dialects: "Indo-Aryan", *the Dialect which remained in the homeland after all the others had left.*

The very first argument usually made by most OIT writers (that the oldest texts and traditions of the Vedic Aryans give no evidence whatsoever of any consciousness of foreign origin) is not as simple or simplistic as it would appear to be at first sight: the Vedic Aryans give no indication of ever having known any land outside India because they *never* indeed *had* known any land outside India. In the words of George Erdosy, *an AIT writer*: "**we reiterate that there is no indication in the Rigveda of the Arya's memory of any ancestral home, and by extension, of migrations. Given the pains taken to create a distinct identity for themselves, it would be surprising if the Aryas neglected such an obvious emotive bond in reinforcing their group cohesion. Thus their silence on the subject of migrations is taken here to indicate that by the time of composition of the Rigveda, any memory of migrations, should they have taken place at all, had been erased from their consciousness**" (ERDOSY 1989:40-41),

Our analysis of the geography of the Rigveda in chapter 3 shows very clearly that the *earliest* areas with which the "Indo-Aryans" of the Rigveda were acquainted were the areas to the *east* of the Sarasvatī (the Sarasvatī of Kurukṣetra, not the Harahvaiti of Afghanistan) in the Early Rigvedic Period, and that it was only towards the *end* of the Early Period that they started expanding *westwards* into areas totally unknown to them before. And, as we saw in chapter 6, the Early Rigvedic Period goes back into *at least* the early third millennium BCE at a conservative estimate. Therefore, even in that *early* period, in the early third millennium BCE or earlier, they were *unacquainted* with any western areas, and, in fact, as we have seen in the chapter on the Geography of the Rigveda, the Rigveda refers, in a hymn of that Early Period, to the area of the Jahnāvī (the Gangā) as "**the ancient homeland**". Therefore, the desperate attempts by scholars like Witzel, to suggest that there are a "**number of vague reminiscences of foreign localities and tribes in the Ṛgveda**", leading as far west as "**the Rhipaean mountains, the modern Urals**" (WITZEL 1995b:320-322: see TALAGERI 2000:461-471), or that "**the IAs, as described in the RV, represent something definitely *new* in the subcontinent** [...] **The obvious conclusion should be that these new elements somehow came from the outside**" (WITZEL 2005:343), remain just that: desperate attempts which are *totally without any basis* in the Rigveda.

But we are not going to start this discussion once more from scratch here: all these things have been repeatedly discussed in detail elsewhere, and, in the light of the *totality* of the evidence presented in Section I of this book, are now pointless issues. The question now is: if the roots of the Indo-Aryans, and indeed the original roots of the Indo-Europeans as a whole, are in India, what are the linguistic indications of this fact?

But before that (and *for* that), we must first understand the term "Indo-Aryan" properly, *and in detail*: in all our discussions in this book and elsewhere, the term is *necessarily* used for *that* branch of the Indo-European family which is represented by the Vedic language (historically spoken in India), *as opposed to* all the other Indo-European branches, including Iranian (historically spoken outside India). This is because the whole discussion is centred around the alleged invasion or *immigration* or "trickle-in" of the Vedic Aryans into India (as per the AIT) versus the *emigration* out of India of the proto-speakers of the other Indo-European branches (as per the OIT in general, and as per the case presented by us in particular).

As we saw earlier on in this chapter, we have two paradigms: the linguistic paradigm with the Indo-Aryans as one of many linguistic groups related to each other, and the Indian historical paradigm with the Vedic Aryans as one of many ethnic (tribal conglomerate) groups related to each other. Therefore, the above proposition can be put in another way: the term "Indo-Aryan" is used for the Pūrus *as opposed to* the Anus and Druhyus. That the Anus and Druhyus of the Rigveda were also, strictly speaking, equally *Indian* at the time is ignored in our use of this term, because all the terms of the linguistic paradigm have been coined keeping in mind the geographical habitats of the twelve branches of Indo-European languages in *later* historical times. In spite of different *nomenclatures*, the *categories* of the two paradigms coincide with each other so far.

But, the same can not be said when we take into consideration *other* groups, in the Indian historical paradigm, which are located to the *interior*, to the *east* and *south* of the Pūrus: i.e., the Yadus, the Turvasus, and possibly others. All these groups were also equally *Indian* at the time, and as there is no reason to believe that major migrations of these groups took them out of India, they, logically, continued to remain *Indian* in later times, even more in the interior of India than the Pūrus. But the term "Indo-Aryan" of the linguistic paradigm is obviously not used for them in our discussions, since the historical tradition places the Yadus and Turvasus even further from the Pūrus than even the Anus and Druhyus (in the Purāṇic mythical traditions, Yadu and Turvasu are the descendants of one queen, while Druhyu, Anu and Pūru are the descendants of a second queen; and, in the Rigveda **I.108**.8, Yadus and Turvasus are mentioned in one breath, and Druhyus, Anus and Pūrus in the next), so the Yadus and Turvasus can not have been *ethnically* a *section* among the

Pūrus, and must have constituted different groups *linguistically* as well. That all the different groups, whatever their original linguistic differences, eventually became "Indo-Aryanized" or Pūru-ized, the Anu groups to the west (the Madras, Kekayas, etc.) as well as the Yadus, Turvasus and others to the east and south of the Pūrus, in the historical process of "Sanskritization" of the subcontinent, does not detract from the fact that the original linguistic situation, as per the historical paradigm, must have been different.

However, all this has no place in the linguistic paradigm of the AIT: from among all the different branches of Indo-European languages, the "Indo-Aryan" as represented by the Vedic language is, strictly speaking, the easternmost branch. In the AIT paradigm, all the roots of the tree of the Indo-European family of languages are in the west: in the region "**from East Central Europe to Eastern Russia**" (HOCK 1999a:16-17). All the major action, including the development of the isoglosses and the division of the branches into Satem and Kentum groups, took place in that broad region, and almost all the branches and shoots of this tree are also restricted to areas west and south of that region. The "Indo-Iranian" branch was the only isolated branch which moved out east into Central Asia; the discovery of (the long extinct) Tocharian in Central Asia in archaeological excavations in the last century was a difficult pill to swallow, but it was accepted as a totally separate and later event unrelated to the isolated "Indo-Iranian" movement eastward. All the rest of the action, even *within* "Indo-Iranian", was also restricted to Central Asia: the separation of the Mitanni, the split between the Indo-Aryans and Iranians, and possibly also the separation of a third group, the "Kaffir" languages. The entry of one ultra-isolated linguistic shoot, "Indo-Aryan", into the northwest of India was the *only* connection of India with the Indo-European world. So, in the AIT linguistic paradigm, there is just *no logical place whatsoever* for any other Indo-European group to be found to the *east* of the "Indo-Aryan" of our discourse. *If* the

Indian historical paradigm is wrong, and the AIT paradigm right, there should not be any logical possibility at all for the existence of any other such Indo-European groups in the east.

But, as we have been pointing out from our first book (TALAGERI 1993:231-235), circumstance after circumstance keeps arising, in the study of "Indo-Aryan" history, which compels the linguists and historians to postulate the existence of Indo-European groups, *separate* from the "Indo-Aryans" of our discourse (i.e. from the Vedic Aryans), in the *interior* of India to the *east* of the Vedic Aryans, who are even postulated to be the remnants of an *earlier* wave of Aryan immigrants. Therefore, the linguists and historians are compelled to postulate two separate waves of Aryan immigrants, different from each other. The scholars get away with referring to these "other" Aryans only when convenient (to make some point of their own on some issue) or unavoidable (when faced with some otherwise inexplicable fact or circumstance), without bothering to clarify how and when they entered the country (see the section on "The Archaeological Case against the AIT" in the next chapter, and see the great difficulty with which the entry of even the "Vedic Aryans" into India has to be literally *pleaded*), and *without clarifying their linguistic position within the broader Indo-European family*: were they just one more sub-section among the "Indo-Iranian" branch, or were they the speakers of languages belonging to a *totally new and different Indo-European branch, or branches, not included in the present count of branches*? [Ironically, S.K. Chatterjee, the *linguist*, even gives us the racial distinction between these two groups — the earlier Aryans were "**Alpines: brachycephalic, leptorrhine**", and the later, Vedic, Aryans were "**Nordics: leptorrhine dolichocephals**" (MAJUMDAR ed.1951/1996:144) — but not the linguistic distinction].

The AIT writers manage to get away with giving the impression that these "other" Aryans were probably just a different group among the "Indo-Iranians", in fact, among the "Indo-Aryans" (which term now acquires a broader connotation beyond the Vedic Aryans) who spoke different "Indo-Aryan" "dialects" of which the Vedic dialect was just one: "**The Aryan came to India , assuredly not as a single, uniform or standardized speech, but rather as a group of dialects** [...] **only one of these dialects or dialect-groups has mainly been represented in the language of the Vedas — other dialects** [...] **(might) have been ultimately transformed into one or the other of the various New Indo-Aryan languages and dialects. The mutual relationship of these Old Indo-Aryan dialects, their individual traits and number as well as location, will perhaps never be settled** [...] **The true significance of the various Prakrits as preserved in literary and other records, their origin and interrelations, and their true connection with the modern languages, forms one of the most baffling problems of Indo-Aryan linguistics** [...] **and there has been admixture among the various dialects to an extent which has completely changed their original appearance, and which makes their affiliation to forms of Middle Indo-Aryan as in our records at times rather problematical**" (CHATTERJEE 1970:20-21). [This is a fair description of the language situation in the "Indo-Aryan" language speaking parts of North India (following the long process of Sanskritization of Indian culture), except for the linguistically ambiguous and unspecified use of the word "Indo-Aryan"].

K.R. Norman, in his study of the variations between the OIA (Old Indo-Aryan: Vedic and Classical Sanskrit) and MIA (Middle Indo-Aryan: Prakrits), finds MIA dialects contain many forms "**which are clearly of IA, or even IE, origin, but have no attested Skt equivalent, e.g. suffixes not, or only rarely, found in Skt, or those words which show a different grade of root from that found in Skt, but can be shown not to be MIA innovations, because the formation could only have evolved in a pre-MIA phonetic form, or because a direct equivalent is found in an IE language other than Skt**", and he suggests that these forms "**support a belief in the existence of**

different dialects of OIA, since we may assume that the forms in that category go back to 'lost' OIA dialects" (NORMAN 1995:282).

He concludes that "**MIA preserves forms which give evidence for the existence of dialects of OIA which differed in some respects from those attested in literature**", and opines: "**I know of no attempt to make a complete and comprehensive collection of the evidence for this interesting category of forms in MIA, and it remains scattered through the pages of Indological writings. I believe that, until such a collection is made, the amount of material available will be underestimated.**" (NORMAN 1995:283).

Thus, even when these forms or roots in MIA are not found in Vedic or Classical Sanskrit, but direct equivalents are found "**in an IE language other than Skt**", Norman still identifies the source of these forms and roots as "**'lost' OIA dialects**": *i.e. still within the "Indo-Aryan" entity*. But closer examination shows this position to be not quite in sync with the facts:

1. Linguists, from the days of Meillet have recognized a phenomenon which is very difficult to fit into the AIT paradigm: the fact that "**all of Indo-Iranian tended to confuse r and l** [...] **Every IE *l* becomes *r* in Iranian. This phenomenon is to be observed in the Northwest of India, and, consequently, in the Rigveda, which is based on idioms of the Northwest**". However, "**initial and intervocalic *l* was present in Indic dialects of other regions. Numerous elements of these dialects were gradually introduced into the literary language, which became fixed in Classical Sanskrit. This explains the appearance of l in more recent parts of the Rigveda and its subsequent rise in frequency.**" (MEILLET 1906/1967:47).

This phenomenon has been studied by many scholars, and it will be useful to see what M. M. Deshpande (not an Indian writer of the OIT brand, but a western academician and close colleague of Witzel) has to say on the subject: "**the Vedic dialect, like the Iranian, is an *r*-only dialect in which the**

Indo-European **l* merged into *r*, but the dialect of the redactors of the Vedas was an *r*-and-*l* dialect, where the original Indo-European **r* and **l* were retained; the redactors of the Vedic texts have put this *l* back into some of the Vedic words, where the original Vedic dialect had an *r*". Later in time, we have the Māgadhī dialect in the east, which was a "**pure *l*-only dialect**", whereas the northwestern dialects were "**almost devoid of *l***". Deshpande, therefore, sees the need to "**explore the difference between the *r*-only dialect and the *r*-and-*l* dialect (and possibly an *l*-only dialect)**" (DESHPANDE 1995:70-71).

Significantly, when we examine the wider "Indo-Iranian" scenario, we find that "**all three groups — the Proto-Iranians, the Western branch of the Proto-Indo-Aryans and the Eastern branch of the Proto-Indo-Aryans — represent the *r*-only dialects of common Indo-Iranian heritage**" (DESHPANDE 1995:71): i.e. *the Proto-Iranians, the Mitanni* (the *Western* branch of the Proto-Indo-Aryans) and *the Vedic Aryans* (the *Eastern* branch of the Proto-Indo-Aryans), *all three of them*, were *r*-only dialects.

Then *who* were the speakers of the *l*-and-*r* and *l*-only dialects in the east within India who very clearly fall *outside* the common Indo-Iranian heritage? This question is raised by Deshpande as well, with no logical answer within the AIT paradigm: Deshpande suggests that "**there was a branch of Indo-Aryan which, like the parent Indo-European, had retained the distinction between *r* and *l***", and that this branch entered India "**before the migrations of the standard Indo-Aryan branch**", but admits to being unable to answer basic questions on this point: "**Where did they come from? Did they reach India via Iran? If so, did they leave any trace of themselves in Iran? Were the speakers of the *r*-and-*l* dialect of pre-Vedic Indo-Aryan a totally different branch from the Indo-Iranian? These are difficult questions.** [...] **Anyway, one would still have to assume the entry of *r*-and-*l* dialects of Indo-Aryan into India before the arrival of the Ṛgvedic Aryans to account for the fact that *r*-and-*l* dialects in India**

were more easterly in relation to the Ṛgvedic dialect" (DESHPANDE 1995:71-72).

The significance of one fact must be noted: the eastern redactors of the Vedic texts (who, it must be kept in mind, changed *only* in "**limited cases certain sounds — but not words, tonal accents, sentences**": WITZEL 2000a:§8), who spoke an *r*-and-*l* language, did not indiscriminately change *every*, or *any*, *r* to *l*: they changed only those *rs* to *ls* which were originally ls in the parent Indo-European language. As Deshpande puts it, their dialect "**like the parent Indo-European, had retained the** [*original*] **distinction between *r* and *l***" and not just coincidentally created a new distinction between *r* and *l* unrelated to the original distinction. They, therefore, represent a linguistic stage within Indo-European *earlier* than the alleged joint linguistic stage of the "Indo-Aryan" (Vedic) + Iranian + Mitanni combine *before* the three separated from each other.

As per the AIT, all the joint action in the Vedic + Iranian + Mitanni combine took place well outside India in Central Asia. And any Indo-European forms of speech representing an earlier linguistic stage (whether as part of this combine or as a separate branch of Indo-European) should be found *well to the west* of Central Asia at a point of time *far earlier* even than the entry of this combine into Central Asia. But we find these forms *well to the east* of this combine, and (as per the joint consensus of a large number of western scholars named by Deshpande, including Hoernle, Grierson, Risley and Oldenberg) still *far earlier* than at least the alleged entry of the Vedic Aryans into India, *with complete confusion, on the AIT side, as regards the exact time and mode of their alleged arrival into India, and, even more important, as regards the evidence for this alleged entry into India from outside.*

What the evidence definitely shows is that the earlier roots of the "Indo-Iranian" combine lie, not to the *west* of Central Asia, but in the *eastern parts* of North India.

2. But we find *even earlier* forms of Indo-European speech in India, going not only beyond the "Indo-Iranian" combine,

but even beyond the joint "Satem" combine (Indo-Aryan + Iranian + Armenian + Baltic + Slavic). As Norman points out, above, there are words surviving in Indian languages, in the so-called MIA period as well as the so-called NIA (or "New Indo-Aryan") period, for which "**a direct equivalent is found in an IE language other than Skt**", and for which "**a complete and comprehensive collection of the evidence**" has not been done. It *could* be argued that such words could merely be words which may have existed in Vedic as well, only they happened to not have been used in any Vedic text (since, after all, every single word in the spoken Vedic language did not necessarily make it into the texts), but *not* when the words clearly represent linguistic forms which are not "Indo-Aryan" or "Indo-Iranian" at all, but forms found in other distant branches which represent a *much older* linguistic stage.

It is difficult to sift out the linguistic evidence in India today, since, as Chatterjee points out, above, "**there has been admixture among the various dialects to an extent which has completely changed their original appearance**", but it is not impossible. As we have pointed out in our earlier book (TALAGERI 2000:319-323), the Sinhalese language may well represent the survivor of one such form of early Indo-European speech. The language, due to its early migration from the northwest to an area to the south of the Dravidian-speaking areas, may have escaped much of this "**admixture**", although it may also have undergone many other types of losses of original features due to a change in environment, the influence of unfamiliar non-Indo-European languages in Sri Lanka, and an excessive Pali-ization in a long Buddhist history. One very significant word in Sinhalese is the word *watura* for "water". It clearly represents a definitely *pre-Indo-Iranian* form of the Sanskrit *uda(-ka)* closely resembling the forms in such very distant and long-separated branches as Anatolian (Hittite *watar*) and Germanic (English *water*). The Sinhalese evidence must be examined in detail to detect all such ultra-archaic forms which may have survived the ravages of time and history.

But, "admixture" notwithstanding, one such archaic survivor with linguistic features going back to the level of the Kentum languages has been discovered, analysed and accepted even by the AIT scholars: the Bangāṇi language spoken in the Garhwal area in Uttarakhand in North India. Claus P. Zoller, a German linguist, announced in 1987 that this language contained three historical layers of words: words in common with the other neighbouring Indo-Aryan languages, words belonging to the level of Vedic Sanskrit, and finally words going back to the level of the Kentum languages. After some bitter initial controversies, the findings have finally been almost universally accepted in the western academic world.

The Bangāṇi language has features which, in the AIT paradigm, should not be found to the *east* of Eastern Europe where Witzel, for example, places the "**fault line between the western Centum and eastern Satem languages**" (WITZEL 2005:361). Although Tocharian was discovered and accepted in the last century, it was very difficult to fit it into the AIT paradigm: as Childe put it: "**To identify a wandering of Aryans across Turkestan from Europe in a relatively late prehistorical period is frankly difficult**" (CHILDE 1926:95-96). It is *much* more difficult to identify a wandering of proto-Bangāṇi all the way from Europe to the Himalayan areas of Garhwal deep inside North India.

Bangāṇi, Sinhalese, the *r*-and-*l* dialects, and any other such archaic speech forms which may still be discovered in India, if they have somehow managed to survive the ravages of time and history, have no place whatsoever in the AIT paradigm, even if they are still sought to be argued and pleaded into the paradigm (as survivals of archaic speech forms of groups who *accompanied* the "Indo-Aryans" all the way from South Russia to the interior of India, some curiously *preceding* them into India). However, they do have a very definite place in the

Indian historical paradigm, where they represent survivals of the speech forms of other groups (Yadus, Turvasus, Ikṣvākus, etc.) who lived to the east and south of the Pūrus (the Vedic Aryans), and also include surviving remnants of varieties of the Anu and Druhyu forms of speech of the north and west. They are not the remnants of mysterious unconnected *immigrant* groups from Europe in the ancient past: they are the remnants of archaic speech forms of *local* origin.

The picture we get is *not* of a language family from a far-off land which sent *one isolated linguistic shoot* into India, but of a language family with *all its earliest roots* going deep into the Indian soil.

3. Going deeper into the matter, we can detect even older traces of the Indo-European roots in India: contacts with a non-Indo-European family of languages which could only have taken place in the interior of India in the most primitive stage of early language development.

We have already seen how the contacts between Indo-European languages and different non-Indo-European languages all fit in with the Indian Homeland (OIT) scenario: the linguistic evidence of contacts of the early European Dialects with different Eurasian languages on different sides of Central Asia and the path leading from Central Asia to East Europe, and with Tocharian, all of which is *missing* in "Indo-Iranian"; and the *one-way* "Indo-Iranian" borrowings into Uralic. Now we will see evidence for contacts between the Indo-European family *as a whole* and another language family *as a whole*, when both were in their most primitive stages, consisting of the most basic vocabulary which would be likely to survive a *total lack of contacts in later times*. This other language family is the Austronesian family (see also TALAGERI 1993:167-169, and TALAGERI 2000:292-293).

Isidore Dyen, in a paper presented in 1966 and published in 1970, makes out a case showing the similarities between many basic words reconstructed in the proto-Indo-European and proto-Austronesian languages, including such basic words as the first four numerals, many of the personal pronouns, and the words for "water" and "land". And Dyen points out that "**the number of comparisons could be increased at least slightly, perhaps even substantially, without a severe loss of quality**" (DYEN 1970:439).

But Dyen is not, by any stretch of the imagination, an OIT writer, and an Indian homeland theory does not even remotely strike him even after he notes these similarities: "**The hypothesis to be dealt with is not favoured by considerations of the distribution of the two families** [...] **The probable homelands of the respective families appear to be very distant; that of the Indo-European is probably in Europe, whereas that of the Austronesian is no further west than the longitude of the Malay Peninsula in any reasonable hypothesis, and has been placed considerably further east in at least one hypothesis. The hypothesis suggested by linguistic evidence is not thus facilitated by a single homeland hypothesis**" (DYEN 1970:431).

But the hypothesis suggested by "**linguistic evidence**" *actually is* facilitated by a single homeland hypothesis: the Indian homeland hypothesis. Apart from the Indian homeland hypothesis for the Indo-European family of languages, which has always been on the cards from the very first day of speculations on the subject, *and which has been confirmed with irrefutable evidence in this present book*, there is also an Indian homeland hypothesis for the ultimate origins of the Austronesian family of languages. S.K.Chatterjee, the well known linguist puts it as follows: "**India was the centre from which the Austric speech spread into the lands and islands of the east and Pacific**" (MAJUMDAR ed.1951/1996:156), and "**the Austric speech** [...] **in its original form (as the ultimate source of both the Austro-Asiatic and Austronesian branches)** [...] **could very well have been characterized within India**" (MAJUMDAR ed.1951/1996:150).

We have, in this chapter, presented a complete linguistic case for the Indian Homeland or Out-of-India theory; and examined the linguistic evidence in all its relevant aspects, starting with the Evidence of the Isoglosses. There is little scope left for claiming that the linguistic evidence is against the OIT: on the contrary, it fully supports the OIT case, and fits in perfectly with the irrefutable textual evidence presented in Section I of this book.

7G
APPENDIX: WITZEL'S LINGUISTIC ARGUMENTS AGAINST THE OIT

Any linguistic arguments against the Indian Homeland and OIT, which may not have been touched upon in the course of our discussion on the Evidence of the Isoglosses, will very likely have been dealt with in our two earlier books (TALAGERI 1993 and TALAGERI 2000). But, just to round off the chapter, we will examine the article presented by Michael Witzel (WITZEL 2005) in a volume edited by Edwin Bryant and Laurie Patton, published in 2005, which claims to present the linguistic case against the OIT.

This volume includes an article by this writer (TALAGERI 2005b), written and presented to the editors in 1998. After delaying the publication for so long, it was sent to me for final correction in 2004, and I was told not to make any changes beyond correcting printing errors, etc. Naturally, I received the impression that all the other articles would be similarly dated. However, Witzel's article was apparently allowed to be updated: he refers repeatedly not only to my book printed in 2000 (TALAGERI 2000), but even to his "review" of that book on his internet site in 2001(WITZEL 2001b). The footnote to the Introduction to the volume by the editors (p. 17), likewise, refers directly, and in detail, to this "review", and only very indirectly to my very detailed reply to it (TALAGERI 2001, which, of course, Witzel himself does not refer to at all in his article). This seems to me a little unfair. Here, however, we will only examine the purported *linguistic* arguments against the OIT in the article by Witzel, ignoring not only personal comments but also his arguments based on textual references, which are *totally irrelevant* after the evidence presented in Section I of this present book.

Witzel begins his linguistic arguments with an inadvertent admission that the AIT linguistic case is based on argumentative points rather than concrete evidence: "**The direction of the spread of languages and linguistic innovations cannot *easily* be determined, unless we have written materials (preferably inscriptions). Therefore, *theoretically*, a scenario of an IE emigration from the Panjab is possible. But some linguistic observations such as the distribution of languages, dialect features, substrate languages, linguistic paleontology, words for cultural and natural features in the languages concerned, etc. all argue against the Out of India scenario**" (WITZEL 2005:355). Ironically, the case presented in Section I of this book (which I *challenge* Witzel to refute), *for* the Out-of-India scenario, is actually based on a combination of the Mitanni "***inscriptions***" and the evidence of the Rigveda and the Avesta, of which the material in the Rigveda has also frequently been referred to by Witzel as being "**equivalent to *inscriptions***" (see section 8C in the next chapter). Among corollary "**linguistic observations**", we have already seen, earlier on in this chapter, the conclusions of Johanna Nichols on the location of the "locus of the IE spread" in the "vicinity of ancient Bactria-Sogdiana" on the basis of, among other things, "**the distribution of** [the Indo-European] **languages**"; we have already seen that the evidence of the "**dialect features**" as represented by the isoglosses can only be logically explained in an Indian homeland scenario; and we have seen the evidence of various "**substrate languages**" (using the phrase *substrate* in the same loose sense in which it is used by Witzel and Lubotsky, to include *adstrate* words) in the European Dialects which show the migrations of those dialects by a route leading from Central Asia towards East Europe. An examination of Witzel's *arguments* allegedly based on "**linguistic observations**" proves to be revealing:

1. Witzel's first linguistic arguments, in section 11.5 (WITZEL 2005:344-346) have to do with what he calls "Linguistic substrates". This issue has been discussed in great detail in TALAGERI 2000:293-308 (and earlier in TALAGERI 1993:197-215). We will not repeat all the arguments and counter-arguments here, except for stressing the difference between "substrate" words and "adstrate" words (see section 6B of chapter 6 earlier in this book). In fact, let us accept that there may be some *adstrate* words of Dravidian or Austric origin in "Indo-Aryan" — perhaps we protested a bit too much in our earlier books, due to the implications sought to be drawn from such alleged "non-Indo-Aryan" words in Classical or even Vedic Sanskrit. The word *kāṇa* "one-eyed", in the RV, for example, is obviously derived from the Dravidian word *kaṇ* "eye". Other, not implausible suggestions include the words *daṇḍa* and *kuṭa*. But this does not excuse the mad hunt for Dravidian and Austric words in the Vedic language: the word *paṇi/vaṇi*, for example, is cognate to Greek *Pan* and Teutonic *Vanir* (see TALAGERI 2000:477-495), but it is regularly portrayed as a "non-Indo-Aryan" word.

In fact, if Witzel's claims that these "non-Indo-Aryan" words include the names of Vedic "**noblemen and chiefs (Balbūtha, Bṛbu) and occasionally of poets (Kavaṣa, Kaṇva, Agastya, Kaśyapa)**" (WITZEL 2005:343) are accepted, it only shows that the Vedic Aryans were very much an integral part of the Indian scene, and adds a multiplier effect to the force of the case presented by us in Section I of this book: *it means that the Pūrus, who expanded from the areas to the east of the Sarasvatī to the areas further west, leading to the westward expansions of the Anus (the proto-Iranians), were an integral part of the interior areas of India to its east long before the development of the joint Indo-Iranian culture of the Late Rigvedic period.* These Dravidian and Austric elements did not spread to the Iranians to the west (except for the pronoun *tanū* common to "Indo-Iranian" and proto-Dravidian?), much less to the other IE Dialects to the west, since these were particularly *eastern* and *southern* developments in the speech of the Pūrus.

2. Witzel's next section on specific linguistic arguments, section 11.13 (WITZEL 2005:356-358) criticizes S.S.Misra's case for dating the Rigveda to 5000 BCE on the basis of Indo-Iranian loan words in Uralic languages. We have already dealt with the Uralic evidence earlier on in this chapter; and, as postulating concrete dates for the borrowed words is not part of our case, we can move on to Witzel's next arguments. In section 11.14 (WITZEL 2005:358-360), Witzel refers to various Indian writers who insist on treating Indo-Aryan and Dravidian languages as related language groups within one family. Again, as such a plea has never been part of *our* case, we can likewise ignore the discussion.

Witzel next, in section 11.15 (WITZEL 2005:360-361), refers to Hock's case for the evidence of the isoglosses, which we have already dealt with in this chapter; and in the next section, 11.16 (WITZEL 2005:361-363), to the Mitanni evidence, already dealt with in Section I of this book.

3. The next section, 11.17 (WITZEL 2005:363-364), deals with the absence of retroflexes west of India, which Witzel treats as evidence that the other branches of Indo-European outside India could not have emigrated from India since they do not have retroflex (cerebral) sounds. This argument is a representative of Witzel's arguments in the following sections, where any Indian or Sanskrit element missing in the Indo-European languages outside India is automatic proof of those Indo-European languages not having originally emigrated from India.

We will deal with that general category of arguments presently. About the particular case of retroflex sounds, it is incredible that Witzel can seriously present such an argument when we have the living example of the Romany language of the Gypsies of Europe *who are known and officially accepted as emigrants from India*, who left from *deeper* inside India at a *later* point of time when retroflex sounds were *much more integral* a part of the Indian languages than they were even in the language of the Rigveda, and yet who have not preserved even a trace of retroflex sounds in their speech. The other Indo-European Dialects were spoken well outside the borders of present day India already by the Early Rigvedic period, and even the proto-Iranians, who were in the areas of northern Pakistan in the Early Rigvedic period, had already shifted their centre to Afghanistan well before the Late Rigvedic period. How can the absence of retroflex sounds in the later historical descendants of these Dialects in distant lands constitute even an *argument*, let alone *evidence*, against their ultimate origin in India?

Witzel gives linguistic arguments based on the linear development of certain words, to show that retroflexion was not an original feature of proto-Indo-European, but a "**late and localizable, that is Ved. *innovation* (in the Hindukush area?) that is not shared by Iranian and the other IE languages** [...] **an *innovation* — in this case, one that separates Ved.IA/OIA from the rest of IA, IIr, and IE**" (WITZEL 2005:364). At this point, we may note Deshpande's 1995 article, already referred to earlier in this chapter and in the chapter on the Mitanni evidence, where he writes: "**My own conclusion regarding retroflexes in the Ṛgveda is that the original compositions were either free from retroflexion of fricatives, liquids and nasals, or that these sounds had only marginal retroflexion. The retroflexion we see in the available recension of the Ṛgveda is a result of the changes which crept into the text during centuries of oral transmission.**" (DESHPANDE 1995:70).

Far from proving that the other IE branches did not emigrate from India, doesn't all this in fact explain how they *could* indeed have emigrated from India without taking retroflex sounds with them? Witzel's next words explain what he is arguing against, not only in this section, but in the article as a whole: "**In other words, Vedic Sanskrit does not represent the oldest form of IE, as autochthonists often claim.**" (WITZEL 2005.364). In other words, all of Witzel's arguments are basically directed against the "**Sanskrit-origin**" hypothesis which is the favourite of most Indian writers, and not against the "**PIE-in-India**" case presented by us. Witzel is a past master of the tactic of attacking soft targets: prove the "**Sanskrit-origin**" hypothesis wrong, and claim to have disproved the "**PIE-in-India**" case!

4. In the next section, 11.18 (WITZEL 2005:364-366), Witzel argues that if the other Indo-European branches had their origins in India, they should have preserved traces of the local words for specifically Indian plants and animals not found outside India. But, again, when even the Gypsies have *not* preserved local names of Indian plants and animals not found outside India, although they originally migrated from areas inside India where those plants and animals were common, and spoke Indo-Aryan dialects of the late 1st millennium CE which are known to have had words for these plants and animals, why should the Indo-European dialects, which developed their earliest isoglosses, thousands of years ago, in areas outside the northwestern borders of India, have preserved traces of such names?

But Witzel tells us that the Gypsies have indeed preserved such names: "**The *hypothetical* emigrants from the subcontinent would have taken with them a host of ' Indian' words — as the gypsies (Roma, Sinti) indeed have done. But we do not find any typical Old Indian words beyond South Asia, neither in the closely related Old Iranian, nor in Eastern or Western IE** [...] **In an OIT scenario, one would expect 'emigrant' Indian words such as those for lion, tiger, elephant, leopard, lotus, bamboo, or some local Indian trees, even if some of them would have been preserved, not for the original item, but for a similar one (e.g. English [red] squirrel > North American [gray] squirrel)**" (WITZEL 2005:364-365).

It would be interesting to know all about the "'**emigrant' Indian words such as those for lion, tiger, elephant, leopard, lotus, bamboo, or some local Indian trees**" preserved in the

Gypsy speech; but Witzel does not enlighten us on this point, although it would not have been unnatural if the Gypsies had indeed preserved such names, since those animals must have been native to the areas from which their ancestors departed. Instead, Witzel tells us: "**The Gypsies, after all, have kept a large IA vocabulary alive, over the past 1000 years or so, during their wanderings all over the Near East, North Africa and Europe (e.g. *phral* 'brother', *pani* 'water', *karal* 'he does')**" (WITZEL 2005:366).

And here we have the *totally unscrupulous* nature of Witzel's arguments in a nutshell: he asks us to *reject* the IE migrations from India by pointing out the failure of the IE languages to preserve Indian words for lion, tiger, elephant, etc; and asks us to *accept* the Gypsy migrations from India by pointing out the preservation in the Gypsy languages of Indian words for brother, water, and certain verbal forms. But, actually, the IE languages have also preserved cognate words of this nature, e.g. the English *brother* (Skt. *bhrātar*), *water* (Skt. *uda-*, Sinhalese *watura*), etc., while the Gypsy languages have also not preserved Indian words for lion, tiger, elephant, etc., although Witzel dates their departure from India to just over a thousand years ago. What the whole thing shows is that Witzel himself is aware of the hollowness of his argument, and therefore employs this unscrupulous jugglery to try to push the argument through.

What is even more ironical is that the IE languages *have* indeed preserved words for the elephant and the ape, two animals typical *not* of the area from "**from East Central Europe to Eastern Russia**", but of either Africa or India (and areas further east), although Gamkrelidze somehow argues them into his Anatolian homeland. The Vedic *ibha* (elephant) is clearly cognate to the Greek el-*ephas* (elephant) and Latin *ebur* (ebony or elephant-tusks), and *kapi* (ape/monkey) is cognate to English *ape* and Irish *apa* (ape); and perhaps *pṛdāku* (spotted animal/leopard) to Greek *pardos* and Hittite *parsana* (leopard) (GAMKRELIDZE 1995:420-426, 442-444, TALAGERI 2000:311-313). But Witzel simply dismisses them, with specious objections, as "**rather dubious cases**" (WITZEL 2005:365, 391).

5. In the next section, 11.19 (WITZEL 2005:366-368), Witzel takes up linguistic features where Iranian has preserved certain original IE linguistic features which have already disappeared in the Vedic language due to linguistic innovations. He tells us that "**Avest. often is quite archaic, both in grammar and also in vocabulary, while Ved. seems to have progressed much towards Epic and Classical Sanskrit (loss of injunctive, moods of the perfect, aorist, etc.) The Avest. combination of neuter plural nouns with the singular of the verb is hardly retained even in the other older IE languages. The Old Avest. of Zaraθuštra thus, is frequently even more archaic than the RV and therefore simply too old to have moved out of India after the composition of the RV (supposedly 2600-5000 BCE). In other words, Iranian simply lacks the many innovations that characterize Ved., innovations that are not found among the other IE languages either**" (WITZEL 2005:367). He concludes: "**In one phrase, *the Iranian languages simply miss the Indianization of IIr,* with all its concurrent innovations in grammar and vocabulary**" (WITZEL 2005:368). [Here, a misprint, he probably means "***the Indianization of IA***"]

Witzel's argument is like that of a non-linguist claiming that modern Lithuanian is older than ancient Latin because it has, to this day, preserved certain Indo-European archaisms lost in Latin, such as the dual number. *Of course* Avestan has preserved certain archaisms that are lost in Vedic. But, as, Witzel himself notes: "**Old Iranian preserved some archaic features while also developing innovations of its own**" (WITZEL 2005:367). Iranian and Vedic "Indo-Aryan" were two different branches of IE languages, and *naturally*, each would preserve archaisms of its own, while developing innovations of its own. So naturally, in some respects, Iranian would be more archaic, and in others, Vedic would be more archaic. Again, we see that Witzel is basically arguing against a "**Sanskrit-origin**" hypothesis, where innovations in Sanskrit must necessarily be found in its daughter languages (which would then include Avestan, ancient Greek, Latin, etc.), and archaisms in other Indo-European languages must necessarily have been preserved in Sanskrit as well. Our analysis of the relative chronology of the Rigveda and the Avesta, in Section I of this book, which I *again* challenge Witzel to refute, gives the lie not only to his insinuation that Avestan is older than Vedic, but consequently also to his claim that the two belong to one single branch of IE languages.

As already pointed out, the other Indo-European Dialects were *different* from the Vedic dialect (and not *descended* from it), and had already moved out into the northwest in the pre-Rigvedic period, and proto-Iranian by the Middle Rigvedic period. Just as there were different isoglosses developing between different sets of Indo-European Dialects, there were innovations developing in individual Dialects, which were unique to them. So why should innovations developed by the Vedic Dialect within itself, or isoglosses developed in common with the Other Dialects to its east and south, be necessarily found in the Dialects to the west and beyond?

6. The next section, 11.20 (WITZEL 2005:368-370), deals with the supposed anomaly between the chronology of the departure from India (in the OIT scenario) of Iranian and the chronology of the invention or adoption of the chariot by the "Indo-Iranians". Witzel gives the chronology of the chariot around "**c2000 BCE, in Ural Russia and at Sintashta**". Witzel's question is: "**The autochthonous theory would have the RV at c5000 BCE or before the start of the Indus civilization at 2600 BCE** [...] **If according to the autochthonous theory, the Iranians had emigrated**

westwards out of India well before the RV (2600-5000 BCE), how could both the Indians (in the Panjab) and the Iranians (from Ukraine to Xinjiang) have a common, inherited word for the — not yet invented — horse-drawn chariot as well as a rather ancient word for the charioteer?"

Here, again, Witzel is not arguing against the OIT scenario put forward in our books: he is arguing against an OIT scenario which includes "**Misra's new dating of the RV at 5000 BCE**" (WITZEL 2005:358), and, which not only has the Iranians migrating out from India "**well before**" 2600 BCE, but, curiously, seems to have the Iranians out of touch with India, and already spread out all over the area "**from Ukraine to Xinjiang**", by 2000 BCE.

About the chariot, there is nothing in the Rigveda to indicate that the word *ratha* originally indicates a horse-drawn spoked-wheeled vehicle: cognate words in other IE branches, as Witzel points out, mean "wheel", and it is only in the Indo-Aryan and the Iranian branches that it acquired the specialized meaning "wheeled vehicle". In the Late Rigvedic period, spoked-wheels were introduced, and the word *ratha* became even more restricted in its meaning: it *now* came to mean the spoked-wheeled horse-drawn chariot, and became an important part of the joint "Indo-Iranian" culture of the Late Rigvedic period. It is only in the Books and hymns of the Late Period, and in the Avesta and the Mitanni records, that we find references to spokes or to a large array of names ending in *-aśva* and *-ratha*; and in fact, the new chariot may have been the catalyst in the Kassite-Mitanni migrations to West Asia. By this time, all the other IE branches had moved out of the sphere of Central Asia, and were exposed to spoked-wheeled chariots from different sources: "**On lexical ground there is no convincing evidence for the assignment of the spoked-wheel to PIE; the earliest terms for 'spoke' in the various IE stocks are at least metaphoric extensions of other words**

[...] **there is no close connection between the Greek and Old Indic chariot terms although both stocks attest chariotry from the second millennium BC**" (MALLORY 1997:627).

The Iranians certainly did not leave India in a pre-Rigvedic period: they expanded westwards from the areas of present-day northern Pakistan towards the end of the Early Rigvedic Period; but were centred in and around Afghanistan in the Late Rigvedic Period, which is when the Avesta was composed and the common "Indo-Iranian" culture was developed (see Section I of this book). So naturally, the Vedic "Indo-Aryans" and the proto-Iranians (*before* they spread out all the way "**from Ukraine to Xinjiang**") had "**a common, inherited word for the** [— *by then* invented —] **horse-drawn chariot as well as a rather ancient word for the charioteer**".

7. In the next two sections, 11.21-11.22 (WITZEL 2005; 370-372), Witzel again takes up, this time in relation to the other IE branches beyond Iranian, the question of linguistic innovations found in the Rigveda and common technological developments. According to him: "**The date of dispersal of the earliest, western IE languages** [...] **can be estimated in the early third millennium BCE. Further dates can be supplied by a study of important cultural features such as the common IE reconstructed word for copper/bronze, or the vocabulary connected with the heavy oxen-drawn wagon** [...] **They point to the end of the fourth or the beginning of the third millennium as a date ad quem, or rather post quem for the last stage of commonly shared PIE**" (WITZEL 2005:370). He also points out (WITZEL 371-372) how different linguistic innovations among different Indo-European branches, many shared by the Vedic language also, can only have taken place after around 3000 BCE. But, according to the OIT scenario, all these cultural features and innovations must have taken place "**after the IE languages would have left the subcontinent**", and so these features and innovations "**would have to be re-imports from their focus in**

Eastern Europe/Central Asia back into India — all convoluted cases of very special pleading." (WITZEL 2005:370).

Here, Witzel, like Hock in delineating his arguments regarding the Evidence of the Isoglosses (discussed earlier in this chapter), whom indeed he refers to again (WITZEL 2005:370), makes a basic mistake: he argues against an alleged OIT scenario where the IE Dialects developed all their isoglosses within India, in a one-time development, and then marched out one by one out of the bottle-neck passes leading out of India, more or less never to come into contact with each other again until later historical times. Witzel compounds this mistake further by pitching all his arguments against what he calls "**Misra's new dating of the RV at 5000 BCE**" (WITZEL 2005:358), and has even the Iranians in any OIT scenario completely "out" of India and out of touch with the Vedic Indo-Aryans "**well before**" 2600 BCE.

Witzel not only repeats this alleged OIT chronology with each argument, but he even tries to suggest that the chronology, and the one-time mode and schedule of emigration, he is arguing against is part of *our* OIT scenario: "**According to the autochthonous theories the various IE peoples (the "*Anu*, *Druhyu*" of Talageri 1993, 2000) and their languages hypothetically left India (c.5000-4000 BCE).**" (WITZEL 2005:371)!

But we have *nothing whatsoever* to object to in the chronological estimates put forward by Witzel for the migrations of the IE Dialects, which are reasonably logical. In our scenario, the different Indo-European Dialects were moving out from Afghanistan into Central Asia (as shown in Figures 2-7 earlier in this chapter) at around this time, while the hymns of the Early Books of the Rigveda were being composed in the areas around the Sarasvatī. And the different isoglosses, including the "**common IE reconstructed word for copper/bronze**" and "**the vocabulary connected with the**

heavy oxen-drawn wagon", and the different cultural features and innovations, were being developed in common among all, or most, or many, or different permutations and combinations, of the Indo-European Dialects, in slow, gradual ("**complex**") stages over a period of time over a large area spreading from northernmost India to Central Asia. There is no question of "**re-imports**" of features from distant areas.

8. In the next section, 11.23 (WITZEL 372-375), Witzel takes up the question of animal and plant names common to different IE branches, a study of which, he claims, disproves the Indian homeland case:

a) One argument in this context is: "**the search for Indian plant names in the west, such as lotus, bamboo, Indian trees (*aśvattha, bilva, jambu,* etc.), comes up with nothing. Such names are simply not to be found, also not in a new meaning**" (WITZEL 2005:373). As we have already seen (as this point is already raised by Witzel in section 11.18), the search for such names in the language of the Gypsies also "**comes up with nothing**". This is because there is a simple logic behind this: languages which left one area in ancient times, and settled down in other distant areas, tended naturally, in the course of time, to forget plants and animals of their earlier areas not found in the new areas, unless active links were maintained with the earlier areas. Therefore arguments based on this premise prove nothing. Witzel himself, ironically, tells us, on the next page, that "**most of the IE plants and animals are not found in India**", and, as a result, their names "**have simply not been used any longer and have died out**" (WITZEL 2005:374).

b) Witzel here introduces the corollary about words being found "**in a new meaning**". In section 11.18, he also gives the example of how the name of an animal or plant could "**have been preserved, not for the original item, but for a similar one (e.g. English [red] squirrel > North American [gray] squirrel)**". But in such a case, how does one decide whether the original word referred to the *red* squirrel or the *gray* squirrel, unless one already *knows* the direction of movement as one does in this particular example? Armed with this ambiguity, when such a word *does* turn up, Witzel treats it as evidence in the opposite direction: to argue that the Indian name is the later one, and that it represents a transfer of name of a non-Indian animal or plant to an Indian one, and is evidence for the AIT. Witzel thus, for example, repeatedly cites the name of the non-Indian beaver (Old English *bebr, beofor*, Latin *fiber*, Lithuanian *bēbrus*, Russian *bobr*, *bebr*, and Avestan *baβri*) with the name of the Indian mongoose (Sanskrit *babhru*) as evidence for the AIT (WITZEL 2005:374).

The common non-Indian word, in the OIT scenario, can have developed in the region of Afghanistan and Central Asia, among the European dialects and proto-Iranian (see figure 3 in this chapter). And there is no case for any movement of the name *into* India: the word *babhru* occurs in the Rigveda, *and in Mitanni IA*, but as a name for a particular horse-colour. In the east, the word (found in later Sanskrit) was *separately* used as a name for the mongoose, but this cannot be as part of an Aryan movement into India in an AIT scenario, because in that case, the Aryans would have remembered the Rigvedic word *babhru* (which, seeing that it is also found in the Mitanni IA language, supposed, in the AIT scenario, to have separated from Vedic in Central Asia itself *before* the separation of the proto-Iranians, makes the meaning quite old and consistent) rather than a long-forgotten non-Indian use of the word in a distant land before an immigration already forgotten even in the Rigveda. And, as Gamkrelidze points out, after a short discussion: "**It is notable that the Indo-Iranian languages are split by this isogloss: Sanskrit shows the more archaic situation, while Avestan displays the innovation**" (GAMKRELIDZE 1995:448).

c) Witzel's primary argument in this context is based on the fact that "**Generally, the PIE plants and animals are those of the temperate climate**" (WITZEL 2005:372). Only some of them are found in Indo-Aryan. About these words, Witzel writes: "**It is *theoretically* possible that these words belonged to the *supposed* original IE/IA vocabulary of the northwestern Himalayas. Even if we take into account that the Panjab has cool winters with some frost and that the adjoining Afghani and Himalayan mountains have a long winter season, neither snow nor birch are typical for the Panjab or the Indian plains. Therefore, words such as those for 'wolf' and 'snow' rather indicate linguistic memories of a colder climate than an export of words, such as that for the high altitude Kashmirian birch tree, to Iran, Central Asia and Europe**" (WITZEL 2005:373).

The point about linguistic memories is obviously ridiculous: when the Rigveda refers to wolves or snow, it is not referring to wolves and snow of distant lands of "**linguistic memory**", but wolves and snow in their contemporary surroundings. And snow appears in the Rigveda only in the Late Books after the Vedic Aryans expanded westwards and northwards, while the birch is mentioned only in post-Rigvedic texts: rather too late for the awakening of memories of names from distant lands forgotten even before the composition of the Rigveda.

But Witzel is not completely wrong when he points out, for example, that a tree, the Indian birch, only found in India in the high altitude areas of Kashmir, and therefore not likely to be a very common tree in an original Indian homeland, would not be a likely source for a name carried by emigrants all the way to Europe. Or when he asks: "**how *did* the IE tree names belonging to a cooler climate ever get exported out of India where those trees do *not* exist?** [...] **some of the typical temperate PIE trees are *not* found in the South Asian mountains. Yet they have good Iranian and IE names, *all* with proper IE word formation.** [...] **In other words, these cool climate, temperate trees and their names are already PIE**".

But they *did not* "**get exported out of India**". The name of the birch did not originate in the high altitude area of Kashmir *inside* India (let alone in "**the Panjab or the Indian plains**") and spread westwards; it developed in the broad area (*including* the high altitude areas of Kashmir) from northwestern India to Central Asia, which was the area over which the isoglosses were developed, and was taken westwards by the emigrating IE Dialects. Most of the words, for trees, animals or natural phenomena of the more western parts of this broad area, developed among groups of Dialects which did *not* include "Indo-Aryan", but a few of them (of which the name *bhūrja* for the birch, or *parkaṭi* for the oak, may be examples), again, may have entered Sanskrit as *substrate* words after the emigration of the major IE Dialects of the northwest and the subsequent "Indo-Aryanization" or "Sanskritization" of the remnants of these Anus and Druhyus.

The reason why Witzel finds it difficult to understand this is because, as we have already seen, he is arguing against an alleged OIT scenario where the IE Dialects developed all their isoglosses within India, in a one-time development, and then marched out one by one out of the bottle-neck passes leading out of India, more or less never to come into contact with each other again until later historical times. Therefore he writes: "**According to the autochthonous theory, these temperate climate, non-Indian plant and animal names would have to be new words that were coined only when the various IE tribes had already migrated out of India. However, again, all of them are proper IE names, with IE roots and suffixes, and with proper IE word formation. It would require extraordinary special pleading to assume that they all were created *independently* by the various emigrant IE tribes, at different times, on different paths, but always from the *same* IE root in question and (often) with the same suffixes. How could these 'emigrants' know or remember exactly which roots/suffixes to choose on encountering a new plant or animal?**" (WITZEL 2005:374-375).

Witzel, therefore also fails to understand the logistical significance of the development of certain other words (e.g.

the words for wine), common to most other western IE languages, but absent in IndoAryan, and even refers to them as if they somehow (it is not explained how) prove the *AIT*, when actually they fit in with the *OIT*: "**early IE loans from Semitic somewhere in the Near East such as **wVjñ, IE *woin (Nichols 1997:143), words that are not found in India.**" (WITZEL 2005:360). Obviously, since they were borrowed into the western IE languages as they moved *away* from India. In fact, this particular word, borrowed from Semitic, is found in three grades, according to Gamkrelidze, which, in fact fit in with the migrations from India: the word is not found in Indo-Aryan, Iranian and Tocharian, which remained in the east; it is found in Anatolian (Hittite), the Early Dialect emigrating westwards, from "**PIE *wi(o)no-, with zero grade**"; in the European Dialects (Italic, Celtic, Germanic, Slavic) from "**PIE *weino- with e-grade vocalism**"; and, in the Late Dialects migrating westwards (Greek, Albanian, Armenian), from "**PIE *woino- with *o* grade**" (GAMKRELIDZE 1995:557-558).

In sum, *all* of Witzel's linguistic arguments are basically directed against *three* hypotheses which are treated as the core of the OIT case, *but which form no part whatsoever of the case presented by us*: (1) the "**Sanskrit-origin**" hypothesis, which treats the proto-Indo-European language as identical, or almost identical, with Vedic Sanskrit; (2) the "**sequential movement of different groups**" Out-of-India hypothesis (postulated by *no-one*, so far as I know) argued against by Hock (HOCK 1999a), which would treat the various Indo-European Dialects as moving, one by one, out of the bottle-neck routes leading out from northwestern India to the outside world, after having developed all the isoglosses within India; and (3) "**Misra's new dating of the RV at 5000 BCE**" (WITZEL 2005:358), from which Witzel decides: "**The autochthonous theory would have the RV at c.5000 BCE or before the start of the Indus civilization at 2600 BCE**", and

"according to the autochthonous theory, the Iranians had migrated westwards out of India well before the RV (2600-5000 BCE)" (WITZEL 2005:369).

Therefore, to sum up, there is no linguistic case at all, worth the name, against the OIT case presented by us in our earlier books, and presented again with much more detail in this present book, especially in this chapter. The Indian homeland case presented by us answers all the linguistic requirements perfectly, while the AIT completely fails to answer any of them.

Chapter 8

The Archaeological Case

As we have seen in the course of this book, the case for an Indo-European homeland in India is *complete* and *final*. But, it has long been ignored or vilified in official and academic circles in favour of the prevalent AIT or Aryan Invasion Theory, and politics and vested interests will see to it that this continues to be the case for quite some time more. But we have presented new, and *irrefutable*, textual evidence in Section I of this book, and presented a *complete* linguistic case in the previous chapter; and the AIT will ultimately *have* to collapse and make way for the OIT or the Out-of-India Theory (or the Indian Homeland Theory) even in western academic circles — though, of course, not without a bitter struggle. But there are a few points to be made, and a few loose ends to be tied. Hence this final chapter to sum up the case and present it in final perspective.

From the very beginning, i.e. from the first moment that the academic search for the Indo-European homeland began, there have been three broad academic disciplines involved in this field of study: linguistics, textual analysis, and archaeology. We have already examined the linguistic evidence and the textual evidence in detail. Now, in summing up, we will mainly examine the OIT case from the archaeological perspective. This is important, since archaeology has always been the *weakest* link in the AIT chain.

In fact, so weak, or rather so negative, has been the archaeological evidence for the AIT that archaeologists as a class reject the AIT as it stands today. And this is not only Indian archaeologists, but even most of the *western* archaeologists involved in the study of India's past. So much so that (to take just one such example) in an academic volume of papers devoted to the subject by western academicians, George Erdosy, in his preface to the volume, stresses that this is a subject of dispute between linguists and archaeologists, and that the idea of an Aryan invasion of India in the second millennium BCE "**has recently been challenged by archaeologists, who — along with linguists — are best qualified to evaluate its validity. Lack of convincing material (or osteological) traces left behind by the incoming Indo-Aryan speakers, the possibility of explaining cultural change without reference to external factors and — above all — an altered world-view (Shaffer 1984) have all contributed to a questioning of assumptions long taken for granted and buttressed by the accumulated weight of two centuries of scholarship**" (ERDOSY 1995:x).

Of the papers presented by archaeologists in the volume (being papers presented at a conference on Archaeological and Linguistic approaches to Ethnicity in Ancient South Asia, held in Toronto from 4-6/10/1991), the paper by K.A.R. Kennedy concludes that "**while discontinuities in physical types have certainly been found in South Asia, they are dated to the 5th/4th, and to the 1st millennium B.C. respectively, too early and too late to have any connection with 'Aryans'**" (ERDOSY 1995:xii); the paper by J. Shaffer and D. Lichtenstein stresses on "**the indigenous development of South Asian civilization from the Neolithic onward**" (ERDOSY 1995:xiii); and the paper by J.M. Kenoyer stresses that "**the cultural history of South Asia in the 2nd millennium B.C. may be explained without reference to external agents**" (ERDOSY 1995:xiv).

Erdosy points out that the perspective offered by archaeology, "**that of material culture** [...] **is in direct conflict with the findings of the other discipline claiming a key to the solution of the 'Aryan Problem', linguistics** [...] **In the face of such conflict, it may be difficult to find avenues of**

cooperation, yet a satisfactory resolution of the puzzles set by the distribution of Indo-Aryan languages in South Asia demands it [...] **to bridge the disciplinary divide** [...]" (ERDOSY 1995:xi).

In short, archaeology not only does not form part of any genuine case for the AIT, but it actually stands in sharp *opposition* to the AIT.

The basic fact that archaeology fails to provide any evidence for the AIT is often acknowledged even by scholars who represent the AIT side in the AIT-vs.-OIT crusades. In the above volume, for example, it is Witzel's papers which are pitted against the papers of the archaeologists. But note what Witzel, in a separate paper elsewhere, has to say on the matter:

> **"To begin with, the *details* for the import of IA language and culture still escape us** [...] **None of the archaeologically identified post-Harappan cultures so far found, from Cemetery H, Sarai Kala III, the early Gandhara and Gomal Grave Cultures, does make a good fit for the culture of the speakers of Vedic** [...] **At the present moment, we can only state that linguistic and textual studies confirm the presence of an outside, Indo-Aryan speaking element, whose language and spiritual culture has definitely been introduced, along with the horse and the spoked wheel chariot, via the BMAC area into northwestern South Asia. However, much of present-day Archaeology denies that. To put it in the words of Shaffer (1999:245) 'A diffusion or migration of a culturally complex 'Indo-Aryan' people into South Asia is *not* described by the archaeological record'** [...] **[But] the importation of their spiritual and material culture *must be explained*. So far, clear archaeological evidence has just not been found**" (WITZEL 2000a:§15).

Therefore, the question is: should the evidence of archaeology be treated as standing in sharp opposition to the AIT *or* should archaeology merely be treated as having no role to play in the AIT-vs.-OIT debate (until actual *decipherable inscriptional evidence* is discovered, either in the Harappan sites, conclusively proving the language of the Harappans to be Indo-European *or* non-Indo-European, or in archaeological sites further west and north, in Central Asia or further, revealing a language which can be conclusively shown to be a form of *pre*-Rigvedic)?

[Either way, it means that the entire AIT case is based only on linguistic and textual arguments. If so, the battle is already won: the textual case we have presented in Section I of this book is invincible and irrefutable; and so is the linguistic case presented by us in the previous chapter (chapter seven), in contrast with the textual and linguistic cases presented by the AIT scholars. We have already exposed most of their arguments in our two earlier books — arguments which are based on wholly subjective and extremely flawed interpretations, and formulated by sweeping numerous inexplicable facts under the carpet. But even if the textual and linguistic *arguments* presented by the scholars are still to be considered to be in the running, they are definitely weak and subjective compared to the massive textual and linguistic *evidence* presented in this book].

If the AIT scholars were to accept the latter proposition, that archaeology has no role to play in the AIT-vs.-OIT debate, we could rest our case at this point. But AIT scholars leave no stone unturned in trying to demonstrate an archaeological case for the AIT. At the same time, for example, Witzel tries to turn the tables on the OIT, on the principle that attack is the best form of defence, by demanding archaeological evidence for the OIT: "**Further, if the Iranians (and IEs) emigrated from India, why do we not find 'Indian bones' of this massive emigration in Iran and beyond?** [...] **Again, autochthonists would have to argue that mysteriously only that section of the Panjab population left westwards which had (then actually not attested!) 'non-Indian' physical characteristics, — very special pleading indeed**" (WITZEL 2005:368). [Witzel, as usual, decides for himself what the "autochthonists" or OIT writers would argue, and *then* goes on to show that "their" arguments amount to "**special pleading**"!]

Therefore it becomes necessary for us to demonstrate conclusively that archaeology is *not* neutral in the debate so far as the AIT case is concerned: archaeology stands in sharp *opposition* to the AIT and conclusively disproves it. At the same time, archaeology is more or less *neutral* so far as the OIT case is concerned: although there is obviously no conclusive archaeological evidence for the OIT scenario, this circumstance does not disprove the OIT. There are many basic reasons why archaeological evidence is *vital* for the *AIT* to be accepted as valid, but archaeological evidence is *not* vital for the *OIT* to be accepted as valid, and we will see this in detail in this chapter.

We will examine the case under the following heads:

8A. The Archaeological Case Against the AIT.

8B. The Case for the OIT.

- 8B-1. The PGW (painted grey ware) Culture as the Vedic Culture.
- 8B-2. The Harappan Civilization as the Rigvedic Culture.
- 8B-3. The Indo-European Emigrations.

8C. The Importance of the Rigveda.

8A
THE ARCHAEOLOGICAL CASE AGAINST THE AIT

As we have seen, the archaeologists are almost unanimous on the point that there is *absolutely no archaeological evidence* for any change in the ethnic composition and the material culture in the Harappan areas between "**the 5th/4th and** [...] **the 1st millennium B.C.**", and that there was "**indigenous development of South Asian civilization from the Neolithic onward**"; and further that any change which took place before "**the 5th/4th** [...] **millennium B.C.**" and after "**the 1st millennium B.C.**" is "**too early and too late to have any connection with 'Aryans'**".

This deals a death blow to the AIT, since there is no way in which the postulates of the AIT can be readjusted so as to bring the "Aryans" into India before the 5th/4th millennium

BCE or after the 1st millennium BCE. Therefore, the *main* concern of historians and linguists involved in the AIT-vs.-OIT debate, or even merely in the study of ancient Indian history in the light of the Aryan problem, is to find ways and means by which the AIT can still be maintained within the required time-frame without prejudice to the archaeological situation.

Witzel, for example, suggests that the Aryan arrival into, and subsequent presence in and domination of, the region resulted in a change in *language* and *spiritual culture* rather than in *material* culture, and that, therefore, it would not necessarily reflect in the archaeological record: "**much or most of the IA cultural and spiritual data can simply not be 'seen' by Archaeology: it would look just like the remains of any other group of second millennium pastoralists** [...] **the South Asian discontinuity of the second millennium is not one of the local food (or pottery) producing cultures, but one of language, poetry, spiritual culture, though it also includes some material culture, such as the — not yet discovered — Vedic chariots**" (WITZEL 2000a:§15).

This is clearly "**special pleading**": Aryan "language, poetry and spiritual culture" did not come into northwestern India in the form of telepathic waves which mysteriously engulfed the entire population of the northwest (and later, progressively, the whole rest of northern India), rather like in modern Hollywood blockbusters about alien invasions, resulting in a *complete* collective amnesia in the local population and replacing their earlier "language, poetry and spiritual culture" with the new Aryan ones. *If* these came from outside, they *must* have been brought in by new people, who, in any reasonable hypothesis must have been of a distinctly different race from the indigenous population, numerous and powerful enough to affect the change. So we *have* to very definitely find evidence of this complete transformation reflected in the archaeological and anthropological record — *if it ever occurred.* The fact that no such evidence is found (not even the Vedic chariots, whose "material" nature at least is accepted by Witzel above) *is evidence in itself* — evidence *against* the AIT.

To fully comprehend the *utterly incredible and impossible* nature of the scenario that the AIT wants us to accept, it is important to first examine certain *fundamental* aspects, the *where, what, when* and *how* of the AIT case. A transformation is alleged to have taken place in the Harappan areas in the second millennium BCE. But *where* is this transformation alleged to have taken place? *What* is the exact transformation that is alleged to have taken place? *When*, or within how long a period of time, is this transformation alleged to have taken place? And *how* is this transformation alleged to have taken place?

1. *Where is this transformation alleged to have taken place*? This transformation is alleged to have taken place in the area of one of the Great Civilizations of the ancient world: a full-fledged, highly developed (in terms of technology as well as civic organization) and highly populated civilization, *the largest and most organized civilization of the time.*

2. *What is the exact transformation that is alleged to have taken place*? The first and foremost point is that the people of the Harappan areas, who were allegedly speaking a totally unrelated (to Indo-European) language, or languages, Munda, Dravidian, proto-Burushaski or Language X, *completely* abandoned that language, or those languages, and switched over to speaking Indo-European (specifically "Indo-Aryan") languages. And this switchover was *so total* that not a trace remains of the original language (except stray words in Vedic or later Indo-Aryan, which are alleged by certain linguists to be *substrate* words from those languages, but which, by their nature, would appear, if anything, more to be *non*-basic *adstrate* words adopted from neighbour or visitor languages: for example, a word which appears to be undoubtedly of Dravidian origin, the Vedic word *kāṇa*, "one-eyed", from Dravidian *kaṇ*, "eye").

This situation is unique, extraordinary and unparalleled in more ways than one: the linguistic transformation was allegedly so complete that even the *names of places and rivers in the area* were so *completely* Indo-Europeanized or "Aryanized" that not a trace remains, even in the oldest hymns, of any alleged earlier "non-Aryan" names.

About place names, Witzel points out that most of the place-names in England (including all names ending in *-don*, *-chester*, *-ton*, *-ham*, *-ey*, *-wick*, etc. like *London*, *Winchester*, *Uppington*, *Downham*, *Westrey*, *Lerwick*, etc) and America (like *Massachussetts*, *Wachussetts*, *Mississippi*, *Missouri*, *Chicago*, etc.), are remnants of older languages spoken in these areas. But about India, he writes: "**In South Asia, relatively few pre-Indo-Aryan place-names survive in the North; however, many more in central and southern India. Indo-Aryan place-names are generally not very old, since the towns themselves are relatively late**" (WITZEL 1995a:104). Witzel talks about "**relatively few pre-Indo-Aryan names**" in the North, but does not bother to give details about these "**few**" names. That there should be "**many more in central and southern India**", in and close to the Munda and Dravidian speaking areas, is not surprising, and is irrelevant to the discussion here. The excuse that the paucity or lack of "**pre-Indo-Aryan**" place-names in the North is due to "**the towns themselves**" being "**relatively late**" is extremely strange: it is the allegedly "**pre-Indo-Aryan**" Harappans who had innumerable towns and cities, while the Vedic "**Indo-Aryans**" were allegedly pastoral nomads "**on the move**", and yet Witzel proffers the above excuse, after having just pointed out that the pre-colonial place-names of the native American Indians of the USA, *who had no towns and cities*, have survived in large numbers to this day!

About river-names, likewise, Witzel writes: "**A better case for the early linguistic and ethnic history of India can be made by investigating the names of rivers. In Europe, river names were found to reflect the languages spoken before the**

influx of Indo-European speaking populations. They are thus older than c. 4500-2500 B.C. (depending on the date of the spread of Indo-European languages in various parts of Europe)." (WITZEL 1995a:104-105). But, in sharp contrast, "**in northern India rivers in general have early Sanskrit names from the Vedic period, and names derived from the daughter languages of Sanskrit later on.**" (WITZEL 1995a:105).

Witzel makes the situation very clear: "**To sum up, what does the evidence of hydronomy tell us? Clearly there has been an almost complete Indo-Aryanization in northern India** [...] **This leads to the conclusion that the Indo-Aryan influence, whether due to actual settlement, acculturation or, if one prefers, the substitution of Indo-Aryan names for local ones, was powerful enough from early on to replace local names, in spite of the well-known conservatism of river names. This is especially surprising in the area once occupied by the Indus Civilisation where one would have expected the survival of older names, as has been the case in Europe and the Near East. At the least, one would expect a palimpsest, as found in New England with the name of the state of Massachussetts next to the Charles river, formerly called the Massachussetts river, and such new adaptations as Stony Brook, Muddy Creek, Red River, etc., next to the adaptations of Indian names such as the Mississippi and the Missouri**". According to Witzel, this alleged "**failure to preserve old hydronomes even in the Indus Valley**" is indicative of "**the extent of the social and political collapse experienced by the local population**" (WITZEL 1995a:106-107).

What is more, the transformation is not restricted to *language* alone: "**What is relatively rare is the adoption of *complete* systems of belief, mythology and language from neighbouring peoples** [...] **Yet, in South Asia we are dealing precisely with the absorption of not only new languages but also of an entire complex of material and spiritual culture,**

ranging from chariotry and horsemanship to Indo-Iranian poetry whose complicated conventions are still actively used in the Ṛgveda. The old Indo-Iranian religion, centred on the opposition of Devas and Asuras, was also adopted, along with Indo-European systems of ancestor worship." (WITZEL 1995a:112).

Therefore, the transformation that is alleged to have taken place in the Harappan areas was *absolutely total.* It is alleged to have left almost no traces whatsoever of the original "**belief, mythology and language**", or of the original "**complex** of **material and spiritual culture**", other than "**complex**" clues that scholars like Witzel, and his predecessors and colleagues in the AIT cottage industry, have occasionally managed to dig out for our benefit. The local people not only adopted "**Indo-European systems of ancestor worship**", they completely abandoned and forgot their own actual ancestors and their own actual ancestral history, and adopted the ancestors and ancestral history of the "**Indo-Aryans**" as their own.

3. *When, or within how long a period of time, is this transformation alleged to have taken place*? It is alleged to have commenced some time after 1500 BCE, and was more or less completed within a period of 200 to 400 years.

4. *How is this transformation alleged to have taken place*? The earlier versions of the manner in which this transformation took place (outright old-fashioned invasion and conquest) have been progressively watered down in the face of the open rejection by archaeologists and anthropologists: from invasion to immigration, and from immigration to "trickling in".

Here is Witzel's now standard version of how this transformation took place (note that he, typically, refers to the unanimous scientific observations of Indian *and* western archaeologists and anthropologists as the views of "autochthonists"):

> **"Autochthonists** [...] **maintain that there is no evidence of demographic discontinuity in archaeological remains during the period from 4500 to 800 BCE, and that an influx of foreign populations is not visible in the archaeological record.**

> **The revisionists and autochthonists overlook, however, that such refutations of an immigration by 'racially' determined IAs still depend on the old, nineteenth century idea of a massive *invasion* of outsiders who would have left a definite mark on the genetic set-up of the local Panjab population. Presently we do not know how large this particular influx of linguistically attested outsiders was. It can have been relatively small, if we apply Ehret's model (1988, derived from Africa, cf. Diakonoff 1985) which stresses the *osmosis* (or a 'billiard ball', or Mallory's *Kulturkugel*) effect of cultural transmission.**
>
> **Ehret (1988) underlines the relative ease with which ethnicity and language shift in small societies, due to the cultural/economic/military *choices* made by the local population in question. The intruding/influencing group bringing new traits may initially be small and the features it contributes can be fewer in number than those of the preexisting local culture. The newly formed, combined ethnic group may then initiate a recurrent, *expansionist* process of ethnic and language shift. The material record of such shifts is visible only insofar as new prestige equipment or animals (the 'status kit', with new intrusive vocabulary!) are concerned. This is especially so if pottery — normally culture-specific — continues to be made by local specialists of a class-based society**
>
> [...] **the descriptions given just now fit the Indus/Ved. evidence perfectly.**" (WITZEL 2005:347).

Elsewhere Witzel adds another fairy-tale dimension to this story:

> **"small-scale semi-annual transhumance movements between the Indus plains and the Afghan and Baluchi highlands continue to this day (Witzel 1995:322, 2000)** [...] **Just one 'Afghan' IA tribe that did not return to the highlands but stayed in their Panjab winter quarters in spring was needed to set off a wave of acculturation in the plains by transmitting its 'status kit' (Ehret) to its neighbors"** (WITZEL 2005:342).

The above attempt, to downplay or bypass the archaeological evidence by trying to suggest a way in which the "Indo-Aryans" could have brought about the alleged transformation in the Harappan areas in the 2nd millennium BCE without leaving any trace of it in the archaeological record, is full of anomalies, contradictions and *impossible* assumptions:

1. The totality of the alleged transformation *itself* is clearly unparalleled and unprecedented, and in every way *contrary* to the normal: Witzel himself, see above, repeatedly describes different aspects of it as "**surprising**", "**relatively rare**" and *against* what "**one would have expected**" in such cases. The case becomes *impossible* when we consider all the aspects together: (a) the transformation was *total*, (b) the people who brought about this transformation were illiterate, pastoral nomadic tribes "**on the move**" who "**trickled**" into the area in miniscule numbers, (c) the people who were transformed were the inhabitants of the most densely populated urban civilization of the time, covering a larger area, and having a relatively longer continuity without much change, than any other contemporary civilization, (d) the change took place within a few hundred years, and (e) it left *absolutely* no traces in the archaeological record, either of the conflicts and struggles involved *or* the necessarily resultant changes in ethnic and material composition of the areas after the transformation. It requires *extraordinary* "**special pleading**" to advocate such a case.

What is particularly notable in this special pleading is that it asks us to believe in a *combination* of abnormal phenomena and lack of evidence. Thus, for example, we could have accepted, in principle, that the river names of the Harappan areas (in an AIT scenario) may have been "**Indo-Aryanised**", if transformation of river names were the norm in such cases, even in the *absence* of evidence in this case of any earlier names. But it is *not* the norm: as Witzel points out, the names of most European rivers, *to this day*, "**reflect the languages spoken before the influx of Indo-European speaking populations** [and] **are thus older than c. 4500-2500 B.C.**" Again, we would have *had* to accept that such a transformation took place here, even if it went contrary to the norm, if earlier "non-Indo-Aryan" names of these rivers were on record at least in the texts. But there is not the faintest clue, even in the oldest hymns, that any such names ever existed. This pleading therefore goes both against the *norm* as well as against the available *evidence*.

What adds to the force of the archaeological evidence (of continuity in material and ethnic culture) is the fact that there *is* considerable acceptable archaeological, as also hydronomic, evidence, for the Indo-European intrusions, in the case of the earliest habitats of most of the other Indo-European branches, although the immigrants either entered over long periods of time into totally prehistoric or primitive areas (in most of Europe), or they entered historic, civilized areas but were quickly absorbed into the local culture and gradually became extinct (e.g. the Hittites etc. in West Asia). So *here*, more than in any of the other cases, we *should* have found massive and unambiguous evidence of the "Indo-Aryan" intrusions, *if they ever took place*. The *total* absence of *any* indications in the material remains of the area, of such a cataclysmic transformation, constitutes *massive* evidence for the rejection of the very idea that such a transformation took place at all.

2. Witzel's attempt to co-opt Ehret's theory (whatever its supposed merits), which pertained to cultural transmissions in Africa, to the situation in northern India, proves, at the very outset, to be untenable. There are many obvious points, in Witzel's *own* description of his so-called "**Ehret's model**", which show it, far from "**fit**[ting] **the Indus/Ved. evidence perfectly**" as he claims, to be totally *inapplicable* as an analogy to the "Indus/Ved." situation:

(a) The Harappan civilization was not a "**small society**": it was a *densely populated* civilization, covering a *larger* area, and remaining unchanged over a *longer* period of time, than *any* other contemporary civilization of the time.

(b) The "**local population**", inhabitants of one of the world's largest, most organized and advanced civilizations of the time, would be extremely unlikely to have made conscious "**choices**" to replace their culture and language with the culture and language of miniscule (*invisible to the archaeological record*) intruding groups of a pastoral, illiterate, nomadic people "**on the move**".

(c) The *total* replacement of the "**preexisting local culture**" and language with the new culture and language (so total that not a *shred* remains of the earlier culture or language), which is alleged to have taken place in the Harappan areas, clearly can not be analogical to a situation where an "**intruding/influencing group**" brings "**new traits** [which] **may initially be small and** [where] **the features it contributes can be fewer in number than those of the preexisting local culture**".

(d) When Witzel himself repeatedly accepts that the horses and chariots of the "Aryans" are yet to be found in the archaeological record, how is it analogical to a situation where apparently "**the material record of such shifts is visible only insofar as new prestige equipment or animals (the 'status kit', with new intrusive vocabulary!) are concerned**"? (Note, also, that here Witzel cites the evidence of horses and chariots, when admittedly *not found*, as "**visible**" evidence, while explaining away the *actually visible* evidence found, of continuation in pottery types, as culture-irrelevant in this case even when he admits it to be "**normally culture-specific**").

3. Moreover, Witzel cites "**Ehret's model**" (totally inappropriate and inadequate as we have just seen it to be) when he is dealing with the *archaeological* evidence *against* the AIT, to try to illustrate how linguistic and cultural transformations can take place with minimum effect on the visible material environment, and even goes so far as to suggest that the *total* transformation of the Harappan areas was due to a "**wave of acculturation**" set off by one small tribe of "Indo-Aryans" from Afghanistan, who overstayed their

annual migration from Afghanistan to Punjab and back. Fully aware that "**a massive *invasion* of outsiders** [...] **would have left a definite mark on the genetic set-up of the local Panjab population**", which is totally *missing*, he dismisses the very idea of such an invasion as an "**old, nineteenth century idea**". In his earlier paper in 1995, he tells us that the "**idea of a cataclysmic invasion has, in fact, been given up long ago by Vedic scholars** [...] **In view of these facts, it would not be surprising if physical anthropologists failed to unearth any 'Aryan skeletons'** [...]" (WITZEL 1995b:323).

But, when he is analyzing the *textual* data to try to find evidence for the AIT, it is a different story. In typical Witzellian style, i.e. *in the very same pages* where he is disowning the idea of a "**cataclysmic invasion**", Witzel presents us with a full-fledged *invasionist* account of the Aryan intrusion in the Harappan areas: as per this account, the "Indo-Aryans" fought their way through the mountains of Afghanistan, storming innumerable mountain fortresses, sometimes after long and bitter 40-year campaigns, and finally reached the Harappan areas. "**On the plains of the Panjab, the Indo-Aryans had further battles to fight**", with numerous "**explicit descriptions of campaigns**", recorded in the Rigveda, in which the "Indo-Aryans" "**destroyed**" hundreds of forts and, on different occasions, "**put to sleep**", "**put down**" or "**dispersed**" 30,000, 50,000 and 100,000 natives (WITZEL 1995b:322, 324). Ultimately, there was a total "**social and political collapse experienced by the local population**" (WITZEL 1995a:106-107).

So, clearly, the make-believe "model" of a magical transformation brought about by "**a process of acculturation**" "**triggered**" by "**a limited number of Indo-Aryan speakers**" (WITZEL 1995b:323) is meant to be brought out only when required as a counter to the undeniable evidence of an undisturbed archaeological and anthropological continuity in the Harappan areas between "**the 5th/4th and** [...] **the 1st millennium B.C.**" In *other* contexts, there are *other* "models".

Witzel is finally compelled to fall back on open pleading as follows: "**any archaeologist should know from experience that the unexpected occurs and that one has to look at the right place**" (WITZEL 2000a:§15). In other words, "there is no archaeological evidence, true. But it must be there somewhere, it is just that no-one has found it as yet; it is only just waiting to be found"! As if some *yet-to-be-discovered* sites could provide the archaeological and anthropological evidence, for a *total* transformation which affected the *entire* region, which is missing in all the *discovered* sites from the same region. This is the sort of wishful appeal-to-faith pleading that Indians are (not unjustly) accused of resorting to when their ideas of ancient India are out of tune with the material evidence: see discussion on spoked wheels in section 6B of this book. By Witzel's logic, even the claim of many Indians that ancient India had aeroplanes should not be dismissed simply because aeroplanes have not yet been found in any archaeological record!

In continuation of the above, Witzel pleads: "**people on the move (such as the Huns) leave few traces**" (WITZEL 2000a:§15). This explanation does not apply to the alleged immigrations, since the alleged immigrants were *not* "**on the move**": they allegedly came to a halt in northwestern India, their earliest attested historical habitat, where they completely transformed the linguistic, social and cultural ethos of the area and established the historically important Vedic civilization depicted in the Rigveda. [On the other hand, *emigrants* from India would be more likely to be "**on the move**" and therefore to "**leave few traces**" in Afghanistan or Central Asia].

This was the evidence against the AIT from the point of view of the alleged transformation in the Harappan areas: i.e. we examined certain *fundamental* aspects, the *where, what, when* and *how* of the AIT case for the transformation that is alleged to have taken place in the Harappan areas in the second millennium BCE, and found that the case is *utterly untenable* in view of the undisturbed archaeological and anthropological continuity in the Harappan areas between "**the 5th/4th and** [...] **the 1st millennium B.C.**".

But the case can be seen from another point of view: from the point of view of the reconstructed proto-Indo-European language and culture. For this, we will examine two more fundamental aspects of the AIT case: the *who*, and another *what*, of the AIT case: *Who* exactly were the people who brought about this alleged transformation (apart from the fact that they were "Indo-Aryans")? And *what* was the relationship of this transformed culture (as reflected in the Rigveda) with the reconstructed proto-Indo-European culture?

1. *Who exactly were the people who brought about this alleged transformation*? They were, of course, "Indo-Aryans"; but what exactly does this mean?

As per the AIT, the original homeland of the Indo-European family of languages was in South Russia, or "**somewhere within a vast area 'from East Central Europe to Eastern Russia'**" (HOCK 1999a:16); and it was in this area that the original proto-Indo-European language split up into various different Dialects (the later branches), two of which were proto-Iranian and proto-Indo-Aryan, or, according to some, one of which was proto-Indo-Iranian. The *original Indo-Iranians* were the original speakers of this proto-Indo-Iranian Dialect in South Russia:

a) These *original Indo-Iranians* were separated from the other Indo-European groups at very early periods: according to Victor H. Mair (MAIR 1998:847-853), for example, the Indo-Iranians were already separated from the speakers of the Anatolian and Tocharian Dialects by 3700 BCE, from the speakers of the Italic, Celtic, Germanic, Baltic, Slavic and Albanian Dialects by 3200 BCE, from the speakers of the Greek Dialect by 2500 BCE, and from the speakers of the Armenian Dialect by 2000 BCE.

b) After separating from most of the other Indo-European groups (perhaps only the Armenians remained with them for some time after), these original Indo-Iranians started migrating eastwards from South Russia. In the course of their long and stage-wise journey from South Russia to Central Asia, they were part of different cultural complexes on the way at different points of time: suggested stages in the Indo-Iranian migrations have the Indo-Iranians as part of the Andronovo Culture in the Pontic-Caspian area and later the Afanas'evo Culture to the north of Central Asia. All along the way, the original Indo-Iranians underwent ethnic changes as they mixed with different local populations.

c) Finally, they reached Central Asia, where they formed part of the BMAC or Bactria-Margiana Cultural Complex. Here, the original Indo-Iranians, now differentiated into two distinct groups, proto-Iranians and proto-Indo-Aryans, merged into the local population. As Witzel puts it, by the time the Indo-Aryans "**reached the Subcontinent they were already racially mixed** [...] **they may have had the typical somatic characteristics of the ancient populations of the Turanian/Iranian/Afghan areas** [...] **even before their immigration into South Asia** [they] **completely 'Aryanized' a local population, for example, in the Turkmenian-Bactrian area which yielded the BMAC, involving both their language and culture. This is only imaginable as the result of the complete acculturation of both groups. To an outside observer, the local Bactrians would have appeared as a typically 'Vedic' people with a Vedic civilization. Later on, (part of) this new people would have moved into the Panjab, assimilating ('Aryanizing') the local population**" (WITZEL 1995a:113).

Hock also makes the same plea: "**it is unrealistic to believe that the āryas descended on India in a sudden movement, and from far-away lands. It is more likely that they migrated slowly, in small tribal groups** [...] **from one**

habitable area to the next, settling for a while, and in the process, assimilating to the local population in terms of phenotype, culture, and perhaps also religion. By the time they reached northwestern India they would, therefore, have been fairly similar to the population of that area in terms of their physical appearance and culture" (HOCK 1999b:160-161).

Therefore, the "**Indo-Aryans**" who brought about the transformation in the Harappan areas were *not the original Indo-Aryans at all.* They were a "**new people**" totally unrelated to the other Indo-European groups, except perhaps the Iranians of the BMAC areas, and only related to the *original proto-Indo-Aryans* of the original homeland (who were themselves separated from the other Indo-European groups at very early periods in distant lands) to the same extent as a drop of homoeopathic tincture many times diluted in water is related to the original tincture.

It was *this* "**new people**", these highly diluted new "Indo-Aryans", who "trickled into" the Harappan areas in miniscule groups and, gradually over a period of time, brought about the total transformation that we saw earlier. The Rigveda was composed *at the end* of this whole process, *after* the whole transformation had more or less taken place: Witzel quotes and endorses F.B.J. Kuiper's linguistic opinion that "**between the arrival of the Aryans ... and the formation of the oldest hymns of the Rigveda a much longer period must have elapsed than is normally thought**", and insists that "**Vedic Sanskrit is already an *Indian* language**" (WITZEL 1995a:108).

[Incidentally, Hock, quoted above, goes on to argue, like Witzel, that this model of Aryan entry into India explains the skeletal continuity in the second millennium BCE, and he even gives other supposedly parallel cases in India: "**Interestingly, skeletal continuity seems also to hold for later, historical periods — even though we know for certain that there were numerous migrations or invasions into South Asia, by**

groups as diverse as the Greeks, the Central Asian Huns, the Iranian Sakas, and Muslims from Iran, Central Asia, and even the Arab world" (HOCK 1999b:161). As in all such AIT arguments, the parallels cited prove exactly the *opposite* of what is claimed. The Greeks, Huns and Sakas were genuinely small in number, and they simply got merged into the local populations, in terms of "**phenotype, culture, and** [...] **religion**", *and language*, and lost their original identity; unlike the "Indo-Aryans" who are supposed to have *preserved* their original identity: in fact it is the *local populations all over northern India* who are alleged to have got merged into the small group of Aryan immigrants in terms of at least "**culture, and** [...] **religion**", *and language*, and to have completely lost their original identity! Likewise, the Muslims were also small in number, but, unlike the Vedic Aryans, they were armed with a militant proselytizing ideology which *compelled* them to merge local populations into themselves in terms of at least "**culture, and** [...] **religion**", in spite of which the local populations managed to retain their original "**culture, and** [...] **religion**" on a major scale. And in *all* these instances, detailed records and memories, and other factors like the original hydronomy and languages, have remained as witnesses to these numerous "**migrations or invasions**"; unlike in the case of the alleged Indo-Aryan "**migrations or invasions**", which have had to be repeatedly sought to be "proved" in the course of the last two centuries to a bemused Indian populace, in the *absence* of such witnesses].

2. *What was the relationship of this transformed culture (as reflected in the Rigveda) with the reconstructed proto-Indo-European culture*? The answer is that this transformed culture was extremely *close* to, and most *representative* of, the reconstructed proto-Indo-European culture, both in language as well as in religion and mythology. As Griffith puts it in the preface to the first edition of his translation of the Rigveda: "**The great interest of the *Ṛgveda* is, in fact, historical rather than poetical. As in its original language we see the**

roots and shoots of the languages of Greek and Latin, of Kelt, Teuton and Slavonian, so the deities, the myths, and the religious beliefs and practices of the Veda throw a flood of light upon the religions of all European countries before the introduction of Christianity."

Any number of detailed quotes can be cited here, from linguists and historians through two centuries, to show how Vedic is the *most archaic*, and the *most representative*, of the different Indo-European languages. This is totally without prejudice to the fact that it is also supposed to represent many changes from the original; and that other archaisms, of different kinds, are found preserved in different other branches of Indo-European languages so that, for example, even the Avestan language contains certain phonetic archaisms not found in Vedic.

Here we are concerned with the nature of the culture of the Rigveda as represented in what Griffith above calls "**the deities, the myths, and the religious beliefs and practices of the Veda**". Rigvedic mythology is undoubtedly the *most archaic and representative of all the Indo-European mythologies* [This subject has already been dealt with in detail in earlier books (TALAGERI 1993:377-399, TALAGERI 2000:477-495; TALAGERI 2005:334-336), and what follows is mainly taken from the last, which summarizes the situation in brief. *AIT scholars have determinedly persisted in failing to recognize the vital significance, importance and relevance of this actual evidence of comparative mythology*, their idea of comparative Indo-European mythology being restricted to purely subjective, and *allegedly* mythological, concepts like "tripartite functions"]:

a) The mythology of the Rigveda represents the most primitive form of Indo-European mythology: as Macdonell puts it, for example, the Vedic gods "**are nearer to the physical phenomena which they represent, than the gods of any other Indo-European mythology**" (MACDONELL 1963:15).

In fact, in the majority of cases, the *original* nature myths, in which the mythological entities and the mythological events are rooted, can be identified or traced *only* through the form in which the myths are represented in the Rigveda.

b) *All* the other Indo-European mythologies, *individually*, have *numerous* mythological elements in common with Vedic mythology, but *very few* with each other; and even these few (except those borrowed from each other in ancient but historical times, such as the Greek god Apollo, borrowed by the Romans) are ones which are also found in Vedic mythology.

Thus, the only Indo-European element in Hittite mythology is the god *Inar*, cognate to the Vedic *Indra*. Likewise, Baltic *Perkunas* (*Parjanya*) and Slavic *Pyerun* (*Parjanya*), *Svarog* (*Svarga*), *Ogon* (*Agni*) and *Bog* (*Bhaga*) have their parallels in the Rigveda.

In many cases, it is almost *impossible* to recognize the connections between related mythological entities and events in two Indo-European mythologies without a comparison of the two with the related Vedic versions. Thus, for example, the Teutonic *Vanir* are connected with the Greek *Hermes* and *Pan*, but it is impossible to connect the two except through the Vedic *Saramā* and *Paṇi* (see TALAGERI 2000:477-495 for details).

The main Vedic myth which relates to the Saramā-Paṇi theme is found in the Rigveda in **X**.108, and it is found in later developed forms in the Jaiminīya Brāhmaṇa (II.440-442) and the Bṛhaddevatā (VIII 24-36). And it is found in both the Teutonic and Greek mythologies in versions which bear absolutely no similarities with each other, but which are both, *individually*, clearly recognizable as *developments* of the original Vedic myth.

The myth, as it is found in **X**.108, incidentally, is itself an evolved and anthropomorphized form, located in the *latest* of the ten Books of the Rigveda, of an original nature-myth, found referred to at various places in earlier parts of the

Rigveda, according to which "**Saramā is the Dawn who recovers the rays of the Sun that have been carried away by night**" (Griffith's note to **I.62**.3) or by the Paṇis who are "**fiends of darkness**" or "**demons who carry away and conceal the cows or rays of light**" (Griffith's note to **I.151**.9).

c) Iranian mythology, which should share to some extent at least the same character as Vedic mythology (since it is held that it was the *undivided Indo-Iranians*, and not the Indo-Aryans alone, who separated from the other Indo-European groups in South Russia and migrated to Central Asia where they shared a common culture and religion), on the contrary, *has no elements in common with other Indo-European mythologies* (other than with Vedic mythology itself).

To sum up: AIT scholars seek to explain away the archaeological evidence (of an undisturbed archaeological and anthropological continuity in the Harappan areas between "**the 5th/4th and** [...] **the 1st millennium B.C.**") by postulating an impossible scenario (that the population over the entire vast area of the most densely populated and highly organized civilization of ancient times, was *completely* transformed in language, religion and culture to an extent unparalleled anywhere else in the world and contrary to all norms, by a small group of nomads "trickling" into their midst, within a few centuries, without leaving *any* trace of it in the archaeological and anthropological record or in the memories of either of the peoples concerned or of their joint progeny — further, note that this process continued in a similar manner in successive stages till it covered most of northern India). Then they compound this further with an equally impossible corollary scenario (that this small group of nomads, who were the *highly diluted* cultural-linguistic *descendants* of a totally different "Indo-Aryan" race which lived in a far off land many centuries earlier, transformed this ancient civilization into an extraordinarily close and representative version of the ancient proto-culture of the "proto-Indo-European" *ancestors* of that different "Indo-Aryan" race in that far-off land)!

As we can see, *the AIT case is made up of a great number of different extremely unlikely to impossible scenarios and postulates which contradict each other hopelessly*: each scenario or postulate is concocted in order to explain away certain very valid objections to the AIT, but it ends up contradicting most of the other scenarios or postulates concocted to explain away various other equally valid objections. The net result is a "**complex**" mess of chaotic scenarios and postulates which explain nothing and lead nowhere: except that all of them are intended to somehow prove the AIT case. But this does not affect the credibility of the AIT scholars because each scenario or postulate is dealt with in isolation, and no-one is expected to raise uncomfortable questions about the *other* scenarios and postulates when discussing any *one* particular scenario or postulate. Any one foolish enough to do so would, of course, only be exposing his own unscholarly inability to comprehend "**complex**" scenarios. [Incidentally, there are many more "**complex**" postulates, equally integral parts of the AIT case, which have not been taken into account here, such as for example the postulate about two or more "waves" of Aryan invasions (or "trickles"), which would compound the case further: see section 7F in chapter 7].

But it is time this state of affairs came to an end and accountability is brought into the AIT-vs.-OIT debate. AIT scholars can not be allowed to get away with this kind of compartmentalized discussions any more, where they can postulate any theory or situation to answer the objection, or the uncomfortable fact which cannot be swept under the carpet, that is before them at the moment, even when this theory or postulated situation sharply contradicts, or is totally incompatible with, what they postulate in other contexts.

So far as the archaeological evidence is concerned, the only possible conclusion that can be reached is that *the undisturbed archaeological and anthropological continuity in the Harappan areas* between "**the 5th/4th and** [...] **the 1st**

millennium B.C." constitutes formidable, and lethal, evidence against the AIT, which *just simply can not* be explained away.

8B
THE CASE FOR THE OIT

The AIT-vs.-OIT debate must, strictly speaking, be conducted totally without reference to archaeology, until *actual decipherable inscriptional evidence* is discovered, either in the Harappan sites, conclusively proving the language of the Harappans to be Indo-European *or* non-Indo-European, or in archaeological sites further west and north, in Central Asia or further, in a language which can be *conclusively* shown to be a form of *pre*-Rigvedic.

However, if we *must* consider and discuss provisional archaeological possibilities (keeping the above proviso in mind), we have definite archaeological candidates in India: the Harappan civilization for the "Indo-Iranian"/Rigvedic phase, and the PGW or painted grey ware culture for the post-Rigvedic Vedic phase.

8B-1.The PGW (painted grey ware) Culture as the Vedic Culture

The PGW or painted grey ware culture has often been mooted as a candidate for the Vedic culture, but the main argument against this identification has been that this culture is a totally indigenous development and does not show any connections with any movement into India from the northwest (i.e., it can not be connected with any earlier culture outside India). This is clearly a circular argument. The identification fails to explain anything when we try to identify it with the culture of the Vedic Aryans of the AIT: i.e. as the culture of the early Rigvedic people who entered India from the northwest, transformed the local population completely, and became the linguistic ancestors of the major part of the subcontinent. But it *does* explain everything when we identify it with the *later* culture of the Vedic Aryans of the OIT hypothesis outlined by us (and confirmed by the textual and linguistic evidence): i.e. as the *post*-Rigvedic phase of the culture of the Vedic Aryans, the Pūrus.

Curiously, Southworth makes this identification, combining linguistic, textual and archaeological identities, while describing the classification of Indo-Aryan dialects or languages into "Inner IA" (Vedic) and "Outer IA" (non-Vedic):

> "**The linguistic division correlates fairly closely with the other divisions: 1. that between PGW (or Painted Gray Ware) and BRW (Black and Red Ware), and 2. the locations of two major lineages as described in the Puranas (OIA *purāṇa-*), namely the Pauravas or descendants of Pūru, who by tradition inherited the *madhyadeśa* ('middle country') and the Yādavas or descendants of Yadu, who according to the tradition was banished by his father Yayāti to the south/west (Thapar 1978:243)**" (SOUTHWORTH 1995:266).
>
> [Further, Southworth points out the proximity of the Yadus to the southern interior of India by deriving their name, very plausibly, from Dravidian: "**This word, which has no Indo-European etymology, may well be Dravidian, meaning 'herder' (from a PDI *yātu-van 'goat/sheep-herd, see DED 5152 * *yātu* 'sheep/goat'). This would imply that the term *yādava-* is original, and the mythical Yadu derived from it by back-formation** [...])" (SOUTHWORTH 1995:266)].

8B-2. The Harappan Civilization as the Rigvedic Culture.

The idea that the Harappan civilization could represent the Rigvedic culture has always been rejected on specious grounds: mainly the lack of conclusive evidence for the substantial presence of horses in the Harappan sites, and the urban nature of the Harappan civilization as opposed to the allegedly "pastoral" nature of the Rigvedic-Avestan culture, etc. However, the basic fact is that the only real objection to the identification of the Harappan civilization with the Rigvedic culture has been the *utter incompatibility* of the chronology of the Harappan sites with the hitherto accepted theoretical chronology of the Rigveda (and its coordination with the known chronology of other Indo-European cultures outside India in the context of the prevalent homeland theories).

We have already seen (in chapter seven) the utter inapplicability of the so-called "equine argument" as an objection to identifying the Rigvedic culture with the culture of the Harappan civilization. The same goes for the claims about the opposition between the urban nature of the Harappan civilization and the "pastoral" nature of the Rigvedic culture. The Harappan civilization consisted of numerous cities, which form the most well-known feature of the civilization, but the vast area covered by the civilization included thousands of villages as well, without which the civilization would never have survived. The culture of the hymns — religious hymns embodying myths, rituals and prayers — undoubtedly reflects the atmosphere of the rural or forest settings, or perhaps just the orthodox sacrificial settings, in which they were composed, but there is nothing in the hymns to show that the ṛṣis were unacquainted with urban culture.

But, it has become mandatory to interpret the Rigveda through AIT glasses. And when established scholars can discover west-to-east movements, "extra-territorial memories" (leading west as far as the Ural mountains), "non-Aryan" native enemies, and even an "Iranian" Vasiṣṭha (crossing the Indus from west to east, from Iran), in the hymns of the Rigveda, it can not have been too difficult to establish and maintain the dogma that the cultural ethos of the texts is incompatible with the cultural ethos of the Harappan civilization.

Although the Vedic culture had been interpreted as pastoral from the beginning (because of the obvious importance of cows and dairying in the Vedic texts), it was earlier recognized that pastoral cultures could be a part of larger civilizations (as, for example, the pastoral ethos of Krishna in Braj, Vrindavan and Gokul, within a larger urban civilizational framework):

> "**Pischel and Geldner have done well to point out that these poems are not the productions of ignorant peasants, but of a highly cultured professional class, encouraged by the gifts of kings and the applause of courts (Einleitung p.xxiv). Just the same may be said of the Homeric bards and of those of Arthur's court [...]**" (ARNOLD 1904:217)
>
> "[The Rigvedic collection] **reflects not so much a wandering life in a desert as a life stable and fixed, a life of halls and cities, and shows sacrificial cases in such detail as to lead one to suppose that the hymnists were not on the tramp but were comfortable well-fed priests**" (HOPKINS 1898:20).

But this interpretation of the Vedic ethos was swiftly abandoned after the discovery of the Harappan civilization: Before its discovery (and the necessity of declaring it to be "pre-Aryan" and "non-Aryan", since it would have led to a complete overturning of the AIT if it was held to be "Aryan", as the "Aryan invasion" had been dated to around 1500 BCE), it was generally assumed that the invading "Aryans" were a highly civilized and cultured race who invaded a mainly barbaric and uncivilized native populace. This conclusion was allegedly based on the logical analysis and interpretation of the Vedic texts. And *every Vedic reference was interpreted according to this paradigm.*

But after the discovery of the Harappan sites, and their early dating to the fourth and third millennia BCE, the "Aryans" suddenly became the barbarians and the native populace became the civilized and cultured ones.

The *very same texts,* and the *very same references in these texts,* which apparently showed that the Vedic Aryans were civilized and their "indigenous" enemies barbarians, now suddenly showed exactly the opposite: that the Vedic Aryans were barbarians, and their "indigenous" enemies civilized! No explanations were found necessary for this complete volte face.

In the process, there was a *further* gross violation of normal scholarly practice on at least two counts:

1. The very fact that the Harappan sites were discovered in roughly the same broad geographical area which had been postulated for the Vedic Aryan civilization (on the basis of the references in the Vedic literature) should have led to their identification as Vedic sites. They were, of course, dated to a period (fourth to mid-second millennium BCE) earlier than the period (late second millennium BCE) *postulated* for the Vedic civilization; but this (*even if the postulated dates for the Rigveda were to be treated as sacrosanct*) should merely have been taken to mean that the Vedic civilization succeeded the Harappan civilization in that area.

Just as an accused is to be presumed innocent until proved guilty, the linguistic identity of any archaeologically excavated ancient civilization is to be assumed to be the same as the linguistic identity of the civilizations which succeeded it on that site, unless and until there is *specific linguistic evidence* (decipherable records within that ancient civilization itself, or clear testimony in the records of other contemporary civilizations, or unambiguous and detailed accounts in the traditional records of the succeeding civilizations) testifying to the identity of the language of that ancient civilization being different, or there is *unchallengeable archaeological and anthropological evidence* showing that the population of that ancient civilization was supplanted by ethnically and *linguistically* different populations found in the subsequent civilizations in that area.

In the absence of such evidence, it does not require any prejudice or pleading to assume the language to be the same, but it does indeed require a great deal of deep prejudice and special pleading to assume that the language was different. In the absence of such evidence, the burden of proof does not lie on the persons assuming the language to have been the *same*, it lies on the persons claiming it to have been *different*.

If sites of an ancient civilization, dateable from the fourth to the second millennium BCE, are discovered in the heart of

Tamilnadu, it will be logical to assume, in the absence of evidence to the contrary, that the sites represent a Dravidian language speaking civilization. Likewise if prehistoric sites are discovered in the heart of China or Saudi Arabia, it will be logical to assume that they are Sinitic or Semitic language speaking civilizations respectively. Pre-Greek and pre-Roman civilizations (Etruscan, etc.) are accepted as non-Indo-European, and the Sumerian and Hittite civilizations in West Asia are accepted as non-Semitic, *only* because linguistic evidence to this effect is available.

The Harappan civilization is situated deep within Indo-European ("Indo-Aryan") territory. The closest non-Indo-European families are at some distance: Semitic far to the west, Burushaski well to the north, Austric considerably to the east, and Dravidian far to the south [Brahui does not change the picture, since, as Witzel points out, "**its presence has now been explained by a late migration that took place within this millennium (Elfenbeim 1987)**" (WITZEL 2000a:§1). Likewise, Southworth, even while urging a Dravidian presence in the Harappan areas, admits that: "**Hock (1975:87-8), among others, has noted that the current locations of Brahui, Kurux and Malto may be recent**" (SOUTHWORTH 1995:272, fn22)]. There is no linguistic, archaeological or anthropological evidence indicating that the Harappan civilization was supplanted by a linguistically different race of people: on the contrary, archaeologists and anthropologists insist on continuity in the anthropological situation from Harappan times well into post-Vedic times. In these circumstances, the Harappan civilization should have been assumed to be Indo-European until proved otherwise. However, in gross violation of normal scholarly practice, it has been assumed to be *non*-Indo-European.

2. Secondly, all the above questions arise only in the circumstance that the chronological position of the Vedic civilization stands *archaeologically* established as post-Harappan. But the postulated dates of the Vedic civilization as a *post*-Harappan civilization have not been *archaeologically*

proved, only linguistically assumed. There is no archaeological evidence that the Vedic civilization *succeeded* the Harappan civilization in the area.

The Vedic civilization has produced a vast corpus of literature which gives a detailed picture of the religio-cultural ethos of the Vedic Aryans; and this picture has been elaborated by mainly western Vedic scholars in over two centuries of scholarship. That this is not a fictional civilization has been confirmed by comparative studies with the known religio-cultural evidence of other Indo-European cultures outside India. However, this civilization, reconstructed from the literature, has not been archaeologically traced in any period. Yet, as pointed out earlier on in this chapter, no scholar has ever doubted that the Vedic Aryans, and their culture depicted in the Rigveda, *did* exist, but they are treated as having existed *in a total archaeological vacuum.*

So we have scholars accepting two different paradigms, both of which complement each other and should therefore have been treated as two parts of a whole: *on the one hand*, a widespread network of archaeological sites of a vast, highly-developed civilization (the Harappan civilization) lasting over thousands of years, which has allegedly left no literary records at all *although it had a writing system*; and, *on the other*, a full-fledged developed culture and civilization (the Vedic civilization) which has left a vast and detailed body of organized literature (unparalleled by any other known civilization of the same period) *although it had no system of writing at all*, but which has left absolutely no archaeological traces behind, *both located in more or less the very same area*! [This contradiction was first pointed out by David Frawley].

Clearly, this unreasoning refusal to consider the obvious represents another gross violation of normal scholarly practice.

In the circumstance, it is clear that the archaeological situation should have been treated as neutral in the entire AIT-vs.-OIT debate, until unambiguous and dateable linguistic evidence was found. Or, as a secondary alternative, at least until a material culture was found "**that presents us with exactly those material remains described above (chariots, handmade pottery used in rituals, fire altars, Soma residue, etc.)**" (WITZEL 2000a:§15). However, no sites have been found in India with exactly those material remains interpreted from the Rigveda.

But this has not prevented some linguists and historians (with support from stray archaeologists involved in the excavations of the particular sites concerned) from trying (in the absence of actual linguistic evidence) to identify Indo-Iranians, or Indo-Aryans on their way towards India, on the basis of material evidence (or symbolic or imaginative interpretations of that material evidence) in archaeological sites in *Central Asia and beyond* which fit into their hypothetical time/space predictions of where the migrating Indo-Iranians should have been at a particular time: i.e., in the BMAC (Bactria-Margiana Archaeological Complex, also called the Oxus Civilization) in Central Asia, in the Afanas'evo Culture to the north of Central Asia, and in the Andronovo Culture in the Pontic-Caspian area. And each of these efforts has attracted a large number of adherents in certain academic circles. However, most archaeologists completely reject these attempts, and many of them have made their rejection very clear in detailed studies: we will take here, as examples, papers by **H.P.Francfort** (FRANCFORT 2001:151-163) and **Carl C. Lamberg-Karlovsky** (LAMBERG-KARLOVSKY 2005:142-177). These papers should be read in full, but here we will only note the main substance.

As these archaeologists point out, these identifications by linguists and historians are not based on intrinsic evidence, but on forced attempts to substantiate their linguistic and historical theories by providing archaeological illustrations for them:

> **"The question of identifying archaeological remains of Indo-European populations in Central Asia has been one of the main**

> **questions that has occupied a number of linguists and historians for many years [...] when written records are not available, a reconstructed time-space framework is generally used to substantiate the reconstruction with some relevant illustrative material. The linguistic attributes are mapped onto archaeological correlates: artifacts are selected, like the chariot, as well as ecofacts, like agriculture, or whole archaeological cultures (material assemblages). The archaeological correlates become some sort of labels or tags that one may employ in order to trace the supposed Indo-European populations. But, in fact, very little of the illustrative archaeological material actually exhibits specific Indo-European or Indo-Iranian traits; a question therefore arises: what is the relevance of archaeological material if any sort of assemblage present at the expected or supposed time/space spot can function as the tag of a linguistic group?**" (FRANCFORT 2001:151).

As he repeatedly makes clear: "**apart from the time-space expectations, there is not much in the archaeological material that could be taken as tags for tracing the Indo-Iranians/ Indo-Aryans** [...] **no one of these archaeological correlates is beyond question** [...] **Briefly, not only have they nothing strictly Indo-European or Indo-Iranian or Indo-Aryan in them, but if we look closely at them in their general cultural context, they appear to be selected isolated traits not always compatible with each other** [...and] **are attested in various cultural contexts, not all necessarily Indo-European**" (FRANCFORT 2001:153-154).

He points out that the whole process is based on "**the simple linguistic space-time argument for locating the speakers, in which case a study of the archaeological record is useless since *anything goes*** [...] **there is no factual evidence apart from the linguistically reconstructed time-space predictions** [...] **There is no point in trying to illustrate ethno-linguistic theories by irrelevant or uninterpretable archaeological material**" (FRANCFORT 2001:163).

The interpretations of the archaeological material are sought to be made by "**drawing parallels between the archaeological record and the Rigvedic and Avestan texts.**

The parallels drawn are, at best, of a most general nature and do not convince, that is, Andronovo houses were large (80-300 square meters), capable of accommodating extended families. A 'reading' of the Indo-Iranian texts, the Avesta and Rigveda, attests to the existence of extended families, thus, the Andronovo were Indo-Iranian" (LAMBERG-KARLOVSKY 2005:155) Or, "**the ethnohistorical parallels and the textual citations are of such general nature that they do not convince. Thus, in the Rigveda there is an injunction against the use of the wheel in the production of pottery. As Andronovo pottery is handmade, this is taken as evidence of their Indo-Iranian identity. Ethnic and linguistic correlates are generally not based on vigorous methodology; they are merely asserted**" (LAMBERG-KARLOVSKY 2005:144).

The archaeological material is culturally so ambiguous that it can very well be representative of *almost any* linguistic group: Francfort points out that the material culture cited "**proves nothing about the language of their owners. Otherwise we would have to admit that the Bronze Age Chinese were Indo-European**" (FRANCFORT 2001:157). Likewise, Lamberg-Karlovsky points out that the "ethnic indicators" cited, "**horse-breeding, horse rituals, shared ceramic types, avoidance of pig, sherd burial patterns, and architectural templates, can be used to identify the Arab, the Turk and the Iranian; three completely distinct types**" (LAMBERG-KARLOVSKY 2005:145). "**Passages from the Avesta and the Rigveda are quoted by different authors to support the Indo-Iranian identity of both the BMAC and the Andronovo. The passages are sufficiently general to permit the Plains Indians of North America an Indo-Iranian identity**" (LAMBERG-KARLOVSKY 2005:168).

And, in fact, as both these archaeologists point out, the cultural features of the said archaeological sites are actually distinctly *non*-Indo-European, and could actually be more compatible with a Uralo-Altaic culture than an Indo-European one: the concluding section of Francfort's paper is titled: "**Iconography and symbolic systems: pointing to non-Indo-European worlds, possibly Uralic or Altaic**" (FRANCFORT 2001:157-163). Lamberg-Karlovsky (LAMBERG KARLOVSKY 2005:169) also accepts this possibility.

In such circumstances, it becomes clear that the *only* logic behind identifying these archaeological cultures as Indo-Iranian or Indo-Aryan is that they fit in with the *time-space expectations* of the linguists and historians as to where the Indo-Iranians/Indo-Aryans must have been at a particular period of time: "**they are 'in the right place at the right time'**" (LAMBERG-KARLOVSKY 2005:157). "**In short, apart from the time-space expectations, there is nothing in the archaeological material that could be taken as tags for tracing the Indo-Iranians/Indo-Aryans**" (FRANCFORT 2001:153).

But these time-space predictions and expectations are based wholly on *purely hypothetical estimates* of the chronological dates of the Rigveda and the Avesta, or rather mainly of the Rigveda (with the Avesta being dated in accordance with it): "**Iron is found only in later Vedic (Ved.) texts** [...] **It makes its appearance in South Asia only by c.1200 or 1000 BCE. The RV, thus, must be earlier than that. The RV also does not know of large cities such as that of the Indus civilization but only of ruins (*armaka*, Falk 1981) and of small forts (*pur*, Rau 1976). Therefore it must be *later* than the disintegration of the Indus cities in the Panjab, at c.1900 BCE**" (WITZEL 2005:342). Apart from the fact that the ruins of the Indus sites (*armaka*) appear only in one hymn in the *latest* part of the Rigveda (see Section I of this book), the general subjective manner in which Witzel dates the Rigveda *as a whole* to *later* than 1900 BCE smacks of the kind of free-style analysis referred to by Francfort and Lamberg-Karlovsky above. It is on such criteria that the dates of the Rigveda are calculated and the dates of the allegedly earlier Indo-Iranian phases backtracked!

However, in the case of the Harappan civilization, we have (apart from all the points noted earlier) a time-space schedule which is based on *solidly established archaeological dates* from West Asia, and *massive and uni-directional textual evidence* from the Rigveda and the Avesta. Let us go over this time-space schedule again step by step:

1. Firstly, we have the *solidly established* dating of the Mitanni kingdom in northern Iraq/Syria to *at least* 1460-1330 BCE (WITZEL 2005:361) and the *even earlier dating* of the Kassite conquest of Mesopotamia by *at least* 1677 BCE (WITZEL 2005:362).

2. Secondly, we have the established fact that in the case of the Mitanni (and possibly also in the case of the Kassites, since the Kassites, like the Mitanni, spoke non-Indo-Aryan, and non-Indo-European, languages), "**the Indic elements seem to be little more than the residue of a dead language in Hurrian, and that the symbiosis that produced the Mitanni may have taken place centuries earlier**" (MALLORY 1989:42). Centuries earlier than 1460 BCE, perhaps even than 1677 BCE.

3. Thirdly, we have the irrefutable fact (see Section I of this book) that the Indo-Aryan elements in the Mitanni and Kassite records are cultural elements which are found massively distributed in the Books of the Late Rigvedic period composed in areas of northern India (including present-day northern Pakistan), but are *completely missing* in the earlier Books of the Middle Rigvedic period and the Early Rigvedic period which were composed *in areas of northern India further east, and which show no acquaintance with western areas*. So these cultural elements undoubtedly *developed* inside northern India in the *Late* Rigvedic period.

If cultural elements which *developed* wholly within northern India appear in West Asia, then they were undoubtedly *brought* into West Asia by migrants from northern India.

Since they are found *already* as "**the residue of a dead language**" in 1677 BCE among non-Indo-Aryan peoples in a symbiosis which took place centuries earlier, then those migrants from northern India *arrived* in West Asia centuries earlier than 1677 BCE: by the very early second millennium BCE at the most conservative estimate.

Further, the migrants must have left India much earlier, and this Late Rigvedic culture must have been fully developed in northern India *by the time* the migrants *departed* from India, perhaps sometime in the late third millennium BCE.

Further, this Late Rigvedic culture, fully *developed* in northern India by the time the migrants left, must have *started developing* in northern India *long before* the migrants left India: i.e. well into the mid third millennium BCE at the least.

4. Finally, if these cultural elements *started developing* in northern India in the mid-third millennium BCE, then the Middle Rigvedic period, and, before that, the Early Rigvedic period, in the Books of which these cultural elements are *completely missing*, must go back well into the early third millennium BCE at the very least.

It is in this Early Rigvedic Period, in the early third millennium BCE at the most conservative estimate, that the testimony of the geographical data in the Rigveda shows the Vedic Aryans long settled in the area to the east of the Sarasvatī, and the proto-Iranians (let alone certain other Indo-European groups identified by us in the last chapter, and in our earlier books) long settled in the central parts of the Land of the Seven Rivers in present-day northern Pakistan.

These time-space correlates, at reasonably conservative estimates, place the joint Indo-Iranians exactly in, and all over, the area of the Harappan civilization, exactly in the period of the heyday of that civilization.

These time-space correlates are based on solid chronological evidence from West Asia, and massive textual evidence from the Rigveda and the Avesta, unlike the purely hypothetical time-space estimates of the historians discussed earlier, and they conclusively establish the identity of the Harappans and the Indo-Iranians.

With the Indo-Iranian nature of the Harappan civilization thus established, the culture of the Harappans=Indo-Iranians will have to be examined in a new light. Already, we have textual studies (e.g. BHAGWAN SINGH:1995) which have established (allowing for some exaggerations) the highly developed technological and commercial nature of the Rigvedic civilization; we have archaeological excavations which have revealed the presence of fire altars and other elements of Rigvedic/Iranian religion and ritual in the material remains of the Harappan sites; we have literary-epigraphical analyses which have established the depiction of certain Vedic themes in the pictorial representations on the Indus seals; and there are various other categories of evidence which have, likewise, not been treated with the seriousness they deserve. All these need to be re-examined very seriously indeed.

8B-3. The Indo-European Emigrations

As we saw, Witzel, on the principle that attack is the best form of defence, asks: "**if the Iranians (and IEs) emigrated from India, why do we not find 'Indian bones' of this massive emigration in Iran and beyond?**" (WITZEL 2005:368).

We could, of course, argue that since the AIT has been consistently maintained and upheld for centuries *without* any valid archaeological evidence being cited for it, such evidence can not be demanded from the OIT after such an irrefutable textual and linguistic case has been made for it: archaeology should be left out of the debate. But we need not leave it at that. The fact is that there are several very basic reasons why archaeological evidence is *vital* for the *AIT* to be accepted as valid, but archaeological evidence is *not* vital for the *OIT* to be accepted as valid:

To begin with, analogical comparison should be between immigrations and immigrations, not between immigrations and emigrations. Archaeological evidence is to be found at the *immigratory* ending point of a migration where the arrival of a totally new people with a totally different culture should cause major changes in the ethnic and cultural composition of the material remains after the migration, not at the *emigratory* starting point. Any archaeological evidence to be found for the migration of white Europeans to America during the colonization of the Americas will be found in America, not in Europe. If anything, literary evidence is found in Europe (as also in America) for these migrations, since these migrations took place consciously in literate historical times, in which there continued to be communication between the areas of the starting point and the ending point of the migrations. Analogically, here we *can* and *do* find acceptable archaeological evidence for the *immigration* of Indo-Europeans in Europe, and in most of the other earliest historical habitats of the other Indo-European groups outside India, but not for their *emigration* from northern India (although, as we saw, we do incidentally find *literary* evidence of their emigrations from northern India). So there would obviously be little to expect by way of archaeological evidence of emigrations in the Harappan areas proper.

So far as the areas to its west are concerned (Afghanistan and the Bactria-Margiana areas of southern Central Asia to its immediate north), we have seen (in the OIT scenario in Chapter 7) that this was already Indo-European in the pre-Rigvedic period: the various Druhyu tribes were already inhabitants of these areas in *pre*-Rigvedic times, and it was an extension of the Indian homeland in the sense that the Indo-European Dialects had already slowly expanded into these areas and were moving off further north in a gradual process which must have occurred over a long period. As all these peoples were presumably ethnically related to each other in a chain of ethnic connections, and, in *this* scenario the process of continuous acculturation and assimilation must certainly have been in play, we can genuinely excuse the lack of substantial archaeological and anthropological evidence of any cataclysmic transformations (unlike in the case of the AIT scenario for the Harappan areas, where two *totally different* civilizations in every sense, *including the ethnic sense*, are supposed to have occupied the same vast area in quick succession). All this, it must be remembered, took place in an earlier and more primitive period, and yet we have the Purāṇic traditions of these emigrations; while the alleged *immigrations* of the AIT scenario are alleged to have taken place in a later and more civilized period, and yet have left not a trace of a memory anywhere.

After the various Indo-European groups entered deeper into Central Asia, they were in an area which Nichols (see section 7D-2 of chapter 7) calls the "**central Eurasian spread zone**" which "**was part of a standing pattern whereby languages were drawn into the spread zone, spread westward, and were eventually succeeded by the next spreading family**" (NICHOLS 1997:137). The further migrations of the Indo-Europeans through Eurasia all the way to Europe were long and gradual processes through primitive areas, and we have archaeological records of movements of people, who can be identified as Indo-Europeans at least because they fulfill the time-space requirements, but also for other more substantial reasons, like the movements of the various pre-Kurgan and Kurgan expansions. While the movements of the European Dialects into Europe are more or less archaeologically established, the first arrival or presence of other groups like the Hittites (as also the Mitanni and Kassites) in West Asia, and even of the Iranians (who moved into their historical areas "**from the east**": Encyclopaedia Britannica, 1974, Vol.9, 832) in Iran are well documented.

8C.
THE IMPORTANCE OF THE RIGVEDA

We have examined more or less all the different aspects of the question, linguistic, archaeological, and textual, but *the central focus of our entire study has been the Rigveda*. This one ancient text has provided us with the key to solve the biggest historical problem of all time — the problem of the geographical location of the original homeland of the numerically and historically most important language family in the world, the Indo-European family of languages.

Our earlier book (TALAGERI 2000) also dealt with the same subject; but, thanks to some very effective needling by AIT scholars like Michael Witzel, it became necessary to go even more deeply into, and into many more aspects of, the Rigvedic evidence.

Before resting our case, it is necessary to fully understand once and for all: Why is the Rigveda so important as the final authority in the matter of ancient Indian, Indo-Aryan, Indo-Iranian and Indo-European proto-history?

After our last book (TALAGERI 2000), Michael Witzel, in particular, launched a major campaign against what he called my use of "**what is essentially the wrong Ṛgveda text — the late Vedic compilation by Śākalya, which had already been subjected to several earlier redactions, and which mixed up materials from several eras in each of the books. Talageri, unlike all serious Vedic scholars after Oldenberg, makes no attempt to reconstruct the more ancient text on which that compilation was based. The result is that all the far-flung historical conclusions that he draws regarding the time and location of individual books, their authors, etc., are totally unreliable. Many of his individual items of 'proofs' (such as the designation of the Gangā in RV 6, Gāngya) immediately fall off the board as late, not as being part of the 'earliest RV' as T. claims**" (WITZEL 2001b:§1).

We have already seen, earlier on in this book (in chapter 3, F-2), Witzel's writings on the subject of "**the Gangā in RV 6, Gāngya**" *before* the publication of TALAGERI 2000 as contrasted with his writings on the same subject *after* the publication of TALAGERI 2000. His writings on the subject of the "right" Rigveda, as opposed to the "wrong" Rigveda, follow the same pattern.

He now claims that the Rigvedic text used by me — the only Rigvedic text in existence, and the only Rigvedic text known (leaving aside the usual traditional claims about there originally having been many different Rigvedas) to any analyst of the Rigveda, right down from the days of Śākalya through Sāyaṇa through Oldenberg down to Witzel and "**T.**" — is the "**wrong Ṛgveda text**", a "**late Vedic compilation**" dateable to "**say, 500 BCE**" (WITZEL 2005:386, fn 75). Because of this, I "**repeatedly confuse late-Vedic redactions and interpretations with what is found in the original RV text**" (WITZEL 2001b: Critique Summary), and arrive at wrong, "**unreliable**" and "**far-flung historical conclusions**"

The proof of the pudding is in the eating: our analysis of the Avestan names in chapter 1 of this present volume would not have yielded results fully in tune with our earlier chronological analysis of the Rigveda if our analysis in TALAGERI 2000 was wrong: the way in which the Avestan names and name-elements fall into distinct categories in line with our classification of the Books of the Rigveda into Early, Middle and Late would not have been the case if there were "**mixed up materials from several eras in each of the books**". As Witzel himself pontificates, when writing about the science of linguistics (WITZEL 2005:352), the correctness of the set of rules established by a theory, when it is based on hard scientific criteria, is established and proved by the ability to make "predictions" based on that set of rules. Witzel writes: "**just as the existence of the planet Pluto was predicted by astronomy, so were the laryngeals, in both cases decades before the actual discovery**" (WITZEL 2005:352). So, also, the correctness of our classification (in TALAGERI 2000) of the Books of the Rigveda into Early, Middle and Late, and the fact that this is the "*right* Rigveda", is established and proved by the way in which it "predicted" the pattern of distribution of the Avestan names and name-elements (and other important words like *ara*, "spokes") years before that distribution was demonstrated in this present book. A more fitting reply to Witzel's criticism could not have been found.

Nevertheless, because it is so well put (and stands so sharply in contrast to what he writes *after* TALAGERI 2000), here is what WITZEL had to say about the Rigveda (yes, basically about the present Rigveda of 1028 hymns!) *before* TALAGERI 2000 [and indeed, knowing Witzel, he may *still* be saying all this when speaking or writing in contexts other than the AIT-vs.-OIT debate! Note that one of the quotations is from an article or paper published in 2006, but which was already included in an earlier *pre-print* version entitled "**Early Loan Words in Western Central Asia: Substrates, Migrations and Trade**" already out in 2002 and probably written much earlier. Along with the ability to write contradictory things, often even on one and the same page, without any apparent loss of credibility in the eyes of his admirers, Witzel also has the tendency to just go on lazily and print what he has already prepared before even when circumstances, in the meanwhile, suggest that some change is necessary]:

"**Right from the beginning, in Ṛgvedic times, elaborate steps were taken to insure the exact reproduction of the words of the ancient poets. As a result, the Ṛgveda still has the exact same wording in such distant regions as Kashmir, Kerala and Orissa, and even the long-extinct musical accents have been preserved. Vedic transmission is thus superior to that of the Hebrew or Greek Bible, or the Greek, Latin and Chinese classics. We can actually regard present-day Ṛgveda recitation as a *tape recording* of what was composed and recited some 3000 years ago. In addition, unlike the constantly reformulated Epics and Purāṇas, the Vedic texts contain *contemporary* materials. They can serve as snapshots of the political and cultural situation of the particular period and area in which they were composed.** [...] **as they are contemporary, and faithfully preserved, these texts are equivalent to inscriptions.** [...] **they are immediate and unchanged evidence, a sort of oral history — and sometimes autobiography — of the period, frequently fixed and 'taped' immediately after the event by poetic formulation. These aspects of the Vedas have never been sufficiently stressed** [...]" (WITZEL 1995a:91).

"[...] **the Vedas were composed orally and they always were and still are, to some extent, *oral literature*. They must be regarded as *tape recordings*, made during the Vedic period and transmitted orally, and usually without the change of a single word.**" (WITZEL 1997b:258).

"**It must be underlined that just like an ancient inscription, these words have not changed since the composition of these hymns c.1500 BCE, as the RV has been transmitted almost without any change** [...] **The modern oral recitation of the RV is a *tape recording of c.1700-1200 BCE*.**" (WITZEL 2000a:§8).

"**The language of the RV is an archaic form of Indo-European. Its 1028 hymns are addressed to the gods and most of them are used in ritual. They were orally composed and strictly preserved by exact repetition through by rote learning, until today. It must be underlined that the Vedic texts are 'tape recordings' of this archaic period. Not one word, not a syllable, not even a tonal accent were allowed to be changed. The texts are therefore better than any manuscript, and as good as any well preserved contemporary inscription. We can therefore rely on the Vedic texts as contemporary sources for names of persons, places, rivers (WITZEL 1999c)**" (WITZEL 2006:64-65).

In all these assertions, it must be noted very carefully that:

1. Witzel is talking very, very specifically about the Rigveda of "**present-day Ṛgveda recitation**": the "**modern oral recitation of the RV**" with "**its 1028 hymns**".
2. It is *this* Rigveda that Witzel tells us "**still has the exact same wording in such distant regions as Kashmir, Kerala and Orissa**", words which "**have not changed since the composition of these hymns**" and have been so "**faithfully preserved**" that "**not one word, not a syllable, not even a tonal accent were allowed to be changed**".

3. It is *this* Rigveda that Witzel describes as "**equivalent to inscriptions**" or "**just like an ancient inscription**" or "**better than any manuscript, and as good as any well preserved contemporary inscription**". Or, even more categorically, as "**a *tape recording* of what was composed and recited some 3000 years ago**" or "***tape recordings*, made during the Vedic period and transmitted orally, and usually without the change of a single word**" or "**'tape recordings' of this archaic period**" or "***a tape recording of c.1700-1200 BC***" which has been "**strictly preserved by exact repetition through by rote learning, until today**".
4. And it is *this* Rigveda on whose hymns Witzel tells us we can "**rely** [...] **as contemporary sources for names of persons, places, rivers**".

Does Witzel qualify these assertions in any way? Or does he perhaps, while repeatedly making each and every one of these above *very specific, detailed and categorical* assertions, just *happen* to not mention major, and vital, exceptions or qualifications to what he is saying, so that OIT yokels *fail* to understand what Witzel is talking about: that what Witzel really means is that there are actually *many* interpolations and late additions in the present day Rigveda, dating to as late as "**say, 500 BCE**", which it was not necessary for him to touch upon while making the above assertions, because what he was writing was only "a short summary" of the full picture which was intended for "later" publications?

Not really. Witzel *does* provide us with qualifications for all the above assertions, but these are qualifications, *equally specific, detailed and categorical*, which only *emphasize and strengthen* the above assertions:

"**We have to distinguish, it is true, between the composition of a Vedic text, for example of the RV which was composed until c. 1200 B.C., and its redaction sometime**

in the Brāhmaṇa period (ca. 700 B.C.?). But the redaction only selected from already existing collections and was mainly responsible only for the present phonetical shape of the texts. The RV of late Brāhmaṇa times only differed from the one recited in Ṛgvedic times in minor details such as the pronunciation of svar instead of suvar, etc. The text remained the same" (WITZEL 1995a:91, fn 13).

"[...] **transmitted almost without any change. i.e. we know exactly in which limited cases certain sounds — but not words, tonal accents, sentences — have changed.**" (WITZEL 2000a:§8).

"**The middle/late Vedic redaction of the texts influenced only a very small, well known number of cases, such as the development *Cuv* > *Cv***" (WITZEL 2002:§1.2, fn 18).

In short: "**The text remained the same**", the *same "**tape recording of c.1700-1200 BC**"*.

As Witzel tells us elsewhere, "**we need to take the texts seriously, at their *own* word. A *paradigm shift* is necessary** [...]" (WITZEL 2000b:332).

Unfortunately, instead of taking the texts seriously at their *own* word, writers like Witzel have spent umpteen years and plenty of energy in producing *voluminous* piles of pure and incomprehensible nonsense based only on wild flights of their imagination, full of masses of chaotic details, wild speculations, mutually contradictory interpretations and conclusions, and ludicrous fairy tales, all of it leading *nowhere*.

We have presented the whole case for the Indian Homeland Theory, and it only remains to be seen how it is received by the established AIT scholars, especially those directly or indirectly involved in the AIT- vs.-OIT debate. Will they continue to steadfastly ignore it (at their own peril, as I pointed out in the preface)? Will they fall back on a haughty dismissal, without bothering (or daring) to take up specific issues, and without bothering to examine, or even acknowledge, the irrefutable evidence presented in this book? Or will they launch an all-out blistering campaign of character-vilification and name-calling?

Or will they show an open-mindedness and willingness to examine issues afresh and undertake, if necessary, an honest and thorough reappraisal of what Erdosy calls "**assumptions long taken for granted and buttressed by the accumulated weight of two centuries of scholarship**" (ERDOSY 1995:x)? We can only wait and see.

And on this point, we rest our case.

Postscript:
Identities Past and Present

The book is completed, but a few minor points need to be made, for which this postscript seems to be necessary and appropriate. This is because, firstly, there was no particular point, in the main chapters, where these side-issues could have been conveniently inserted, and they remained till the end. Secondly, the issues which will be dealt with seem to have a common thread: a connection with identities and identity-based biases; so it seems appropriate that they should be clubbed together, although the issues are different from each other. And, thirdly, they are proper at the end of the book, since at least the second of the two issues deals with general and subjective questions that may arise after the rest of the book is read.

The two issues are:

1. Ancient "communal" words.
2. Ancient vis-à-vis modern identities.

1. ANCIENT "COMMUNAL" WORDS.

There are certain words, referred to earlier in chapter 1 (section 1A-4), which are important in any historical study of the Rigveda: they are the words *ārya*, *dāsa* and *dasyu*. As pointed out, these words (along with the words *deva* and *asura*) are important words in both the Rigveda and the Avesta, and (again, like the words *deva* and *asura*) they obviously have historical connotations which have something to do with differences or conflicts between the Vedic Aryans and the Iranians.

However, the words have always been treated by AIT scholars as words having historical connotations which have something to do with differences or conflicts between "Indo-Aryans" and "native non-Aryans". The word *ārya* has always been interpreted as referring to *non-native* people linguistically and racially "Indo-European" or at least "Indo-Iranian", and, by contrast, the words *dāsa* and *dasyu* to the "non-Indo-Iranian", and therefore "non-Indo-European", *native* people of India. Even when some scholars (e.g. HOCK 1999b) now emphatically reject the idea of the *āryas* being *racially* different from the *dāsas* and *dasyus* (in terms of skin-colour, hair, eyes and cranium), since this goes against the anthropological evidence (see chapter 8), they continue to assume that the words refer to an original *linguistic* difference between incoming "Indo-Aryans" and native "non-Aryans".

It is not that no serious scholar has ever comprehended the real meanings of the words: Dr. B.R. (Babasaheb) Ambedkar, for example, emphatically rejected the idea that Dasas and Dasyus were linguistically "non-Indo-European"; and concluded, instead, that the words were merely indicative of "**different communities of Aryas who were not only different but opposed and inimical to each other**" (AMBEDKAR 1990:87), and even that the *dāsas* were *Iranians* (AMBEDKAR 1990:104). George Erdosy, an AIT scholar, accepts that "**Arya and Dasa were only horizontal divisions, denoting groups of people living in their separate territories in north-western India**" (ERDOSY 1989:39), that *dasyus* were only "**a segment of Dasas**" (ERDOSY 1989:37), and also that the term *paṇi* was used for people who were "**rich and niggardly**" and possibly "**usurers**", and that the group of *paṇis* "**cross-cuts the otherwise horizontal stratification of non-Aryas,** [...] **and may denote either an occupation or simply a set of values attributable to anyone**" (ERDOSY 1989:37).

The real meanings of these three words has been dealt with in detail in our second book (TALAGERI 2000:154-160, 176-180, 206-208, 250-254, etc.), but this important issue has been mainly overlooked by the AIT scholars (who have neither accepted nor tried to disprove, but have simply ignored, the detailed evidence in the above-cited pages), and perhaps not been really noted by most other readers as well. Hence, this reiteration of the basic evidence here:

1. The word *ārya*, which occurs 36 times in 34 hymns in the Rigveda, is used in the Rigveda in reference to Pūrus as opposed to non-Pūrus. In the Avesta, it is used in reference to Iranians as opposed to non-Iranians. It is nowhere used in reference to Indo-European language speaking people as opposed to non-Indo-European language speaking people. The connotation of the word, whatever its etymological origin, is "belonging to our community", and in that sense it is a "communal" word.

The word is generally found in the hymns in general contexts where it is not identity-specific, except that it is clear that it is used for the People of the Book. However, when it is used in specific contexts, it is clearly in reference to Pūrus: e.g. in reference to individuals, it refers to Divodāsa in **I.130**.8; **IV.26**.2 and **VIII.103**.1. In a tribal sense, it clearly refers only to Pūrus: in **I.59**.2, Agni is said to be produced by the God to be a light unto the *ārya*, and in the sixth verse of the hymn, it is clear that the hymn is composed on behalf of the Pūrus. Likewise, in **VII.5**.6, Agni is said to drive away the Dasyus and bring forth broad light for the *ārya*, and in the third verse of the hymn the deed is said to be done for the Pūrus. The word is *never* used for non-Pūrus: e.g. although the Tṛkṣi kings Purukutsa and Trasadasyu are praised to the skies, and Trasadasyu is even described as a "demi-god" in **IV.42**.8,9, in recognition for some crucial help rendered by them to the Pūrus (**I.63**.7; **IV.38**.1; **VI.20**.10; **VII.19**.3), neither of them is ever called an *ārya*. Nor are any of the other non-Pūru patrons of the ṛṣis in the Late Books (**VIII.1**.31; **4**.19; **5**.37; **6**.46,48; **19**.32,36; **65**.12, etc) ever referred to as *āryas*.

Likewise (see TALAGERI 2000:156-157 for details) the word is used, in 28 of the 34 hymns which use this word, by composers belonging to the Bharata family or its two closely affiliated ṛṣi families, the Angirases and the Vasiṣṭhas. It is used in 4 hymns by partially affiliated families like the Gṛtsamadas, Kaśyapas and Viśvāmitras, and in 2 hymns by totally neutral families like the Atris, Kaṇvas, Bhṛgus and Agastyas. Of these last, both the references are by Kaṇvas, and the two references again emphasize the fact that the *āryas* are the Pūrus: the Kaṇvas were a neutral family with patron kings from all the different tribes, and **VIII.51**.9 diplomatically refers to both the *āryas* and the *dāsas* as being the beneficiaries of Indra's bounty, while **VIII.103**.1 refers, as we saw, to Divodāsa, so that even Kaṇvas, who never refer to a single one of their non-Pūru patrons as an *ārya*, reserve the word for Pūrus.

Even more significant is the fact that there are nine hymns which refer to *āryas* among the *enemies* of the particular hymns. These references make little sense in the AIT interpretation, except for the generalized conclusion that the "Aryans fought among themselves" as also with the Dāsas. What the AIT scholars fail to realize is that all these hymns establish a pattern, which logically shows that there was only *one* section, from among the people calling themselves (and recognizing each other as) *ārya*, which were the real People of the Book in the Rigveda, while there were other sections, also recognized as *ārya*, which were *not*. Of course, those determined to find "**complex**" situations in the Rigveda could argue that the different hymns referring to *ārya* enemies could each have a different group of protagonist *āryas* and enemy *āryas*, so that the protagonist *āryas* of one hymn could be the enemy *āryas* of another, and vice versa. But logic shows that this would be unlikely, since the hymns are clearly a collection belonging to *one* particular group of people.

The references, however, make sense in our analysis, where the particular People of the Book are the *Bharata* Pūrus alone, so that there are other sections of Pūrus, also recognized and referred to as *ārya*, who are not directly among the People of the Book. These references to enemy *āryas* prove our case to the hilt: of the nine references to enemy *āryas* (**IV.30**.18; **VI.22**.10; **33**.3; **60**.6; **VII.83**.1; **X.38**.3; **69**.6; **83**.1; **102**.3), *two* are by Bharata composers, and *all the remaining seven* by the two ṛṣi families closely affiliated to them, the Angirases and Vasiṣṭhas.

This is not *only* by chance, or simply because most of the references to *āryas* (also by chance?) are by these three families of composers. There are seven other hymns which again refer to the same situation in different words: they refer to *jāmi* (kinsmen) and *ajāmi* (non-kinsmen) enemies. Of these seven references (**I.100**.11; **111**.3; **IV.4**.5; **VI.19**.8; **25**.3; **44**.17; **X.69**.12), one is by a Bharata composer (a descendant of Sudās, who attributes this late hymn, **X**.69, to Sudās himself; and this hymn, it may be noted, also has one of the *ārya*-enemy references given above) and *all the remaining six* are by Angirases and Vasiṣṭhas.

There is more. There is one hymn which refers to the same situation in yet other words: **X.133**.5 refers to *sanābhi* (kinsmen) and *niṣṭya* (non-kinsmen) enemies. This *single* reference is by a Bharata composer. The force of all this evidence will be even clearer when we see that there are only 19 hymns composed by Bharata composers out of a total of 1028 hymns in the Rigveda.

Finally, as if all this were not clear enough, we have *one* more reference, this one by the Viśvāmitras, which clinches the case: it is in one of the two hymns (**III**.33, 53) which directly refers to the period when the Viśvāmitras, *before* the Vasiṣṭhas, were closely affiliated to the Bharatas as the priests of Sudās, and it is the only hymn in this Book which actually mentions Sudās by name. It refers to *prapitvam* (relationship) and *apapitvam* (non-relationship). The last verse, **III.53**.24, tells us that the Bharatas (specifically named as such) do not recognize non-relationship or relationship when dealing with their enemies in battle.

Therefore, it is clear that the protagonist *āryas* of the Rigveda are the *Bharatas*, and the enemy *āryas* in a few hymns are the other, *non*-Bharata, sections among the *greater* conglomeration of tribes of which the Bharatas are a part, i.e. among the *Pūrus*, who are otherwise clearly the People of the Book in a broader sense (which the Anus, Druhyus, Yadus and Turvasus are not): we have already seen (in *Pūrus as the Vedic Aryans* in section 7E-1 of chapter 7) that the word Pūru (which includes the Bharatas) is undoubtedly used in the first-person sense for the People of the Book in the Rigveda, except in two hymns which specifically differentiate between protagonist Bharatas and *other* hostile Pūrus.

2. The words *dāsa* and *dasyu*, on the other hand, clearly refer to the *Others* in the Rigveda: i.e. to the *Other*-than-the-Pūrus. But it is clear, from *two* circumstances, that the words *originally and primarily referred to the proto-Iranians* (the Anus), even though used as a general term for all non-Pūrus:

One: the words *dā°ŋha* (by itself) and *daŋju/daŋhзuš* (in suffixes), the Avestan equivalents of *dāsa* and *dasyu*, are found in personal names in the Avesta (see chapter 1), and both the words have pleasant or neutral meanings. The word *daha* in certain Iranian languages (e.g. Khotanese), even today, has the meaning "man". And Greek texts refer to an Iranian people known as the *Dahae*.

Two: the word *dāsa* is used in a friendly sense in only *three* references in the Rigveda (see TALAGERI 2000:206-208), and as *all* three of them are *dānastutis*, or hymns in praise of patron or donor kings, it is clear that the uncharacteristic friendly sense of the word has to do with the identity of the donor kings. In *two* of these hymns, the names of the patron kings have been identified by many western scholars, *incuding* Witzel, as proto-Iranian names: *Kaśu Caidya* in **VIII**.5 and *Pṛthuśravas Kānīta* in **VIII**.46. And the name of the patron king in the third hymn, *Ruśama Pavīru* in **VIII**.51, may well be a proto-Iranian name too.

In the Rigveda, moreover, it is clear that *dasyu* was a name for a *section* among the *dāsas*: this is specifically stated in **IV.28**.4, and is noted by scholars like Erdosy (ERDOSY 1989:37). But the exact nature of this sectional identity is not comprehended by the scholars: *the dasyus were the priestly class among the non-Purus*, and this is crystal clear from the references:

a) The *dasyus* are referred to in terms of hostility which have to do with *religious* differences: *ayajvan* (**I.33**.4), *anyavrata* (**VIII.70**.11; **X.22**.8), *adevayu* (**VIII.70**.11), *akarman* (**X.22**.8), *abrahman* (**IV.16**.9), *avrata* (**I.51**.8; **175**.3; **VI.14**.3; **IX.41**.2), *amanyamāna* (**I.33**.9; **II.12**.10), *grathin* (**VII.6**.3), *ayajña* (**VII.6**.3), *avṛdha* (**VII.6**.3), *aśraddha* (**VII.6**.3), *akratu* (**VII.6**.3), *māyāvat* (**IV.16**.9).

Not *one* of these words is used even *once* in reference to *dāsas*.

b) The *dāsas* find mention in all the Books of the Rigveda, except the most ritualistic Book (Book 9), and in the hymns of all the families of ṛṣis except the most ritualistic priestly family, the Kaśyapas.

By contrast, *dasyus* find mention in the hymns of all the families of ṛṣis, except the one *non*-priestly family, the Bharatas.

c) The *dāsas* (being tribes and kings) frequently figure as powerful entities to be feared, whether the word is used for human enemies or symbolically for atmospheric demons: in seven hymns (**I.104**.2; **158**.5; **VIII.24**.27; **X.22**.8; **54**.1; **69**.6; **102**.3), the composers ask for protection from *dāsas*, or are rescued from them by the Gods. In three others (**I.32**.11; **V.30**.5; **VIII.96**.18), the *dāsas* are powerful demons who hold the celestial waters in their thrall.

The *dasyus*, on the other hand, are rarely shown as particularly powerful. In fact, they are sly creatures who incite others to hostile acts (**V.24**.18).

d) The *dāsas* are sometimes depicted together in *one* bracket with the *āryas*, with *both* depicted as enemies (in

VI.20.10; **33**.3; **60**.6; **VII.83**.1; **X.38**.3; **69**.6; **83**.1; **102**.3) or *both* as friendly entities (in **VIII.51**.9).

The *dasyus*, however, do not figure even *once* with *āryas* in such references. The logic behind this is obvious: only same-category entities can normally be bracketed together. Thus, we would say "Muslims and Christians" (communities of people), or "*mullahs* and *padres*" (priestly groups), but normally *not* "Muslims and *padres*" or "*mullahs* and Christians". Clearly, in the Rigveda, *āryas* and *dāsas* are communities, and can therefore be bracketed together, but *dasyus* are priestly groups and can *not* be similarly bracketed together with *āryas*.

The Rigvedic hymns are basically the compositions of priests, and hence the hostility towards rival classes of priests (*dasyus*) is sharper in the hymns than the hostility towards non-Pūrus (*dāsas*). Thus the word *dāsa*, like the related Avestan words, must have originally had a *good* connotation, and this is found in its use in the early name *Divodāsa*. Likewise, of the 63 or so verses which refer to *dāsas*, only 38 talk of direct physical violence against them; and, as we saw, *three* are even friendly references by donation-accepting priestly composers.

On the other hand, *every single* one of the 80 or so verses which refer to *dasyus* is uncompromisingly hostile, and 76 of them talk of direct physical violence against them. And, although, like the word *dāsa*, the word *dasyu* must also have had an originally *good* etymological connotation, it is never used in a good sense even when it is part of a name (e.g. *Trasadasyu*: "tormentor of the *dasyus*").

[Incidentally, the reference in **X.49**.3, where the composer expresses his refusal to call a *dasyu* by the name "*ārya*" makes sense only in the above contexts. If *ārya* and *dasyu* were ethnic-linguistic terms, the question of calling a "non-Aryan" *dasyu* an *ārya* would never arise at all, and the verse makes no sense. But *ārya* means a Pūru, and the *dasyu* referred to in this particular verse may be a Pūru (an *ārya* by community) who has joined a rival priestly class of the non-Pūrus, just as a branch of the Bhṛgus after Jamadagni, who were Anus, joined the priestly classes of the Pūrus].

The three words, *ārya*, *dāsa* and *dasyu*, therefore, have nothing to do with any "non-Aryan", *in the sense of "non-Indo-European*", contexts.

2. ANCIENT VIS-À-VIS MODERN IDENTITIES.

Our analysis of the Rigveda refers to people who lived, and events which took place, thousands of years ago. But it is important in the present day as well, from a purely historical point of view, since it has to do with the early history of existing civilizations and actual living language families, particularly the Indo-European language family which, in numerical terms (of the number of people who have an Indo-European language as their mother-tongue, as well as people who otherwise use an Indo-European language as a second or third language), is the most important family of languages in the world today.

It is particularly important for Indian civilization because the Indo-European theory in its AIT version, which stands disproved by our analysis, was a major source for subversive political activities in India. This is noteworthy because in *no* other country which has people speaking an Indo-European language (the Nazi experience being a weird aberration) has the Indo-European theory been used for subversive political activity, and (*even* in the Nazi case) certainly *never* as a tool to *undermine* and destroy the national identity. India, for various reasons, is particularly susceptible to such subversive manipulations, and for this very reason it is necessary to sound a word of caution or sanity here: i.e. *there is no direct ethnic connection between the identities of different peoples of the Rigvedic period and the identities of actual different peoples living in present-day India, or indeed in the world today.*

Thus, we saw the history of the Pūrus, Anus, Druhyus, Yadus and Turvasus of the Rigvedic period, but there is no logical way in which any modern or present-day group of people can be identified with any of those ancient groups. This fact is instantly clear in the case of the groups which migrated out of India: obviously the present-day speakers of Germanic languages in northern Europe are not direct lineal ethnic descendants of the ancient Druhyus of northwestern India even though their languages are distant descendants of the speech-forms of those Druhyus. It is nobody's case that the ancient Druhyus of northwestern India were blonde, blue-eyed Nordics (although Witzel presumptuously assumes that such would be the argument of OIT writers: "**autochthonists would have to argue that mysteriously only that section of the Panjab population left westwards which had (then actually not attested!)364 non-Indian physical characteristics, — very special pleading indeed**": WITZEL 2005:368), and it would be as ridiculous for a present day Germanic speaker to personally identify with the trials, triumphs *and biases* of the ancient Druhyus (vis-à-vis the other peoples mentioned in the Rigveda) as it would be for an English language speaking black or native (Red) Indian of present day America to personally identify with the trials, triumphs *and biases* of the Anglo-Saxons of mediaeval England (vis-à-vis, say, the Normans).

Likewise, the Zoroastrians of the present day (the Parsis) are not only the inheritors of the Iranian language descended from the speech-forms of the ancient Anus (although almost all of them now speak the Indo-Aryan Gujarati language due to a long stay of many centuries in Gujarat), they are also the proud and direct inheritors of the Zoroastrian religion and traditions which developed among the ancient Anus. But, ethnically, they are definitely not linear descendants of the Anus of Kashmir, or later of the Punjab, or even later of Afghanistan, in the "racial" or biological sense. They are basically linear descendants of different ethnic groups in ancient Iran which, at different times, adopted the language and culture of the expanding Anus.

What is so clearly true in the case of the ancient Druhyus and Anus is equally true, if not so instantly clear, in the case of the other ancient peoples closer to home as well. No caste, community or ethnic group of the present day is identifiable with the tribal or communal groups in the Rigveda. Not even when they bear the name of Rigvedic groups: the Yadus of the Rigveda, for example, have nothing whatsoever to do with the different caste groups, found in different parts of the country, including in the southern and eastern states of India, who are known as Yadavs. Nor are the Anus identifiable with the inhabitants of present-day Punjab or Pakistan.

Nor is there any group, caste or community in India which can be directly identified *ethnically* with the Pūrus: neither the inhabitants (or particular castes from among them) of present day Haryana, U.P. or the Punjab, nor the different Brahmin groups, found in every part of India, which claim direct descent from the different families of ṛṣis of the Rigveda. To take a direct example, the Saraswat Brahmins of the south (to which community this writer belongs) has a strong traditional history of having migrated from the areas of Kashmir and the Sarasvatī river, and even the name of the community testifies to this claim. Moreover, a linguistic analysis of the Konkani language spoken by the Saraswats shows different archaic features (pitch accents, an inflexional morphological structure, and many crucial items of vocabulary) which corroborate this tradition. But are the Saraswats themselves actually direct ethnic linear descendants of the Pūrus or their priestly classes? Clearly not: the physical features of the Saraswats are clearly identifiable with the physical features of other castes and communities of Maharashtra, Goa and Karnataka.

In short, the history of Vedic times is just that: *the history of Vedic times*. It has to do with the history of civilizations and language families, and must be recognized as such; but it does not have *anything whatsoever* to do with relations between different ethnic, linguistic, caste or communal groups of the present day. The biases and the conflicts of ancient times are the biases and conflicts of ancient peoples *with whom present day peoples have no direct ethnic connections.*

But even when there are clear *traditional* connections with the *traditions* of any of those ancient groups, modern people (when political manipulations do nothing to stir up troubles) have fortunately tended to adopt a logical and unbiased approach, *even when these traditions represent memories of ancient biases and conflicts.* For example, it has been known for far more than a century now that the opposite use of the words *asura* and *deva* in the Hindu and Zoroastrian traditions represents memories of ancient conflicts between the Vedic Aryans and the proto-Iranians. And yet, it has not prevented a single devout Zoroastrian from visiting and praying at Hindu temples and treating the word *deva* as a synonym for "God", or even the term *asura* as a synonym for "demon". Nor has it prevented a single devout Hindu (who is only prevented from offering worship at Zoroastrian temples by a rigidly observed Zoroastrian tradition in India which prohibits any non-Zoroastrian from entering a Zoroastrian temple) from treating the name of the Zoroastrian *Ahura* Mazda as a synonym for "God" and the name of the Zoroastrian Angra Mainyu *Daēva* as a synonym for "demon". Even the most erudite but devout scholar, Hindu or Zoroastrian, treats both the words *deva* and *ahura* as synonyms for "God" and both the words *asura* and *daēva* as synonyms for "demon".

This is not just due to the casual force of habit by which a confirmed atheist (or agnostic like this writer) may still continue to use exclamatory phrases like "Oh God!" or even "My God!" or "God knows!". Rather, this is due to a mature outlook which understands that conflicts and biases of the past have no place in present day relations or even in our simultaneous acceptance of originally mutually hostile traditions.

Incidentally, as pointed out in our earlier book, the religious traditions of the Purus of the Rigveda themselves include important elements borrowed from the Anus (proto-Iranians), including elements central to Vedic tradition like Soma rituals (now long extinct) and fire worship (still the central core of Vedic ritual) (TALAGERI 2000:132-135, 172-174). Further, as pointed out in detail, Hinduism owes the preservation and development of most of its Vedic heritage to a family of priests originally belonging to the priestly classes among the Anus (proto-Iranians): the Bhṛgus (see TALAGERI 2000:174-176). And even the later Purānic and Epic traditions, which speak of *deva-asura* conflicts, treat the priests of the *asuras* with the greatest respect: Śukrācārya, the head priest of the *asuras* (the ancestral Usan of the Avestan traditions) is, in many ways (e.g. in his knowledge of the *sanjīvanī* mantra which can bring the dead to life), even shown as superior to the high priest of the *devas*. Likewise, the ideal king, celebrated in stories of his goodness and generosity in the Purāṇas and Epics, is Śivi, an *Anu* king.

And Hinduism itself represents, as *repeatedly* pointed out in our earlier books, a pan-Indian religion which has Vedic tradition as its elite layer, but incorporates elements and traditions from all the different parts of India within itself, even when some of these elements may represent originally rival traditions. And all these elements and traditions are *equally intrinsic* parts of Hinduism, and *totally* acceptable as such to the traditional Hindu. In this writer's opinion, the Mahābhārata story of Krishna lifting up the Govardhan hill to protect the tree-and-forest worshippers from the wrath of Indra may actually represent a Yadu rebellion against Pūru *domination* in the field of religion; but to any true Hindu, both the Vedic traditions and the Yadu traditions are equally intrinsic parts of his religious heritage, and, as becomes clear from other parts of the Mahābhārata, even Krishna apparently felt the same!

This mature outlook is basically intrinsic to human nature, along with the opposite tendency to harbour biases and prejudices, and both Hindus and Parsis have, by and large, attained this level of religious maturity. However, other religious groups have not: Christian Proselytization activities, based on an original inherent hatred and intolerance for other traditions and a desire to wipe them out of existence, are in full swing in different parts of the country. Likewise, within Hindus, the biases and prejudices of caste, community, region and language are still rampant, and provide breeding ground for political manipulations of every kind. In this postscript, *I can only hope that nothing written in this book is used as fodder for manipulative politics of any kind seeking to revive supposed biases, prejudices and putative identities of the past.*

Finally, I must say a word on the biases involved in analyzing history or in looking at (real or mythical) events from the past as recorded in textual or oral traditions. The main ancient text analyzed in this book, as well as in our earlier book, is the Rigveda; and, as I have pointed out repeatedly, the Pūrus (the Vedic Aryans) are the People of the Book in the Rigveda. However, they are not necessarily the People of the Book in this present volume: that is, they are not the unqualified heroes of *this* book.

Many OIT writers write from the point of view of the Vedic Aryans: to them the Vedic Aryans are unqualified heroes, a highly righteous, spiritual, "good" people; while their enemies, or whoever is described in unfriendly or critical terms in the hymns of the Rigveda, are "bad" people, unspiritual or materialistic, in fact they are often "fallen Aryans" (whatever that means). And the battles between the Vedic Aryans and their enemies were somehow battles between Good and Evil.

However, our analysis of the Rigveda and Vedic history is not based on this rosy viewpoint. As pointed out in our earlier book:

> **"there is nothing to indicate that the Āryas were more civilized and cultured than the Dāsas, or that the Ārya kings were more noble and idealistic than the Dāsa kings, or that the priests of the Āryas were more spiritual and righteous than the priests of the Dāsas. Nor**

> **that the struggles between the Āryas and Dāsas involved any noble social, moral or ethical issues.**
>
> **Rigvedic history, which forms the backdrop of the Rigveda, is like the history of any ancient civilization: in ancient China (not coterminous with modern China), during the period of the Warring States (403-221 BC), the land was divided into seven kingdoms (Chu, Chin, Chi, Yen, Chao, Han and Wei) which were constantly at war with each other. Likewise, ancient India was divided into various kingdoms, not necessarily constantly at war with each other, but certainly with often sharp political differences, rivalries and enmities.**
>
> **In Chinese tradition, the soul-stirring poems of Chu Yuan, a poet, thinker and statesman of the kingdom of Chu, have survived to this day. In India, a collection of hymns composed among the Pūrus has survived to this day. But this does not render all the kingdoms other than the kingdom of Chu, or all tribes other than the Pūrus, as the villains of the piece.**
>
> **The Pūru text, of course, later became the primary text of a Pan-Indian religion which came to encompass and incorporate the religious traditions of all parts of India; and some of the non-Pūru tribes, in the course of time, emigrated from India. But neither of these facts justifies a partisan attitude in the study of Rigvedic history."** (TALAGERI 2000:405).

This has been our attitude in this book as well. This book sets out the history of the Rigvedic period as the data shows it. There are no heroes in this analysis, although there are heroes in the Rigveda. Thus, Sudās is definitely the unqualified hero of the Rigveda (or at least of Books 3 and 7, or of certain particular hymns in those books), but he is not necessarily a hero from the point of view of our analysis. In fact, from the moral or ethical point of view, he is an imperialist who conquers the lands and kingdoms of other tribes; and in this case, the moral ground is definitely with the Anus who form an alliance to defend their lands from this "Aryan invader". Nevertheless, from the objective and unbiased point of view of history, he is an extremely *important* person, not only from the point of view of Vedic history, but even from the point of view of world history: after all, it is possible that the Battle of the Ten Kings, provoked by him, provided the catalyst for the westward movements of various Anu tribes, which included the Greeks and the Iranians. Can we imagine how different the history of the world would have been, and how different the civilization of Europe, and indeed of the modern world, if the Iranian and Greek civilizations had never come into existence?

It is necessary that ancient texts be analyzed objectively and honestly, to arrive at the truth, and, at the same time, biases and prejudices within those texts should neither be masked, camouflaged or denied, nor nurtured and carried forward into present times. And all this can be done with full respect for the texts, their composers, the persons depicted in those texts, and the traditions derived from those texts.

Index

General Index

Sanskrit Word Index